Economic Development among the Aboriginal Peoples in Canada:

The Hope for the Future

Robert Brent Anderson

Captus Press

Economic Development among the Aboriginal Peoples in Canada: The Hope for the Future

Canadian Cataloguing in Publication Data

Anderson, Robert Brent, 1951–
Economic development among the aboriginal peoples in Canada: the hope for the future

Includes bibliographical references and index.
ISBN 1-896691-56-0

1. Native peoples — Canada — Economic conditions.
2. Native peoples — Industries — Canada. I. Title.

E78.C2A475 1998 338.9'0089'97071 C98-932616-0

Captus Press Inc.
Units 14 & 15
1600 Steeles Avenue West
Concord, Ontario
Canada L4K 4M2
Telephone: (416) 736-5537
Fax: (416) 736-5793
Email: info@captus.com
Website: http://www.captus.com

Canada We acknowledge the financial support of the Government of Canada through the Book Publishing Industry Development Program (BPIDP) for our publishing activities.

0 9 8 7 6 5 4 3 2
Printed and bound in Canada

Table of Contents

Appendices

List of Figures

List of Tables

Acknowledgments

More people than I can thank individually played an important role in the events that resulted in the completion of this book. Two individuals deserve special recognition — Dr. Bob Bone for his endless patience and invaluable advice and my wife, Bev, for her continuous support in this and my prior educational endeavours. I would also like to thank Dr. Jim Randall, Professor John McConnell, Dr. George Baxter, Dr. Robin Armstrong, and Professor Paul Dudgeon. Thanks also to Randy Hoffman, Pauline Lai, and Ania Czyznielewski at Captus Press.

I would like to dedicate this work to the people of the First Nations in Canada. During the past 10 years, while with the Saskatchewan Indian Federated College, I have come to appreciate the traditional cultural characteristics that the people of the First Nations have preserved in the face of centuries of assimilation, and still exhibit today. In spite of extraordinarily trying circumstances, the people of the First Nations continue to demonstrate endless patience, a wonderful sense of humour, respect for the promises they and others have made in the past, a respectful inclusion of all in decision-making regardless of their position or power, and a profound concern about family, community, and their "Mother Earth" now and for the generations yet to come.

1 Introduction

The United Nations declared 1995 to 2005 to be "The International Decade of Indigenous People." The significance of this declaration is that it acknowledges that Indigenous people around the world share in a common struggle for the recognition and realization of their rights. These rights include: "the right to ownership and control of their territories; the right to self-determination; and the right to representation through their own institutions" (Colchester 1994, 73). Economic development is emerging as a key component of this struggle in two ways. First, gaining control of land and resources is considered critical to improving the socioeconomic circumstances of Indigenous people. Such control improves the potential for the creation of businesses essential to the development of a viable Indigenous economy. Second, a robust and sustainable economy is regarded as essential to self-determination and the exercise of a measure of real control over the relationship between Indigenous people and the non-Indigenous governments and institutions of the global economy. This book deals with the aspirations and activities of a particular group of Indigenous People — the Aboriginal Peoples in Canada — as they pursue their self-reliance and self-determination through economic development.

The recently concluded Royal Commission on Aboriginal Peoples addressed the circumstances and aspirations of the Indigenous people in Canada. Not surprisingly, the Royal Commission found that Aboriginal people in Canada suffer the same consequences of colonialism; are struggling for the same outcomes; and have reached the same conclusions about ownership and control of their territories, and the relationship between economic development and self-determination, as their Indigenous counterparts around the world. The Commission summarizes its view as follows:

- *The time is right for Canadians and their governments to recognize the inherent right of Aboriginal peoples to self-government and to make room in the Canadian federation for its exercise.*
- *A more equitable and just allocation of lands and resources to Aboriginal peoples is a fundamental prerequisite for pre-*

serving Aboriginal culture and identity and for the effective operation of Aboriginal self-government.

- *An adequate land and resource base by itself is not enough to support self-government: the challenge of Aboriginal economic development must also be met through the combined efforts of Aboriginal and non-Aboriginal people governments and institutions.* (RCAP(2) 1996, 8)

The report of the Royal Commission goes on to stress that redressing the ills of colonialism in this fashion will benefit all Canadians, not just the Aboriginal people. The Commission estimated that the cost to the Canadian economy of the underdevelopment of Aboriginal people and their communities was $7.5-billion in 1996. This cost is expected to increase to $11-billion by 2016 unless the socioeconomic circumstance of Aboriginal people improve dramatically. The Royal Commission report goes on to estimate that economic development activities that reduce by 50% the economic gap between Aboriginal and non-Aboriginal people by the year 2016 would result in the Aboriginal people making a $375-million annual contribution to the Canadian economy instead of imposing this $11-billion burden.

In the context just described, this book explores the economic development objectives, strategies and activities of the Aboriginal people in Canada with the following four objectives:

1. Identify the approach to economic development that is emerging among them.
2. Develop a theoretical perspective capable of providing insight into this approach.
3. Investigate their economic development activities to determine if these activities are consistent with the identified approach to development and the proposed theoretical perspective, and
4. Identify actual development outcomes and compare these outcomes with expectations to determine if the adopted approach is effective.

A common and important thread running throughout the consideration of these objectives is the role that mutually beneficial alliances between Aboriginal and non-Aboriginal people in Canada and their institutions can play in the economic development process in the context of an increasingly flexible global capitalist economic system. The mutual benefits occur at two levels — business and societal. At the business level, alliances can bring into existence a venture that is stronger and more successful than any individual member of the alliance could have created alone. More broadly, as has aptly been demonstrated by the Royal Commission on Aboriginal Peoples and others,[1] improving the socioeconomic circumstances of Aboriginal people will benefit all Canadians while fail-

1 For example, see Appendix 1 for the comments of Michael Wong, Vice-President of the Hong Kong Bank of Canada, to the Select Standing Committee on Aboriginal Affairs of the legislature of British Columbia. See also Appendix 4, *The Summary Report on the Social and Economic Impacts of Aboriginal Land Claims.*

1

ure to do so will result in an ever increasing economic and social costs that will be borne by all.

This book contains nine chapters. The next chapter begins by briefly identifying and describing the Aboriginal people in Canada. It continues with an overview of the development objectives and strategies of this group as garnered from numerous Aboriginal sources. Based on this overview, eight characteristics of the emerging Aboriginal approach to development are proposed. The chapter ends with the suggestion that there are three key questions related to this emerging Aboriginal approach to development that must be addressed in order to satisfy objectives 2, 3 and 4:

1. Does the economic development theory support the goals, strategies and structures adopted by Aboriginal people? If so, are the outcomes they expect consistent with those anticipated by theory?
2. What strategies and structures have Aboriginal people established to retain control over economic and business development, and to assure that an appropriate proportion of the benefits of that development accrue to their people? What role do mutually beneficial alliances play in these strategies and structures?
3. Are the actual outcomes consistent with theoretical expectations and/or Aboriginal people's expectations?

Chapter 3 addresses the first of the three questions. It begins with a review of economic development theory as it evolves in response to changes in the global economic system. Then, a "contingency perspective" on the economic development of Aboriginal people is developed that is an amalgam of three of these emerging theoretical perspectives — the regulation theory, the postimperial perspective and the alternative/Indigenous development approaches.

The other two questions are addressed in four ways: (i) a review of the comprehensive land claims and modern treaties (chapter 4) and other economic development capacity-building activities of Aboriginal people in Canada (chapters 4 to 8); (ii) an investigation of the approach to Aboriginal economic development being adopted by selected non-Aboriginal companies (chapter 5); (iii) an investigation of the economic development activities of the 70 First Nations in Saskatchewan in order to identify the strategies adopted, structures created and activities undertaken (chapter 7); and (iv) an in-depth case study of the economic development activities of the Meadow Lake Tribal Council (chapter 8). Chapter 6 is a discussion of entrepreneurship, innovation and new venture creation in an Aboriginal context.

The final chapter is a look into the future. Based on the research results, the prospect is hopeful. If the Aboriginal people of Canada continue the development journey they have begun in partnership with non-Aboriginal people, particularly in business, there is hope for the future. This hope is for all members of the Canadian federation, not just for the Aboriginal people. As the Royal Commission on Aboriginal Peoples concluded, the investment required to create viable and self-reliant Aboriginal communities pales in significance when compared to the financial and human costs to all Canadians for failing to do so.

There are two things not included in this book and their omission is intentional. First, there is no review of the history of economic development activities among Aboriginal people, not because such a review is unimportant but rather because such reviews have already been done by several authors.[2] There is no need to duplicate their efforts in this work, which is essentially a look into the future.

For similar reasons, a discussion of the nature of economic development is also missing here. This activity has been the subject of innumerable works.[3] In spite of these efforts, defining development still remains problematic. Rather than add to these endless discussions, I have chosen to start with development as defined by the Aboriginal people and to evaluate this approach in light of the current development theory. Rather than compare or contrast the Aboriginal approach with other approaches or with some theoretical ideal, my objective is simply to answer the first of the key questions mentioned earlier in this chapter.

---

2 Three that come to mind are the works of Elias (1991 & 1995), Tough (1996) and Knight (1996).

3 So (1990), Wilbur and Jameson (1975) and Brohman (1996) provide particularly good overviews of the nature of economic development and the contending and evolving development theories.

2 Aboriginal Economic Development

The purpose of this chapter is to develop an understanding of the approach to development that is emerging among the Aboriginal people in Canada. This understanding will form the basis of the subsequent review of economic development theory in the search for a relevant perspective and investigation of actual development activities.

This chapter contains three sections. The first describes the study area and subjects. The second section is a description of the development objectives that Indigenous people internationally and the Aboriginal people in Canada have, and the approach to economic development that is emerging as they pursue these objectives. The final section summarizes the challenge facing Aboriginal people as they pursue their development objectives and identifies three critical questions arising from this challenge. These questions must be answered in order to assess the likelihood that the Aboriginal people will attain their economic development objectives by following their approach.

2.1. The Aboriginal Peoples in Canada

Before continuing, here are some words about terminology. The terms "Aboriginal" and "native" are general and refer to persons descended, at least in part, from the original inhabitants of North America. The terms "Indian," "Inuit" and "Metis" have more specific meanings. All three groups are recognized as Aboriginal people in the Canadian Constitution and all are acknowledged as having "Aboriginal rights." Increasingly, the term "First Nation" has been adopted as an accepted alternative to Indian. The people of the First Nations (Indians) have a particular relationship with the Government of Canada and before that with the British Crown. The same is true with the Inuit. Both trace their existence as distinct people or nations to pre-colonial times. Both possess specific rights to land and other resources flowing from this original occupancy. In the case of the First Nations, these rights were often captured in historic treaties. These same Aboriginal rights are at the core of current court battles, land claims negotiations and modern treaties. Both the First Nations and the Inuit are aggressively pursuing their rights through negotiation and litigation and, as a result, are acquiring title to and control over vast tracts of land as well as receiving large financial settlements.[1]

The Metis are of mixed Aboriginal and European descent. While they have a rich and distinct history and culture, their existence as a people began in colonial, not pre-colonial, times. Their relationship with the Government of Canada and before that the British Crown was not clearly captured in "nation to nation" treaties to the same extent as the relationship between these non-Aboriginal governments and the Indians. The Metis are recognized as Aboriginal people in the constitution of Canada and they are making claims to rights, land and financial resources as Aboriginal people. Their claims are meeting with some success in Canadian courts. A recent and ongoing example is the Grumbo case in Saskatchewan. The trial judge found that the Metis, as one of Canada's Aboriginal people, have the same Aboriginal hunting rights as the people of the First Nations in Saskatchewan (Indians). The case was appealed to the Saskatchewan Court of Appeal which ordered a new trial. Similar court cases are in process in other jurisdictions across Canada.

The Aboriginal people in Canada have a well-developed political system. Among the First Nations, each individual Nations forms the cornerstone of this structure. Each First Nation has its own government, controls its own land base, and determines its own membership. Access to, control of and responsibility for federal funding is at the First Nation level. Within Saskatchewan, the First Nations have created a provincial body, the Federation of Saskatchewan Indian Nations (FSIN) to deal with common concerns (e.g. the negotiation of an agreement on gaming with the provincial government). To deal with regional concerns (e.g. larger economic development projects, health services and education), the FSIN is subdivided into 10 districts or tribal councils. The FSIN and similar bodies from the other provinces and the territories have joined together to form the Assembly of First Nations (AFN) to represent their interests at the federal level.

The Metis have adopted a similar structure consisting of community based locals, provincial associations and a national body — The Metis Nation of Canada. The Inuit also have a similar structure with a national body called the Inuit Tapirisat. Internationally, the interests of Indigenous people are served by the World Council of Indigenous Peoples.

2.2. Indigenous People and Economic Development

The United Nations announced the beginning of the International Decade of Indigenous People in 1995. This announcement is significant in that it acknowledges that Indigenous peoples around the world share in a common struggle for the recognition and realization of their rights. These rights include

1 See Appendix 2, *Comprehensive Claims Policy and the Status of Claims.*

"the right to ownership and control of their territories; the right to self-determination; and the right to representation through their own institutions" (Colchester 1994, 73). In Panama, in 1984, the World Council of Indigenous Peoples ratified a Declaration of Principles (see Figure 2–1) that it feels must be accepted by all the states and peoples of the world for this struggle to succeed.

FIGURE 2–1: World Council of Indigenous Peoples: Declaration of Principles

1. All human rights of indigenous people must be respected. No form of discrimination against indigenous people shall be allowed.
2. All Indigenous Peoples have the right to self-determination. By virtue of this right they can freely determine their political, economic, social, religious and cultural development, in agreement with the principles stated in this declaration.
3. Every nation-state within which Indigenous Peoples live shall recognize the population, territory and institutions belonging to said peoples.
4. The culture of Indigenous Peoples are part of mankind's cultural patrimony.
5. The customs and usages of the Indigenous Peoples must be respected by the nation-states and recognized as a legitimate source of rights.
6. Indigenous peoples have the right to determine which person(s) or group(s) is (are) included in its population.
7. All Indigenous Peoples have the right to determine the form, structure and jurisdiction of their own institutions.
8. The institutions of Indigenous Peoples, like those of a nation-state, must conform to internationally recognized human rights, both individual and collective.
9. Indigenous peoples, and their individual members, have the right to participate in the political life of the nation-state in which they are located.
10. Indigenous peoples have inalienable rights over their traditional lands and resources. All lands and resources which have been usurped, or taken away without the free and knowledgeable consent of Indian peoples, shall be restored to them.
11. The rights of the Indigenous Peoples to their lands includes: the soil, the subsoil, coastal economic zones all within the limits specified by international legislation.
12. All Indigenous Peoples have the right to freely use their natural wealth and resources in order to satisfy their needs, and, in agreement with principles 10 and 11 above.
13. No action or process shall be implemented which directly and/or indirectly would result in the destruction of land, air, water, glaciers, animal life, environment or natural resources, without the free and well informed consent of the affected Indigenous Peoples.
14. Indigenous peoples will reassume original rights over their material culture, including archeological zones, artifacts, designs and other artistic expressions.

FIGURE 2–1 (continued)

15. All Indigenous Peoples have the right to be educated in their own language and to establish their own education institutions. Indian people's languages shall be respected by nation-states in all dealings between them on the basis of equality and nondiscrimination.
16. All treaties reached through agreement between Indigenous Peoples and representatives of the nation-states will have total validity before national and international law.
17. Indigenous peoples have the right, by virtue of their traditions, to freely travel across international boundaries, to conduct traditional activities and maintain family links.
18. Indigenous peoples and their designated authorities have the right to be consulted and to authorize the implementation of technological and scientific research conducted within their territories and the right to be informed about the results of such activities.
19. The aforementioned principles constitute the minimal rights to which Indigenous Peoples are entitled and must be complemented by all nation-states.

In March 1996, a United Nations seminar was held in Whitehorse, Yukon, to discuss Indigenous land rights and claims. The meeting produced over 30 conclusions and recommendations, all of which are consistent with and supportive of the principles declared by the World Council of Indigenous Peoples. A complete text of these conclusions and recommendations can be found in Appendix 3.

Economic development is emerging as a key component of the struggle by Indigenous people for their rights in two ways. First, gaining control of land and resources is considered critical to improving the socioeconomic circumstances of Indigenous people. Control over such resources improves the potential for the creation of businesses essential to the development of a viable Indigenous economy. Second, a robust and sustainable economy is regarded as essential to self-determination and the exercise of a measure of real control over the relationship between Indigenous people and non-Indigenous governments and transnational corporations (TNCs).

While attending the Council for the Advancement of Native Development Officers (CANDO) Conference held in Winnipeg, Manitoba in the fall of 1995, Jorge Valente (CANDO 1995c), President of the World Council of Indigenous Peoples, spoke of the relationship between economic development and the struggle by Indigenous people to reassert their rights. He and other international Indigenous leaders[2] at the conference emphasized that Indigenous control

---

2 Sam Mercado, President of the Corporation for Indigenous Economic Development, Nicaragua; Brooklyn Rivera, Miskito Indian leader and Vice Minister of the Nicaraguan national government; Reginaldo Marroquin, Guatemalan Mayan leader; and Simon Brascoupe and Wayne Dunn of the Apikan Indigenous Network.

over their lands and resources and a return by them to their pre-colonial practices of trade and commerce will be essential to the rebuilding of robust and sustainable Indigenous economies. Recognizing current world realities, the World Council believes that the creation of businesses and other institutions necessary to restoring these patterns and practices of trade and commerce will require partnerships between Indigenous people and non-Indigenous people, businesses and state governments in various combinations.

2.3. Economic Development and the Aboriginal Peoples in Canada

As with all Indigenous people, the Aboriginal people of Canada are understandably unhappy with their circumstances and are striving to improve them. In the words of George Erasmus, past National Chief of the Assembly of First Nations of Canada and Co-Chair of the Royal Commission on Aboriginal Peoples:

> *Our people have been relegated to the lowest rung on the ladder of Canadian society; suffer the worst conditions of life, the lowest incomes, the poorest education, and health; and can envision only the most depressing futures for our children.*
> (Erasmus 1989, 1)

Elaborating on the current socioeconomic state of the people of the First Nations, according to the Federation of Saskatchewan Indian Nations (FSIN), "only one of every three First Nations citizens in Saskatchewan is employed and over 60% of the province's First Nations people are classified as living in poverty — roughly four times the average found in non-Aboriginal communities" (Peters 1996, 8). The circumstances of the Metis and the Inuit are similar. A sense of the scale of the employment circumstances of Aboriginal people Canada-wide was captured by the Royal Commission on Aboriginal Peoples, which says in its final report that

> *more than 300,000 jobs will need to be created for Aboriginal people in the period 1991–2016 to accommodate the growth in the Aboriginal working-age population and to bring employment levels among Aboriginal people up to the Canadian standard.*
> (RCAP 1997, 275)

Erasmus says that the Aboriginal people in Canada believe that this dismal situation can be turned around. He says to do so will require a return to the self-government principles underlying the treaties between the Aboriginal people and the Europeans. In a manner consistent with the aspirations of Indigenous people around the world, Erasmus states that

> *All across North America today First Nations share a common perception of what was then agreed: we would allow Europeans*

> *to stay among us and use a certain amount of our land, while in our own lands we would continue to exercise our own laws and maintain our own institutions and systems of government. We all believe that that vision is still very possible today, that as First Nations we should have our own governments with jurisdiction over our own lands and people.*
>
> (Erasmus 1989, 1–2)

Similarly, the recently released report of the Royal Commission on Aboriginal Peoples (RCAP 1997) concluded that

- *The treaty process is the most appropriate vehicle for embodying the new relationship between Aboriginal and non-Aboriginal people in Canada.*
- *The time is right for Canadians and their governments to recognize the inherent right of Aboriginal peoples to self-government and to make room in the Canadian federation for its exercise.*
- *A more equitable and just allocation of lands and resources to Aboriginal peoples is a fundamental prerequisite for preserving Aboriginal culture and identity and for the effective operation of Aboriginal self-government.*
- *An adequate land and resource base by itself is not enough to support self-government: the challenge of Aboriginal economic development must also be met through the combined efforts of Aboriginal and non-Aboriginal people governments and institutions.* (RCAP(2) 1996, 8)

Aboriginal people want control over their traditional lands through self-government so that they can "decide about and benefit from the type of development we want in our own territories, not have such development forced on us to serve outside interests" (Erasmus, 1989, 2).[3] According to Lester Lafond, a respected First Nations leader from the Muskeg Lake First Nation in Saskatchewan, such control will:

> *Create an environment in which Indians can deal more effectively with their social and economic problems in a positive manner. Do not be misled, however, it will not, and I repeat, will not in itself make those problems disappear...* [Aboriginal people must] *make the necessary adjustments in our thinking so that we will eventually become self-reliant.*
>
> (Lafond 1985, 16)

From these and other Aboriginal sources (e.g. FSIN 1993, MLTC 1991–5a, PATC 1993, SIAP 1992), it is clear that self-government and the related con-

---

3 See chapters 5 and 6 for a discussion of the role land claims play in building the economic development capacity of the First Nations.

trol of lands and resources are expected to play a powerful enabling role in Aboriginal socioeconomic development.

At the same time, Aboriginal people consider economic self-sufficiency to be critically important to the realization and ongoing support of self-government and to the preservation and strengthening of traditional values and practices. Ovide Mercredi, past Grand Chief of the AFN, succinctly summarizes the First Nations' view of the relationship between economic development and the realization of self-government when he states that "If we gain [political] power for the community but we don't get the economy, we have power that cannot exercise itself" (Mercredi 1994, 7). With respect to the relationship between economic development and traditional values and practices,[4] he says "without an economic base the culture is either dying or dead. So what we have to do is restore an economic base ... everything else will fall in place in terms of self-esteem, in terms of community spirit and in terms of improving the standard of living in our community" (Mercredi 1994, 7).

From the two preceding paragraphs, it is apparent that Aboriginal people realize regaining jurisdiction over their traditional lands will not result in an automatic improvement of their socioeconomic circumstances. Instead, they acknowledge that the relationship between such self-government and socioeconomic development is much more complex with the former enabling the latter and the latter supporting the former.

Figure 2–2 captures the essence of the Aboriginal view of the relationship between self-government and control of traditional lands, economic and business development and economic self-sufficiency. Gains in any one area lead to improvement in others. In turn, these improvements impact positively on the area where the initial improvements occurred, and so on and so on. This view of the development process is entirely consistent with Gunnar Myrdal's concept of cumulative causation and the "virtuous circle" (Myrdal 1968). At the same time, it reflects the "Circle World View" that is widely held among Aboriginal cultures in North America and Indigenous people elsewhere.

There is general agreement among Aboriginal people that building economic self-sufficiency requires participation in the global economy through business development, often in partnership with others (Decter and Kowall 1989; FSIN 1993; MLTC 1991–5a & b; PATC 1993; SIAP 1992; TFHQ 1993). A sense of this agreement was captured by the National Aboriginal Financing Task Force in its report *The Promise of the Future: Achieving Economic Self-Sufficiency Through Access to Capital* (NAFT 1996). The report identified seven essential steps to economic self-sufficiency. The third step says:

---

4 For an example of the relationship between traditional values and practices and development see chapter 7. It contains a description of the key traditional values that are to guide all of the economic development activities of the Meadow Lake Tribal Council as well as the process used to determine these guiding principles (itself an example of traditional practices in action). The principles include: self-reliance as communities, families and individuals rather than dependency on "welfare" programs, sharing, community decision-making, respect for the environment and consultation with Elders.

FIGURE 2–2: The Aboriginal Development Circle

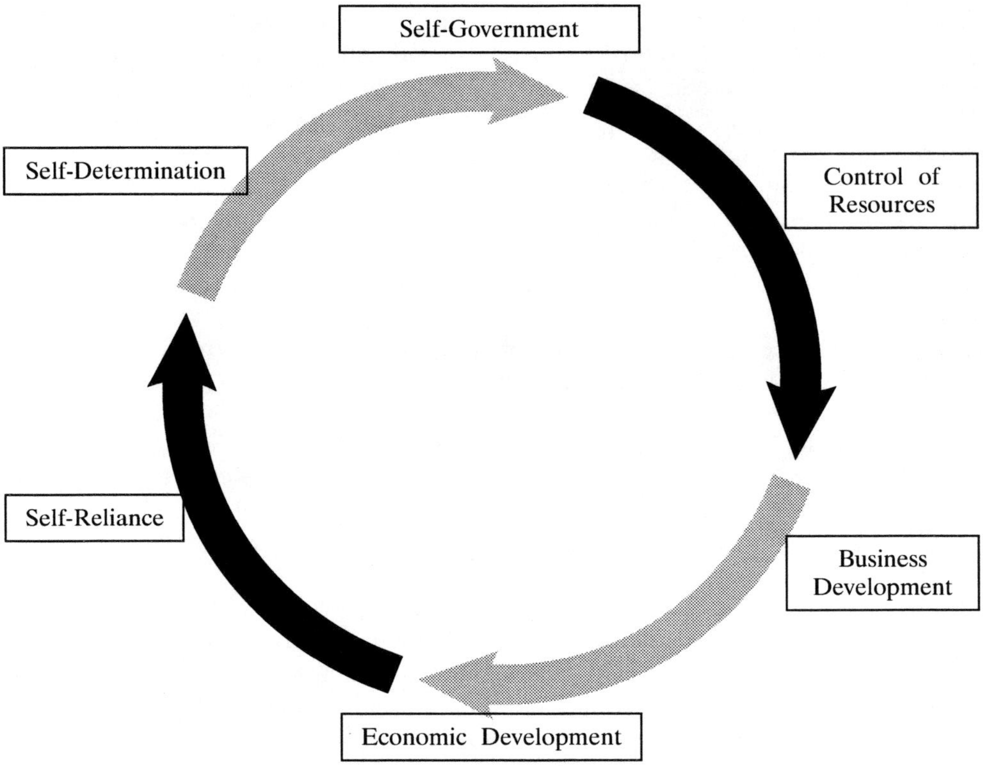

> *The most effective way (and probably the only way) for Aboriginal communities to address their current socioeconomic challenges is to create wealth through business activity.*
> (NAFT 1996, 9)

While the NAFT's seventh step says:

> *To achieve economic self-sufficiency, Aboriginal communities must promote coordination and partnership among many groups and individuals, both within the Aboriginal community and outside it.* (NAFT 1996, 11)

Aboriginal people recognize that planning to create successful business in the search for self-sufficiency is an intellectual exercise. Going beyond planning, to actually create such businesses and operate them successfully requires capacity — human, financial and physical. Participants at an Aboriginal corporate roundtable conducted by the Council for the Advancement of Native Develop-

FIGURE 2–3: The Eight Characteristics of Economic Development among Aboriginal People in Canada

The Aboriginal people's approach to economic development is

1. A predominantly collective one centered on the individual Nation or community.

For the purposes of

2. Attaining economic self-sufficiency as a necessary condition for the realization of self-government.
3. Improving the socioeconomic circumstances of Aboriginal people.
4. Preserving and strengthening traditional culture, values and languages and reflecting the same in development activities

Involving the following processes:

5. Creating and operating businesses to exercise the control over the economic development process.
6. Creating and operating businesses that can compete profitably over the long-run in the global economy, to build the economy necessary to support self-government and improve socioeconomic conditions.
7. Forming alliances and joint ventures among themselves and with non-Indigenous partners to create businesses that can compete profitably in the global economy.
8. Building capacity for economic development through (i) education, training and institution-building and (ii) the realization of the treaty and Indigenous rights to land and resources.

Source: Adapted from Anderson and Bone, 1995a.

ment Officers were asked to identify critical capacity issues relating to economic development. The top three capacity-related issues identified by Aboriginal participants were:

> *1. Stable and culturally appropriate institutions of government.*
> *2. Recognition of Aboriginal rights regarding land and resources.*
> *3. Education initiatives* (CANDO 1995d, 2)

Responding to these issues, Aboriginal people are creating administrative structures, negotiating the settlement of outstanding Treaty and Aboriginal rights claims, and developing financial and education institutions.

Based on the preceding, it appears that the approach to economic development being adopted by the Aboriginal people in Canada has eight key characteristics (see Figure 2–3).

Overall, individual First Nations and Inuit and Metis communities exhibit a predominately collective approach to economic development that is closely tied to each group's traditional lands, its identity as a nation and its desire to be self-governing. This collective development approach is intended to serve three purposes: the attainment of economic self-sufficiency, the improvement of socioeconomic circumstances, and the preservation and strengthening of traditional culture, values and languages. It is this strong collective aspect with its "national" focus and its emphasis placed on culture, values and languages that distinguishes the approach to economic development of Aboriginal people and communities from the approach of other Canadian communities of a similar size and in similar locations.

Aboriginal people in Canada believe that they can achieve these purposes through participation in the global economy and have adopted processes that reflect this belief.

Aboriginal people are creating businesses to compete in the global economy in order to generate the wealth necessary to support self-government and improve socioeconomic conditions. At the same time, through business ownership, Aboriginal people expect to exercise greater control over activities in their traditional territories. They recognize that the success of this approach depends on the long-term profitability of the businesses that they create. Therefore, they are devoting considerable efforts to capacity building to enhance their ability to develop and manage businesses. These capacity building goals and strategies fit well with the "four capitals" of ecological economics: ecological, human, manufactured and institutional (Straussfogel 1997, 122–23).[5] They are striving to improve their capacity for development on all four fronts.

More importantly, in spite of their national status, individual First Nations and Metis and Inuit communities exhibit many characteristics associated with the local/regional scale (population, size and location of land base, etc.) as opposed to those commonly expected at the national scale. Acknowledging this, they realize that to succeed in the global economic system they will often have to form alliances with other people and groups (Aboriginal and non-Aboriginal). This gives Aboriginal economic development a unique geographic character. It is simultaneously a local/regional (from a geographic perspective), national (from the First Nation, Inuit and Metis perspective) and global process.

2.4. The Issues and Questions

Aboriginal people in Canada want to develop an economic system that will improve their peoples' socioeconomic circumstances, build economic self-reliance, support self-government, and preserve and strengthen the traditional aspects of their society. Aboriginal control over their own development is an essential char-

5 Straussfogel (1997) suggests replacing the usual core-periphery continuum used to describe the relative levels of development among people/places with a set of four continuums — one for each of the capitals. A description of relative development would be based on the aggregate of a people'/place's position on all four continuums. This leads to a much richer and more descriptive system for comparing relative levels of development and provides better guidance for policy and program development.

acteristic of this system. At the same time, Aboriginal people acknowledge that their economy must be integrated with the global economic system. The challenge facing Aboriginal people is to successfully integrate their economic activities into the global economy while retaining adequate control over development on their lands and attaining their development objectives.

This challenge raises three critical questions that will be addressed in the subsequent chapters:

1. Does the economic development theory support the goals, strategies and structures adopted by Aboriginal people? If so, are the outcomes they expect consistent with those anticipated by theory?
2. What strategies and structures have Aboriginal people established to retain control over economic and business development, and to assure that an appropriate proportion of the benefits of that development accrue to their people? What role do mutually beneficial alliances play in these strategies and structures?
3. Are the actual outcomes consistent with theoretical expectations and/or Aboriginal people's expectations?

In answering these questions, objectives 2, 3 and 4 (indicated in chapter 1) will be met.

2.5. The Aboriginal Approach to Development: Cases

The following seven cases document the development activities occurring among Aboriginal people from coast to coast. They were selected to give a sense of the range of projects being undertaken, their purpose and connection with Aboriginal cultures and values, which are key aspects of the Aboriginal approach to development. Other cases elaborating these and other aspects of the Aboriginal development approach can be found in chapters 5, 7 and 8.

Case 2–1: Essipit's Economic Development: For Our Fathers and Our Children (1997)[6]

It all began some 20 years ago, on the shores of the Gulf of Saint Lawrence. Seated around a campfire, much like their ancestors once did, three young Montagnais made a pact that would change their community's way of life.

Armed with university degrees and the determination to make a difference, Denis Ross, his brother, Bernard, and their friend, Réginald Moreau, devised a plan that would help improve Essipit's socioeconomic situation.

"The rates of unemployment and social assistance were extremely high in our community," Réginald remembered. "We were becoming increasingly

---

6 Source: DIAND Website, *http://www.inac.gc.ca/ecdev/entre/pq/Essipi.html* [edited].

dependent on the white people for survival, and as a result, we were losing our Montagnais culture."

"Les petits gars," as they were often referred to by others, realized that the community had limited experience in economic development and management. "It was important to start with a small project that would respond to the immediate needs of the community," said Denis Ross, who has been band chief of Essipit since 1979. "There was no sense of solidarity within the community. We needed a place where families could gather, to improve morality."

At the annual meeting, they proposed the construction of a community centre that would include an administration office for the Band Council as well as a small restaurant and pool tables. After convincing the skeptical community to take out a loan, the project was approved. The first step toward economic development was made and, in 1978, the Montagnais Community Centre opened.

In 1979, Bernard was named director general and, with the help of band chief Denis, the evolution of a new community focused on economic development began. The community centre has continued to expand and now offers a wide variety of services including an outdoor swimming pool, a rink for both ice skating and roller-blading, tennis courts and a baseball field. Inside the centre, there is a racquetball court, a weight room and bowling alley. Sauna and showers were also installed.

The band council continues to implement projects that respond to the immediate needs of the community. The Montagnais Community Centre Bar was established to provide members of the community with a more informal, relaxed meeting place. Today, the Montagnais Community Centre employs more than 35 Aboriginal people on a full-time basis.

In keeping with the emphasis on creating jobs while meeting the immediate needs of the band members, Le Dépanneur was also built. "The main objectives of this project were to offer better services to the community and to limit off-reserve spending," Sylvain Ross, Director of Business Administration, explained.

The Band Council is also responsible for the management of CHEM FM 94.9, a radio station serving Quebec's north shore. "We are a pop rock music station with an audience of approximately 3,000 listeners," said Daniel Ross, director general of the station. The radio station also enables the Band Council to inform its members of activities that are being held.

The tourism industry has also played a significant part in the economic development of the 0.5 sq. km reserve. "As the economic situation of the community continued to improve, we observed an increase in tourists who were curious about our way of life and anxious to experience it," said Réginald Moreau, who was named director general of the band in 1995.

Le Tipi campground and the l'Anse-à-Jos chalets were built to offer tourists the opportunity to stay on the reserve. Campers can go for nature walks along the Gulf of Saint Lawrence, kayaking and even whale watching.

Since 1993, Les croisières SMB 93 inc. have been enabling tourists to get a closer look at the world's largest mammals. The MV Cap Bon Désir schooner, which holds up to 76 passengers, goes on several guided excursions each day. For the more adventuresome, Les croisières TGB inc. lets tourists experience whale watching from inflatable rafts that glide across the gulf, providing a close-up shot of finback and beluga whales.

"It is definitely an unforgettable experience. Schools of whales measuring anywhere from 3 to 8 m in length, surface for air and breach before plummeting to the bottom of the gulf; tourists often describe their experience as a rush," said Sylvain.

In 1983, the Essipit Band Council became the first band in Quebec to acquire an outfitter's camp — Lac des Coeurs. "The Montagnais have always relied on hunting and trapping as a means of survival. It was difficult to convince people that our primary objective was economic development and not a playing field for hunters in the community," Réginald remembered.

The acquisition of the 142 sq. km camp has led to that of four other sites: Club du Lac Claire, Club des Lacs Jumeaux, Domaine sportif du Lac Loup, and Lac Gilles (which is an expansion of Domaine du Lac des Coeurs).

Each site is managed by the band council and has been developed so as to benefit from the unique physical, natural and human resources that each has to offer. "Each of the sites is unique in that it offers a different adventure based on the characteristics of its setting. This helps to insure that the camp will suit the client's needs," explained Réginald. For those who wish to remain within close proximity to the town, Club du Lac Claire is situated 41 km from Escoumins (the local town), while Domaine du Lac des Coeurs is situated 80 km in the forest.

"It is obvious that the emphasis has been placed on economic development but it is equally important to improve the socioeconomic situation of the reserve," said Réginald.

In an attempt to regain the Montagnais culture that was being lost, the Essipit Band Council hired and trained six Montagnais to fabricate traditional moccasins, clothing and other handicrafts. "It used to be that when the Montagnais girls married a white man, they would lose their status and as a result, we would lose part of our culture. Even though the language is lost, the craft shop is helping us to conserve an important part of the Montagnais culture," said Sylvain.

In the past 20 years, "les petits gars" have managed to build a community with a thriving economy and much potential for the future. "Our motto expresses the spirit in which our Band Council operates; 'Pour nos pères et nos enfants' (for our fathers and our children)," explained Réginald.

Case 2–2: Where the Buffalo Roam: Brokenhead Ojibway Nation Building on Tradition (1997)[7]

The world is waking up to the richness to be found in indigenous cultures. Past generations of European colonists tried to eradicate Aboriginal customs and traditions in the territories they conquered. Now, some of their descendants are trying to learn about these traditions, to discover what Aboriginal culture has to offer.

---

7 Source: DIAND Website, *http://www.inac.gc.ca/ecdev/entre/mb/broken.html* [edited].

In recent years, interest in Aboriginal culture and history has been growing, not only in North America but in Europe as well. This growth translates into opportunities for tourism development in Aboriginal communities. People don't just want to read about Aboriginal culture in books; they want to see and experience it themselves.

The Brokenhead Ojibway Nation in Manitoba was hoping to attract tourists from Canada and abroad when they opened the Brokenhead Ojibway Nation Historic Village in summer 1997. The village would feature camping facilities for teepees and tents, as well as a sweat lodge display, wigwams (dome-shaped huts built of wood and covered with hides), plains bison, traditional Ojibway food, interpretive sessions on topics ranging from history and culture to modern-day politics, and other attractions. There would also be guided tours ranging from a few hours to a four- or five-day camp-out.

Harvey Olson, the general manager of the historic village project, says the Brokenhead Ojibway Nation developed the idea for the historic village in 1985 and presented a proposal to the province and the federal government in 1986. However, the result was not what they'd hoped for. "At that time, people weren't even thinking of tourism," Olson says. "As a result of that, it was just basically looked at and then shelved. I think it was ahead of its time."

It was also what Olson refers to as a "mega-project." The proposal was not only for a village, but also included a theatre centre, restaurant and museum, all housed in one giant building. It would have cost more than $5-million to build.

In 1993, the band returned to its original proposal and decided to go with a scaled-down version. They determined that culture had the greatest tourism potential, so it made the most sense to concentrate on the historic village. This time, they were successful in getting the funding they needed. Human Resources Development Canada (HRDC) provided some funding initially. In fact, they suggested that if the community combined the historic village with its plan for a bison ranch, the funding could be used most efficiently.

"We brought both projects together because it was an easy fit. That's how we were able to obtain the funding to kick this project off and get it going," Olson says. Eventually, they decided to separate the two ventures again for practical reasons. They incorporated the bison ranch and made it financially independent of the village. It is still owned by the band, though managed now by community member Allen Hocaluk.

"Now the ranch has to try to sustain itself, but the village is still going to utilize some of the bison for viewing purposes," Olson says. The bison ranch is presently concentrating on increasing its stock, which currently numbers around 30 head. After that, its focus will be on raising bison to sell in the lucrative livestock market.

Now that the bison ranch is a separate entity, Olson and the other band members involved are free to focus their energies on the completion of the village. Olson estimates the total cost of the village project will be around $600,000. The band has provided some of its own funding for the project, and will take out some loans for further development. They have also taken advantage of section 25 of the Unemployment Insurance Program, which provides wage subsidies for workers who are collecting Unemployment Insurance [now Employment Insurance] benefits. They continue to collect Unemployment Insurance plus an additional wage while working at temporary jobs.

The Brokenhead Ojibway Nation also received some help from Aboriginal Business Canada, in the form of funds for a 12-day promotional trip to Berlin in March 1996. Representatives from the band attended an international tourism business conference and made contacts with German travel agencies. These agencies expressed an interest in developing tour packages for the village, and are arranging to visit the village after it opens.

While the prospect of owning a profitable tourist attraction is exciting, Olson emphasizes that money is not the Brokenhead Ojibway Nation's only priority when it comes to the historic village. Traditional values will play a major role in the way the village operates. Respect for nature and the environment is an important part of Aboriginal society, and will be incorporated into the village's program. Spirituality will also be a part of the village experience. There will be a sweat lodge display, and some visitors may be able to take part in an actual sweat lodge ceremony.

However, the First Nation is protective of this aspect of its culture. "It's not for everyone," Olson says. "We'd like to have the opportunity to decline some requests. We're thinking of a screening process so we'd know right off whether people are sincere. We don't encourage curiosity seekers. We want them to respect it. We want it to be personal for them."

Elders are playing an important role in the process of both sharing and preserving traditional culture. Olson says, that in the past, Elders have been wary of plans to market culture to tourists. But attitudes are changing, and Olson says the Elders at Brokenhead are supportive of the project.

"Even six years ago, their response [to the project] would have been an outright no, you shouldn't do that, it's like selling our culture. But recently there has been deep concern regarding the financial portion of putting on large ceremonies. There's cost involved. We're finding that now they're saying we have to start looking at ways to generate revenue, and hopefully funnel it back into our culture and ceremonies."

But the need to generate revenue will be carefully balanced against preserving culture and spirituality. The Brokenhead Ojibway Nation does not want the village to be a tourist trap, and they aren't marketing themselves to the kind of tourists who seek superficial thrills. Olson sums up their marketing strategy this way: "The clientele we're looking at is eco-tourists. This is not Disneyland."

Case 2–3: Prince Albert Development Corporation: First Nations Working Together Toward Economic Development (1997)[8]

Eleven years ago the Prince Albert Grand Council (PAGC) was sitting on the sidelines when it came to economic development. First Nation members were pouring money into Prince Albert's economy, but the PAGC had no venues through which it could participate in the city's economic development. Today

8 Source: DIAND Website, *http://www.inac.gc.ca/ecdev/entre/sk/padc.html* [edited].

the PAGC is playing an active role in Prince Albert's economy through the Prince Albert Development Corporation (PADC).

The PADC, with its head office located 10 km north of Prince Albert on the Wahpeton First Nation, was established in 1985 and is equally owned by the 12 First Nations that comprise the PAGC. Since its establishment, the PADC has ventured into real estate, security and janitorial services, the hotel and service industries, construction and employment referral services.

Wesley Daniels sat on PADC's board of directors as chief of Sturgeon Lake First Nation, was general manager for over a year and now sits on the management board which deals with the day-to-day business operations. Mr. Daniels believes PADC has grown as a result of a good business philosophy.

Strength in unity is the philosophy of PADC. In striving for economic self-sufficiency, PADC gives priority to First Nations people, but the corporation combines this with good business sense and always attempts to secure the best qualified people.

Mr. Daniels believes PADC has helped to change the way people think about First Nations in the business sector.

"We've shown that First Nations have management capabilities when it comes to business. It used to be that every time a First Nation business went under it was big news. We've been holding our own and doing it nicely and proving some myths wrong."

PADC's first business venture was in the area of real estate. During the 1980s, the PAGC took over the administration of many programs and services formerly administered by Indian and Northern Affairs Canada (INAC). As a result, the Grand Council was hiring new staff while INAC was reducing staffing requirements. The First Nations saw an opportunity in developing a new office complex to house its own staff, as well as those of INAC and Medical Services Branch (MSB) of Health Canada. The First Nations pooled their economic resources in order to provide the equity the newly formed development corporation needed to finance construction of the John E. MacDonald building. The PADC also signed long-term leases with the Grand Council, INAC and MSB. Since constructing this first office building in 1986, PADC has purchased one more office complex in the city of Prince Albert and two properties in the surrounding area.

PADC also started a security and janitorial services company in 1986. Over the past 10 years, this company has continued to grow. Today they have contracts with Cogema Resources Inc., Cameco Corporation and Millar Western Pulp to provide security and janitorial services to mine sites, pulp mills and office buildings.

In 1993, PADC saw that there was a great deal of potential for the corporation in Prince Albert's hotel and service industry. First Nations organizations often met in Prince Albert and required hotel and meeting accommodations. Rather than letting someone else gain the economic and employment benefits of First Nation business, PADC decided to purchase the Prince Albert Inn. The PADC has upgraded the inn by adding over $750,000 worth of improvements. The inn includes 108 rooms, a pool, conference and banquet facilities, nightclub, lounge, cold beer and wine store and restaurant.

In its first year of operation under PADC ownership, the inn's total sales increased by 14%. Trevor Ives, the General Manager and Director of Finance of PADC, says that First Nation ownership has a great deal to do with the hotel's success.

"As a general rule the owners of a business will support that business. Having a base of approximately 23,000 owners helps in developing a large market," says Mr. Ives. "This market, combined with sound management, committed staff and the support of a strong board of directors has been key to our accomplishments in business."

Recently, PADC has used its service industry experience gained at the Prince Albert Inn to operate the Northstar restaurant and lounge at the Northern Lights Casino and its real-estate knowledge to act as the developer for the casino building.

In 1994, PADC entered into a joint venture agreement with PCL Construction Management Inc. to bid on upcoming construction projects. In 1995, PADC/PCL-Maxam, a joint venture, successfully bid on the construction of the new multi-million dollar uranium mill near McClean Lake, 45 km west of the community of Wollaston Lake.

Mr. Ives says that joint ventures between Aboriginal and non-Aboriginal groups have many advantages. While PADC benefits from PCL's expertise and size, PCL benefits from PADC's influence in the market as an Aboriginally owned corporation as well as PADC's access to the northern labour market.

PADC has capitalized further on the McClean Lake mine construction by signing a two-year contract with Cogema to provide an employment referral service for construction through a PADC agency known as Northern Employment Services (NES). This agency has compiled an up-to-date database of over 400 northerners available to work on the project. Instead of having to bring in workers from other parts of Saskatchewan or other provinces or having to search the North for a qualified workforce, the contractor is supplied with a list of available workers by NES. PADC will be paid a fee based on the number of hours worked by employees hired through NES. In the space of one year over 160 employees have been hired through NES generating in excess of 170,000 man-hours of work for residents of northern Saskatchewan.

Mr. Daniels says that creating job opportunities for Aboriginal people is one of the corporation's goals. For him, creating employment goes hand-in-hand with business success.

"Success is going into a business and making it pay; you make it pay and you create employment and you make it pay more and you create more employment," says Mr. Daniels. "The Prince Albert Inn is a good example. We increased occupancy and by doing so increased employment. As you get bigger, you create more jobs."

With a sales estimate in excess of $10-million per year and over 200 employees, the majority of whom are Aboriginal, it would seem that PADC has reached success.

But, Mr. Daniels says, "PADC hasn't reached success. I don't think anyone ever reaches success. If you say you've reached success you start to coast. Success is an ongoing venture."

If PADC hasn't achieved success, they've certainly made a great deal of progress. Prince Albert's business community has recognized this and made

PADC a finalist in the city's Samuel McLeod Business Awards in four categories including business of the year, job creation, new business and investment. Not bad for a corporation that only 11 years ago was watching Prince Albert's economic development from the sidelines.

Case 2–4: Aboriginal Culture Shines at Nakoda Lodge (1997)[9]

Running a successful lodge is not always easy, but Dave Drews, manager of Nakoda Lodge, explains that the key to success at this lodge lies with the people. "Nakoda Lodge is unique because it hasn't been taken over by a large company, instead it is the Wesley people that make it a success." This conference centre and guest lodge, located in Morley, Alberta, is owned and operated by the Wesley First Nation of the Stoney Tribal Administration.

Eighty percent of the 50 employees at the lodge are Aboriginal. "The spirit of Nakoda is to employ as many people as possible from the Wesley First Nation," said Mr. Drews. A management team has been created that allows supervisors and managers from Nakoda to work with Elders from the Wesley First Nation to discover new ways to motivate community members to work at the lodge.

Community members also make sure the Aboriginal culture has a strong role at the lodge. "Guests want to learn about our ways," explained Roxanne House, Assistant Manager. "They are always asking questions about our culture." There is an archives and museum area where people can see interesting Aboriginal artifacts and art. There is also a library featuring books about the history of all the First Nations in Canada and films about the history of the Stoney Bands. At the restaurant, guests can try traditional food like bannock, buffalo steak and potatoes. On special request, people from the Wesley community will hold a mini pow-wow for the guests.

The fly-fishing lake, which has a catch-and-release policy, is another big attraction for the guests. "It has been a tremendous boom," explained Mr. Drews. "We have even had a couple of fly-fishing television shows produced out here." Outdoor activities such as canoeing, skiing, riding and hiking also keep guests busy at the lodge.

Nakoda Lodge was originally opened as a conference centre in 1981, but it has since expanded to include a guest lodge with 50 rooms and executive suites with fireplaces. The lodge is fully equipped with a restaurant, swimming pool, sauna, Jacuzzi and gift shop.

Named after the living language of the Wesley band, Nakoda Lodge is a place where guests can learn about Canada's Aboriginal culture, but also where employees can gain experience.

Roxanne House is a Wesley First Nation member. She feels she is getting valuable experience working at the lodge. She started as a kitchen helper and has worked her way up to assistant manager. She is currently being trained on the job to become a manager and plans to go back to school to take formal management training.

---

9 Source: DIAND Website, *http://www.inac.gc.ca/ecdev/entre/ab/nakoda.html* [edited].

Ms. House is a role model for the younger generation of her community. She encourages them to get an education and start businesses in their future. "Every chance we get, we say we are doing this for our community and they need to help us," said Ms. House.

Pam Hunter is also a member of the band. She started working at Nakoda Lodge out of necessity. "When I first started working, I was here for the money, but as the years go on, it gets more interesting and I want to learn more," said Ms. Hunter. Her first job was in housekeeping and she is now the front desk supervisor. "Working here makes me feel like I could go out there and work someplace else because of the help and encouragement I have received here, " she added.

Since its opening, Nakoda Lodge has experienced some growing pains, but 1996 has been a banner year. In fact, another six rooms are being built in the hotel for the spring season. There are also plans to expand the existing museum into a cultural centre within the next five years.

The lodge was an economic development initiative of the Wesley First Nation that has turned out to be a success for its members, both financially and personally. Nakoda Lodge is looking toward a bright future. As Mr. Drews explains: "The lodge is growing slowly but surely — step by step."

Case 2–5: Trapping the Future (1996)[10]

The T'Sou-ke First Nation is reclaiming a part of its heritage for the future of its people and its salmon resource. The First Nation is reviving the abandoned practice of trapping salmon in large nets for the purpose of acquiring fish for food, societal and ceremonial purposes.

The T'Sou-ke First Nation people used a reef net, or SXOLE, years ago, and a pile-secured salmon trap later, before decreased fishing times increased operating costs and the development of the modern seine fleet made it necessary to discontinue in 1958. Many similar traps are still used around the world, most notably the Newfoundland cod trap and the Japanese salmon trap. The new trap's name, Glung-Us, was chosen in memory of the last T'Sou-ke chief to fish with a reef net at their traditional territory of Sooke, a small community 64 km west of Victoria, British Columbia.

Designing and testing the trap took place in the flume tank at the Marine Institute of the Memorial University of Newfoundland. While there, the T'Sou-ke people met some local fishers, including Tom Best, president of the Association of Newfoundland and Labrador Fisheries Cooperators. These fishers were hired and brought to Sooke as consultants on the project, because of their experience with fish traps, specifically the east coast cod trap.

There are vast advantages to using these traps over using drift nets or gill nets. The trap allows fish to remain alive until harvest or release, which in turn, enables harvesting of top condition, or "ocean bright" fish. Since the traps are in a fixed location, they can be used for stock assessment, tagging and

10 Source: DIAND Website, *http://www.inac.gc.ca/ecdev/entre/bc/Glungu.html* [edited].

monitoring. The traps are a renewable product, can be used year after year, with only minor repairs to any section that needs it.

Another great benefit is that this trap will allow the First Nation's people to begin fishing in their traditional territory again, employing people from their own community. Currently they are meeting their fish needs by hiring a seine boat which does not fish in their territory and does not employ any T'Sou-ke people. David Mannix, T'Sou-ke forestry consultant, says about 12 new jobs will be created by the trap. He also mentioned that there has been discussion regarding patenting the design of Glung-Us. "There is interest from other Native bands. They're watching what we're doing," remarks Mannix.

The trap net is a funny-looking contraption. It is large, about 35 fathoms long, and about 12 fathoms at its widest point. (To all landlubbers: a fathom is the length from fingertip to fingertip of an average man's outstretched arms, or six feet.) It has four distinct sections called the diamond, the heart, the pot and the spiller. The fish swim up along a very long section of lead net, which encourages them right into the first section of the trap; the diamond. Gordon Curry, the Department of Fisheries and Oceans officer who worked with the T'Sou-ke First Nation on this project, explains it this way: "The salmon tend to swim against the current when trapped and, when further guided by deflecting panels, the fish swim through funnel-shaped openings into the heart, pot and spiller. This style of trap net only fishes on the flood tide so when the tide changes, the entrance into the spiller is closed to prevent the catch from escaping." Sounds simple?

Well, it isn't. David Lightly, T'Sou-ke First Nation's biologist, says that "anchoring it was a big problem." They originally used 100 pound anchors, but they needed to increase the weight to 1025 pounds. Fred George, a T'Sou-ke Elder, says they experimented using railroad wheels as anchors, and even tried an old car engine.

Another major problem using the Glung-Us was sea lions. Local Steller's sea lions were no trouble, but migrating California sea lions were always trying to eat the salmon, and posing a threat to the nets. "Four or five of them habituated to the trap, going in and out. They're smart as a wolf," explains Lightly, mentioning that the name for sea lions in Uruguay translates to "sea wolves." DFO representative Curry provided this answer to the problem: "The California Sea Lions migrate back through the Juan de Fuca Strait about the second week of September. The current target species for harvest are sockeye and pink, which are mostly through the Sooke area by the end of August. By fishing to about early September, the interaction with sea lions can be avoided."

There is a great deal of concern for the state of the west coast fisheries, by those both inside and outside of the fishing industry. Conservation and revitalization of west coast salmon stocks are a priority of Fisheries and Oceans Minister Fred Mifflin, resulting in the closings of many commercial fisheries along British Columbia's coast. Numerous British Columbia fishers are in danger of losing their livelihoods. With this new approach to harvesting salmon, fishers could begin to contribute to the revitalization of weak stocks of salmon while harvesting from those strong enough to sustain it.

Case 2–6: Techs Unlimited (1997)[11]

Mapping, surveying, wildlife research and management, forest appraisals, rough terrain research: the field of environmental technology includes these and many other areas. There is an open market for firms with a new approach, and Techs Unlimited, based out of Tagish, Yukon, is such a company. This young firm is on the road to success with the right equipment, an impressive background, and an innovative approach to environmental technology.

Four equal partners own this environmental consulting firm and a host of support staff work on contracts. Both the partners and the peripheral workers have extensive training in assorted fields of environmental consulting and management.

This amalgamation of experience has produced a team that can meet all requirements in environmental technology. Some of the approaches that Techs Unlimited take to solve problems they faced can be seen as unconventional; for instance, when studying a piece of land, the Techs team is as likely to consult local Elders and trappers as they do with maps and aerial photographs. "These people are out in the wilderness all the time," says Linda Coffey, contract administrator, "it seems so simple to talk to them."

Traditional knowledge is very important to the company because it contributes to the company's holistic approach to the environmental management industry. When dealing with the environment, Techs Unlimited tries to look at the "big picture," instead of simply the area in question. In doing this, they do things like consult the Elders of the area to find out how things were in the past in regards to the environment, such as climate, wildlife, and migratory patterns. "If we can find out what has changed," says Danny "we can predict what will."

On the scientific side, the Techs team tries to stay ahead of the competition by maintaining a technological edge. Their equipment includes an assortment of computers and specialized mapping equipment, including a stereometrograph, a device that allows the conversion of aerial photographs into topographical landscapes that can be viewed from a variety of angles.

The four partners all come from varying backgrounds that complement each other's skills and experiences. Frank James is a member of the Carcross Tagish First Nation with an education in renewable resource management. He spent six years working for Parks Canada before joining Techs Unlimited, and is a skilled timber cruiser and forest appraiser. Fred Green also has extensive forestry experience and has worked with Frank in the past. Fred has often represented Yukon First Nations on different boards and committees. He has also contributed technical support and counseling for the Umbrella Final Agreement between the federal government, the Yukon territorial government, and Yukon First Nations.

Danny Cresswell is a director of the Carcross Tagish Development Corporation and is also the manager of the highly successful Southern Lakes Caribou Recovery Program. He spent 10 years on the Chilkoot trail working for Parks Canada, where he gained immense outdoors experience.

---

11 Source: DIAND Web Site, *http://www.inac.gc.ca/ecdev/entre/yt/Techs.html* [edited].

The latest member of the Techs Unlimited team is Steve Williams. Steve is the former chief of Six Nations of the Grand River, Ontario and has extensive knowledge of both federal and First Nations governments. Steve has earned respect through exposure gained while serving on several national boards and committees representing First Nation interests.

Linda Coffey is the administrator of the company. She is in charge of all contract administration and other administrative details thus enabling the partners to work where they do best: in the field.

Despite their qualifications, the company has had their share of barriers along their road to success. The first was probably the reluctance of the territorial government to allow them to call themselves Techs Unlimited. It was thought that "Techs Unlimited" was not specific enough. After almost a month of fighting, the legal name "4Techs Unlimited" was agreed upon. The company is currently in the process of registering under the jurisdiction of all of the Yukon First Nations, in recognition of these new governments.

With the abilities and experience of the partners, the right equipment for the job, combined with an innovative approach, Techs Unlimited is positioned to change with the field of environmental management.

3

Theory Review and Development

The objective in this chapter is to find or develop a theoretical framework for interpreting the economic development taking place among Indigenous people in Canada. In doing so, I address the first of the key questions posed in chapter 1. That is, "Does economic development theory support the goals, strategies and structures adopted by Indigenous people. If so, are the outcomes they expect consistent with those anticipated by theory?"

The chapter begins with a brief review of the orthodox (modernization) and radical (dependency, world system and modes of production) perspectives on development. Both are rejected as incomplete and incapable of offering adequate insight into the prospects for the emerging Aboriginal approach to economic development.

Questions about the usefulness of the orthodox and radical perspectives are not restricted to an Indigenous context. There is a strong and growing body of theory that rejects both and instead proposes a less dogmatic and deterministic view of the development process within a global capitalist economy. According to these emerging perspectives, the outcome of interaction with the global economy experienced by a developing area at a particular time is determined by (contingent upon) the actions and characteristics of the parties involved and not preordained by some inviolable law of capitalism.

In the second part of this chapter, three of these perspectives — regulation theory, the postimperial perspective and alternative/Indigenous approaches to development — are reviewed. Following this review, a contingency (as opposed to a modernization or dependency) perspective on development is proposed. Finally, the emerging Aboriginal approach to development is evaluated in light of this theoretical perspective.

3.1. The Orthodox and Radical Perspectives

The orthodox and radical perspectives, in particular their modernization and dependency variants, have commonly been used to describe and analyze the process of development and its outcomes among the Aboriginal people in

Canada. Given this dominance, these two perspectives will serve as a starting point for the search for a perspective capable of providing insight into the emerging approach to development as described in the chapter 2 (see Figure 2–2).

The dependency argument goes as follows. The objective of the Europeans since first contact has been assimilation through modernization or elimination through genocide of the Aboriginal people in North America. Indirectly as a result of the former or directly as a result of the later, the once self-reliant Aboriginal people have been reduced to a state of underdevelopment and dependency.

Alternatively, the modernist argument holds that the process of modernization, far from being the cause of these current circumstances, is its cure. The problem, according to those who espouse this perspective, is that the process of modernization has not been allowed to run its course. They argue that only when Aboriginal people have shed their traditional ways and become fully adjusted to the modern world can they be expected to reap its socioeconomic benefits. The policy of the Reform Party of Canada with respect to Aboriginal people is an example of this perspective and indicates of its continuing and, perhaps, even growing acceptance among some.

3.1.1. The Modernization Perspective

The classic modernization (orthodox) perspective emerged in the years following the Second World War to address the development in newly independent countries of the Third World. According to Rostow (1953), an early and leading proponent of the perspective, a developing country or region passes through a series of stages during which its people build economic capacity, shed traditional and adopt modern ways, and from which they emerge as fully modern, prosperous states.

Dube (1988, 2–4), drawing heavily on the work of Huntington identifies nine characteristics of the modernization/development process. Combining his first three characteristics, modernization is a complex, revolutionary and systematic process affecting all aspects of a society resulting in its transformation from a traditional to a modern one. Dube's fourth, fifth and sixth characteristics combine to suggest that the modernization/development process is a lengthy and phased one that involves the diffusion of modern characteristics from the core or First World to the traditional or Third World. According to his seventh and eighth characteristics, development is a homogenizing and irreversible process resulting in the decline in the differences between nations as they all adopt modern (western European) characteristics. Finally, The ninth suggests that modernization is considered to be progressive and desirable in its own right, as well as inevitable and essential to socioeconomic development.

Brohman (1996, 16–17) describes six features of the classic modernization theory (circa 1965) that are consistent with the views of Dube and Huntington. He is even more explicit about the theory's position on the relationship between traditional culture and practices and development saying that its proponents hold that

> *Especially important for the overall process* [development] *is the removal of various social and cultural 'barriers' to modern-*

> *ization, many of which are linked to the continuing existence of a traditional sector.* (Brohman 1996, 17)

Development involved much more than simply instituting economic changes

> *new values, norms, institutions, and organizations had to be introduced to transform the old social order. Elements of traditional societies that constitute obstacles to modernization had to be replaced.* (Brohman 1996, 20)

Recently, and largely as a result of the experience of the rapidly developing countries of the Far East, proponents of the modernization perspective have been forced to modify their views. According to So (1990), new modernization studies differ from classic ones on the following grounds:

> 1. *They avoid treating tradition and modernity as a set of mutually exclusive concepts ... instead of arguing that tradition is an obstacle to development, the new modernization studies attempt to show the beneficial role of tradition.*
> 2. *The new modernization studies do not assume a unidirectional path of development toward a Western model.*
> 3. *The new modernization studies lay more emphasis on external factors than before.... They often incorporate the factors of class conflict, ideological domination, and religious revolution into their analyses.* (So 1990, 61)

3.1.2. The Radical Perspectives

3.1.2.1. The Dependency Perspective

The dependency perspective arose in the early 1960s in response to the obvious failure of Third World development efforts based on the modernization approach (Frank 1966; Cardoso 1979; others). Results since the end of the Second World War were not those expected by modernists. The newly independent colonies, particularly those in Central and South America and in Africa, were not developing along the western path into fully modern economies. In fact, while per capita GNP growth did occur in some cases, the gap between the standard of living of the mass of people in the developing countries and those in the developed ones widened. Frank and others sought an alternate view of the development process that would explain this failure to modernize. They found their answer in the operation of the capitalist economy and in particular in the principle of unequal exchange.

According to the dependency perspective, the capitalist economy in the core evolved naturally as the merchant class wrested control of the economic surplus from the landowners through commercial activity. Through the reinvestment of this surplus in productive activities, a new class which controlled the means of production (the capitalist) and a new mode of production (capitalism) began to emerge. This process continued and culminated with the creation of the capitalist economy in the core. An important element in the development of capitalism in its later stages was the reaching of an accommodation between capital and labour (as a result of government intervention and/or collective action by labour — the "Keynesian compromise") to "share" the surplus, leading to a mass consumption society based in large part on the purchasing power of labour.

This process has been absent in the periphery. Instead, capitalism "invaded" from the outside. The elites (the landholders) of the periphery formed alliances with the external capitalists that satisfied the needs of both, but usually not the needs of the masses in the periphery. As a result, the economy that emerged in the periphery operated to suit the needs of the core and the local elites. The decisions that drove the system were made in the core and all the surplus generated by activities in the periphery was appropriated by the core or the elites of the periphery — the process of unequal exchange. The result was that the very forces that fostered and sustained development at the core at the same time, and as part of the same process, created underdevelopment and dependency in the periphery.

The dependency view was anticipated much earlier by Innes in his work on the staple theory (Drache 1982; Laxer 1991; Watkins 1963). His work and the work of those following his lead suggest a range of possible outcomes extending from the full development of the regional economy at one extreme to "an ever-deepening arc of dependency of the hinterland on the metropole" (Drache 1982, 22) at the other as a result of a peripheral region's interaction with core. Actual outcomes are attributed to the operation of linkages (forward, backward and final demands) between the core and the periphery and within the peripheral region. The first outcome (full development) occurs when a significant proportion of the linkages operates within the region and the latter (dependency) when the bulk of the linkages extends from the region to the metropole or core.

As with the modernization school, actual development outcomes contrary to their expectations have forced proponents of the dependency perspective to modify their views. So (1990) describes the characteristic of the new dependency studies saying that

> 1. *The new dependency studies have paid more attention to historically specific situations.*
> 2. *The state of the Third World is no longer perceived as a dependent state for foreigners, but as an active agency that tacitly works together with local capital and international capital. In addition, it is the political struggle among the state, local capital, and international capital that shapes the ever-changing situations of dependency.*
> 3. *The final characteristic of the new dependency studies is their willingness to acknowledge the existence of two contradictory processes — dependency and development.*
>
> (So 1990, 164–165)

3.1.2.2. The World System Perspective

The world-system perspective (Wallerstein, 1979) arose in response to dissatisfaction with the conflicting modernization and dependency perspectives on development. It addresses the regional development process within the context of a global economic system. Though an outgrowth of the dependency perspective, it differs from it in several respects.

The world-system perspective asserts that the capitalist economy has evolved into a single worldwide economic system that accommodates all manner of cultural and political systems and to which all such systems must adapt. The world system perspective rejects the conflicting bi-modal, unidirectional structure of the dependency and modernization perspectives in favour of a tri-modal one consisting of the periphery, the semiperiphery and the core. It anticipates movements in both directions among the three stages of development and stresses that the current circumstances of a particular state or region are transitory and potentially reversible. The perspective accommodates the possibility of a unique outcome in a particular region shaped in part by the characteristics of the region, its people and their culture.

3.1.2.3. The Modes of Production School

The modes of production school arose from dissatisfaction with the dependency perspective of Frank and others and the world system perspective of Wallerstein (both often characterized as being "neo-Marxist" in their approach). Corbridge (1989) says that the "modes" school is a return to a more classic Marxist approach from these neo-Marxist ones.

The classic Marxist criticism of the dependency perspective centres on the nature and source of the surplus that is exploited by the capitalist economic system. They (classic Marxists) hold that this surplus is generated not by unequal exchange (as argued by the "dependenistas") but from production; hence the emphasis on modes of production. Those arguing for a classic Marxist approach also criticize Frank and Wallerstein for seeing the capitalist mode of production everywhere and not acknowledging the presence and role of other pre- and co-existing modes of production.

The modes of production school has three variants: (i) the articulation of modes, (ii) the peripheral mode, and (iii) the internationalization of capital. All three variants have in common a core/periphery view of the world and seek to explain the reasons for the development of the former and the persistent chronic underdevelopment of the latter. All view the global capitalist economy (a particular mode of production) as the integral factor in their explanation. The three differ about the mechanism through which the global capitalist system imposes and maintains the inequality between the core and the periphery.

The articulation of modes variant sees the capitalist mode from the core entering a peripheral area where other modes exist (traditional and/or feudal/plantation). Initially, the capitalist mode draws on these other modes for its benefit (i.e. surplus "free" labour, required resources). Over time, the externally controlled capitalist mode grows in strength supplanting or marginalizing the other modes. In supplanting or marginalizing the other modes, the capitalist mode *does not* reproduce a "modern economy" in the periphery but rather one that is integrated (articulated) into the global economy in a dependent fashion. This process is lengthy and may never be complete with traditional and/or feudal/plantation modes persisting alongside the capitalist mode indefinitely.

The peripheral mode of production school sees the same economy in the periphery; that is, a combination of capitalism, feudalism/plantation, and traditional modes. It differs from the "articulation variant" in that it does not see this as a transitional stage during which one mode, capitalism, is in articulation with one or two other modes. Rather, this variant views the entire package as a "mode" in its own right — one consisting of a combination of pre-capitalist modes locked in an unequal and persistently dependent relationship with the core through the workings of the global capitalist economy.

The internationalization of capital variant takes the view (as do Frank and Wallerstein) that capitalism is globally pervasive and that the economies of peripheral countries are part of the capitalist mode. Their underdevelopment is an outcome of their place/role in that mode. Of the three variants, this last one is the closest to Frank's original dependency perspective.

In summary, the dependency and world system perspectives focus on unequal exchange between the core and the periphery and the expropriation of the surplus from that exchange by the core. In contrast, the modes school focuses on the surplus from production and its tendency to accrue to the capitalist mode and, through its control of this mode, to the core. However, all three radical perspectives paint the same bleak picture of the prospects for the people of the periphery as an outcome of interaction with the global capitalist economy — chronic dependency and underdevelopment.

3.1.3. Concluding Comments on the Orthodox and Radical Perspectives

In spite of the recent modifications to each, the expectations of the (orthodox) modernization and radical perspectives remain irreconcilable, one with the other and with many of the actual outcomes in developing regions. Is the outcome of interaction with the capitalist economic system full development with the possible retention of unique aspects of traditional culture (neo-modernization), or is it dependency with the chronic poverty allayed to some degree by incomplete development (neo-dependency)? The modes of production school does little to resolve this dilemma. Its three variants all see the periphery as a creature of the capitalist core with its economic activity controlled by, and subservient to, that core.

A resolution of this seemingly irreconcilable difference between the orthodox and radical perspectives is essential before the likelihood of success of the emerging Aboriginal approach to economic development can be assessed. It is comforting to note that concern about the limitations of the orthodox and radical perspectives is not limited to an Aboriginal context. For example, Brohman says that there has been a realization that

> *neither mainstream nor radical frameworks offer viable solutions to critical Third World problems.... Tired old conceptual dichotomies (e.g. modernization-dependency, internal-external) seem no longer to afford needed explanatory power. On a more practical level, none of the traditional approaches seems capable of offering a coherent alternative strategy or viable way out of the present crisis.* (Brohman 1996, 24)

The search for a solution to the impasse between the orthodox and radical perspectives has been widespread. This search and the views on development flowing from it are the subjects of the next section.

3

3.2. The Emergence of Contingent Perspectives on Development

Faced with the conflict between both the orthodox and radical perspectives, many have rejected them as incomplete with each describing a possible, but not inevitable, outcome of interaction between a developing region and the global capitalist economy.[1] For example, Stuart Corbridge says that

> *The changing contours of global production are no more accessible to accounts of modernization theory and neoclassical economics than they are to MDS* [Marxist development studies]*: indeed, a metatheoretical commitment to the logic of diffusion or to freely functioning markets is even less fitted to the task than is a faith in the development of underdevelopment.*
> (Corbridge 1989, 624)

Instead, many argue that the outcome experienced at a particular time and in a particular place is contingent on a variety of factors, many of which are under at least the partial control of the people of the developing region. In this vein, Corbridge says that there is a powerful trend "towards theories of capitalist development which emphasize contingency ... a new emphasis on human agency and the provisional and highly skilled task of reproducing social relations" (Corbridge 1989, 633). Figure 3–1 summarizes this trend. If these new theories are correct, then Aboriginal people can chart a development course that suits their purposes. Whether they succeed or not will depend in a large part on the development approach they adopt.

In the following sections, three of the emerging perspectives that emphasize the contingent nature of the development process are reviewed in search of a greater insight into the Aboriginal approach to development and the likelihood of its success. Following this review, a "contingency perspective" on development is proposed that is an amalgam of the three perspectives.

3.2.1 Regulation Theory

Regulation theory is one of the new approaches to development that emphasize contingency and human agency. Hirst and Zeitlin say that it executes

> *a slalom between the orthodoxies of neo-classical equilibrium theory and classical Marxism to produce a rigorous but non-deterministic account of the phases of capitalist development that leaves considerable scope for historical variation and national diversity.* (Hirst and Zeitlin 1992, 84)

---

1 See Bertramsen 1991; Brohman 1996; Corbridge 1989 & 1990; Friedman 1992; Thomsen 1991; Shatz 1987a & 1987b; Stander and Becker 1990; Straussfogel 1997; and Torfing 1991.

FIGURE 3–1: The Emergence of a Contingency Perspective

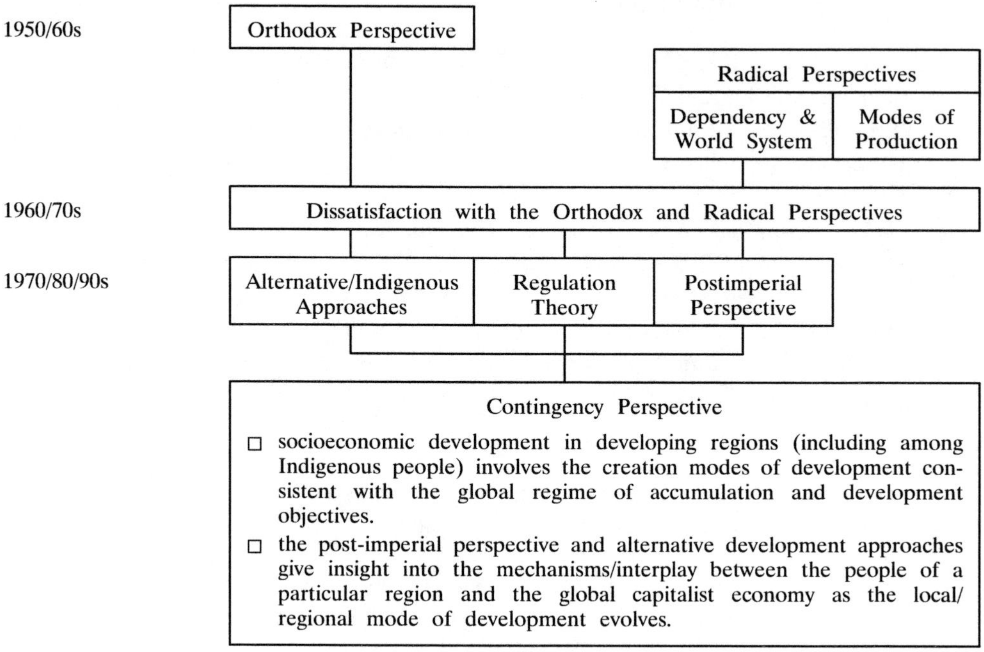

Source: Anderson and Bone 1995a, 124.

Several authors expand on the notion of historical variation and national diversity. Elam says that regulation theory addresses the complex interrelationship between national and subnational units and global capitalist economy. On one hand, national and regional units are seen as constantly in a state of flux as they adjust to broader processes of influence in the global economy. On the other hand, these broader global influences "are seen as having essentially local origins" (Elam 1994, 66). Extending the discussion, Torfing (1991) says that regulation theory refuses to explain the dynamics and outcomes of capitalism in terms of necessary and abstract "laws." Instead, the economy is seen as an evolving social system created by people with its "laws" at a particular time "socially determinate and always related to a precise specification of the historical conditions of their validity" (Torfing 1991, 68). The process of regulation involves the "dynamic formation of rules, norms and institutions which are ... constantly altered as we progress. The contingent process of regulation reflects the contingent nature of what is regulated" (Torfing 1991, 73). In other words, it is the actions of people that determine the characteristics of the economic system rather than the system that determines the actions of people.

Regulation theory analyses the evolution of the capitalist economy "in terms of a series of modes of development based on a combination of regimes of accumulation and modes of regulation" (Hirst and Zeitlin 1992, 84–85). These three concepts are the key to understanding regulation theory and are discussed in the following paragraphs.

The regime of accumulation determines the general possibilities for the capitalist economy (Torfing 1991). Peck and Tickell describe the regime of accumulation as

> *The dominant mode of economic growth and distribution. Elements of the accumulation system include the conditions of production (such as the amount of capital invested, the distribution of capital among the various branches and the norms of production) and the conditions of consumption.*
> (Peck and Tickell 1992, 349)

In the same vein, Scott says that

> *A regime of accumulation can be rather simply defined as a historically specific production apparatus (in capitalism) through which surplus is generated, appropriated, and redeployed* ... [it has] *four distinctive elements:*
> *(a) a set of production techniques,*
> *(b) a characteristic way of organizing production and labor relations,*
> *(c) a distributional mechanism governing the appropriation and redeployment of the surplus,*
> *(d) a process of aggregate demand driving forward the evolution of productive capacity.* (Scott 1988, 8–9)

Finally, the regime of accumulation is a "relationship between production and consumption defined at the level of the international economy as a whole" (Hirst and Zeitlin 1992, 85).

Speaking of the modes of social regulation, Scott says that stability in the economic system is

> *dependent on the emergence of a further set of social relations that preserve it, for a time at least, from catastrophic internal collisions and breakdowns. These relations constitute a mode of social regulation. They are made up of a series of formal and informal structures of governance and stabilization ranging from the state through business and labor associations, to modes of socialization which create ingrained habits of behaviour, and so on.* (Scott 1988, 9)

Hirst and Zeitlin agree, saying that a mode of social regulation (MSR)

> *is a complex of institutions and norms which secure, at least for a certain period, the adjustment of individual agents and social groups to the over-arching principle of the accumulation regime ... composed of a number of interrelated elements: the*

> *form of monetary and credit relationships; the wage-labor nexis; the type of competition; the mode of adhesion to the international regime; and the form of state intervention.*
> (Hirst and Zeitlin 1992, 85)

While regulation theory does not prescribe the exact nature of a particular mode of social regulation, the authors reviewed generally agree that

1. A regime of accumulation does not create or require a particular mode of social regulation, "each regime, in short, may be regulated in a multiplicity of ways" (Scott 1988, 9).
2. Because modes of social regulation are based on such things as "habits and customs, social norms, enforceable laws and state forms" (Peck and Tickell 1992, 349), unique modes "can exist at virtually any territorial level — local, regional, national, global" (Storper and Walker 1989, 215).

A mode of development is the coupling of a particular mode of regulation with the currently dominant global regime of accumulation. Torfing describes it as the articulation of "a regime of accumulation with the institutional features of a mode of regulation into a regulatory ensemble capable of generating growth, prosperity and social peace in the context of the international division of labor" (Torfing 1991, 77). Hirsh and Zeitlin (1992) echo this definition and then go on to stress that "each mode of development also contains its own internal limits — reflecting the deeper contradictions of capitalism as a mode of production — and eventually comes to decay over time" (Hirsh and Zeitlin 1992, 85).

According to regulation theory, this decay periodically causes a system-wide crisis that in turn results in the emergence of a new regime of accumulation and modes of social regulation. This process is neither automatic nor are its outcomes preordained. Instead, the new modes of development that emerge depend "on the strategic choices and political struggles of the major social actors" (Hirst and Zeitlin 1992, 85). Corbridge (1989) says regulation theory indicates that the capitalist system has gone through four stages in the twentieth century (see Figure 3–2).

This evolution of the capitalist economic system has implications for First Nations and others who are developing and pursuing an economic development strategy. The emergence of a new regime of accumulation following a period of crisis creates the need and opportunity to develop new modes of social regulation and resulting modes of development. As the following material indicates, the global economy is in the midst of just such a period of adjustment.

In stage one, the system was in equilibrium. Stage two was a period of crisis or disequilibrium resulting from a shift from the extensive to the Fordist regime of accumulation. Equilibrium returned in stage three when a suitable mode of social regulation emerged. The fourth (current) stage is also one of crisis. Most authors (Dicken 1992; Getimis and Kafkalas 1992; Gottdiener and Komninos 1989; Komninos 1989; Peck and Tickell 1992; Scott 1988; Storper and Walker 1989) suggest this crisis — the collapse of the Fordist equilibrium — was caused by a failure of the monopolistic mode of social regulation to

FIGURE 3–2: The Evolution of the Capitalist Economic System

Date	Regime of Accumulation	Modes of Social Regulation
Stage 1: Prior to 1920	extensive: expanded reproduction of the capitalist system, sharp international divisions of labour, orientation to external markets; colonial or imperialistic capitalism	competitive: national regimes of accumulation adjust to one another through exchange and interest rates; output is adjusted and wages are adjusted to changes in price; classic economics
Stage 2: 1920 to 1945	intensive: emergence of Fordism, mass production based on the principles of Henry Ford and Frederick Taylor, growth of vertically integrated corporations	competitive: as above; is in crisis, unable to regulate Fordist regime of accumulation; economic 1930s collapse; early emergence of Keynesian policies; World War II
Stage 3: 1945 to 1965	intensive: expansion of Fordism, growing importance of multinational corporations, international trade, increased mobility of capital	monopolistic: increase in productivity matched by increase in consumption through sharing of surplus and promotion of mass consumption; collective bargaining, minimum wage laws, unemployment insurance, etc. to share surplus and support mass consumption; Keynesian economic policies re: business cycle; international regulation of capital — Bretton Woods, International Monetary Fund
Stage 4: 1965 to present	flexible accumulation	monopolistic: as above; is in crisis, unable to regulate flexible accumulation; collapse of Bretton Woods in the face of capital mobility; demise of Keynesian economic policy because of growing government deficits, recurring periods of inflation and recession, Third World Debt crisis, etc.

Source: Based on Corbridge 1989.

accommodate changes in the nature of the regime of accumulation. This collapse, and the equilibrium that is struggling to emerge from it, are discussed in some detail in the remainder of this section.

The Fordist equilibrium is well described by Getimis and Kafkalas (1992, 74) as consisting of

> *The Fordist compromise, a regime of accumulation according to which mass production was matched with mass consumption through a constant sharing-out of value added and the parallel growth of real income and productivity.*

and

> *Keynesian policies, a mode of regulation whereby social legislation, collective bargaining, and welfare measure, together with credit controls,* [that] *allowed the regulation of demand and investment.*

Storper and Walker (1989, 151) provide a typical description of the characteristics of the Fordist regime of accumulation:

- *Large capital-intensive factories organized around either continuous flow processes (e.g. petrochemicals, steel) or assembly-line processes (e.g. cars, electrical machinery).*
- *Production and marketing posited on standardization of output, long production runs, and dedicated, non-adaptable capital equipment.*
- *Large firms internalizing large parts of production systems, seeking to enhance internal economies of scale.*
- *The factory of the large corporation occupying the critical position between upstream suppliers and downstream fabricators, who often manufacture using batch production methods.*
- *Multiplant oligopolistic corporations operating within a relatively stable competitive framework.*
- *Industry-wide unions with national contracts.*

While Peck and Tickell (1992, 349) offer insight into the mode of social regulation associated with Fordism, saying that

> *The Fordist system of accumulation was complemented by a monopolistic MSR* [mode of social regulation], *which served to secure the conditions appropriate to the maintenance of mass labor and consumer demand. The state played a particularly important role here, as through Keynesian policies it sought to minimize the vulnerability of the accumulation system to cyclical recessions.*

Under the broad umbrella of the global Keynesian mode of social regulation, distinctive national and regional variants emerged (for example the "free enterprise" approach of the United States and the "social democratic" approach of the Scandinavian countries).

The Fordist coupling began to collapse in the 1970s. Causes of this collapse include technical limits to rigid fixed capital production techniques; working class resistance to Taylorist and Fordist forms of work organization (Jessop 1989); a change in consumption patterns "toward a greater variety of use values ... [that] cannot be easily satisfied through mass production" (Amin 1994, 12), the increasing mobility of capital and the resulting ability of transnational corporations (TNCs) to move among spatially bounded regulatory jurisdictions in the pursuit of greater profits (Leyshon 1989); and, in the face of this internationalization of capital, the inability of national Keynesian policies to avert crisis (Komninos 1989).

According to regulation theory, the crisis in Fordism has ushered in a period of turmoil (that continues still) in the capitalist economic system, as a new regime of accumulation and associated modes of social regulation struggle to emerge. Most authors agree that the restructuring of the global economy in response to the crisis in Fordism has involved, and continues to involve, a "selective move from mass production to various forms of flexible production" (Norcliffe 1994, 2).

For example, Amin and Malmberg (1994, 119) say that the "irreversible growth in recent decades of consumer sovereignty, market volatility and fragmentation, and shortened life cycles for products require that production be organized on an extremely flexible basis." In a similar vein, Ash Amin says that the ongoing transition to a post-Fordist economy has resulted in companies:

> *Shifting emphasis in production from scale economies, rigid technologies and compartmentalization toward scope economies, flexible manufacturing systems and the integration of design, production and marketing.* (Amin 1994, 17)

Storper and Walker (1989, 152), compare the emerging flexible regime with Fordism, saying that flexible production systems have:

- *More general purpose equipment and machinery, especially machines based around variable labor processes and/or programmable computerized equipment.*
- *Smaller, more specialized workplaces and firms and greater reliance on subcontracting.*
- *Greater attention to demand variations, to which the quantity of inputs and outputs can be rapidly adjusted by altering the procedures or the mix of participants.*
- *Collective social and institutional order in place of hierarchical control exercised by the mass production corporation.*
- *More temporary and part-time hiring and more relaxed internal rules for assigning workers and managers to various tasks.*

Business literature echoes regulation theory's view that the capitalist economy is passing through a period of crisis from which a flexible regime of accumulation is emerging. For example, Steven Goldman (1995) in an issue paper examining leading edge management processes and practices for the Society of Management Accountants of Canada, says that

> *A new system of creation, production and distribution of goods and services has begun to take shape. It is defined by a distinct set of relationships, interdependencies, and forms of interaction among suppliers, producers, distributors, and customers. It demands new approaches to organizing, operating, and measuring the performance of both individual companies and clusters of cooperating companies. It will entail sweeping changes in social institutions, as well as social and personal values.*
> (Goldman 1995, 1)

Goldman calls this new system "agile production" and the companies exhibiting these characteristics "agile corporations." He elaborates on the changes in companies associated with the shift to agile (flexible) production, saying that they include:

> - *Organizing the operational workforce into cross-functional teams, ranging from manager-led to self-directing.*
> - *Distributing decision-making authority much more widely, reducing the levels of middle management.*
> - *Systematically bench-marking business process and production operations against external standards.*
> - *Integrating the flow of information across divisions within the company and between the company and other companies, especially suppliers and customers.*
> - *Creating a more open internal information environment, and a culture of universal workforce accountability and mutual responsibility for the company's success.*
> - *Introducing concurrent engineering, that is, integrating the design, engineering, manufacturing, marketing, finance, and service dimensions of new product development.*
> - *Highlighting customer responsiveness as a primary and universal company value.*
> - *Developing new products cooperatively with suppliers, and even collaboratively with competitors.* (Goldman 1995, 5)

He expands on the final point stressing that strategic and interactive relationships among networks of companies are often the most effective way of producing complex goods and services in "a competitive environment of continuous and unanticipated change." In such an environment it may "be advantageous on the grounds of cost, speed, or market penetration, to utilize only some company-owned resources, combining them with others available in other companies" (Goldman 1995, 6–7). This shift to a strategy of alliances and networks suggests that the emphasis in the Aboriginal approach to development on joint ventures with non-Aboriginal companies is well-founded.

A number of authors offer observations about the nature of the modes of social regulation and the resulting modes of development that emerge in various places as people struggle to adapt to the demands of the emerging flexible regime of accumulation. Two aspects of these emerging modes are particularly significant. First, there is evidence of an increasing emphasis on local/regional and global strategies at the expense of national approaches. For example, Amin and Malmberg (1994, 222) say the crisis in the global economy has resulted in "new opportunities for the location of economic activities" and that "the geography of post-Fordist production is said to be at once local and global." Second, many of the emerging modes of development attempt a seemingly incompatible simultaneous emphasis on competition and on coordination, cooperation and trust. These efforts seek to create networks, alliances and other methods of cooperation among various local and global players as they seek a competitive advantage in the global economy at the expense of other networks and alliances.

With respect to the local/global aspect of the emerging modes of development, Peck and Tickell (1992, 352) suggest that "geographies of accumulation interact with one another (as well as pre-existing spatial structures), to produce unique regional couplings." Peck and Tickell's observations about unique regional flexible accumulation couplings (modes of development) are echoed by other authors. For example, Gottdiener and Komninos (1989) suggest that different societies have embarked on their own modes of development which stand in subtle contrast despite similarities. Komninos (1989), writing separately, says that there has been a shift to the local as an important level of regulation as a result of the collapse of the national modes associated with Fordism. He suggests that development initiatives are increasingly in the hands of local or regional institutions and enterprises, often in joint venture. Scott (1988, 108) says that new industrial spaces result from a "very specific articulation of local social conditions with wider coordinates of capitalist development in general." Finally, Dicken (1992, 307) emphasizes that successful participation in the global economic system "is created and sustained through a highly localized process" and that "economic structures, values, cultures, institutions and histories contribute profoundly to that success." The strategy adopted by Aboriginal people is an example of this "highly localized process" of development involving participation in the global economy.

Moving from the local to the global level, Peck and Tickell and others caution against overestimating the power of, and the prospects for, particular localities in the face of the fierce competition that is part of the emerging global accumulation system, saying that

> *It is difficult to see how local strategies can do anything other than bend to the will of global competition.... The basic difficulty lies in trying to establish local order in the face of global disorder.* (Peck and Tickell 1994, 298)

Jessop agrees saying that the "local economy can only be seen as a node within a global economic network" (Jessop 1994, 271). Expanding on this, Amin and Malmberg suggest that because transnational corporations (TNCs) have emerged as the prime players in the global economy there is a "growing dependence of such development [at the local level] on the events and decisions within a wider corporate division of labour" (Amin and Malmberg 1994, 235). Dicken (1993) says that it is folly to assume that the local will have significant power and control in the emerging regime of accumulation unless it possesses unique resources. It follows that an effective mode of development is more likely to emerge among a people or in a region that controls key resources. Further, such a mode must involve interaction directly or indirectly with the key players in the global economy — the TNCs. Again, the First Nations appear to be on the right track with their strategy of business development through alliances and joint ventures and capacity building through resource acquisition.

As a note of caution, several authors warn that the success of one locality in the global system is often achieved at the expense of failure in other places. Such success can be transitory in the face of the power of global actors and the competitive reaction of other localities as they in turn woo these global players. This spectre emphasizes the need for mechanisms of cooperation and coordination to curb destructive competition among developing regions.

Peck and Tickell (1994, 311) suggest that "solutions to the crisis of uneven development in *after*-Fordism are unlikely to come from the bottom — through local competition — but must begin with action from above, through national and global coordination." Expanding on this notion, they say that a post-Fordist mode of social regulation "capable of restoring *sustainable* growth requires the reining in of the destructive processes of deregulated competition" (Peck and Tickell 1994, 282). To do so, the relations within and between localities must be reconstituted through the establishment of coordinating mechanisms. For example, Jessop (1994, 272) suggests that "efforts to make regional economies more competitive in the new global economy" must involve strategies to foster cooperation and coordination including such things as "labour market policies, education and training, technology transfer, venture capital, innovation centres, science parks, and so forth." Amin and Malmberg (1994, 230) express similar sentiments about the necessary local/regional coordinating responses saying that they involve a

> *local pool of expertise and know-how; a social structure and a culture which encourages labour flexibility and social cooperation as a result of face to face contact and the build up of communal ties; and the growth of a local infrastructure of specialized services, distribution networks and supply structures.*

While Hirsch and Zeitlin say that

> *Flexible specialization depends for its long-term success on an irreducible minimum of trust and cooperation among economic actors ... the establishment of rules limiting certain forms of competition ... as well as on collective institutions for the supply of nonmarket inputs such as technological information and trained labor* [and] ... *the resolution of disputes.*
> (Hirst and Zeitlin 1992, 76)

Aboriginal people, in their approach to development, address the issues of cooperation and coordination through (i) the organizational structures they have created within Canada (for example, among the First Nations their Tribal Councils, the FSIN and similar bodies in other provinces and the AFN); (ii) their international activities at the United Nations and other international bodies (particularly through the World Council of Indigenous Peoples); (iii) their capacity-building efforts; and (iv) their emphasis on competition through cooperation using business alliances and joint ventures.

In summary, regulation theory holds that communities, regions and nations are all part of the global economic system and must accommodate themselves to the requirements of that system's currently dominant regime of accumulation. The present period is one of transition from the Fordist to a flexible regime. This time of transition provides a particular developing people with an opportunity to establish their place in the new global economy through the creation of a mode of development that reflects their values, cultures, institutions and histories and can meet their needs and objectives. The potential for success in a particular instance is enhanced through the control resources valued by key players in the global economic system. As a particular region or people strive for success they will be competing with others with similar objectives. Destructive competition between regions has the potential to result in arrangements highly skewed to the benefit of the transnational players in the economy at the expense of developing people. Therefore, a set supralocal regulatory mechanisms complementary to the modes of social regulation adopted by particular peoples must be established to mediate competition among them and limit its destructiveness. Only if this can be done will the potential for development consistent with local/regional needs that is inherent in the emerging flexible global regime be realized.

According to a number of authors (Bertramsen 1991; Corbridge 1989; Jessop 1989; Thomsen 1991; Torfing 1991), regulation theory does not provide much insight into how a particular mode of social regulation, consistent with the nature and needs of a particular people, can be developed and successfully coupled with the dominant regime of accumulation to form a successful mode of development. However, alternative development strategies and the postimperial perspective, the subjects of the next subsections, do offer such insight.

3.2.2. The Postimperial Perspective

Becker and Sklar (1987, ix) describe postimperialism as "an idea about the political and social organization of international capitalism." It is a

> *paradigmatic conception of late 20th-century international capitalism ... it seeks to explain what notions of capitalist imperialism cannot: the observation that in the world's fully industrialized capitalist countries, national interests are increasingly distinct from the interests of dominant classes; whereas in the countries of the third world, the two sets of interests are increasingly congruent.* (Stander and Becker, 1990)

A key characteristic of the postimperial perspective is its emphasis on class. Rather than treating developing and developed areas as monolithic wholes that interact with one another, the perspective contends that the relationship between such areas is shaped by the actions of, and interactions among, certain groups or classes.

According to Becker and Sklar (1987), within developing regions a managerial bourgeoisie, consisting of the entrepreneurial and the bureaucratic elite (the managers of firms, politicians, professionals and the like), has emerged as the dominant class. Members of this class make the decisions about economic development goals, strategies and structures, including the approach taken to participate in the global economy (mode of development). They also direct and control the activities intended to attain these development objectives. At the same time, with the emergence of TNCs as the dominant force in the capitalist economy, the authors suggest that an international corporate bourgeoisie has appeared that exercises significant control over the activities of the global economy.

The mode of development that emerges in a particular place is largely determined by the objectives established and strategies adopted by the managerial bourgeoisie and the corporate international bourgeoisie, the arrangements negotiated among them, and the actions taken by them. This view of the role played by key players is supported by others, including Hirst and Zeitlin who noted that "which of the possible [post-Fordist] outcomes or scenarios prevails will depend ultimately on the struggles of the key players: state decision makers, capitalist managers, and trade union leaders" (Hirst and Zeitlin 1992, 86).

The postimperial perspective offers insight into the likely behaviour of the corporate international bourgeoisie in developing regions. Proponents of the perspective contend that the managers of TNCs have no particular national allegiance but rather "are ideologically disposed to have each branch of the corporation behave like a "good corporate citizen" of the country in which it is domiciled." (Stander and Becker 1990, 197). According to Stander and Becker, this behavioural disposition of TNCs, called "The Doctrine of Domicile" by R. L. Sklar (1987), arises because:

> *The TNC's interest in maximizing global profitability and avoiding suboptimization at a subsidiary level will be weighed against another, equally important interest: the corporation must legitimize its host-country presence in order to obtain the stability it needs to plan the maximization of capital accumulation under its control.* (Stander and Becker 1990, 198)

In their observations about the behaviour of TNCs in developing regions, Tavis and Glade (1988) offer support for the Doctrine of Domicile. They suggest that there are three possible approaches to interaction with developing regions available to TNCs: power-based, participative and combined strategies. The authors contend that while power-based strategies dominated in the past, participative strategies are now necessary if TNCs are to assure their long-term survival. The authors attribute this shift to a number of factors including:

1. Changing expectations about what constitutes ethical and responsible TNC behaviour.
2. Increased TNC experience in developing regions and especially the partial naturalization of multinational management in overseas subsidiaries.
3. The growth of a business infrastructure in developing regions.
4. More experienced, technically competent, and self-confident organizations for negotiation and economic administration in developing regions.

This TNC behaviour (the Doctrine of Domicile) is a manifestation of the approach to corporate social responsibility adopted by a firm's managers/owners. Various authors address the subject of the changing nature of corporate social responsibility as it is perceived by people at large and by those within the corporation. James Brummer (1991) and Ahmed Belkaoui (1987) provide particularly useful and comprehensive reviews of the subject.

In his analysis of corporate social responsibility, James Brummer (1991) suggests that there are four perspectives on the issue: classical, stakeholder, social demandingness and social activist. According to the classical perspective, economic performance is greatest when corporate executives respond only to the economic interests of the company's shareholders. It is argued that society's best interests are served when its specialized institutions (for-profit businesses, non-profit organizations, governments, and others) focus exclusively on their particular functions. The social obligations of businesses are confined to satisfying legal and economic criteria. Socially responsible behaviour not mandated by law will not be pursued because it imposes unnecessary costs on the business and therefore reduces profits. Proponents argue that if a segment of society desires some good or service, they should build a market for it, or urge government to either supply it or require business to do so.

The stakeholder approach suggests that a business's responsibilities extend beyond shareholders to include those who (i) are, or are likely to be, directly affected by the decisions and activities of the business; (ii) have an explicit contractual relationship with it; and/or (iii) can directly affect the corporation. Corporate executives may respond to the interests of stakeholders out of corporate and/or individual self-interest, because such a response is demanded by law; in response to, or in anticipation of, public pressure; and/or from a genuine desire to benefit the lives of stakeholders.

According to the social demandingness theory, corporations are responsible to carry out those activities that are expected or demanded of them by society. Managers should solicit and consider the opinions, demands and/or expectations of members of the public (not just stakeholders) regarding corporate activities and respond to the interests and needs expressed. Most theorists adopting this perspective contend that society's social and moral demands on businesses have been increasing over the past decades. It is no longer enough for firms to provide goods and services to the public for profit; they are expected to meet social and moral responsibilities as well.

The social activist approach holds that there is a universal standard for determining responsible corporate conduct that is independent of the interests of stockholders and the claims of stakeholders. This standard demands concern for the ideal or rational interests of the public, rather than their expressed or present interests. Therefore, the standard of responsible corporate conduct is independent of current circumstances and even current interests of various groups and is absolute and universal — it has an ethical, religious and/or metaphysical basis.

In a similar vein, Belkaoui (1987), in his book *Corporate Social Accounting,* suggests that society increasingly expects businesses to consider issues beyond profit maximization and that these expectations have resulted in three new and related paradigms: (i) the new economic paradigm, (ii) the rectification paradigm, and (iii) the ethical paradigm.

The new economic paradigm seeks to rationalize two differing views — libertarianism and radical economics. These views represent the extremes on a continuum of opinion concerning the pre-eminence of either the market or the state. Each of these views has its own rigid set of solutions to complex economic and social problems. Social and institutional economists occupy a more moderate position on this continuum holding that

> *The economic paradigm governing the relationships of the corporation and society need not be the role or importance of the market and/or the state as in libertarianism or radical economics but a clear statement of national and social goals based on*

> *a commitment to human and welfare and social justice and experimentation with institutional arrangements to solve economic and social problems.* (Belkaoui 1987, 13)

The basis of the rectification paradigm is the premise that the corporation is an active market and social agent whose actions will either worsen or improve the socioeconomic conditions. The continuum of rectification options available to the organization extends from complete indifference to an active role in rectifying social problems. Belkaoui suggests that

> *Complete indifference would definitely be harmful to the long-term interests of the firm. Involvement in some forms of rectification is a way of ensuring mutual acceptance by society and a role in securing social order and affluence.*
> (Belkaoui 1987, 14)

The ethical paradigm is similar to the rectification paradigm in that it also recognizes that a corporation's actions have the potential to impact positively or negatively on society. Again, a continuum of possible responses exists. At one extreme are the constructionists who argue that a business serves society best when it concentrates on the objective of profit maximization. The company should undertake social activities only if they aid in the pursuit of this objective or are imposed by law. At the other end of the continuum are those who argue that an ethical corporation has an obligation to behave in a socially responsible manner even if that behaviour interferes with profit maximization. Such a firm pursues a set of goals including social objectives and fair profits.

A synthesis of the three paradigms described by Belkaoui and the approaches to corporate social responsibility described by Brummer is possible. In that synthesis, corporate approaches to social responsibility and long-term survival range between two extremes (see Figure 3–3).

Belkaoui, Brummer and others (Armstrong 1982; Davis 1991; Goldman 1995) suggest that society's expectations and the requirements of flexible or agile competition are combining to force businesses to shift their approach toward the right end of the continuum. For instance, Goldman says that

> *Management must support a proactive posture toward operations-relevant social values.... Agility* [flexible competition] *reflects a competitive environment that links producers and consumers far*

FIGURE 3–3: Corporate Social Responsibility and Long-Term Survival

◄────────────────────────────────────►

Profit Maximization as the objective with the satisfaction of social responsibilities considered as a constraint.	Satisfaction of social responsibilities as an objective essential to the earning of returns adequate for long-term survival.

> *more closely than the mass production environment does. A hostile internal or external social environment precludes agility. A company cannot routinely reconfigure itself in response to changing market opportunities if it must continually fight battles ... over the environmental and community impact of its operations.*
>
> (Goldman 1995, 20)

He goes on to say that it is "advantageous for companies to internalize social values, rather than having them constrain their operations from the outside" (Goldman 1995, 30). These arguments flowing from the Doctrine of Domicile suggest that at least some companies will be receptive to arrangements intended to satisfy the development objectives of the people of Aboriginal people so long as such arrangements do not impair the companies' ability to survive in the global economy.

According to Sayre Shatz (1987b), the development strategies adopted and the actions taken by people in developing regions indicate that they believe that businesses' approach to social responsibility is shifting in the manner described. He suggests that people in developing regions exhibit one of three approaches to interaction with TNCs — the acceptance, the rejection, or the pragmatic. He characterizes the approaches as follows:

> *The acceptance approach conceives of MNE* [multinational enterprise] *expansion as economically rational, with benefits considerably outweighing costs for the host as well as home country. The rejection approach sees MNE activities as essentially baleful, with harm to the host countries overshadowing benefits. Between these two is the pragmatic approach which views MNE operations as mixed in effect; which believes that feasible government pressures can produce a worthwhile improvement in the benefit-cost mix; and which therefore advocates intelligent bargaining by host governments.*
>
> (Shatz 1987b, 108–109)

It is Shatz's contention, which is supported by others, that the pragmatic approach has become the strategy of choice for most developing people including Aboriginal people in Canada[2]. The assertively pragmatic approach of the Tahltan people of British Columbia toward companies wishing to develop natural resources on their traditional lands is typical.

> *We wish to make it very clear that the Tahltan People and the Tahltan Tribal Council are not inherently opposed to any specific type of business or resource development within our country. However, we do feel strongly that any development within our tribal territory must adhere to some basic principles.*

---

2 See Anderson and Bone 1995a & 1995b; Anderson 1995; Friedman 1992; Decter and Kowall 1989; MLTC 1993, 1994, 1995a & 1995b; Notzke 1994; and Pitelis 1991.

Before a resource development project can commence within Tahltan territory, it will be necessary for the developer and the Tahltan Tribal Council to enter into a project participation agreement that encompasses the following elements and basic principles:

1. *assurance that the development will not pose a threat of irreparable environmental damage;*
2. *assurance that the development will not jeopardize, prejudice or otherwise compromise the outstanding Tahltan Aboriginal rights claim;*
3. *assurance that the project will provide more positive than negative social impacts on the Tahltan people;*
4. *provision for the widest possible opportunity for education and direct employment-related training for Tahltan people in connection with the project;*
5. *provision of the widest possible employment opportunities for the Tahltan people with respect to all phases of the development;*
6. *provision for substantial equity participation by Tahltans in the total project;*
7. *provision for the widest possible development of Tahltan business opportunities over which the developer may have control or influence;*
8. *provision for the developer to assist the Tahltans to accomplish the objectives stated above by providing financial and managerial assistance and advice where deemed necessary*

(Notzke 1994, 215)

Even allowing for TNC behaviour consistent with the Doctrine of Domicile, nothing in the postimperial perspective (or in the regulation theory) suggests that the mode of development that emerges in a particular place among a particular people will deliver benefits beyond its elites to the general population. In fact, the plight of the masses could be worsened, as has been the case for much of the "development" that has occurred in the Third World to date. Alternative development approaches have emerged as a result of this failure and are discussed in the next subsection.

3.2.3. Alternative and Indigenous Development Approaches

According to Friedmann (1992), alternative or "grassroots" approaches to development began to emerge in underdeveloped regions in the 1970s as a result of the failure of the growth maximization strategies pursued since the end of the Second World War. In describing this failure, he quotes from the Cocoyoc Declaration (issued at the conclusion of a United Nations-sponsored conference in Cocoyoc, Mexico, in 1974):

Thirty years have passed since the signing of the United Nations Charter launched the effort to establish a new international or-

> *der. Today that order has reached a critical turning point. Its hopes for creating a better life for the whole human family have been largely frustrated. It has proved impossible to meet the "inner limits" of satisfying fundamental human needs. On the contrary, more people are hungry, sick, shelterless and illiterate today than when the United Nations was first set up.*
> (Friedmann 1992, 2)

Throughout the 1980s and into the 1990s, this failure continued and the circumstances of the world's poor deteriorated further. De Janvry and Sadoulet (1993, 663) observed that during the 1980s there was:

1. A sharp rise in the incidence of poverty.
2. A deepening of dualism in the types of employment (precarious versus formal) and forms of economic activity (informal versus formal).
3. A sharp rise in inequality.
4. As part of austerity programs, a disproportionately large reduction in government social expenditures.

According to De Janvry and Sadoulet, the focus of the development strategies that failed to meet the needs of the poor of the world has shifted from an emphasis on the market to state and back over time. The market dominated during the liberal period from 1850 to 1930. The Great Depression during the 1930s and the emergence of newly independent nations following the Second World War resulted in a shift in emphasis to the state (Keynesian policies) which lasted until the late 1970s. During the late 1970s, the 1980s and the early 1990s, the market (and its principal players, the TNCs) regained ascendancy following the failure of Keynesian policies (deficits in developed countries, Third World debt crisis, recurring recessions and inflation, etc.). Although couched in different terms, this description of change over time in the capitalist economic system is similar to that offered by the regulation theory (see Figure 4–2).

Beginning in the 1970s and continuing to date, supporters of alternative or "grassroots" development strategies have argued that in the face of the failure of development strategies centered on the market or the state to improve the circumstances of the world's poor, emphasis must shift to a third previously neglected sector — the civil. For example, Nugent says:

> *Neither direct state intervention or indirect state influence through macro policies is a sufficient condition for success. Nor are the best efforts to utilize existing markets ... guaranteed to lead rural residents out of pervasive poverty.... Failure can be attributed to the lack of vibrant, functional, and healthy local organizations and institutions* [the civil sector] *and can be overcome by their presence.* (Nugent 1993, 623)

In a similar vein, according to De Janvry, Sadoulet and Thorbecke:

> *Many civil organizations have emerged as substitutes for the state and the market. When the state fails to deliver public*

> *goods, insurance, management of externalities, minimum basic needs and democratic rights, civil organizations may develop to fill the vacuum. The same holds for the market, where market failures may lead to the emergence of* [civil] *institutions.*
> (De Janvry, Sadoulet and Thorbecke 1993, 567)

On the other hand, Peet and Watt note that the

> *Failings of neoliberal and authoritarian and bureaucratic development provided considerable momentum for a focus on institutions within civil society, especially agreements based on bargaining, cooperation, and persuasion.*
> (Peet and Watt 1993, 236)

Proponents of alternative development do not suggest that this third or civil sector can or should replace the market or state. Rather, according to Friedman, alternative development

> *accepts the existing system of global accumulation as a fact. It does not propose to turn away from it and shut the door.... Broadly speaking, the objective of an alternative development is to humanize a system that has shut them* [the poor] *out.... Its central objective is their inclusion in a restructured system that does not make them redundant* (Friedmann 1992, 12–13)

Parallel to, in fact, part of, the emergence of alternative approaches to development, there has been increasing attention paid to what are called "Indigenous" approaches to development where Indigenous people and groups perform the role of the "civil sector." Agrawal says that the failure of neoliberal (market) and authoritarian and bureaucratic (state) approaches to development has led to a "focus on Indigenous knowledge and production systems" (Agrawal 1995, 414). He goes on to say that these efforts are an attempt "to reorient and reverse state policies and market forces to permit members of threatened populations to determine their own future" (Agrawal 1995, 432).

Wiarda (1988) expresses a similar view saying that among Indigenous people there has been

> *A rejection of the basic developmental models and paradigms originating in the West, both Marxian and non-Marxian varieties, and a corresponding assertion of non-Western, nonethnocentric and Indigenous ones.* (Wiarda 1988, 59)

He goes on to suggest that Indigenous people (and others) believe and behave as if there is "not just one or two (First and Second World) paths to development but many and diverse ones ... where a blending and fusion of these [traditional and modern] is both likely and more widespread" (Wiarda 1988, 60).

Bebbington suggests that "like it or not, Indigenous peoples are firmly integrated into a capricious and changing market. Their well-being and survival depends on how well they handle and negotiate this integration" (Bebbington

1993, 275). He goes on to say that the Indigenous approach is not to reject outright participation in the modern economy

> *but rather to pursue local and grassroots control over modernization ...* [and] *over the economic and social relationships that traditionally have contributed to the transfer of income and value from the locality to other places and social groups*
> (Bebbington 1993, 281)

This view is consistent with regulation theory's view that successful participation in the global economy "is created and sustained through a highly localized process ... values, cultures, institutions and histories contribute profoundly" (Dicken 1992, 307).

In two papers discussing economic development among Aboriginal people in Canada, Robinson and Ghostkeeper suggest that Aboriginal people are rejecting industrial development from the outside in favour of development strategies originating in, and controlled by, the community "with the sanction of Indigenous culture" (Robinson and Ghostkeeper 1987, 139). The authors argue that "a wide range of cultures may enable entrepreneurship and economic development to flourish" (Robinson and Ghostkeeper 1988, 173). They go on to suggest that the key to successful Indigenous development lies in recognizing in each culture those forces conducive to development and "designing development plans accordingly" (Robinson and Ghostkeeper 1988, 173).

Case 3–1 that follows shows how Aboriginal and "mainstream" strengths can be combined as part of a strategy of tourism development that builds on and supports Aboriginal values and provides employment for Aboriginal people.

Case 3–1: FirstHosts for First Nations Tourism (1996)[3]

At last Sandra White will see the fruits of her labour. For more than three years she has been developing a British Columbia First Nations tourism initiative. "The whole object of developing a customer service program was to provide Aboriginal businesses with information which was relevant and accessible to Aboriginal needs," says FirstHost Project Manager White.

Lynn Phelan of the Senklip Native Theatre group delivered the premiere FirstHost workshops on June 4, 1996, held at the Cherry Grove Golf Course, owned by the Osoyoos First Nation. FirstHost Leader Katherine Robinson of the Nuu-Chah-Nulth Economic Development Corporation delivered a simultaneous eight-hour customer service and tourism training program at the Victoria Indian Centre.

What distinguishes FirstHost from other customer service programs is its focus on cultural tourism products. FirstHost explains to its participants the sort of cultural tourism products on the market and the issues that arise because of them.

Most of the participants, called "circle members," are already involved in the tourism industry, as frontline customer service workers, business owners and

---

3 Source: DIAND Website, *http://www.inac.gc.ca/ecdev/entre/bc/1sthos.html* [edited].

First Nation staff members. Still others are career changers, looking for an introduction to the world of Aboriginal tourism. FirstHost workshops are open to the public.

The workshop consists of four modules called "learning circles." The first learning circle focuses on tourism — what is tourism, who has been involved historically, and what businesses are involved in Aboriginal tourism in British Columbia. The second learning circle is about the guest — how to identify your guests, how to meet their needs and expectations, and how to build a service relationship with them. This section also highlights British Columbia's tourism market, and how to appreciate cultural differences. "It's about sharing culture," says White.

The third learning circle is one of the most important, perhaps the most beneficial for universal learning. Customer service — communications skills, greetings, first impressions and complaint handling — are covered in a theory lesson, followed by intensive role play practice. At the end of this long day, the fourth learning circle focuses on the tourism market in the community where each circle member lives and works in, so the new FirstHosts can provide accurate information to their guests.

FirstHost initially needed to build a team of First Nations trainers. In March of this year, 12 First Nations people, selected from various regions across British Columbia, were led through a comprehensive curriculum to become FirstHost Leaders. Each circle member pays $35 to attend a workshop, explains FirstHost Leader Beverley O'Neil, a marketing entrepreneur of Ktunaxa ancestry. Each workshop can accommodate 13 to 21 circle members. If it has fewer than the 13 minimum, the business can opt to pay a flat fee of $455. For instance, a small business or organization with at least 13 people interested in taking FirstHost can host a workshop. Alternatively, the host organization can open the workshop up to the public to fill the required 13 seats and make the workshop more affordable.

"I have a lot of requests from other jurisdictions," says White, discussing the future of FirstHost. "There is a great deal of interest." She mentions that she has received requests from other provinces and territories, including Saskatchewan, Manitoba and the Yukon.

"I have projected that there are over 250 First Nations tourism-related businesses in British Columbia now," says White. "There are probably over 1,500 people currently employed in the First Nations tourism industry." A projected 1,301 British Columbia First Nations people will be trained in the arts of customer service and tourism by the end of FirstHost's first year of operations.

FirstHost's logo was designed with the First Nations market in mind. It makes use of traditional icons such as the circle and the four directions, which, when pictured with four human figures facing each other, represent the unity among peoples and the four learning circles of the workshop. The two eagle feathers also incorporated into the design signify love, peace and harmony.

The Urban Native Indian Education Society (UNIES) developed FirstHost in conjunction with Human Resources Development Canada and British Columbia's Ministry of Skills, Training and Labour. FirstHost is owned by UNIES.

FIGURE 3–4: The Contingency Perspective

- Communities, regions and nations are all part of the global economy and must accommodate themselves to its dominant regime of accumulation.
- The nature of this accommodation with the global economy (mode of development) can reflect the needs and objectives of a particular developing people/region.
- The potential exists for negotiation of mutually beneficial arrangements (as part of the mode of development) between the leaders of a developing region and those who control the global economy.
- An active civil sector capable of articulating the needs of their people and a leadership capable of developing the strategies and negotiating the arrangements necessary to address those needs, are essential to the creation of a mode of development that will deliver benefits beyond the elites to the general population of a developing region.
- Supralocal regulatory mechanisms are necessary to coordinate the activities of developing regions and peoples and reduce destructive competition among them.

Source: Adapted from Anderson 1995.

3.3. The Contingency Perspective

Regulation theory, the postimperial perspective and alternative development approaches have emerged from the impasse between the modernization and dependency perspectives. Common to all three perspectives is a focus on the relationship between a developing region and the global economy. All take the view that economic activity in a particular region, while it is and must be integrated into the global economy, can exhibit characteristics unique to that region and serve the particular needs of its people. The three perspectives can be combined to form a contingency perspective on economic development (see Figure 3–4).

From the regulation theory, the proposed contingency perspective adopts five key concepts. First, at any particular time, the global capitalist economy is dominated by a regime of accumulation and the current period is one of transition from the Fordist to a flexible regime. Second, all communities, regions and nations are part of the global economy and must accommodate themselves to the requirements of its emerging dominant regime of accumulation. Third, the development of an appropriate mode of social regulation is the key to successful interaction with that regime; that is, the creation of an effective mode of development. Fourth, such a mode is "is created and sustained through a highly localized process" where "economic structures, values, cultures, institutions and histories contribute profoundly to that success [the creation of an effective mode]" (Dicken 1992, 307). Control of resources valued by the key players in the global economic system (the TNCs) greatly increases the likelihood of success. Finally, while the local plays a key role in the development of a particular mode of development, supralocal mechanisms are necessary to coordinate and regulate the global economic system in order to minimize destructive competition between localities.

From the postimperial perspective, the contingency perspective holds that the relationship between a particular developing region and the global economy (the mode of development) emerges as a result of the interaction between the leaders of the developing region (the managerial bourgeoisie) and the capitalist economy (the corporate international bourgeoisie). More importantly, this interaction is not carried out in the abstract. Rather, it is played out in real time and in real places by real people with unique outcomes. Further, based on the Doctrine of Domicile (and the characteristics of flexible accumulation), the proposed perspective contends that there is the potential for the formation of mutually beneficial alliances of various types between developing regions and the main players in the global economy — the TNCs — as part of the mode of development. However, nothing in the postimperial perspective suggests that the mode of development that emerges in a particular situation will necessarily deliver benefits beyond the elites to the general population of a particular developing region.

Alternative/Indigenous development approaches are concerned with how the relationship between a developing region and the global economy can be structured to increase the likelihood that the needs of the people of the region will be met and not just the requirements of the regime of accumulation and interests of the managerial and corporate international bourgeoisies. These approaches emphasize that there are "not just one or two paths to development but many and diverse ones" (Wiarda 1988, 60) shaped by a people's culture, values, history and resources. From alternative/Indigenous development approaches, the contingency perspective holds that creation of a successful mode of development requires an active civil sector capable of articulating the needs of the people, a leadership capable of devising the strategies and negotiating the arrangements necessary to address those needs, and a mechanism for the people to modify these arrangements should the outcomes prove unacceptable.

According to the contingency perspective on economic development, participation in the capitalist economy can serve the interests of a developing region or people. Whether a particular situation actually results in the realization of the benefits sought will depend on the characteristics and actions of the parties involved. The outcome is not preordained by some fundamental "law" of capitalism as it is assumed to be by both the orthodox and radical perspectives.

3.4. The Contingency Perspective and Aboriginal Development

According to the contingency perspective, the answers to the two parts of the question raised at the beginning of this chapter are both in the affirmative. Yes, the emerging Aboriginal approach to economic development is well conceived and is consistent with development theory; and, yes, Aboriginal peoples' expectations are realistic and potentially realizable.

Aboriginal people acknowledge the necessity of participation in the global economy and are attempting to create a distinct mode of development that will permit them to do so. Central to this mode is a strategy of business creation in various forms of partnership and alliance (supply contracts, subcontracting, joint ventures, etc.) with other Aboriginal and non-Aboriginal businesses. In support of this approach, Aboriginal people are actively pursuing capacity-building activities to increase their human, financial and physical resources. As a result, they are becoming more attractive to corporations as prospective partners. This strategy is clearly consistent with the characteristics of flexible accumulation. It also anticipates behaviour by at least some non-Aboriginal companies consistent with the Doctrine of Domicile.

Arrangements intended to implement the mode of development have involved, and will continue to involve, negotiations between key Aboriginal and non-Aboriginal leaders. Aboriginal people also acknowledge the need for and have developed mechanisms to coordinate their activities and reduce destructive competition among them. They have formed organizations to that end (the Tribal Councils, the FSIN, the AFN, etc.). Aboriginal peoples' values, traditions and organizational structures demand input from, and control by, people at the "grassroots" (the civil sector). If the arrangements established through negotiation between Aboriginal and non-Aboriginal leaders produce outcomes unacceptable to a significant portion of the Aboriginal community, their reaction should cause (and has caused) Aboriginal and non-Aboriginal leaders to modify these arrangements.[4]

Chapters 4 through 8 explore in more detail Aboriginal people's development strategies and activities to (i) confirm that they are consistent with the proposed eight characteristics, and (ii) address in depth the three key questions raised in chapter 2.

---

4 See chapter 8 for a discussion of the blockade by members of the First Nations of the Meadow Lake Tribal Council of the Tribal Council's forestry company's operations caused by their dissatisfaction with certain company decisions and practices.

4

Aboriginal Rights, Land Claims and Treaties

As discussed in chapter 2, Aboriginal people in Canada have been actively engaged in capacity-building activities as they pursue their goal of economic self-sufficiency and self-determination. These capacity-building efforts have been particularly significant in three areas: (i) the acquisition of financial and physical resources through the realization of treaty and Aboriginal rights, (ii) financial institution building, and (iii) post-secondary education focusing on economic/business development and business management. The first of the three areas is particularly significant and is the subject of this chapter. The other two areas are dealt with through examples in chapters 5, 7 and 8.

The modern drive by Aboriginal people to regain control over their traditional lands and resources began in earnest in the mid-1970s with three landmark events: (i) the Calder decision of the Supreme Court of Canada, (ii) the Mackenzie Valley Pipeline Inquiry and (iii) the James Bay and Northern Quebec Agreement.

The Calder decision is extremely significant because in it

> *[t]he Supreme Court of Canada in 1973 first recognized land rights based on Aboriginal title* [and that] *Aboriginal title is based on an Aboriginal group's traditional use and occupancy of that land.* (DIAND 1996, 1)

As a result of the Calder decision, a federal policy for the settlement of land claims was adopted in 1973. The thrust of the policy "was to exchange claims to undefined Aboriginal rights for a clearly defined package of rights and benefits set out in a settlement agreement" (DIAND 1997, 1).[1]

According to Peter Usher, the Mackenzie Valley Pipeline Inquiry is important because the inquiry and the resulting report by Justice Thomas Berger brought about "a new paradigm of development and social change" (Usher

1 See Appendix 2 for background on comprehensive claims.

1993, 99) relating to economic development involving Aboriginal people and lands in Canada. The inquiry and its conclusions are discussed in depth in section 1 of this chapter.

The third item, the James Bay and Northern Quebec Agreement, is included among the landmark events because it is the first comprehensive claims agreement to be reached following the Calder decision and the federal government's adoption of its comprehensive claims policy. Further discussion of the agreement follows in section 2.

Following these three events, there has been a series of land claims agreements and treaties that have moved the Aboriginal people in Canada a considerable distance toward their goal of control over their traditional land resources. In fact, during the period 1973 to 1996, 10 comprehensive claims were settled. They include

- the James Bay and Northern Quebec Agreement and the Northeastern Quebec Agreement,
- the Inuvialuit Final Agreement,
- the Gwich'in Agreement,
- the Nunavut Land Claims Agreement, the Council of Yukon Indians Umbrella Agreement (presently encompassing four final agreements),
- the Sahtu Dene and Metis Agreement, and
- the Nisga'a Agreement in Principle.[2]

In these comprehensive agreements, attempts were made to address the twin issues of Aboriginal control over activities on their traditional lands and the building of capacity for economic development. According to J. Rick Ponting (1986, 194), these agreements were intended to

> *carry Indians forward with both a viable traditional sector for those who chose that way of life, and an adequate share of political-economic power or local influence to be used to protect Indian interests and to create enduring economic opportunity of the nontraditional type.*

Two of these agreements have been selected for more in-depth review: the Inuvialuit Final Agreement and the Nisga'a Final Agreement.

The Inuvialuit Agreement was reached 10 years after the James Bay and Northern Quebec Agreement and the Nisga'a Final Agreement another 10 years later. Both are reviewed with particular attention to their terms with respect to (i) economic development, (ii) arrangements providing Aboriginal people a measure of control over activities on their traditional lands, and (iii) the issue of extinguishment of Aboriginal rights. Over time, one finds an evolution in the terms relating to these three issues. In addition, the Nisga'a Agreement provides insight into the likely outcomes of the other ongoing treaty

2 See Appendix 2 for a brief description of each agreement.

negotiations in British Columbia.[3] These two agreements are considered in more detail in sections 3 and 4 of this chapter.

In closing, the evolution of the terms in the comprehensive land claims agreements and the ongoing refinement of the definition of Aboriginal rights are results of the ongoing struggle of Aboriginal people for the realization of their rights. The "civil sector" has been active and done its work well.

4.1. The Mackenzie Valley Pipeline Inquiry

In 1974, a consortium of multinational oil companies (Arctic Gas) made application to the Canadian government to build a pipeline to carry natural gas from the fields in the Mackenzie Delta and Prudhoe Bay in Alaska to markets in southern Canada and the United States. According to Gurston Dacks, the federal government

> *favoured and indeed had actively promoted the construction of the Mackenzie Valley pipeline. However, for public-relations reasons and to mollify the New Democratic Party, which at that time held the balance of power in the House of Commons, the cabinet decided that a public inquiry should be held to study the questions surrounding the pipeline.* (Dacks 1981, 135)

As a result, in March 1994, Mr. Justice Thomas Berger was appointed to head the inquiry established to consider the issues surrounding the pipeline.

According to Dacks, "Justice Berger was known to be sympathetic to native people" (Dacks 1981, 136). In fact, he was one of the lawyers who argued the Calder case before the Supreme Court on behalf of the Nisga'a. On the face of it, this would seem to make him an unusual choice for the government, given its support for the project. However, these were the very reasons he was chosen. According to Robert Page:

> *The Trudeau government [lacked] credibility with native groups as a result of its white paper and its court actions ... the inquiry had to be headed by someone who commanded their respect.... If native groups participated fully and with some faith in the commissioner, they were more likely to abide by his recommendations in authorizing the pipeline.* (Page 1986, 92)

Justice Berger's terms of reference required him to

> *inquire into and report on the terms and conditions for granting a pipeline right-of-way under two specific headings: the social, environmental, and economic impacts regionally of the construction, operation, and subsequent abandonment of the*

---

3 See Appendices 1, 2, 3 and 7 for additional information on the comprehensive claims process underway in British Columbia.

> *proposed pipeline and any proposals to meet the specific environmental and social concerns.* (Page 1983, 93)

According to proponents of the pipeline, Berger was not being asked to determine if the line should be built. In their view, he was only to determine the terms and conditions that would apply to its construction and operation, and to do so quickly. Berger took a broader view of his mandate. He ruled against the proponents on both counts. With regard to timing, he refused to rush the process to suit their commercial interests. He ruled that all parties should have a fair opportunity to prepare for the hearings and have an opportunity to be heard. According to Page:

> *On the scope of the hearings he was even more emphatic. "I take no narrow view of my terms of reference" ... not confined to the consideration of a pipeline application but related "to the whole future of the North."* (Page 1983, 102–3)

From the beginning, there were contending views on the project and, in particular, its possible benefits to the people of the region and those of Canada as a whole. The proponents espoused the modernization perspective on development. Their views were challenged by Aboriginal groups and others arguing from the neo-Marxist perspective.[4] According to Peter Usher, the latter view triumphed, and "there emerged from those years both a new paradigm of development and social change ... and new processes of directing their course" (Usher 1993, 99). The new paradigm that emerged in this instance was a part of the broader trend toward alternative/Indigenous/contingent approaches occurring worldwide, described in chapter 3 and incorporated into the contingency perspective on development.

Arctic Gas and other proponents of the pipeline put the modernization case. They argued that industrialization in northern Canada was "inevitable, desirable, and beneficial — the more the better" (Usher 1993, 105). They did not deny that the process would have negative impacts on the traditions of the Aboriginal society. In fact, in their view, development "required the breakdown and eventual replacements of whatever social forms had existed before" (Usher 1993, 104). They agreed that the process would be painful for Aboriginal people, but from it would emerge "a higher standard of living, a better quality of life, and greater personal choice ... [while] continued blockage could only lead to deepening dependency" (Usher 1993, 104–105). A sense of the modernist view can be found in the words of Mayor R. Sykes of Calgary, who described efforts to protect the traditional Aboriginal way of life as

> *misguided attempts to preserve under the meaningless title of culture a primitive life of insecurity and hardship. If they knew a better way of life* [the modern way of life], *they would hardly wish it* [the traditional way of life] *on their children.*
> (Page 1986, 113)

4 See chapter 3 for a discussion of these contending perspectives on development.

In addition to their views on the desirability of industrialization and the inevitability of modernization, proponents of the project held the view that "all Canadians have an equal interest in the North and its resources" (Page 1986, 114), a view at odds with the position of Aboriginal people and the recent Calder decision.

The views of the proponents were challenged by Aboriginal groups and others arguing from the neo-Marxist perspective. They agreed with the proponents that the pipeline project would introduce "massive development with incalculable and irreversible effects like the settlement of the Prairies" (Usher 1993, 106). However, unlike the proponents, they did not feel that this was a desirable outcome. Instead, it was argued from the dependency perspective that

> *this massive assault on the land base of Native northerners threatened their basic economic resources and the way of life that these resources sustained ... when all the riches were taken out from under them by foreign companies, Native land and culture would have been destroyed and people left with nothing.* (Usher 1993, 106–7)

This alternative view of the development process was accompanied by a different view about the land in question. Far from believing that the lands and resources belonged to all Canadians equally, Aboriginal people felt that these were their traditional lands over which they held "Aboriginal title" and which they had never ceded to the Crown under treaty — a view consistent with the Calder decision and the newly establish federal policy on comprehensive land claims.

In 1976, after an exhaustive and exhausting series of hearings, Berger issued the first volume of his report. He recommended a 10-year moratorium on pipeline construction in the Mackenzie Valley "in order to strengthen native society, the native economy — indeed the whole renewable resource sector — and to enable native claims to be settled" (Berger 1977). In Berger's view, such settlements

> *must be part of a fundamental reordering of the relationship between white and native, in order to entrench their rights to the land and to lay the foundations for native self-determination under the Constitution of Canada.* (Page 1986, 119)

An interesting side issue emerges from the inquiry. Alberta Gas Trunkline withdrew from the Arctic Gas consortium and, together with Westcoast Transmission, formed Foothills Pipe Lines. Foothills made an application to build a smaller pipeline solely for Canadian gas serving the Canadian market. It is not the application itself that is interesting but rather the fact that Foothills

> *recognized the profound changes underway within society and tried to meet Berger on his own ground, taking seriously the criteria he had defined for his inquiry* [whereas] *Arctic Gas assumed his terms and conditions were an aberration from reality.* (Page 1986, 115)

As demonstrated in chapter 6, Foothill's vision of the future, not Arctic Gas's, was correct. Indeed, Westcoast Transmission, which is one of the principals of Foothill, has remained a leader in corporate/Aboriginal relations to this day.

4.2. The James Bay and Northern Quebec Agreement

While the drama of the Mackenzie Valley Pipeline Inquiry was being acted out in the Northwest Territories, an event of equal significance was occurring in the Province of Quebec — the negotiation of the James Bay and Northern Quebec Agreement (JBNQA). This agreement and its companion Northeastern Quebec Agreement (NEQA) are particularly important because they mark the dawning of a new era. According to the Department of Indian Affairs and Northern Development, these agreements were "Canada's first modern land claim settlements" (INAC 1993, 1), while Bob Bone describes the JBNQA agreement as "the first modern treaty" (Bone 1992, 220) between the Government of Canada and an Aboriginal people.

According to J. Rick Ponting, this new treaty and those that followed

> *were designed to provide more than token economic support to Indians. They were framed to do so in a manner that would carry Indians forward with both a viable traditional sector for those who chose that way of life, and an adequate share of political-economic power ... to protect Indian interests and to create enduring economic opportunity of a non-traditional types.*
> (Ponting 1991, 194)

This adequate share of political-economic power was to be achieved through (i) cash compensation, (ii) outright ownership and control over an expanded land base, (iii) a right to participate in the management of activities on a far larger "shared" land base and (iv) the establishment of a variety of governmental and administrative bodies to provide for the exercise of self-government and the pursuit of socioeconomic development.

The forces that gave rise to the JBNQA were the same as those underlying the Mackenzie Valley Inquiry — the struggle by Aboriginal people for control over their tradition lands and recognition of their Aboriginal rights. The event that precipitated the crisis that resulted in the agreement was the 1971 decision of the Province of Quebec to develop the hydroelectric potential of the rivers draining into James Bay. In that year, the province "created the James Bay Development Corporation to develop all the territory's [northern Quebec] resources, including hydro, forestry, mining and tourism" (DIAND 1993b, 1).

Understandably, the Aboriginal Peoples who had occupied the region "since time immemorial" — the Cree, Inuit and Naskapi — objected to the failure of the province to recognize their rights on and to these lands. In the fall of 1972, they petitioned the Quebec Superior Court for an injunction stopping all work on the James Bay hydroelectric project until their lands claims were settled. The injunction was granted and, although it was subsequently overturned, "the determination of Natives to protect their historic land-based interests led to negotiations toward a land claim settlement" (DIAND 1993b, 1).

An agreement-in-principle was reached in 1974 between Canada, Quebec, the Cree and the Inuit, and the final agreement was signed on November 11, 1975. According to Bone:

> *The James Bay Agreement called for $225 million to be paid to the Cree and Inuit over a ten-year period; outright ownership of 13,300 km^2, and exclusive hunting rights over 155,000 km^2.*
>
> (Bone 1992, 220)

Subsequently, the Naskapi of northeastern Quebec reached a similar agreement — the Northeastern Quebec Agreement — which became part of an amended James Bay and Northern Quebec Agreement in 1978. Under the agreement, the Naskapi received $9-million in compensation. Because this agreement is the first of the modern settlements and, as such, "may have set the terms for future modern treaties" (Bone 1992, 220), its terms are worthy of review in some detail.[5]

The land provisions of the agreement were complex, involving three categories, each with a different level of Aboriginal "ownership" and control. Category I lands are set aside for the exclusive use and benefit of the Aboriginal people of the Cree and Inuit communities of the James Bay region. The Cree received 2,158 square miles and the Inuit 3,130 square miles of such land. Title to the land is held by the various community corporations, and the land cannot be sold to anyone other than the Province of Quebec. For example, the JBNQA says the following about Inuit Category I lands:

> *Title to the land shall be transferred to Inuit Community Corporations for Inuit community purposes, which shall include the use of the lands by the Inuit Community Corporations for commercial, industrial, residential or other purposes.*
>
> (JBNQA, Section 7.1.3)

> *Category I lands or any portion thereof may not be sold or otherwise ceded except to the Crown in the right of Quebec.... Subject to the provisions of this section, an Inuit Community Corporation shall enjoy the usual rights of an owner and, more particularly, may make with any person, including a non-Inuit, agreements in respect to servitude, leases and other rights of use and occupation respecting such lands.*
>
> (JBNQA, Section 7.1.5)

Similar terms and conditions apply to the Category I lands of the Cree.

According to Ponting, the issue of mineral rights on Category I lands

---

5 See Appendix 5 for additional information of the history and terms of the JBNQA.

> *was resolved by having the rights remain with the Quebec government but also giving the native people the right to veto the Quebec government's exercise of those rights … compensation must also be paid for the use of such mineral or subsurface rights.* (Ponting 1991, 195)

Ponting goes on to say (and, as shown in chapter 5, others, including corporations, agree) that this treatment of mineral rights "enables the Cree [and the Inuit] to negotiate certain development terms in exchange for suspending their veto" (Ponting 1991, 195).

Category II lands are much larger in area — 25,130 square miles for the Cree, and 35,000 square miles for the Inuit. The Cree and Inuit do not own this land. Instead:

> *Category II lands belong to the province, but Native governments share management for hunting, fishing, trapping, tourism development and forestry. Native people have exclusive hunting, fishing and trapping rights on these lands.* (DIAND 1993b, 2)

In Section 5.2.6.(a), the JBNQA says that non-native people can hunt, fish and/or trap on Category II lands "only with the consent of the native people." As with the right to veto the Quebec government's exercise of its mineral rights on Category I lands, this provision creates development opportunities in tourism and outdoor recreation.

The JBNQA says Category II lands

> *may be appropriated by Quebec for development purposes, provide such lands are replaced or, if the Native people wish, and an agreement can be reached thereon, they are compensated… 'development' shall be defined as any act or deed which precludes hunting, fishing and trapping activities.*
> (JBNQA, Section 5.2.3)

This right of Quebec to pursue development, particularly hydroelectric development, impacting Category II (and Category III) lands has been a controversial aspect of the JBNQA from the outset.

Category III lands, totalling almost 350,000 square miles, are a special category of Quebec public lands:

> *Both Native and non-Native people may hunt and fish here subject to regulations adopted in accordance with the agreements* [JBNQA and NEQA]. *Aboriginal groups have exclusive rights to harvest certain aquatic species and fur-bearing animals and to participate in the administration and development of the land. The Quebec government, the James Bay Energy Corporation, Hydro Quebec and the James Bay Development Corporation have specific rights to develop resources on Category III lands.* (DIAND 1993b, 2)

Controversy over development on Categories II and III lands has emerged most recently with respect to the Great Whale hydroelectric project (James Bay II). While opposition by the Cree and Inuit, as well as from environmental groups and others, resulted in the government of Quebec indefinitely "shelving" the project in 1994, it in no way altered that government's position that it was within its rights to pursue such development even if it impacts Category II lands. In fact, according to the Grand Council of the Cree at its 1997 Annual General Assembly, Hydro-Quebec

> *has recently made public a plan to divert the Whapmagoostuie River and the Rupert River into existing reservoirs of the La Grande complex ... this river diversion would totally submerge Epsikameesh (Lake Bienville), the headwaters of the Great Whale River ... a sacred area, a major calving ground for the inland caribou, and a sanctuary for marine life, water fowl and other forms of wildlife...* [this] *proposed diversion would have the same impact as if the James Bay II scheme (now shelved) had gone ahead.* (GCC 1998(1), 4)

This is one of the "darker sides of the agreement" Grand Chief Mathew Coon Come referred to when he addressed the 1997 General Assembly of the James Bay Cree. Specifically, he said:

> *We have always declared that through the Agreement the Crees gave permission for one hydro electric project in our territory. The governments have stated, however, that they believe we surrendered and gave up all our rights, title, and claims in and to our waters and lands....* (GCC 1998(1), 2)

We will return to the Chief Coon Come's comments on the JBNQA in the concluding segment of this section.

Now on to the financial compensation. The compensation of $235-million provided under the terms of the JBNQA was paid out over 20 years as follows: $75-million paid out in cash over 20 years, $75-million in Quebec bonds maturing in 1995 and $75-million when the hydroelectric project was completed (or by 1996). Of the total, the Inuit received approximately $90-million, and the Cree $135-million. The Naskapi received $9-million. In the case of the Cree and the Inuit, the moneys were paid to the Makivik Corporation and the Cree Regional Authority, respectively. These bodies were the legal entities established under the terms of the JBNQA "to receive and administer the compensation moneys, oversee the implementation of the JBNQA, and ensure the integrity of the agreements" (Makivik 1998a, 1). A brief review of the performance of the two bodies can be found in the following subsections.

4.2.1. Makivik Corporation

The Makivik Corporation was officially created on June 23, 1978 to "administer the implementation of the Agreement [JBNQA], and invest the $90-million in compensation, paid over 20 years from 1975–1996" (Makivik

1998d, 1). The mandate of the corporation is foster socioeconomic development among the 14 Inuit communities[6] that are signatories to the JBNQA. The following philosophy has guided Makivik in the pursuit of such development:

> *Makivik has always treated these compensation moneys as a 'heritage fund' and its financial policies have had the objective of ensuring that these funds are available to future generations of Inuit.* (Makivik 19982, 1)

From its creation to March 1998, the corporation's accomplishments have been considerable. It has increased the value of Inuit compensation funds to $145-million, while at the same time investing more than $40-million in the construction "of much needed municipal facilities such as arenas and community centres to improve social conditions in Nunavik. Furthermore, since 1975 the corporation have made over $6-million in donations to various Nunavik organizations" (Makivik 1998d, 1).

During the same 20-year period, Makivik created several large subsidiary companies that now employ 1,100 people. These companies include:

- *Air Inuit: Nunavik's regional airline. It employs 200 people in its various operations. Its revenues reached $27 million in 1993.*
- *First Air: A major air carrier in Canada's eastern Arctic. It links the north to the south, and the Canadian Arctic to Greenland.*
- *Seaku Fisheries: Exploits shrimp stocks, groundfish, and develops inshore projects with Inuit entrepreneurs. Makivik is also a 50% partner of Unaaq Fisheries with Qikiqtaaluk Corporation.*
- *Nunavik Arctic Foods: Harvests wild meat in Nunavik, processes [it] in four community processing centers, and markets the meat (caribou, seal, ptarmigan, Arctic char) in Nunavik and southern markets.*
- *Pan Arctic Inuit Logistics Inc. (PAIL) is a joint venture company between Makivik, the Labrador Inuit Development Corporation, Nunasi Corporation, the Inuvialuit Development Corporation, and Frontec Logistic Corporation. It operates and maintains radar sites which are part of the North Warning System.* (Makivik 1998b, 1)

The Inuit in Northern Quebec, through the actions of the Makivik Corporation, provide an excellent example of the Aboriginal approach to economic development described in chapter 2. The focus is on the community, its present and future. The objective is socioeconomic development in a manner con-

6 The traditional territory of the people of the 14 Inuit communities that are signatories of the JBNQA is called Nunavik. The current population of the communities is approximately 7,000.

sistent with and supportive of traditional values and practices. For example, Seaku Fisheries and Nunavik Arctic Foods are designed to blend aspects of traditional life on the land and on the modern dollar-based economy to improve the socioeconomic circumstances of those who wish to follow a primarily traditional lifestyle. The development processes adopted involve the creation of businesses to compete in the broader national and global economy (e.g. First Air and Nunavik Arctic Foods) and, often, involve joint ventures with other Aboriginal and non-Aboriginal parties (e.g. Unaaq Fisheries and Pan Arctic Inuit Logistics).

While the accomplishments of the Inuit through the Makivik Corporation over the past 20 years have been impressive, they pale in comparison to the challenge of the future. In 1996, 60% of the Inuit of Nunavik were under 30 years old and the population growth rate was four times the provincial average. As a result, with respect to employment:

> *a recent survey* [1996] *conducted by the Kativik Regional Government's Employment and Training Department concludes that, in order to maintain even today's unacceptably low rate of employment, we will have to create 25% more jobs than presently exist in all of Nunavik by the year 2,000.*
> (Makivik 1998e, 1)

In the following discussion of the activities of the Cree, we will see a similar situation — many accomplishments to date, but much more needed in the future.

4.2.2. The Cree Regional Authority

The Cree Regional Authority (CRA) was established in 1978. Like the Makivik Corporation, its mandate is to administer the terms of the JBNQA and manage the financial compensation received. The Cree Regional Authority has the same membership as that of the Grand Council of the Crees. This was done to assure

> *coordination between political objectives and administrative actions. So the CRA Council, like the Grand Council, is composed of each band chief of the nine communities, and one other member from each community, in addition to the Grand Chief and the deputy Grand Chief, who are elected directly at the Cree Annual General Assemblies.* (CRA 1998a, 1)

The CRA coordinates and administers all programs falling under the JBNQA for the nine communities.[7] It also exercises Cree authority on Category II lands with respect to their exclusive hunting, fishing and trapping rights, and represents Cree interests on Category III lands. Further, "the CRA has broad-

7 Nine Cree communities with a current population of approximately 12,000 are signatories of the JBNQA. They call their traditional territory Eeyou Astchee.

ranging responsibilities for ensuring that the many provisions of the JBNQA designed to protect and enhance Cree life are implemented" (CRA 1998a, 2).

In 1982, the Cree Regional Authority created the Cree Regional Economic Enterprises Company (CREECO), "a holding company for all Cree-owned enterprises in which compensation moneys were invested" (CRA 1998b, 1). CREECO describes its approach as follows:

> *Aside from the objective of creating wealth, the CREECO companies also have a social mission of partnership with the Cree communities. This involves maximizing native employment in its ranks, and to that extent, CREECO has undertaken training programs in each of its companies.*
>
> *The CREECO companies also participate enthusiastically in joint ventures ... provide grants and funding to communities and regional activities... promote support and cooperation in the business community, both in the Cree world and externally.*
>
> (CRA 1998b, 1)

On formation, CREECO assumed ownership of two major companies that had already been formed using compensation money — Air Creebec and the Cree Construction Company. Both companies "had mandates beyond simply servicing the Cree communities themselves ... [and] were envisioned as commercial enterprises that aimed to be competitive in the business world ... [and to] provide work for Cree people" (CRA 1998b, 1). Since its formation, CREECO has established three additional companies — Valpiro Inc. (ground and aircraft service operations) and Servinor and Jessel Foods (food wholesalers).

According to its 1997 annual report, CREECO's assets total $68-million. In the same year, CREECO companies had combined revenues of $86-million and combined expenses and write-offs of over $87-million, resulting in a net loss of after taxes of $1,220,119. It is interesting to note that the new food wholesale companies (in their first full year of operation) accounted for all the losses. In fact, the older, more established companies showed a profit of $1-million. The new companies, Servinor and Jessel Foods, are expected to perform better in their second and subsequent years of operation. The various CREECO companies employed a total of 525 employees, 184 (35%) of whom were native.

Employment growth among the Crees flowing from the JBNQA is not limited to the jobs created by these business ventures. Many Cree found employment in the government and community service sectors, such as the Cree Regional Authority and the local community governments, which assumed control over their own affairs and began delivering their own programs. According to a study by Salisbury (1988), during the 1970s and early 1980s there was a doubling of the number of Cree employed and a five-fold increase in the average wage. As a result, "welfare and family allowance benefits ... dropped from 16 to 5 percent of total income, and salaries have increased from 23 to 52 percent" (Hedican 1995, 150).

As with the Inuit through Makivik, the Cree through the Cree Regional Authority have accomplished much since the signing of the JBNQA 20 years ago. Also, like the Inuit, much remains to be done.

4.2.3. Concluding Comments on the James Bay and Northern Quebec Agreement

A sense of where things stand today for the Cree can be drawn from the 1997 Annual Report of Grand Chief Mathew Coon Come to the Cree people. According to the Chief, the Cree gained important rights under the JBNQA agreement. These include:

> ***Political rights*** *such as guarantees of citizenship, certain aspects of self-government, membership, nation-to-nation relations.*
>
> ***Social rights*** *such as education, health, social services, justice, housing, police and community infrastructures.*
>
> ***Economic rights*** *such as economic development, the hunting, fishing and trapping regime, training and guarantees of employment and preferential access to contracts in the context of development in the territory.*
>
> ***Cultural rights*** *overlap with many other areas, but include education, our right to continue with our language, culture and traditional pursuits.*
>
> ***Other rights*** *including the right to participate in the development of laws and regulations concerning the environment, and to special participation in the assessment of the environmental and social impacts of proposed developments in the territory.* (GCC 1998, 2)

The Grand Chief said that the Cree had hoped that these rights "would provide sufficient guarantees that our people would be able to maintain our society, culture and way of life, and survive as a people" (GCC 1998a, 1). He went on to say that this has not proven to be the case and that the Cree Nation has reached a crossroad in its relation with the Quebec and Canadian governments, and that Cree people are demanding

> *more than ever the full recognition of our status and rights, and the right to benefit meaningfully from the resources and economic potential of Eeyou Astchee, our land.* (GCC 1998a, 1)

The major difficulties the Cree have with the JBNQA and its implementation deal with (i) the extinguishment of their Aboriginal rights; (ii) the "fact that immense wealth — several billion dollars a year — is being taken off land in Eeyou Astchee ... and that we Crees get no share in the wealth; either in the form of royalties, business opportunities or work" (GCC 1998, 1), and (iii) the failure of both the federal and Quebec governments to fulfill their commitments under the agreement. The first and second issues are dealt with in the following paragraphs. The third is complex, and fraught with controversy and claims and counterclaims, and best left for another time and place.[8]

---

8 See Appendix 5 for a description of the issues and negotiations surrounding implementation.

At the time of the negotiations, both the federal and Quebec governments viewed the money, land and other rights the Cree and Inuit received as compensation

> *for the extinguishment of all aboriginal rights and claims, for renouncing the right to collect royalties or mining duties (past, present and future), and for the forfeiture of the right to block the James Bay hydro development project in the courts.*
> (Ponting 1991, 196)

The Cree (and the Inuit) do not take the same view. In his report, Chief Coon Come put the Cree case as follows:

> *The Crees have important rights as an Aboriginal people and as residents in Canada and the province of Quebec. These rights exist independently of the Agreement, and are reflected in Canadian law, including the constitution. The Agreement resulted in the Crees entering into a formal relationship with the two governments, and gave special* [additional] *rights in favour of the Crees.* (GCC 1998, 2)

The view expressed by the Grand Chief on behalf of the Cree is not new. The extinguishment provision was controversial among Aboriginal people at the time of the negotiation and implementation of the JBNQA and has remained so. Indeed, subsequent land claims negotiations have been marked by increasingly effective efforts by Aboriginal people to have extinguishment dropped as a condition of their settlements. These efforts culminated in a 1986 decision by the federal government to drop its policy "to only negotiate treaties if Aboriginal peoples accepted extinguishment of their Aboriginal rights and title" (INAC 1996, 1). Instead, the federal government expressed a willingness to negotiate alternatives to blanket extinguishment and has done so in subsequent agreements.

The second issue, the claim by the Cree "to an ownership and jurisdiction of adequate resources and a direct and fair share of the benefit extracted from our traditional lands" (GCC 1998, 3) gave rise to Resolution 18 at the 1997 General Assembly of the Cree. This resolution states that the Crees have

> *full ownership, titles, claims and interests in all minerals, trees, waters, and other resources in, under and over traditional Cree territory pursuant to their status as a Nation and distinct people; and that the JBNQA did not and does not completely extinguish all ownership, titles, claims and interests in all minerals, tree, waters, and other resources in, under and over traditional Cree territory; and that the JBNQA does not provide a just, fair and appropriate share to the Crees of these resources.*
> (GCC 1998, 4)

The resolution goes on to mandate the Cree Regional Authority to "enter into discussions with the government of Quebec and Canada and with all developers operating in Cree traditional territory, to provide for the most equitable and just Cree participation in the use of the natural resources referred to above" (GCC 1998, 4).

Will the efforts of the Cree and the Inuit be successful? Time will tell, but there is reason to be hopeful. The Cree's view, and the similar view of the Inuit of Nunavik, that their Aboriginal rights to their traditional lands and resources should provide them a sound basis for socioeconomic development as a distinct people, is consistent with the recommendations of the Royal Commission on Aboriginal Peoples. Their desire to participate equitably in the development of these resources in partnership with others "in a manner that is compatible with our traditional pursuits and way of life" is consistent with the Aboriginal approach to development as described in chapter 2, and the contingency perspective discussed in chapter 3. Their efforts to participate in the development of the resources of their lands is likely to find favour with corporations wishing access to those resources, as the following chapter will attest.

4.2.4. Cases: Aboriginal Communities and Hydroelectric Development

The three cases that follow document the experience of other Aboriginal communities with hydroelectric developments in their traditional lands. They indicate that the relationship between an Aboriginal community and a large hydroelectric company need not be confrontational. Projects can be developed in a manner acceptable to Aboriginal people that bring benefits to both parties involved.

Case 4–1: Wawatay Generating Station (1997)[9]

It sits at the bottom of a ravine, surrounded by a neat, grassy lawn trimmed with remnants of the logging days on the Black River. There is an air of calmness about the place, but looks can be deceiving. Somewhere inside this big, tidy building by the river, a heavy rush of water is being converted into power.

Started in 1987 and completed in 1992, the Wawatay Generating Station marks the culmination of years of planning for the Ojibways of the Pic River First Nation. It also marks the beginning of a new plan for the future of the community.

During development, the First Nation owned 50% of the project, while Sunridge Power owned the other half. Sixty band members formed a significant portion of the manpower needed in the building stage.

Creating a weir to collect the water and a huge tunnel with a 148-foot drop to guide it into the station, and purchasing all the components of the station proved to be an expensive undertaking. To facilitate financing the project,

---

9 Source: DIAND Website, *http://www.inac.gc.ca/ecdev/entre/on/Pichyd.html* [edited].

the First Nation sold their interests to Conwest Exploration. They now own a profit-sharing interest in the station. Once the debt has been serviced on the project, the First Nation's interest will be worth approximately $400,000 per year.

Meanwhile, a merger of Conwest Exploration with gas and oil giant Alberta Energy Corporation has allowed the First Nation to pursue the purchase of the facility as the new company divests itself of all "non-core" assets, including its hydro division.

Byron LeClair, economic development officer for the Ojibways of the Pic River, says the band has been working with the Department of Indian and Northern Affairs on a loan or grant arrangement in order to buy into 100% of the station. If they are successful, the generating station will net the band an average of $3.7-million annually, once all loans are paid off.

The place itself is an impressive sight. It's fully automated, which may have something to do with the peaceful atmosphere. An operator and a maintenance man, both members of the First Nation, are the only employees.

Hydro generating stations often have a major impact on the environment around them, both during and after construction, because of their tendency to divert water away from its natural course and increase its speed. Because of their concern for the natural environment that exists on the First Nation, which is located on the north shore of Lake Superior, the Ojibways of the Pic River took pains during the planning of the project to reduce its impact as much as possible.

One environmental obstacle they are very proud to have overcome involved the well-being of local fish species spawning in the Black River. To ensure the continued survival of the fish, the station's outflow area was designed in such a way that newly hatched trout are kept in a separate backwater area away from the outflow, until they are mature enough to join the river's natural course.

The Wawatay Generating Station took years of planning, negotiations and hard work to complete, but it's shaping up into a big success and a source of pride for the First Nation. LeClair recommends similar projects for other First Nations, if the conditions are right. It has proven to be a sustainable, stable business, and now that it's off the ground with a long-term contract, there is little risk involved.

If the community's plan to buy the entire project works out, profits from the sale of power could allow the First Nation the chance to invest in even more business ventures and capital projects. "It's not so much what it's done, it's what it's going to do," LeClair said.

Case 4–2: The Dokis Hydro Project: A First For First Nations (1997)[10]

In 1984, Chief Martin Restoule had a vision while standing on a bridge on the Dokis reserve in northern Ontario, watching the water rush by under his feet. He saw potential, and he didn't want it to go to waste. Restoule is no longer

---

10 Source: DIAND Website, *http://www.inac.gc.ca/ecdev/entre/on/Dokis.html* [edited].

chief, but his dream of harnessing the power of the water for electricity and using it for the benefit of his people is still alive, inching closer to reality. Chiefs who followed him continued to pursue Restoule's dream. Through the years, developments were made through the efforts of Chief Tim Restoule. Chief Jack Restoule and Dokis' Economic Development Team continue the negotiations today.

For decades, Public Works Canada has been operating dam structures, known as the Big Chaudiere Dams, along the French River, using part of the Dokis First Nation's territory and roads. But the Big Chaudiere system needs to be rebuilt in order to continue controlling water levels in nearby Lake Nipissing. That reality has provided a perfect opportunity for Dokis to start its own hydroelectric project. Negotiations have been successful in moving the control structure of the Big Chaudiere dam downstream to maximize the potential of the river. If completed, it would be the first 100% Native-owned hydro project in Canada.

Dokis First Nation has proposed a site for building a new dam, which would allow Public Works to save about $2-million by constructing only one new structure, at a natural narrow down river, rather than refurbishing the two existing structures. At the same time, construction of the dam would be designed in such a way that Dokis would be able to add its own hydroelectric plant to work in conjunction with the structure, at a significantly reduced cost to the First Nation.

About 15 band members would be employed for up to two years during the building stage, and four or five more would have full-time jobs once the project was complete. And it would mean big money. Once all the mortgages were paid off, it is estimated that sales of hydro power could net the band up to $1-million annually. That money would go a long way toward creating an economic development corporation to oversee future business ventures, which is one of the band's main goals for the future.

It's a good idea for all concerned but, like so many good ideas, the Dokis hydro project has had to survive a few challenges along the way.

In 1986, the Province of Ontario declared part of the land around the French River a Heritage Provincial Park, an area where hydro projects are not allowed. However, because one bank of the river is on the Dokis reserve, the band has been able to negotiate with the province to accommodate the project.

Another hurdle involved the eventual sale of the power itself. In 1991, Ontario Hydro placed a moratorium on entering into new contracts for hydro power. Without a buyer, Restoule's dream nearly died. But that moratorium is now scheduled to be lifted within the next five or six years, and Ontario Hydro supports the Dokis project. With that battle won, an environmental assessment is underway, paid for by Public Works Canada, since that department operates the existing dams.

Cory Restoule, Dokis' economic development officer, believes the end to all the red tape may be in sight, and he's determined to get down to business. "Everybody is just really willing to get this job done and they're really willing to help out," Restoule said. "All our homework is done. Now everything has to fall into place."

4

Case 4–3: Dogrib Nation Powerful Players in Development (1997)[11]

After launching the Snare Cascades Hydroelectric Project, the Dogrib people are making further strides toward economic self-sufficiency. The completion in July of the generating facility on the Snare River, 140 km north of Yellowknife, is only the first phase of planned hydro development in the Snare Basin.

The 4.3-megawatt Snare Cascades plant, owned by the Dogrib Power Corporation, is Canada's first 100% Aboriginally owned hydroelectric power project. The company is part of the Dogrib Nation Group of Companies (DNGC), the economic development arm of the Dogrib Treaty 11 Council, representing the communities of Rae-Edzo, Lac La Marte, Rae Lakes and Snare Lake.

Dogrib Power Corporation is developing two more hydro projects: a 10-megawatt plant, at an estimated cost of $80-million, and a 12-megawatt plant, at an estimated cost of $60-million. The 10-megawatt plant, 70 km north of the Snare Cascades plant, is expected to begin construction in the fall of 1997. Depending on their design, the two new plants together will employ upwards of 100 Dogrib people and will generate more than 50% of the installed power capacity of the Northwest Territories Power Corporation.

The electrical power generated by the plants will provide the region with a stabler and more cost-effective and environmentally sensitive alternative to diesel fuel. The 7% added to the Yellowknife power grid by the completion of the Snare-Cascades project is a significant start toward replacing diesel generation dependence with renewable energy sources.

The Snare Cascades plant will be operated by the Northwest Territories Power Corporation under a 65-year power acquisition agreement that will provide the Dogrib Nation with both employment and financial benefits.

Further large scale projects on the horizon for the Dogrib people will build upon the successes of the "partnership-in-development" approach pursued by the Dogrib Treaty 11 Council so far. "The completion of the Snare Cascades Hydro Electric Dam is an example of our commitment toward developing partnerships between Aboriginal people and the public and private sectors," says Al-Nashir Jamal, President and CEO of the Dogrib Nation Group of Companies. "We hope developers will take this as an example of how they can successfully complete projects in partnership with Aboriginal people," adds Jamal.

The Dogrib Nation is also engaged in several joint ventures with prominent Canadian companies. These companies include PCL construction, the country's largest private construction and construction management company; SNC-Lavlin Inc., Canada's leading engineering, environmental and project management group; Canadian Helicopters; and Txi Cho Corporation Ltd., Northwest Territories' premier industrial catering and camp services. As a result of these partnerships, The Dogrib Nation Group of Companies is poised to benefit from mining investment and resource development in the area. As CEO Al-Nashir Jamal explains: "The Dogrib Nation has now become an active player

---

11 Source: DIAND Website, *http://www.inac.gc.ca/ecdev/entre/nt/Dogrib.html* [edited].

in the infrastructure development of the NWT and a major figure in large-scale financing."

The projects and partnerships forged by the Dogrib Nation Group of Companies have built a strong foundation for continued opportunities for the Dogrib people, who are in an advantageous position to be full participants in sustainable economic development in the Dogrib/North Slave Region.

4.3. The Inuvialuit Final Agreement

The Inuvialuit Final Agreement was an outcome of the forces that gave rise to the Berger Inquiry. The Inuvialuit had never signed a treaty with the federal government surrendering ownership of their lands to Canada. Yet, in the drive to develop oil and gas reserves and build the pipeline, neither the government nor the oil companies were acknowledging the Inuvialuit's rights to the land and resources, nor were they concerned with the disruption their activities were causing to the traditional Inuvialuit lifestyle. These were the issues that caused Berger to recommend a 10-year moratorium on development while outstanding claims were settled.

In 1974, the Inuvialuit entered into negotiations with the federal government over their traditional lands. In May 1977, the Committee of Original Peoples' Entitlement (COPE) submitted a formal comprehensive land claim on behalf of the approximately 4,500 Inuvialuit living in the six western Arctic communities of Aklavik, Inuvik, Tuktoyaktuk, Paulatuk, Holman and Sachs Harbour. Negotiations between the Inuvialuit and the federal government continued through the late 1970s and early 1980s, culminating in the Inuvialuit Final Agreements (IFA) in May 1994.

Under the terms of the agreement the Inuvialuit retained title to "91,000 sq. km [35,000 square miles] of land, 13,000 sq. km [5,000 square miles] with full surface and subsurface title; 78,000 sq. km [30,000 square miles] excluding oil and gas and specified mineral rights" (Frideres 1993, 118). The Inuvialuit also received $45-million in cash compensation to be paid out over 13 years (1984 to 1997), wildlife harvesting and management rights, a $7.5-million Social Development Fund (SDF) and a $10-million Economic Enhancement Fund (EEF). In return for the specific rights in the IFAQ, at least in the minds of the federal government, the Inuvialuit relinquished all other rights based on their traditional use and occupancy of the land — extinguishment!

Before going on to discuss details of the IFA (and the actions of the Inuvialuit since its signing), it is useful to compare it with the JBNQA. In the minds of the non-Aboriginal governments involved, both agreements had the Aboriginal people involved giving up their "ill-defined" Aboriginal rights in return for the specific rights contained in the agreement — extinguishment. In both, the Aboriginal people received specific land rights, financial compensation, certain rights pertaining to the maintenance of a traditional lifestyle and the right to participate, in an advisory capacity, in certain decision-making situations and bodies pertaining to their lands. Both the JBNQA and IFA required the Aboriginal people involved to establish regional corporations to receive and manage the lands and financial compensation received — the

Makivik Corporation and the Cree Regional Authority under the JBNQA, and the Inuvialuit Regional Corporation under the IFA.

On a per capita basis, cash compensation for the Inuvialuit was approximately $13,900 paid out over 13 years in 1977 dollars (Frideres 1993, 118), whereas the per capita compensation under the JBNQA was $22,000 over 20 years in 1974 dollars (Hedican 1995, 148–149). The facts that the Inuvialuit received the $10-million EEF and the $7.5-million SDF at the start of the agreement and that the JBNQA agreement was valued in 1974 dollars spread out over a longer time reduce the apparent difference in per capita compensation considerably.

The amount of land received differed in total, with the Inuvialuit receiving 5,000 and 30,000 square miles of Categories I and II lands respectively. Together, the Cree and Inuit of James Bay received 5,300 square miles of Category I lands and 60,000 square miles of Category II lands. However, this works out to just over 7 square miles per person under the IFA, and just less than 7 square miles per person under the JBNQA, based on population at the time the agreements were signed. Under both agreements, the Aboriginal people involved had ownership and "jurisdiction" over Category I lands, and similar special rights and participative co-management mechanisms on Category II lands.

Based on the preceding, it seems fair to conclude that the agreements are similar in their important aspects. Why, then, do the Inuvialuit appear much more satisfied with the IFA than the Cree are with the JBNQA? The answer appears to lie in the implementation of the agreement, as the material in section 4.3.2 shows. Three factors emerge as particularly important: (i) failure by non-Aboriginal governments to implement the terms of the JBNQA, (ii) the non-Aboriginal governments' views on extinguishment and their right to proceed with development outside Category I lands, and (iii) the actions of corporations interested in developing the resources of the region.

4.3.1. The Inuvialuit Regional Corporation

In 1984, the Inuvialuit Regional Corporation "was formed to receive the lands and financial compensation obtained by the Inuvialuit" (IRC 1998a, 1) and given "the overall responsibility of managing the affairs of the settlement to achieve the objectives in the IFA" (ICG 1998, 4). According to the introduction to the 1996 Annual Report of the Inuvialuit Corporate Group (ICG), of which the IRC is the lead organization, these objectives are to:

- *Preserve Inuvialuit cultural identity and values within a changing northern society.*
- *Enable Inuvialuit to be equal and meaningful participants in the northern and national economy and society.*
- *Protect and preserve the Arctic wildlife, environment and biological productivity.* (ICG 1997, 3)

The IRC is controlled by the Aboriginal people of the six communities that are party to the IFA. Each community

> *has a community corporation with elected directors. The chair of each community corporation forms the IRC Board of Directors. The Chair/CEO of IRC is elected by the directors of the six community corporations.* (ICG 1997, 4)

In their objectives — to preserve and enhance culture and traditional practices while participating fully in the local, regional and national economy, and in their approach — collective with the people, which means participating through their communities and the assets held by the communities in common, the Inuvialuit provide a "textbook" example the Aboriginal approach to development described in chapter 2.

Is the Inuvialuit approach working? In an attempt to answer this question, the following three subsections describe the activities of the three major subsidiaries of the IRC (that together with the IRC make up the Inuvialuit Corporate Group) — the Inuvialuit Development Corporation, the Inuvialuit Petroleum Corporation and the Inuvialuit Investment Corporation.

4.3.1.1. The Inuvialuit Development Corporation

The Inuvialuit Development Corporation (IDC) was created to address one of the objectives in the IFA; that is, "to enable the Inuvialuit equal and meaningful participation in the Western Arctic, Circumpolar, and national economies and societies" (IDC 1998, 1). In pursuing this objective, IDC says it will "build and protect a diversified asset base, generate financial returns, create employment, and increase skills and development among the Inuvialuit" (IDC 1998, 1). A sense of the performance of the company and its subsidiaries can be obtained from the IDC and IGC 1996 annual reports.

The IDC owns, wholly or in joint ventures, over 30 companies operating in eight sectors: technology and communications, health and hospital services, environmental services, property management, manufacturing, transportation, northern services and real estate development (see Figure 4–1). The IDC started five new businesses in 1996, three of them joint ventures, and dissolved or sold five others that were underperforming. In total, 14 of the IDC companies are joint ventures and, according to its 1996 Annual Report, "the IDC will continue its strategy of establishing joint ventures with strong partners to take advantage of large contract opportunities" (ICG 1997, 28). The IDC companies operate in the North and throughout southern Canada as well as internationally.

According to Chairman Dennie Lennie in his "Chairman's Message" in the said annual report:

> *1996 was a successful year for the Inuvialuit Development Corporation (IDC). The Company generated the largest profit this decade, achieved record Inuvialuit employment … reported a positive cash flow … the best balance sheet in the company's history; debts lowered, assets and liquidity increased.*
> (IDC 1998b, 1)

In 1996, the combined revenues of these IDC companies and joint ventures was $84.5-million, and the profit after taxes a record $4.6-million. While earning the

FIGURE 4–1: The IDC Companies

Technology and Communication	Health and Hospital Services	Environmental Services	Property Management	Manufacturing	Transportation	Northern Services	Real Estate Development
100% Inuvik Video Convenience Centre (Inuvik)	J.V. Inuvialuit Projects Inc./ Versa Services Ltd. (Inuvik)	100% Inuvialuit Projects Inc. (Western Arctic)	100% Inuvialuit Corporate Centre (Inuvik, NWT)	50% SRI Homes/SRI International (Alberta)	100% Aklak Air Ltd. (Western Arctic)	100% Inuvialuit Sporting Goods Ltd. (Western Arctic)	100% The Village at Port Moodie Dev. Corp. (Port Moodie BC)
J.V. Service Company Ltd. Aboriginal Management (NWT, Yukon)		50% Avati Ltd. (NWT)	100% Stanton Holdings Ltd. (Inuvik, NWT)		100% Aklak Inc. (NWT)	50% Stanton Distributing Co. Ltd. (Western Arctic)	100% Oceanside Village Developments Inc. (Nanaimo BC)
12.5% North Warning Systems J.V. (Labrador, Quebec, Ontario, NWT and the Yukon)		100% Koblunaq Construction Ltd. (BC and NWT)	100% IDC Northern Properties Ltd. (Western Arctic)		50% Northern Transportation Co. Ltd. NORTRAN (NWT & Alaska)	50% Akita Equtak Drilling Ltd. (Western Arctic)	50% Taga-ku Development Group Inc. (Yukon Territory)
8.325% ARDICOM Digital Communications Ltd. (Western Arctic, NWT &Yukon)		25% Pan Arctic Inuit Logistics Inc. (Labrador, Quebec, Ontario, NWT and the Yukon)	50% Begbie Court (New Westminster BC)		50% NorTran Inc. (Baffin Island & Quebec)	100% Arctic Insurance Brokers Ltd. (NWT & Yukon Territories)	
		25% Northern Aboriginal Services Co. Ltd. NASCO (Western Arctic)			J.V. Canadian Helicopters (NWT and Yukon Territories)	80.6% Yukon Aboriginal Business Fund (Yukon)	

Note: JV indicates joint venture; % figures represent size of ownership interest.

Source: Adapted from "IDC's Structure, By Industry Sector," http://www.inuvialuit.com/idc/operate.html.

revenue and profit, IDC employed approximately 200 Inuvialuit, up from only 70 or so in 1992. The IDC and its subsidiary companies paid over $3-million in salary and benefits to these employees in 1996. One of the IDC companies is featured in the following case.

Case 4–4: Inuvialuit Sporting Goods Ltd. (1997)[12]

In the high Arctic, a land covered with snow for eight months of the year, "sporting goods" has little to do with leisure. It is an all-inclusive business consisting of everything from the vehicles needed to get around to the outerwear and equipment required to survive.

Inuvialuit Sporting Goods Ltd. (ISGL) was founded in 1989 to meet the specific supply and service needs of Northerners and Inuvialuit of the Western Arctic. The company is a supplier of sporting goods, snowmobiles, boats, engines, and hunting equipment to the Beaufort-Delta Region with a market of 10,000. Inuvialuit Sporting Goods Ltd. is a company of the Inuvialuit Development Corporation (IDC), a diversified management company operating a portfolio of over 20 subsidiary enterprises. The various northern and southern companies owned by IDC, whose mission is to "fulfill the business goal of the 1984 Inuvialuit Final Agreement," are active in all sectors of the economy.

Situated in the Northern Services business sector of the IDC corporate structure, Inuvialuit Sporting Goods is a strong retail presence in Inuvik, the regional supply base for the Mackenzie Delta.

The business has several dealerships, which allow them to concentrate on specific product lines. Inuvialuit Sporting Goods houses a Yamaha dealership selling snowmobiles, ATVs, Seadoos, boats, and generators; a Polaris dealership selling snowmobiles, ATVs, and Seadoos; a Mercury dealership selling motors; and a Stihl dealership selling chainsaws.

Although ISGL maintains a diverse inventory, the sale and service of snowmobiles and related accessories is the largest part of the business. In a good year ISGL sells between 100 and 200 machines. The majority are utility sleds used for work and hunting. Much of the inventory at Inuvialuit Sporting Goods is geared toward providing everything a person needs, as Sales Manager Hans Lennie says, "to jump on a snowmobile and go." There is some seasonal variation in the products carried, but winterwear, "Sorel" boots, generators, camping equipment and other products required to live on the land are the expansion areas where ISGL is trying to meet local demands.

The company has had to adapt to shifts in the regional economy. In 1994, it underwent an intensive review of its operations. It took steps to bring down high costs and rebuild its image. Part of the restructuring of ISGL involved consolidating the company's operations into one location just over a year ago. Merging the retail section and the service shop permitted ISGL to concentrate on the Yamaha, Polaris and Mercury dealerships. Having everything under one roof made ISGL more competitive and in a position to benefit from dealer advantages.

---

12 Source: DIAND Website, *http://www.inac.gc.ca/ecdev/entre/nt/Inuvi.html* [edited].

New computer ordering and inventory control systems set up for the consolidated operation were also a vital part of the restructuring. Focusing on the products that ISGL carries and services has translated into better customer service. The new systems are paying off, according to Hans Lennie: "Especially in the parts department, things are coming together. When someone calls for a part, we've got to have it."

The service shop at Inuvialuit Sporting Goods Ltd. provides exclusive parts and maintenance on product lines carried by ISGL. A new service contract to repair GNWT vehicles keeps the two full-time mechanics on staff constantly busy. James Day, the Inuvialuit head mechanic, goes to Polaris and Yamaha training centres every year to stay on top of product line technology. Providing training opportunities and involving employees in the business is a high priority at ISGL. "We encourage the guys to go to as many job-related courses as possible," says Danny Smith, Executive Director.

Sales Manager Hans Lennie, who has worked at ISGL for seven years, has grown with the company. He has seen how ISGL has created opportunities for Inuvialuit while meeting the needs of Northerners. "This business really helped the Inuvialuit as a whole," says Lennie.

As an Inuvialuit-owned business, ISGL has maintained its northern and traditional focus, which is intimately connected with the bottom line. As Hans Lennie points out, "we service all the outlying communities, they are the ones who are always out on the land." Knowing the people and the traditions creates community-based service, whether that means comprehensive snowmobile service or carrying soapstone to arts and crafts producers.

One example of meeting local needs has been the addition of supplies for trapping, a vital part of the traditional economy. "Now that fur prices are coming up we're looking into expanding our trapping supplies," says Hans Lennie. So far, these items have moved very well. In terms of both the traditional and modern economies, Inuvialuit Sporting Goods Ltd. is a business closely linked to the Northern way of life. After its first year as a consolidated service and retail operation, it is poised to hold the course as an important fixture in the Mackenzie Delta Region.

4.3.1.2. The Inuvialuit Petroleum Corporation

The Inuvialuit Petroleum Corporation (IPC) was formed in 1985. The objective of the Inuvialuit was "to establish a profitable, medium-sized, integrated Inuvialuit petroleum company" (ICG 1997, 25). IPC began operations by purchasing shares in two small, publicly traded companies, and it had grown steadily through the late 1980s and early 1990s.

In 1994, IPC sold all its oil and gas assets except for one property in northwestern Alberta. "IPC received a total price of $83.4-million which, after the deduction of all associated costs, resulted in an extraordinary profit of $29.5 million. This extraordinary gain is very notable as it was realized for the Inuvialuit on an equity investment of $11.9 million" (IPC 1998, 2). The company ended 1994 with a $50-million investment portfolio to be used "to investigate internally generated oil and gas prospects, pursue acquisition opportunities and finance ongoing commitments for Inuvialuit benefits" (IPC 1998, 2).

Since 1994, the IPC has continued to develop the Alberta property and pursue its other objectives, including the 1995 purchase of the assets of Omega Hydrocarbons and the resulting formation of Inuvialuit Energy Inc., a joint venture 60% owned by the IPC. The IPC's strategy has been successful. In 1996, the company reported a profit of $4.2-million on revenues of almost $20-million. The IPC, through Inuvialuit Energy Inc., "was able to employ 55 Inuvialuit from the communities of Holman, Sachs Harbour, Tuktoyaktuk, Inuvik and Aklavik on this project [on its properties in northern Alberta] and generated approximately $750,000 in employment income for the Inuvialuit" (ICG 1998, 14).

4.3.1.3. The Inuvialuit Investment Corporation

According to the 1996 Annual Report of the ICG, the Inuvialuit Investment Corporation (IIC)

> *was established to receive the bulk* [80%] *of the financial compensation that flows from the IFA. Its mandate is to invest these funds in low risk investments and to preserve the capital for future generations of Inuvialuit, much like a heritage or pension fund.* (ICG 1997, 24)

The company maintains a conservative and diverse portfolio of investments in national and international securities. It has been criticized for not investing compensation funds in the Inuvialuit region. The company defends this investment policy by saying that "IIC recognizes that businesses built on local markets can be successful and profitable. However, in the current market conditions, they do not provide the most secure and best cash and interest rates of return to meets IIC's mandate" (IIC 1998, 1). In 1996, IIC recorded a net income of $2.1-million from interest and dividend on its investments.

In summary, the companies of the Inuvialuit Corporate Group made a considerable contribution to the Inuvialuit people in 1996. The ICG ended 1996 with total assets of $286-million, liabilities of $118-million and beneficiaries equity of $168-million. Of its total assets, fully $150-million were either current assets or marketable securities, the vast majority being Government of Canada bonds. The three economic subsidiaries of the ICG — the Inuvialuit Development Corporation, the Inuvialuit Petroleum Corporation and the Inuvialuit Invest Corporation — earned a combined after tax profit of $11.2-million on revenues of $130.3-million. In earning these profits, the ICG employed approximately 260 Inuvialuit, paying them a total of $4.1-million in wages. In addition to these salaries, the group paid honorariums of $398,682, student financial support of $335,000, payments to Elders and youth of $755,500, donations and the like of $175,427 and payments to community corporations of $565,427. In total, in 1996, "$6,170,264 was provided from the operations of the Inuvialuit Corporate Group" (ICG 1997, 22) to the Inuvialuit, over and above the profit of $11.2-million.

4.3.2. Concluding Comments on the Inuvialuit Final Agreement

In reading materials about the IFA and its implementation, it is striking that there is no significant amount of dissatisfaction on the part of the Inuvialuit about the terms of the agreement itself or its implementation by the non-Aboriginal parties — particularly the federal government and the multinational oil and gas companies. This is in stark contrast to the feelings of the James Bay Cree about the terms and implementation of the JBNQA and, in particular, the actions of the Government of Quebec and Quebec Hydro. Why? The sources of the difference appear to be threefold: (i) failure by non-Aboriginal governments to implement the terms of the JBNQA, (ii) the respective non-Aboriginal governments' views on extinguishment and their right to proceed with development outside Category I lands, and (iii) the actions of corporations interested in developing the resources of the region.

First, among the Cree and the Inuit of James Bay there is a strongly held view that the governments involved (particularly the government of Quebec) did not fulfill their obligations under the terms of the JBNQA. The following statement captures a sense of the frustration of the Cree:

> *Also worrisome for almost all Crees is the flagrant violation of so many of the undertakings made in the JBNQA. Crees were supposed to have some priority in employment in all the lands covered by the Agreement; were supposed to have a role in decision-making about future "developments" in the territory; were supposed to have been protected to some extent against the impact of logging, roads and other disturbances by provisions in the Agreement that guaranteed them their right to hunt, trap and fish and use the forest. In none of these areas has the Quebec government made any effort to implement the agreement.* (GCC 1998a, 1)

There seems to be no similar sense of unfulfilled non-Aboriginal government promises on the part of the Inuvialuit, at least to date. However, the Inuvialuit do express a sense of unfulfilled expectations toward their own government and institutions. Nellie Cournoyea, Chair and Chief Executive Officer of the ICG opened her remarks in the 1996 ICG Annual Report by saying:

> *The Inuvialuit Corporate Group entered 1996 with a very clear message from beneficiaries and community corporations that stressed the need for corporate control, fiscal responsibility and stabilization throughout the organization. The need to restore the trust and confidence of the beneficiaries was closely linked to the need for increased communication to provide a clear picture of the business affairs and financial status of the corporate group* [ICG] *... to fully establish the parent organization* [IRC] *as credible.* (ICG 1997, 2)

The ICG and its subsidiaries devoted considerable efforts during 1996 to address these community concerns; in particular, the feeling that IIC should invest more of the settlement compensation in local business and communities, as was discussed earlier.[13]

The second factor — extinguishment — was discussed at some length in section 4.3. To summarize, the Quebec government is firm in its interpretation of the terms of the JBNQA. In its opinion, the Cree and Inuit surrendered all their Aboriginal rights in the region in exchange for the rights specifically granted under the agreement. The government of Quebec believes it has the right to direct development on the traditional lands of the Cree and the Inuit, subject only to the terms of the JBNQA, and has shown a willingness to act on this belief. On the other hand, the federal government, as the sole non-Aboriginal government party to the IFA, has renounced blanket extinguishment. Although this change in policy occurred after the signing of the IFA, it still guides federal-Inuvialuit interactions. The federal government has shown no inclination to impose or direct development on Inuvialuit lands.

Finally, the corporations involved in development in the regions, indeed in the very projects that resulted in the JBNQA and IFA agreements — Hydro Quebec in the first case and the multinational oil companies in the second — have behaved very differently. Not surprisingly, Hydro Quebec, as a provincial Crown corporation, has adopted the same view of its rights in the James Bay region as the Quebec government. It feels it has the right to proceed with new projects on Categories I and II lands, subject only to replacing any such land expropriated with other land. As a result, the Cree and the Inuit find themselves in constant conflict with Hydro Quebec and the Quebec government over development in their traditional lands.

In contrast, the multinational oil companies withdrew almost entirely from the North following the Berger Inquiry. Oil and gas activity did not resume in the area until the Inuvialuit themselves became active in the industry through IPC. A feeling for the corporate reaction can be garnered from a recent article in the highly conservative magazine *Alberta Report:*

> *Last month ... native leaders did something that would have been unthinkable in 1980: they turned up in Calgary to beat the drum, literally, for northern resource development. The locally-controlled* [Inuit-controlled], *Calgary-based Inuvialuit Petroleum Corp. announced it would be tapping into a gas field in the Mackenzie River delta.*
>
> *Oil and gas exploration is also restarting in the far north. Many Aboriginal claims have been settled or are nearing completion,*[14] *giving producers such as Alberta Energy Co. Ltd. (AEC), Ranger Oil, Imperial Oil Resources Ltd. and others the confidence required to put capital at risk.* (Koch 1998, 1–2)

---

13 A detailed description of these efforts can be found in the 1996 ICG Annual Report.

14 See chapter 5 for a detailed discussion of corporate reactions to land claims and related issues.

It is clear that, as an outcome of the Berger Report (and the resulting IFA), the Inuvialuit have to be active players in the very type of development that gave rise to Mackenzie Valley Pipeline Inquiry in the first place. It appears that Berger was correct when he recommended delaying development until land claims were settled and the Aboriginal people are in a better position to be active participants in the process, rather than victims of it.

4.3.3. Cases: Small Business among the Inuvialuit

The ICG is not responsible for all business development among the Inuvialuit. Neither are the Inuvialuit the only Aboriginal people engaged in business development in the North. There is a vibrant and growing small-business sector north of the 60th parallel as the cases that follow will attest.

Case 4–5: Arctic Tour Company — Tuktoyaktuk (1997)[15]

Arctic Tour Company (ATC) has been giving people the experience of a lifetime for over a decade. The company is owned by Roger and Winnie Gruben of Tuktoyaktuk. They bring their love of the region and its peoples as part of the tours they offer, and a genuine desire to share their traditional lifestyle and culture.

Tours organized by Arctic Tour Company are well planned and well researched. ATC offers base tour packages, tours revolving around summer arts festivals, and a myriad of options, ranging from day trips to nature and wildlife tours lasting three to five days. Whatever the interests of tourists, Roger and Winnie customize packages to meet the needs and budgets of clients. People are given the opportunity to join cultural or add-on tours to base-tour packages or planned excursions.

Since they took over the company three years ago, Roger and Winnie have made the tours more culturally oriented. "We changed tours to reflect more of the region and more of the people and values of the area," says Roger. ATC tours give people a chance to experience and understand the relationship between the landscape and the people of the Western Arctic. Community tours, wildlife viewing, whale watching, boat tours, Mackenzie River cruises, and cultural entertainment are all available to adventure-seekers.

Clients are accompanied on their voyages of discovery by experienced guides, born and raised in the region. Winnie gives personal tours of Tuktoyaktuk. In her role as bus driver, tour guide, and cultural educator, she is knowledgeable, courteous and patient. "We find that our clients really enjoy the tours because we give them personal service," says Winnie. Whether it means inviting people into their home for tea or introducing someone to a member of the community, ATC goes the extra mile to create a personalized tour built around the interests of the clients. Roger explains that "we try to give people their money's worth by providing them with as much of a well-

---

15 Source: DIAND Website, *http://www.inac.gc.ca/ecdev/entre/nt/Atc.html* [edited].

rounded cultural experience as possible, because we want them to learn more about us."

Arctic Tour Company's personalized style of organizing and marketing tours gives them a distinct edge. Roger and Winnie write their promotional materials themselves. Roger also designed a web page to showcase all of the sites and experiences available to the adventurous. The Internet has been a good marketing tool for ATC. It has extended the marketing range by allowing people to make inquiries or bookings from anywhere in the world. Currently Roger is updating the site to include more information about winter tours, dog team excursions, and snowmobile safaris.

Although they market the company themselves, Arctic Tour Company covers all the bases by also marketing tours in association with tour operators in Germany, the United States, and throughout Canada. "They take bookings and bring groups to us. Throughout the year they market and we market," says Roger. ATC explores all avenues to expand their distribution network and let people know what the Arctic has to offer. The company plans to attend trade shows next year in an attempt to attract clients to the growing market of Aboriginal and eco-tourism.

Roger and Winnie know that the best advertising is done by happy customers through word of mouth. Most people's first experience with Canada's Arctic leaves a big impression. Guests of the area return home with a better understanding of the Northern way of life, and on issues facing Aboriginal people. As Roger explains, it is a positive experience for everybody. "A lot of people go away from here with a different perception, because we take a real pride in sharing the details of our lifestyle."

According to feedback that Roger receives from tour-goers, the cultural experience is extremely important to people. "They want to know what makes the people up here, who they are, they want to dip their toe in the Arctic ocean, and sample the food we eat." Aside from the tangible cultural benefits created by a better understanding of how people of the region embrace the modern and the traditional, Arctic Tour Company has created economic opportunities by creating a sustainable market.

The community level impact of tourism development in the Inuvik/Tuk region is significant. Arctic Tour Company has four full-time employees working from the Inuvik office during the summer. In addition, they also bring business to guides who are contracted throughout the region. The trickle-down effects of tourism dollars provide casual income to carvers and arts and crafts producers, while feeding the transportation and hospitality services of the local economies. As the positive economic impacts of tourism flow into the region, tourism is being regarded as an important sector of the economy in which to promote and preserve Inuvialuit culture.

Running the company is a labour of love for Roger and Winnie Gruben. The future looks bright for the company as an increasing volume of people wants to experience the unique character of the Western Arctic. "Tourism is a fledgling industry up here, it's just growing," says Roger, "The potential is as good as you make it." Guided by this philosophy, Arctic Tour Company has opened the window of opportunity to share the natural and cultural bounty of the region.

4

Case 4–6: Kakivak Spearheading Inuit Small Business Development (1997)[16]

Kakivak, an Inuit fishing spear, is a fitting symbol for the Kakivak Association. Their latest enterprise, an innovative concept called an incubator mall, is spearheading Inuit small business development in Iqaluit, NWT.

Kakivak Association is an Inuit economic development society that represents and serves the business interests of all Inuit in the Baffin Region. The idea of the "incubator mall" grew out of a desire to spark the growth of Inuit-owned and -operated businesses.

The completion of 3,000 square feet of retail space for small businesses in the new Parnaivik Building, which also houses the Kakivak Association and the Baffin Business Development Centre, provided entrepreneurs with all the resources for starting a business under one roof. This economic development pilot project has been able to provide ongoing support to help overcome some of the difficulties of getting a small business off the ground.

Kakivak's role in translating the vision of business people into self-sustaining companies is renewed throughout the development of a business. The application process for space is designed to be accessible — with a minimum of red tape — and clients are given the opportunity to develop business plans. The availability of business management services allows the Kakivak economic development officers to meet specific client needs and provide targets for the growth of individual businesses

As Kakivak Programs Manager Leonie Qaumariaq admits: "It's going to be a learning process for our organization and for the small businesses." A flexible approach to finding working solutions is the path followed by Kakivak. "Together we can succeed," says Qaumariaq.

In addition to providing business development assistance, Kakivak provides a strong slate of resources and services available to assist clients of the incubator mall in daily functions or in achieving long-term goals. Clients can use a business resource library, basic bookkeeping assistance, and the benefit of bi-monthly workshops on operating a small business.

Aside from providing access to management expertise, the Kakivak business centre also provides a receptionist. Cost-sharing these services among the tenants, in addition to providing them a chance to develop business skills, is an efficient way to decrease start up costs.

Inuit-owned businesses housed in the incubator mall also enjoy the benefit of subsidized rent. Tenants of the incubator mall are on a flexible schedule to stay for three years in incubator status. However, businesses are reviewed on an annual basis to help prepare them to make the transition to commercial space.

Since the first clients moved into retail space in May, the Kakivak incubator mall has already hatched a success story. The first graduate, Nunanet — a company providing Internet service — moved out way ahead of schedule. Nunanet has grown at an astronomical rate. Since the company moved into the mall in May with 150 customers, its clientele has grown to over 500 clients

16 Source: DIAND Website, *http://www.inac.gc.ca/ecdev/entre/nt/Kakiva.html* [edited].

throughout the Baffin region. Nunanet, which moved in September, has quickly expanded to five employees requiring more space and more room to expand.

Kakivak provided the starting ground for Adamee Itorcheak, the very independent entrepreneur who started Nunanet. Speaking from experience, he knows the value of Kakivak in helping businesses get off the ground: "I think it's fabulous for the present businesses in the mall because they get an opportunity at a reduced rate. They have a bit more of a fighting chance competing against businesses from Southern Canada."

Although the reduced rent was a great benefit in freeing up cash flow, according to Itorcheak, one of the greatest resources was the support of the Kakivak staff, who were instrumental in showing him different ways to find solutions. "That's all that a lot of us need. Every one of us has it inside, we just need a bit of support."

Currently the incubator mall is full, with four clients. Kamagiak jewelry store and Arctic Creations, which sells locally made clothing as well as fabrics and complete sewing supplies, are businesses opening a new way to market goods that are a traditional source of income to Inuit. Another company, Uqsiq Communications, is an Inuit-owned and -operated publishing and design agency providing creative services on all kinds of projects. With the newest addition of a consulting service for the growing outfitting industry, the businesses in the incubator mall represent a diversified microcosm of the future of Inuit-owned businesses in Nunavut.

It is no wonder that there is an air of optimism in the incubator mall about the prospects for Inuit-owned companies. Kakivak Programs Manager Leonie Qaumariaq has a good reason to be hopeful: "I see a bright future. It's a nice feeling to see businesses owned by fellow Inuit. This is just the beginning."

Case 4–7: Inuit Communications Systems Limited Connecting the North (1997)[17]

Inuit Communications Systems Limited (ICSL) is a Northern company dedicated to finding Northern solutions. Since 1982 they have been adapting the latest in communication technologies to the special requirements of northerners.

Fully Aboriginal-owned, ICSL is the for-profit arm of the Inuit Broadcasting Corporation (IBC) which produces five hours of Inuit programming a week for TVNC, the Television Northern Canada network, which spans the entire North, from Yukon to Labrador. Through the video-production facility and service centre located in Iqaluit, NWT, ICSL provides technical coordination and consultation service, designed to meet the communication needs of clients across the North. They also supply comprehensive equipment sales and services on a wide range of professional broadcast and video-conferencing equipment. In addition to helping clients develop communications solutions, ICSL and their marketing office in Ottawa can implement and oversee a project through any and all stages.

The expert ICSL staff in Iqaluit, working in association with IBC, handle video-production projects ranging from providing authentic footage in a North-

---

17 Source: DIAND Website, *http://www.inac.gc.ca/ecdev/entre/nt/Icsl.html* [edited].

ern setting to producing full-length documentary films. ICSL produces local and regional contracts for groups such as Arctic College and the Baffin Regional Health Board, as well as numerous aboriginal organizations and government departments. The company also provides full-broadcast quality production at all stages for a growing international clientele that includes Japan, Europe, and the United States. As their reputation spreads, an increasing number of international companies have been knocking on ICSL's door

The greatest advantage of working with Inuit Communications Systems Limited is the benefit of Northern knowledge and expertise. BBC and other international broadcasters, unable to cope with the harsh Arctic conditions, have discovered that it is more cost-effective to use the crew supplied by ICSL. The Inuit staff possess all the tools to film on the land for extended periods. Local know-how in dealing with extreme weather has proved invaluable to getting jobs done on time. Once companies work with ICSL and see the professional quality of productions they know that nobody does it better in the North. The company goes the extra mile to build constructive working relationships with their clients. "We are always trying to align ourselves with people who have strong international contacts," says ICSL Producer Patty Billings.

When pursuing co-production opportunities, ICSL tries to guarantee the participation of Northerners in productions that tell stories about the Northern people and way of life. In August, ICSL was given permission to send a team to Repulse Bay to film the first legally harvested bowhead whale hunt in over 20 years. The IBC crew captured the return of a significant traditional cultural activity through Inuit eyes. The astonishing footage will be part of a co-production with a southern Canadian company for an international market. Having a well-developed broadcast production team gives the Inuit Broadcasting Corporation an important opportunity to present an authentic representation of Inuit culture and the northern environment.

The most important area of recent expansion for Inuit Communications Systems Limited has been in developing video conferencing. It is an area of communications technology that presents an exciting frontier for meeting the communication challenges of Northerners. ICSL maintains permanent public access video-conferencing centres in Ottawa, Iqaluit, and Rankin Inlet, with plans to expand to Cambridge Bay by the end of the year. The service, which is currently utilized mainly by government and business, represents a new way of doing business in the sparsely populated North.

The video-conferencing technology set-up in the northern centres will be supported by an 18-week intensive training program. Starting in January, six unemployed Inuit will receive specialized training that will cover the technical aspects of video conferencing as well as marketing the service, and management skills required to coordinate conferences. The hands-on training will be conducted using the technology itself, with trainees participating from their own communities.

Video conferencing holds a great potential to connect northerners to each other or with people anywhere in the world. Recently, as part of the Museum of Nature exhibit at the World Conservation Congress, ICSL coordinated a video conference pilot program linking a class of students in Iqaluit with a class in Montreal. The two groups of students shared presentations via live video feed and were given the opportunity to discuss environmental issues, traditional and modern lifestyles, and the management of resources in the modern world. Both groups gained a great deal of understanding from the face-to-face encounter. As producer Patty Billings explains, projects like this are just starting to tap the potential of interactive two-way communication. "It was very successful. This is a way to use the video-conferencing technology to link the world to northerners."

Not only is ICSL making steps toward connecting the North to the world, it is also taking a giant leap toward connecting communities throughout the circumpolar world. A community consultation model is being developed to link communities via video and teleconference. The advantages of the interactive component of the technology, which can encompass a larger symposium beyond the delegates sent to conferences, are within reach. Additional delegates can be linked in via video-conferencing studios, and other groups can be linked through teleconference at hamlet offices. In addition, through broadcast on TVNC, the symposium can link communities throughout the North to the proceedings, and provide the opportunity for input via a 1-800 number. The potential for completely interactive, live simulcasts shows great promise to expand direct community-based decision making and information sharing among Inuit.

As Inuit Communications Systems Limited expands, the greatest challenge is keeping on top of technology. Innovative applications that serve the practical needs of northerners and the cultural needs of Inuit are often found together. "In the North we are able to be on the leading edge of it," explains Patty Billings. "Just because of the distance, we need all the modern equipment just to communicate. Inuit are very accepting of this." Through a willingness to find solutions, ICSL is closing the distances between communities in the North, and providing vital links connecting the Inuit world.

Case 4–8: Indivisual Productions (1997)[18]

"I've got a pretty big playground," says Tookie Mercredi of Indivisual Productions, describing the Yukon and the filming opportunities here.

Mercredi has been working in the industry since 1979 and, over the years, has accumulated experiences that not many other people in the business can compare to. He started working for CBC in Yellowknife before TV came to the North and, since then, has been a part of over 1,200 productions, both in the territories and south of 60. After 14 years of working for CBC, two years training as a Nedaa (Yukon Aboriginal TV program) technical staff, and studying video-editing systems in California, he created Indivisual Productions when he realized that he could continue doing the same work he had been doing, but for himself and not as an employee.

Indivisual Productions is capable of performing all sorts of production demands, but the company specializes in video technology in the North. Mercredi saw that there was a discrepancy between the people whose stories were being told on film and video, and those who were telling them. "People figure that everybody can tell the story of the Yukon by hiring southerners to

18 Source: DIAND Website, *http://www.inac.gc.ca/ecdev/entre/yt/Visual.html* [edited].

do it." There are, however, many extra demands on people filming in the North, since "a good northern cameraman has to be ready for anything," as well as willing to adapt to very remote locations and dealing with the cold. "People from the south are not big on shooting on location up here, but I'm comfortable anywhere as long as I have a good sleeping bag. I'll just sleep with my batteries," says Mercredi, referring to the need to keep batteries warm in order for them to keep their charge.

It is not only the climate and geography that is different in the Yukon; the people are different as well. Much of the filming here involves Aboriginal life and communities, and Mercredi feels that it is easier for a person of Aboriginal descent, like himself, to work with First Nation communities since he knows many people and can communicate without cultural conflicts due to his background and cultural understanding.

Mercredi makes a conscious effort to give back to the First Nation communities that he profiles. He tries to give honorariums to the Elders he talks to. He employs local-based businesses and workers on his projects. He also does this for businesses beyond First Nation communities by employing Yukon businesses when filming for outside companies in order to keep the employment in the Territory.

Over the years, Tookie Mercredi has worked on some very exciting assignments, from filming Beluga whale mating grounds in the Arctic Ocean to filming the Commonwealth Games in Victoria, to filming beer commercials in the mountains around Whitehorse. Of all these assignments, Mercredi says working at the Commonwealth Games was the biggest honour, since all the cameramen who worked at the games were handpicked. This allowed him to work with some of the best professionals in the business. The camera has taken Mercredi to many places, and he has seen a lot through its lens, and it has yet to bore him. As Mercredi attests: "You never see the same thing twice...."

On a more technical side, Mercredi sees Indivisual moving into the next millennium in a trend-setting position. This includes filming in formats that will become standard in the future, like digital video instead of Betacam, and utilizing nonlinear video-editing systems. With this forward-thinking attitude, Mercredi is also working to turn one of his current projects, producing tourism videos of the Yukon, into a series. He also looks forward to one day tapping the feature film and TV series potential of the North. His dream is to eventually be able, through advancements in communications technology, to produce a finished video product in the Yukon and then deliver it to buyers in the South, all without ever leaving the comfort of Yukon's isolated surroundings.

Tookie Mercredi sees the future of Indivisual Productions the same way that he has seen its past and present: through the eye of a camera.

4.4. The Nisga'a Final Agreement

On July 22, 1998, the Nisga'a Tribal Council, the federal government and the government of the Province of British Columbia announced that they had reached a final agreement on the first modern treaty in British Columbia. Many more similar agreements will follow as the treaty-making process continues in British Columbia. In fact, as of March 1998, there were 42 First Nations in the

British Columbia Treaty Consultation Process, representing about two-thirds of the 197 Bands in British Columbia.[19] The Nisga'a Agreement provides insight into likely terms of the agreements that will follow.[20]

Under the terms of the agreement, the Nisga'a will have title to 1,992 sq. km of land in the lower Nass Valley. These lands will be communally owned and include the four communities of Gitlakdamiks[21] (New Aiyansh), Gitwiksihlkw (Canyon City), Lakalzap (Greenville) and Gingolx (Kincolith) and the existing Indian reserves. The Nisga'a will hold both the surface and mineral rights to these lands.

Each of the four communities will have its own village government, and there will be a common Nisga'a government. In these communities and throughout Nisga'a lands, the Nisga'a will have the power to make laws governing culture and language, employment, public works, regulation of traffic and transportation, and land use. They will control and provide health, social services and education. The Nisga'a government will provide full policing service on Nisga'a lands and establish a Nisga'a court with jurisdiction over Nisga'a laws on Nisga'a lands.

On an ongoing basis, the Nisga'a government will receive transfer payments from the federal and provincial governments sufficient to enable them to provide government services at levels generally comparable to those available elsewhere in northwest British Columbia. As with all governments receiving transfer payments, the Nisga'a government's ability to raise revenue through taxation and from other sources will be considered when the transfer amount is determined. In addition to these ongoing transfer payments, the Nisga'a will receive $190-million over a period of 15 years. Over and above this $190-million, the Nisga'a will receive transition and implementation funding totalling $40.4-million, broken down as follows:

1. $15-million over five years for such things as training, building Nisga'a institutions and enhancing resource-management capabilities;
2. $15-million over five years to ensure that existing infrastructures are brought to a level comparable to those of other local governments; and
3. $10.4-million for the funding of necessary activities, such as fishery and forestry studies, the ratification process and the preparation of Nisga'a laws.

The final agreement also deals with fishery rights. The Nisga'a will be entitled to 26% of the Canadian Nass River total allowable salmon catch. The Nisga'a will manage this catch. Their catch can be sold, subject to laws of general applicability. In addition, the Nisga'a will participate in the overall management of the Nass River fishery through membership on a joint management committee. Beyond the Nass fishery, the agreement will provide the Nisga'a

---

19 See Appendices 1, 2, 3 and 7 for additional information on the comprehensive claims process under way in British Columbia.

20 See Appendix 6 for a summary of the terms of the Nisga'a Final Agreement.

21 In recognition of the need to perpetuate the Nisga'a culture and heritage, the agreement calls for key geographic features and places to be renamed with Nisga'a names.

with $11.5-million for participation in the coastal commercial fishery — specifically for the purchase of vessels and licences.

After a transition period, the Nisga'a will manage all forestry activities on their lands. They will have the right to implement and enforce forest management standards so long as they meet or exceed provincial standards. The Nisga'a will collect the stumpage fee from all licence holders operating on Nisga'a lands. In addition to these forestry-related rights on their own lands, the agreement gives the Nisga'a the right to purchase an existing timber licence (to a maximum 150,000 cubic metres) on non-Nisga'a lands. In return, the Nisga'a have agreed not to establish a sawmill in the Nass Valley for at least 10 years.

It is interesting to note the reaction of the forest companies that will be affected by the Nisga'a's gaining control of forestry on their lands. Repap Ltd. has 140,000 cubic metres of allowable cut affected by the agreement. After a transition period, jurisdiction over this resource will pass from the province to the Nisga'a, who will then control such things as annual cut, forestry practices and stumpage fees. Repap "expects that the wood will still flow to the company's mills — it will just be cut at the direction of the Nisga'a and it may cost Repap a bit more" (Terrace Standard Online 1997, 1–2). Overall, according to the *Terrace Standard*:

> *Most industry observers in the northwest said the Nisga'a deal by itself looks workable. But they have grave concerns about the cumulative effects if the same provisions are extended to other native groups like the Tsimshian, Haisla and Gitskan.*
>
> (Terrace Standard Online 1997, 2)

Because the Nisga'a agreement is likely to be a template for those that will follow, the extension of similar terms to these and other Aboriginal people is almost certain.

This concern by forestry companies is echoed throughout British Columbia and extends beyond forestry. Many view the upcoming series of settlements with trepidation, feeling the costs to British Columbia will be immense. To address these concerns, the Province of British Columbia commissioned a report from KPMG.[22] The report concluded the following:

> *When all the financial impacts in B.C. are considered, British Columbia can expect about three dollars worth of total benefit for every dollar of provincial financial costs ... the net financial benefit to British Columbians ... is between $3.9 and $5.3 billion, when totaled over 40 years.*
>
> (B.C. Ministry of Aboriginal Affairs 1998a, 1)

The Berger Commission, the James Bay and Northern Quebec Agreement and the Inuvialuit Final Agreement have characterized land claims and settle-

---

22 For a summary of the KPMG report, see Appendix 7; for a commentary on the report see Appendix 1.

ments over the past two decades. British Columbia, with more than 40 claims in process, is bound to be the center of land claims negotiations for the next several decades. Perhaps, instead of imposing a cost on non-Aboriginal people in order to confer benefits on Aboriginal people, the treaty process in British Columbia will result in a win-win situation for all the people living in British Columbia. The KPMG report and the ARA report, entitled *The Social and Economic Impacts of Aboriginal Land Claims Settlements: A Case Study Analysis*,[23] which are discussed in the conclusion that follows, support this view.

4.5. Conclusions

Four questions flow from this discussion of land claims and modern treaties: (1) Have comprehensive claims agreements served the purposes of the Aboriginal people who signed them? (2) If so, will they continue to do so in the future? (3) If not, what must be done to see that they do? (4) Will and should non-Aboriginal Canadians support the land claims and treaty-making process? These are the questions this concluding section addresses.

A report prepared in 1995 by ARA Consulting for the government of British Columbia summarizes the impact of treaties and land claims settlement in Canada, the United States, New Zealand and Australia. The key findings of that report were:

- *In no case has the resolution of land claims brought political or economic chaos.... People adjusted to the new arrangements, political systems adapted, and businesses quickly found new ways of responding to the post-settlement environment.*
- *The business communities in the areas affected by land claims opposed negotiations initially.... Over time business leaders came around... In the post-settlement era, non-Indigenous business capitalized on new opportunities (often in joint venture with aboriginal companies) and discovered a common interest in sustainable mutually-beneficial economic development.*
- *All the modern treaties have respected and accepted private land holdings and leases. Although Indigenous groups have been forthright in their demand for land and resources, they have in each case accepted the rights of existing property owners.*
- *The most contentious issue surrounding treaty settlements relates to the management of resources. Non-Indigenous fears that final agreements will block access to minerals, timber, fish, wildlife and other resources has, in almost every instance, added fuel to the fires of discontent ... it is vital that the approaches re: resource use and control be fully*

---

23 For a summary of the ARA report, see Appendix 4.

explained in order to alleviate non-Indigenous concerns about the future of businesses and communities that rely on resource development.

- *Treaties have provided Indigenous groups with the financial and administrative means to begin charting a new economic future for their people. The establishment of for-profit companies, joint ventures with non-Indigenous corporations, community development schemes, and the like are an integral part of the settlement process and treaty implementation ... a basis for participating more fully in the broader economy.*
- *Indigenous groups have learned ... that education and training must figure prominently in post-settlement operations.*
- *Underlying the treaty process is a heartfelt desire among the indigenous people to keep their language and culture strong, to recover from the difficulties of the past, and to interest non-indigenous people in their heritage.*

(B.C. Ministry of Aboriginal Affairs 1998b, 5–6)

These findings suggest that, in general, there is reason for optimism. Comprehensive agreements and treaties seem to be having the outcomes expected. In particular, the agreements seem to be fostering economic development among Aboriginal people, often in mutually beneficial alliances with non-Aboriginal people. The findings also provide confirmation about the nature of the Aboriginal approach to development described in chapter 2 and suggest that its practice extends beyond the Aboriginal people in Canada to other Indigenous people around the world.

The ARA findings do not measure the degree to which the settlements have satisfied Aboriginal objectives in the three areas introduced at the start of this chapter: (i) economic development, (ii) arrangements providing control over activities on traditional lands and (iii) extinguishment of Aboriginal rights. The reviews of the James Bay and Northern Quebec Agreement, the Inuvialuit Final Agreement and the Nisga'a Final Agreement help in this respect.

It is fair to conclude that the JBNQA and the IFA have fostered successful economic development. The stories of the Makivik Corporation, CREECO and the Inuvialuit Corporate Group companies attest to this. However, as successful as these activities have been, they fall far short of what is needed to raise employment levels among the affected Aboriginal groups to anything close to the level of non-Aboriginal Canadians. Two things about Aboriginal employment levels must be noted.

First, such levels may never be attained or, even, desired by the Cree and Inuit of James Bay, the Inuvialuit or other Aboriginal people in Canada. Many have chosen to maintain a more traditional way of life and are not pursuing the "Canadian dream" of a full-time, 9-to-5 job. The desired level of employment obviously lies somewhere between today's currently unacceptably low rate and the non-Aboriginal level. Development activities to date have been successful in moving employment toward this desired level.

Second, not all employment for Aboriginal people needs to be provided by Aboriginal-created companies. As their education levels improve and they become an increasingly larger proportion of the labour force, Aboriginal people will make up an increasing proportion of the workforce in non-Aboriginal companies. This is particularly true for companies that view Aboriginal people as an increasingly important target market.[24]

The second and third items, control over activities on traditional lands and the extinguishment of Aboriginal rights, are problematic. As described earlier, the Cree of James Bay are clearly dissatisfied in both respects, with good reason. The Inuit of James Bay seem somewhat less unhappy. On the other hand, the Inuvialuit seem satisfied, at least at this point. The Nisga'a, with the benefit of hindsight, have gone to considerable lengths to build control mechanisms into their agreement to address the issue of jurisdiction and control. This is an area where the evolution in government policy, in response to pressure from Aboriginal people and decisions of the Courts, has been significant. The federal government and, although perhaps more reluctantly, the provincial governments no longer demand blanket extinguishment as a condition for agreement. Both levels of government have also become more willing to (i) acknowledge and support Aboriginal jurisdiction and self-government over their own lands and (ii) create co-management mechanisms in areas of joint Aboriginal/non-Aboriginal concern. As a result, it appears that agreements are becoming increasingly more acceptable to Aboriginal people with respect to items two and three.

The answers to the four questions raised at the beginning of this summary are therefore:

1. Yes, the comprehensive claims agreements have served the purposes of the Aboriginal people who signed them, to some extent, at least. Economic development has followed the signing of the agreements, and valuable rights and powers over activities on traditional lands have been gained, as even the Cree of James Bay concede.
2. Regarding the terms of agreements, they are evolving; and as they do, it seems likely that the Aboriginal people will build on their already considerable success. In particular, the battle to retain traditional rights rather than lose them through extinguishment appears to have been won.
3. As regards to ensure ongoing success, Aboriginal people must continue to pursue development on their terms (i.e. the eight characteristics of Aboriginal development as described in chapter 2).
4. With respect to non-Aboriginal Canadians should support the land claims and treaty process, as the B.C. studies indicate, it is in their own best interests to do so. As the ARA study found, communication is the key. Non-Aboriginal people need to know about the positive outcomes that have emerged following the implementation of previous settlements. In this respect, corporations are clearly ahead of the general public, as the material in the next chapter will attest.

---

24 This issue receives considerable attention in chapter 5.

5 Corporate Aboriginal Alliances

The relationship between corporations and Aboriginal people in Canada has evolved and will continue to evolve in response to changes in the Aboriginal world and the society at large. This has been particularly true since the Calder Supreme Court decision, and the Mackenzie Valley Pipeline Inquiry of the mid-1970s and the resulting series of comprehensive land claims and modern treaties that have followed and will continue.

According to Sloan and Hill (1995), this evolution has resulted in the emergence of corporate Aboriginal relations programs "designed to build constructive partnerships with communities and expand employment and business opportunities for Aboriginal people" (Sloan and Hill 1995, ix). The number of corporations developing and implementing programs of this type has

> *grown significantly in each of the past three decades, with the greatest growth in activity taking place in the last five years ... almost two-thirds of the programs in this book were introduced in the past five years.* (Sloan and Hill 1995, x)

The ARA report discussed in the previous chapter confirms this trend as does the material on corporate social responsibility and flexible production presented in chapter 3.

According to my own research and confirmed by others,[1] this change in corporate attitude and behaviour is emerging as individual corporations respond strategically to five mutually reinforcing factors that have greatly increased the importance of Aboriginal people to the company's profitability and long-term survival (see Figure 5–1).

---

1 Including Sloan and Hill (1995), KPMG (Appendices 1 and 6) and ARA (Appendix 4).

FIGURE 5–1: Factors Influencing Corporate Aboriginal Relations

1. A change in the global competitive environment from a Fordist to a flexible regime of accumulation.
2. A broadening and deepening of society's expectations about what constitutes socially responsible corporate behaviour in general and toward Aboriginal people in particular.
3. The large and growing number of legal and regulatory mechanisms that impose requirements and restrictions on business ventures impacting Aboriginal lands and people.
4. The large and growing Aboriginal population, its increasing affluence and increasing level of education.
5. The already enormous and rapidly growing pool of natural and financial resources (in addition to human resources) that Aboriginal people control or will control in the near future.

The first factor is the change in the global competitive environment that all corporations face and to which all must adjust. As detailed in chapter 3, this change is the shift from the Fordist to a flexible regime of accumulation. As a result, many companies are much more likely to enter into alliances and partnerships now than they were in the past.[2]

Factors 2 through 5 relate to the circumstances that are making Aboriginal people likely potential partners for corporations. I distilled them from a variety of sources including Brooks (1994), CANDO (1995), Jamieson (1994), Newell (1994), Sloan and Hill (1995), Syncrude (1995), Thomas (1994), The Globe and Mail (1996), and the Bank of Montreal (1993). These five factors are responsible for the fact that some corporations have adopted or intend to adopt a strategy of partnership with Aboriginal people in pursuit of competitive advantage and long-term profitability.

This change in corporate approach to Aboriginal people coupled with the approach to development Aboriginal people have adopted (chapter 2) has resulted in the emergence of a variety of alliances between business corporations and First Nations. These alliances take various forms ranging from employment access programs at one extreme to true business joint ventures at the other. In between are:

1. Education and training programs.
2. Public (i.e. Aboriginal) consultation processes.
3. Co-management committees and boards.
4. Preferential procurement policies toward First Nations companies.
5. Programs to assist First Nations (government and individuals) to create businesses to supply corporate needs.

2 See Goldman 1995; Amin 1994; Storper and Walker 1989.

6. Involvement of people from the First Nations, the development of products and services to meet their needs.
7. Joint business ventures to develop a resource and/or serve a market need.

Common to all, and hence the use of the term "alliance," is an element of corporate/Aboriginal cooperation and partnership in the pursuit of goals important to each.

My purpose in this chapter is to explore in greater depth the influence of the five factors on corporate Aboriginal relations over time (1985–1995). To do so, I sent a questionnaire to 33 corporate members of the Canadian Council for Aboriginal Business. The results of this survey are presented in section 5.2. Prior to that, in section 5.1 Factors 2 through 5 are explored in greater depth. In section 5.3, the partnership programs are categorized by type and "best case" examples of each type provided. Chapter 5 concludes with comments about the relevance of the contingency perspective to corporate/Aboriginal relations and the likelihood for success of the Aboriginal approach to economic development.

5.1. Corporate Aboriginal Programs

In this section, the nature of Factors 2 through 5 and the corporate reaction to them are explored in more detail. This is done by drawing on survey responses and other sources as noted.

5.1.1. Factor 2: Social Responsibility

Factor 2 is the general need for corporations to be seen as socially responsible. It has played a role in the emergence of Aboriginal relations programs. A sense of this factor can be found in the following statement by Ron Jamieson, a Mohawk from Six Nations and a vice-president of the Bank of Montreal:

> *Companies should partner with Aboriginal people because it is the right thing to do. After all, the Native people were here first.... The Aboriginal people shared their wealth and taught the newcomers how to survive in a sometimes harsh environment. They were willing partners, but were not treated fairly....*
>
> *We can't right all the wrongs, at least not immediately, but we can work to recover the sense of partnership that prevailed in the beginning. Partnering with Aboriginal communities has the strongest of arguments going for it — justice.*
>
> (Jamieson 1994, 16)

Variants of this argument are found in the literature of almost all companies with Aboriginal relations programs. However, in no case is this factor put forward as the sole or even most important reason for partnering with native people (even by the Bank of Montreal, in spite of Mr. Jamieson's statement).

Instead, this factor finds expression in one of two ways, and often in both — special requirements in law and regulation (Factor 3) and socially responsible corporate behaviour as a source of competitive advantage (relating to Factors 4 and 5).

5.1.2. Factor 3: Legal Requirements

Factor 3 is the growing number of legal and regulatory mechanisms that impose requirements and restrictions on business ventures involving Aboriginal lands and/or impacting Aboriginal people. These laws and regulations are a codification of what society considers to be a minimum acceptable level of corporate social responsibility toward Aboriginal people. They range from specific terms and conditions relating to Aboriginal participation in mineral leases, forest harvesting/management licenses, government contracts, and so forth to laws of general application such as human rights codes and environmental protection legislation.

Beginning in the late 1970s, environmental legislation and the environmental impact assessments that flow from it required the involvement of local people in initial impact assessment and ongoing monitoring and control of resource projects. At the same time, provincial governments began requiring mining and forestry companies granted resource leases in remote areas to put in place preferential hiring and procurement policies for local people.[3] Many of the corporate Aboriginal programs in place today began in response to such legally imposed requirements. For example, according to Eric Newell, President and CEO of Syncrude Canada Ltd.:

> *Our resources are on land that abuts traditional Native hunting grounds. From the beginning — in fact, in order to get the permit to build the property — Syncrude was required to provide opportunities so local Native residents could share equally with others in the benefits of oil sands development.*
>
> (Newell 1994, 6)

Syncrude's Aboriginal programs and alliances emerged in response to Alberta government requirements as did Cameco's[4] in response to similar requirements in Saskatchewan. The programs and alliances of both companies have evolved from an initial focus on equity in employment to include alliances in the areas of education and training; business development; and communication, consultation and negotiation with communities and community leaders. As

---

3 In the remote areas of Canada where most resource projects are located, the local people are overwhelmingly Aboriginal.

4 In 1989, as required by license, Cameco made a commitment to build a mine site workforce that employed at least 50% northerners (the vast majority of whom are Aboriginal). At the time, the employment rate for northerners at the mine sites was 32%. By 1995, 50% of the mine site workforce was from the North and 40% was Aboriginal — a total of 450 Aboriginal people (Cameco 1993, 1995a & 1995b). With these numbers, Cameco became Canada's largest industrial employer of Aboriginal people surpassing Syncrude with approximately 340 Aboriginal employees.

a result of these programs and alliances, these two corporations have become the largest industrial employers of Aboriginal people in Canada and both pump tens of millions of dollars into the Aboriginal economy through purchases from Aboriginal-owned companies. For example, through such measures as "tendering contracts only in the North and encouraging joint ventures between northern firms and southern suppliers" (Cameco 1993, 3), by 1995 "of the $92 million Cameco spent on goods and services in Saskatchewan, 52% was spent on purchases from northern Saskatchewan-based enterprises" (Cameco 1995a, 25). Other resource companies are following suit.[5]

Human rights legislation and the affirmative action programs flowing from it have been another legal/regulatory force behind the emergence of some corporate Aboriginal programs. This is particularly true for Crown corporations, government departments and agencies, and companies wishing to do business with governments. Because of their unique relationship with the government, Crown corporations have been required to develop affirmative action programs (rather than simply being allowed or encouraged to do so, as is the case with other business corporations). As with Aboriginal requirements in resource licenses, affirmative action programs have been the base upon which more elaborate corporate Aboriginal partnerships have been built. As examples, the programs of the Saskatchewan Wheat Pool and SaskEnergy are described in the next section.

Beyond resource companies and Crown corporations (and a few business corporations with affirmative action programs), specific legal and regulatory requirements have had little direct impact on corporate Aboriginal relations. The same cannot be said for the issues that underlie these laws and regulations — the redress of past wrongs and the need for socially responsible corporate behaviour in the future. These issues have had a significant influence on the strategic planning of some corporations as they pursue the business opportunities presented by Aboriginal people (Factors 4 and 5).

A growing number of companies are realizing that a strategy of alliances and partnerships with Aboriginal people that addresses past wrongs and offers them hope for the future is the key to doing business profitably with native people and on "native land" now, and will be even more so in the future. As a result, where laws and regulations exist, companies are going well beyond the minimum requirements and where none are in force, companies are voluntarily including Aboriginal people in their business activities.

5.1.3. Factor 4: Aboriginal Labour Force and Market

Factor 4 is the large and rapidly growing Aboriginal population. This growth has created opportunities in two areas: market and labour force. Aboriginal people are becoming an increasingly significant target market for some companies, particularly given the fact that population growth is coupled with an increasing (albeit very slowly) affluence (The Globe and Mail 1996; Armstrong

5 Examples are Cogema, Placer Dome, Imperial Resources, MacMillan Bloedel, Interfor and Timber West.

1996). Aboriginal people also form a significant and growing segment of the Canadian labour force. As the level of education and training increases, this growing labour force is becoming more competitive in the labour market (Brooks 1994; Thomas 1994).

Companies see these two aspects as intertwined. Those wishing to take advantage of the growing Aboriginal market often view the hiring of Aboriginal people as the mechanism for reaching that market while at the same time addressing the issue of employment equity. The following comments by Ron Jamieson, a Bank of Montreal vice-president, capture the essence of this argument:

> *Native people, with almost 5 percent of Canada's current population, or more than one million customers, make up a large potential market.*
>
> *The valuable pool of Native talent is another reason for corporate Canada to partner with Aboriginal people. Education levels are rising rapidly.... No growth oriented company can afford to ignore this expanding group of well-educated potential employees.*
>
> *Aboriginal workers provide a window on the expanding Native market ... companies had better change or risk being left out of important markets. Implementing workplace equality is the right thing to do, but it is also a smart, profitable move.*
>
> (Jamieson 1994, 14)

As examples, the programs of the Bank of Montreal and SaskEnergy are described later in this chapter.

5.1.4. Factor 5: Natural and Financial Resources

The fifth and final factor, the already enormous and rapidly growing pool of natural and financial resources controlled by Aboriginal people, has a compelling influence on corporation Aboriginal relations. The magnitude of the lands and dollars accruing to the First Nations and the Inuit[6] is revealed by the following statement that appears in the material sent by The Globe and Mail to corporate managers inviting them to a conference on corporate/Aboriginal partnerships:

> *By the year 2000, over one-third of the land in Canada will be returned to First Nation control. Resolution of recent claims has delivered to First Nations approximately $35,000 per Aboriginal person and it has been estimated that the cost to resolve land claims in British Columbia alone will exceed $10 billion.*
>
> (The Globe and Mail 1996, 5)

---

6 To date, the Metis have been much less successful in securing a land-based and/or financial compensation for "lost Aboriginal rights."

The Globe and Mail goes on to say:

> *It is clear that the First Nations community is becoming a substantial economic force in this country and that corporate Canada has moved ... to foster ties with Aboriginal groups and businesses.* (The Globe and Mail 1996, 5)

The companies with Aboriginal relations programs and alliances that go beyond satisfying basic legal and regulatory conditions have often done so for business reasons having to do with Factor 5 alone or in combination with Factor 4. Employment and business development programs along with joint ventures and other partnership arrangements are seen as essential to gaining corporate access to needed resources. The programs of Cameco, Interfor and BC Hydro, described later in this chapter, are typical.

5.1.5. Factor 3 Revisited

The federal government has reacted to the emergence and evolution of corporate Aboriginal alliances in the private sector. On April 3, 1996, the Department of Indian Affairs and Northern Development announced a new program called "A Procurement Strategy for Aboriginal Business." In a letter describing the program, Ronald Irwin, the Minister, said:

> *Beginning April 1st, 1996, qualified Aboriginal businesses and joint ventures will be given the first opportunity to compete for government contracts servicing Aboriginal populations, where Aboriginal capacity exists and normal requirements for quality, best value and competition can be met. Departments will also be encouraged to target certain types of contracts voluntarily* [other than those for services to Aboriginal people] *where this action is appropriate and would assist the governments objectives for Aboriginal business development.*
>
> (DIAND 1996, 1)

Under this policy, an Aboriginal business is one that is 51% Aboriginal-owned and controlled. An Aboriginal joint venture is one in which 51% of the participating companies are Aboriginal-owned. In both cases, 33% of the full-time employees (if there are more than six) must be Aboriginal.

Other recent government actions have combined with this procurement policy to increase the incentive for corporations to form joint ventures with Aboriginal partners. For example, on July 10, 1996, at the Annual Assembly of the AFN, Mr. Irwin announced an 80% increase (some $100-million) in the annual budget for sewer and water and related projects on reserves. In addition, an increase of $140-million over the next five years in the funds allocated to on-reserve housing has also been announced recently (Star Phoenix 1996b, A1). Expenditures of this size create an opportunity that is not lost on non-First Nation construction companies. It is bound to encourage some of them to seek out First Nation partners with whom they can form joint ventures that will qualify as Aboriginal under the new procurement policy.

Evidence of the impact of the policy is already surfacing.[7] On July 8, 1996, the Meadow Lake Tribal Council and Kilborn Western, a large general contractor, announced the formation of a joint venture contracting company — Great Bear Construction. This company will bid on the construction projects of the nine First Nations of the Tribal Council. When announcing the partnership, Ray Ahenakew the Executive Director of the Tribal Council said that over $50-million had been spent on construction by the Meadow Lake First Nations over the past 10 to 15 years. According to Ahenakew, beyond the buildings themselves, the people of the First Nations derived very little economic benefit from this activity. The joint venture is expected to change this by providing permanent employment for a core Aboriginal workforce in the building trades, technical support and management. In addition, a share of the profits of the business will flow back to the MLTC. From Kilborn's perspective, as a result of the joint venture the company will continue to have access to the Aboriginal market under the terms of the new procurement policy. Great Bear Construction has already secured its first contract — a $700,000 health station for the Buffalo River First Nation. (Indigenous Times 1996, 19)

With this program, events have traveled full circle. In a press release from the Minister's Office announcing the new policy, the following statement was made:

> *This new federal initiative borrows from the example set by a number of large businesses which use mentoring, joint venturing, and their own contracting needs in a purposeful way to build a healthy Aboriginal economy.* (DIAND 1996, 2)

Many of the corporate programs that so inspired the government (e.g. those of Syncrude and Cameco) began in response to earlier government requirements. For good business reasons, companies have voluntarily expanded their Aboriginal relations programs beyond the minimum legislated requirements. Most often this expansion has involved the encouragement of Aboriginal business development and the creation of joint ventures. The success of these expanded corporate programs has inspired this new effort by the government. In turn, this new program will stimulate further action by companies wishing to do business with the government on Aboriginal projects.

The emergence of this procurement policy confirms the wisdom of those businesses that have already adopted a partnership approach to relations with Aboriginal people. Their past efforts give them a current and future competitive advantage in competing for government contracts benefiting Aboriginal people.

---

7 See also the purchase of Tron Power by the English River First Nation described in chapter 7.

5.2. Corporate Aboriginal Relations: Survey Results

The results of my corporate survey are presented in this section. An analysis of the responses provides a sense of the importance that corporations attach to each of the five factors. In addition, the results provide an indication about how corporations' views have changed over the past 10 years and, by projection, how they may be expected to change in the future.

Question 1 explores a company's sense of corporate social responsibility as it translates into its approach to alliances with Aboriginal people — Factor 2. Corporations were asked to select from among three choices[8] the one that best reflects the motivating force behind their corporate Aboriginal relations strategy. The results of the responses are summarized in Table 5–1.

Sixteen percent of the respondents said that their approach to corporate Aboriginal relations was primarily motivated by a sense of corporate social responsibility toward Aboriginal and all other "disadvantaged people." These companies indicated that they felt that such "socially responsible behaviour" imposes a cost on their company. Interestingly, none of the respondents indicated the second alternative — compliance with a legislated, license or regulatory requirements — as a primary motivating force. Eighty-four percent indicated that working with Aboriginal people is part of their corporate strategy to improve long-term profitability and is therefore not a cost but an "investment."

The second question asked respondents is: Would their answer to question 1 be the same five and ten years ago (see Table 5–2). They were also asked to comment briefly on the reasons for any change. Eighty-three percent of respondents said that their company's primary motivating force for working with Aboriginal people was the same five years ago as it is today. The figure drops

TABLE 5–1: Aboriginal Relations, Primary Motivating Force

Reason	Proportion (%)
Good corporate citizenship imposing a cost on the company	16
Required by legislation, license requirements, etc. and a cost of doing business	0
Part of corporate strategy intended to improve its long-term competitive performance	84

Source: Corporate survey.

8 The three alternatives are drawn from material on corporate social responsibility as discussed in chapter 3.

TABLE 5–2: Primary Motivating Force, Change Over Time

Response	All Respondents (%)	Respondents Indicating Reason #3 in Table 5–1 (%)
The same answer 5 years ago	83	80
The same answer 10 years ago	39	27

Source: Corporate survey.

to 39% for those who felt their company's motivating force was the same 10 years ago. For companies reporting the third choice as their primary motivation, the proportion reporting the same factor five and ten years ago drops to 80% and 27% respectively. Significantly, this means that 10 years ago only 22% (lower as compared to 84% today) of the companies surveyed would have reported that working with Aboriginal people was a part of their strategy to improve long-term corporate performance. From this, it is clear that corporate attitudes about programs for, and partnerships with, Aboriginal people have shifted over a decade in a manner consistent with theoretical expectations as captured in Figure 3–2.

In their comments relating to questions 1 and 2, several respondents indicated that their company's current approach began as a response to legislative/regulatory requirements. Over time, they said their company came to realize that expanding corporate Aboriginal alliances beyond the minimum legislated requirements was in its best long-term interests. Cameco's experience, as described in the comments section of the questionnaire, is typical:

- *Ten years ago — legislated requirement*
- *Five years ago — began to see the strategic advantages*
- *Now — very much a strategic investment.*

(Cameco survey response, 1996)

These responses provide a partial explanation as to why no companies reported Factor 2 as their primary current/future motivating factor. The companies surveyed have progressed beyond mere compliance with regulations to developing more elaborate approaches to their relationship with Aboriginal people. This shows the long-term value to both corporations and Aboriginal people of legislated requirements. They can force companies to take a reluctant first step toward partnering with Aboriginal people. After that, if conditions warrant, the partnerships may expand and deepen, to the benefit of both.

The next four questions on the survey explored the extent to which Factors 3, 4 and 5 are responsible for the fact that corporations increasingly see working with Aboriginal people as an opportunity for improving long-term corporate performance (a long-term investment) as opposed to a constraint im-

TABLE 5–3: Aboriginal Relations, Primary Motivating Force

Factor	Current (%)	Future (%)	Important to Strategy (%)
Aboriginal people as a significant labour force	79	79	68
Aboriginal people as a significant market	26	32	21
Aboriginal people in control of significant resources	53	79	79

Source: Corporate survey.

posing current costs. Results are described in the following paragraphs and summarized in Table 5–3.

Question 3 asked if the company views Aboriginal people as a significant labour pool from which future employees will be recruited and if the company has an Aboriginal hiring policy or program. Companies were asked to expand on their answer by giving comments about the success of such programs. Seventy-nine percent of respondents indicated that their company viewed Aboriginal people as a significant pool from which future employees will be recruited. Sixty-eight percent of the companies reported having an Aboriginal employment policy or program. Several were also involved in training and education partnerships with others in their industry and Aboriginal groups or institutions intending to prepare people for employment in their industry. Companies commenting on their success to date reported satisfactory outcomes.

Question 4 explored the importance of Aboriginal people as current or future customers of the companies. Of those responding, 26% stated that Aboriginal people and/or communities are currently significant customers. When asked about future prospects, the proportion viewing Aboriginal people and communities as an attractive market increased to 32% of the total. Two-thirds of this 32% stated that market potential was the major reason they have adopted or are considering adopting Aboriginal hiring policies and/or establishing business alliances with Aboriginal people.

The importance to a corporation of the current and potential resources held by Aboriginal people was the subject of the fifth question. Of the companies surveyed, 53% of the respondents felt that Aboriginal people currently control resources important to their company's profitable operation. When the focus shifted to the future in the second part of the question, the proportion of companies that felt that Aboriginal people will acquire control of resources critical to their future, profitability jumped to 79%. All the companies making up this 79% reported that current or potential Aboriginal control of resources was the major reason for the adoption of their policy toward Aboriginal people. From this finding, it is evident that the drive by the Aboriginal people to build economic development capacity through land claims is working. The claims already settled and the prospects for many more being settled in the future have set the stage for the successful implementation of the First Nations' strategy of joint ventures with non-First Nation corporations.[9]

Combining the responses to questions 3, 4 and 5, 89% of the companies indicated that their Aboriginal alliance strategy and programs are motivated by Aboriginal people as a current and/or potential labour pool, market, and/or source of key resources (Factors 4 and 5). Only 11% are motivated solely by a sense of general social responsibility (Factor 2) or legislated requirements (Factor 3). These results differ from those reported in Table 5–1 where 16% of companies say that their current programs are motivated by a sense of general social responsibility. The difference (11% versus 16%) stems from the fact that one of the companies that selected the first response to question 1 (making it part of the 16%) feels Factors 4 and 5 will become very important to them in the future and is therefore developing its Aboriginal relations program accordingly.

In summary, based on corporate responses it is apparent that Factors 4 (Aboriginal people as a labour force and/or market) and 5 (Aboriginal people in control of key resources) are the overwhelming reasons why corporations have adopted a strategy of alliances with Aboriginal people. Factor 2 (the duty to be socially responsible) is often alluded to as a contributing factor, usually in the sense that a company must behave appropriately vis-à-vis Aboriginal people in order to tap into their potential as a market and/or a supplier of human, financial and/or natural resources. Factor 3 is not viewed as significant at present or in the future. The companies responding said that the forces motivating their behaviour and their objectives go far beyond simple compliance with legislated quotas and requirements. Several do, however, attribute the genesis of their current programs to such requirements imposed on them in the past.

Question 6 asked the companies if they have a policy and programs to encourage Aboriginal companies to meet some of their current and future input and other needs. Eighty-four percent of the companies responded that they do. The second part of the question asked if these programs go beyond encouraging existing Aboriginal companies to include assistance to Aboriginal individuals and communities to establish new companies. Seventy-nine percent of the responding corporations indicated that they already have or are developing such a program. This proactive encouragement of First Nations business development provides an indication of the strength of the willingness of some corporations to partner with Aboriginal people and augurs well for future Aboriginal economic development activities.

The final question was the most general of all. It explored the extent to which the companies are pursuing a strategy of alliances and joint ventures in response to Factor 1 — the shift to a flexible global competitive regime in general and not just with respect to Aboriginal people. Fifty-eight percent indicated that they are more likely to pursue such strategies now and in the future than they were five years ago. The proportion jumped to 95% when asked to compare their current and future strategies and arrangements with those of 10

9 The ARA report in Appendix 4 supports this finding.

FIGURE 5–2: Categories of Corporate Aboriginal Relations Programs

1. Employment Equity Programs (legislation/licensing social responsibility).
2. Market-based Programs.
3. Resource-based Programs.
4. Balanced (market and resource) Programs.

years ago. It is clear from their responses that the companies are adopting a more "flexible" mode of operation in response to Factor 1 — global competitive pressures. This general response combined with the significance corporations attach to Factors 4 and 5 has obvious implications for corporate/Aboriginal relations. For sound business reasons, corporations are more likely to pursue alliances with Aboriginal people now and in the future than they were in the past.

In the next section, corporate Aboriginal programs are categorized and one or more examples of each type are provided.

5.3. Corporate Aboriginal Programs: "Best Cases"

A review of the material received from respondents indicates that their corporate Aboriginal relations programs can be grouped into four categories (see Figure 5–2). The first category includes those that have been developed in response to Factors 2 and/or 3. They are generally employment equity programs intended to increase the number of Aboriginal people (as well as the disabled, women, visible minorities, and others) employed by the company to an equitable level. While certainly of value to the individuals who might otherwise not have been employed, such programs play a very minor role in First Nations' economic development.

The other three categories of corporate Aboriginal relations programs are market-based, resource-based and balanced (a combination of market- and resource-based). While they may acknowledge Factors 2 and 3 and may even have begun to respond to them, they are largely the outcome of company strategies motivated by Factors 4 and/or 5. Factor 1 exerts an important influence, because of it, a growing number of companies are willing to pursue a strategy of alliances with Aboriginal people as they respond to Factors 4 and 5. Companies view alliances and programs as an investment that will contribute to profitability, growth and long-term survival. Most Categories 2, 3 and 4 programs have four key features in common: (i) employment; (ii) education and training; (iii) business development programs including joint ventures and other partnering; and (iv) communication, consultation and negotiation between corporate leaders and Aboriginal leaders and communities. Categories 2, 3 and 4 programs are particularly significant because of the "fit" they have with the First Nations' strategy of business development founded on regaining ownership and control of their traditional lands.

5.3.1. Employment Equity Programs

The Aboriginal relations program of the Saskatchewan Wheat Pool falls into this category. According to its response to the survey, the company does not consider Aboriginal people a significant market for its products or services. Neither do they feel that Aboriginal people control resources important to Wheat Pool's profitable operation. To date, the company's program for Aboriginal people is simply a part of a larger employment equity program designed to satisfy human rights legislation.

Interestingly, the Wheat Pool feels that this may change in the future. The company expects the recent Treaty Land Entitlement settlements in Saskatchewan to result in significant growth in Aboriginal agriculture. As a result, the people of the First Nations may become both significant customers and controllers of resources important to the Pool. Based on this expectation, the company has begun to explore possibilities for joint ventures with the Federation of the Saskatchewan Indian Nations. Perhaps this is another case where a limited program begun in response to legislated requirements will blossom into a relationship that includes businesses alliances to the benefit of both the company and Aboriginal people as Factors 4 and 5 come into play.

5.3.2. Market-based Programs

Category 2 programs are those inspired by the fact that Aboriginal people represent a large and growing market for a company's products and services. The programs of Bank of Montreal and SaskEnergy are good examples.

5.3.2.1. The Bank of Montreal

The Bank of Montreal makes no attempt to disguise the motivation for its Aboriginal relations strategy, nor should it. The company's primary objective is to increase the business it does with Aboriginal people. According to its Aboriginal Banking Review, to achieve this objective, Bank of Montreal:

> *Will work hard to build and nurture a relationship that will endure, based on mutual respect and mutual advantage. We will listen, learn and work with Aboriginal communities to find new and creative solutions to satisfy financing and investment needs.*
> (Bank of Montreal 1993, 1)

The bank's key measures of success for its Aboriginal relations strategy include (i) the number of Aboriginal employees in its workforce and the number promoted and (ii) growth in the number and dollar amount of loans to, and deposits from, Aboriginal people and communities. (Jamieson 1994; Sloan and Hill 1995; Bank of Montreal 1993).

The bank has pursued its strategy on two tracks. One is directed toward improving the products and services it markets to Aboriginal people and communities, and the other to increasing the number of Aboriginal employees with the bank. The latter was expected to support the former because:

> *Building a workforce that better reflects the communities it serves gives the bank an enhanced understanding of the needs of those communities, builds mutual trust and respect and enables the bank to provide Aboriginal people with better customer service.* (Sloan and Hill 1995, 42)

This is clearly a case where the company views socially responsible corporate behaviour as a key factor in attaining its long-term business objectives and not simply an obligation imposing costs to be minimized.

The bank's efforts to increase the number of Aboriginal employees began in May of 1991. At that time the bank established a task force on Aboriginal employment. The task force studied the issue for over a year and submitted a report in October of 1992. According to that report, fewer than one-half of 1% of the bank's employees were Aboriginal, whereas the Aboriginal component of the national workforce was 2%. The report identified barriers to the employment of Aboriginal people at the bank and made 31 recommendations for action. The objective of these recommendations was "to develop a national workforce that comprises at least 2% Aboriginal employees by 1995" (Bank of Montreal 1993, 8). To ensure that its Aboriginal employment goals received serious attention, the bank began including accountability for workplace equity in its business planning and performance evaluation processes. Executives and senior managers are expected to set and achieve realistic annual goals. Workplace equality results are assessed as part of a manager's annual performance review.

The bank has been pursuing its employment target with some success. By the end of 1991, there were 118 Aboriginal people employed by the company. By 1993, 122 additional Aboriginal people were hired and, in 1994, another 130. This three-fold increase brought the Aboriginal proportion of the bank's workforce to 1.7%. No final report is available for 1995 but it is expected that the 2% target will have been achieved. As well, during this same period considerable efforts were made to ensure that Aboriginal people had the opportunity to advance within the bank. For example, in 1994, Aboriginal people received 0.9% of promotions even though they made up only 0.6% of the workforce at the start of that year.

The other major track of the bank's strategy to increase its Aboriginal business is to improve the quality and quantity of its products and services for Aboriginal people and to improve access to these services. In pursuit of these ends, the bank established an Aboriginal Banking Unit in 1992. This unit was (and still is) headed by a vice-president, Ron Jamieson, a Mohawk from Six Nations in Ontario. Under Mr. Jamieson, eight Aboriginal banking managers (each Aboriginal) were appointed, one in each of the bank's eight regions. In describing the role of these managers, the bank says that:

> *Managers of Aboriginal banking will provide the bank with counsel and training in matters of Aboriginal community proto-*

> *col, tradition and culture. Aboriginal business is a significant and growing business opportunity, which a major Canadian financial institution would be foolish to neglect. We need to listen and to understand, if we are to earn the right to bank Aboriginal business.* (Bank of Montreal 1993, 6)

The creation of the Aboriginal Unit involves the allocation of considerable corporate resources and is evidence of the importance the bank attaches to its Aboriginal strategy. The bank is "putting its money where its mouth is."

With this structure in place, the bank began a number of initiatives intended to better serve and therefore attract the business of Aboriginal people and communities. These efforts included (and still include):

1. A circle of Aboriginal leaders to advise the bank on Aboriginal banking issues.
2. Branches on reserves.
3. An Aboriginal business support program including conferences and workshops.
4. An Aboriginal credit task force to share specialized knowledge throughout the bank to better serve Aboriginal customers.
5. A legal project to build an expertise in relevant laws and taxation impacts to enable the bank to offer sound and consistent service across the country.
6. A community interaction pilot project to "learn how our front-line customer service staff perceive the opportunity to serve Aboriginal business, and how Aboriginal customers, in turn, perceive banks, bank products, and banking relationships." (Bank of Montreal 1993, 6)

The bank is pleased with business results to date. According to Sloan and Hill, between 1993 and 1994, the bank increased the number of Aboriginal loans by 200% and increased the number of accounts held by Aboriginal people and organizations by 70%. More importantly, the bank has established itself in the Aboriginal market and is poised and prepared to participate in the economic growth that is likely to occur as a result of further land claims settlements and Aboriginal economic development activities.

5.3.2.2. SaskEnergy

SaskEnergy is a Crown corporation of the Province of Saskatchewan. It provides natural gas to households and businesses in the province. Its Aboriginal relations program is motivated in part by the fact that it sees the Aboriginal market as currently important and rapidly growing. In its publication *Doing Business with Aboriginal Business,* SaskEnergy identifies the expanding Aboriginal housing market and reserve gasification as areas of particular potential (SaskEnergy 1995b). In fact, it says that "Aboriginal people constitute the largest market of expanding customer demand for SaskEnergy and TransGas in the province" (Sloan and Hill 1995, 16).

This business motivation is compounded by the fact that SaskEnergy is a Crown corporation. The Government of Saskatchewan's stated objective is to have Aboriginal people become full partners in the processes and benefits of social and economic development in the province. As the owners of SaskEnergy, the province has the power and the right to have the corporation incorporate this objective into its policies, programs and operations, and it has done so.

These two influences are apparent in SaskEnergy's Aboriginal policy that

> *Recognizes the need for the Aboriginal community of Saskatchewan to be integral stakeholders in Canada's economic development; specifically, SaskEnergy will encourage and foster partnership development in three strategic areas: employment, education and training, and business development.*
>
> (SaskEnergy 1995a, 2)

The company goes on to say that its policies are intended to "help facilitate Indian and Metis self-determination ... promote Aboriginal community development and renewal" (SaskEnergy 1995a, 2). Further, in its literature the company states that its partnerships with Aboriginal people intended to accomplish these objectives "make good business sense" because they permit "programs and services to be customized for and by the community they seek to serve" (SaskEnergy 1995a, 2); that is, the current and rapidly growing future Aboriginal market. This approach is consistent with the company's vision of becoming "Canada's leading energy company by anticipating customers changing needs and providing innovative and responsive solutions" (SaskEnergy 1995b, 2).

SaskEnergy is implementing its program on three fronts. The first is employment. In 1994, the company adopted an employment plan involving the following actions:

1. Develop and demonstrate fair and accessible employment practices and planning to ensure that Aboriginal people are considered for employment opportunities.
2. Foster and promote a culturally sensitive and proactive workplace.
3. Employ Aboriginal role models at all business levels of the corporation.
4. Employ Aboriginal post-secondary students for the summer.

As a result of these policies, the company reports that 20% of all new hires in 1994 were of Aboriginal ancestry. By the end of that year, Aboriginal people made up 4.5% of the company's workforce. As well, 17% of the summer students hired in 1994 were Aboriginal.

The second front, education and training, has four elements. The first is the development of partnership programs with Aboriginal post-secondary institutions to promote co-op work/study programs to increase the recruitment and retention of Aboriginal students. The second is a community-based program to encourage students to stay in school. The third is to provide scholarships, bursaries and grants to Aboriginal students who will meet SaskEnergy's future workforce needs. The fourth component is training for current Aboriginal employees to prepare them for advancement opportunities.

The final front is business development. SaskEnergy's objective is to "foster and support Indian and Metis businesses and contractors to do business with and for SaskEnergy" (SaskEnergy 1995a, 3). To develop alliances with current and new Aboriginal businesses, SaskEnergy will:

- *Identify business opportunities.*
- *Advise the Aboriginal business community of opportunities and how to access them.*
- *Include Aboriginal businesses in the Saskatchewan Supplier Development Program.* (SaskEnergy 1995a, 3)

In support of these activities, SaskEnergy prepared a list of Aboriginal companies and contractors in the province. The list is updated continuously as additional business are identified or new ones created.

SaskEnergy, like the Bank of Montreal, has integrated its Aboriginal objectives into its planning and performance evaluation processes. Managers are held accountable for the setting and achieving of goals consistent with these objectives. The second and third elements of SaskEnergy's program are so new that it is not possible to measure their impact. However, the company says it is pleased with progress to date.

In summary, both the Bank of Montreal and SaskEnergy view Aboriginal people and communities as an attractive growth market. Both have concluded that the inclusion of Aboriginal people through employment and business relationships is the key to tapping this potential. Both have invested considerable time and money in their Aboriginal programs with the expectation that the business returns from this market will more than justify the investment. In fact, the word "investment" captures the essence of both companies' attitudes. Aboriginal programs are not seen as a current cost but rather as an investment that is an important component for their strategy for future success.

The Bank of Montreal's program is not unique among financial institutions; nor is SaskEnergy's among Crown corporations. The other major chartered banks see the same market opportunity and are following similar strategies of partnership. One notable initiative involves the Toronto Dominion Bank in a joint venture with the Federation of Saskatchewan Indian Nations to create a new national chartered bank — The First Nations Bank of Canada (see chapter 7 for details). Another is a joint venture between the Canadian Bankers Association and the Saskatchewan Indian Federated College. The two have joined forces to develop and offer an undergraduate business degree with a major in "Aboriginal Banking." Companies in the financial services and accounting field are also developing similar programs. This is particularly true of the major accounting/business consulting firms such as KPMG Peat Marwick and Price Waterhouse that have a history of doing business with Aboriginal communities and organizations. Other Crown corporations in Saskatchewan and across the country have or are developing market-driven programs like SaskEnergy's (e.g. SaskTel, Manitoba Hydro, BC Hydro and BC Tel, Ontario Hydro, Hydro Quebec).

Some companies in the construction industry have developed similar market-driven programs. PCL Construction's excellent program is a case in point. Corporate Aboriginal partnership activity in this sector is certain to increase. With all federally funded construction (houses, schools, water/sewer systems, etc.) on reserves (and elsewhere for the benefit of Aboriginal people) falling under the new procurement policy, there is bound to be a scramble by non-Aboriginal companies to find Aboriginal partners with whom they can establish "Aboriginally controlled" joint ventures to bid on such projects. This will be matched by new Aboriginal companies searching for experienced and well-equipped partners so that they can bid on these large construction projects. The already described Great Bear Construction, a newly formed joint venture between the nine First Nations of the Meadow Lake Tribal Council and Kilborn Western is a case in point.

5.3.3. Resource-based Programs

These programs are motivated by Aboriginal people's control of resources (natural, financial and/or human) critical to a company's profitability and survival. Not surprisingly, the majority of the corporations with programs in this category are resource companies that require access to land and resources in remote areas. Increasingly, control of much of this land is passing, completely or partially, into Aboriginal hands through the comprehensive claims/modern treaty process described in chapter 4. The programs of Cameco and Interfor fall in this category and are described in the following pages.

5.3.3.1. Cameco

Cameco Corporation is the world's largest publicly traded uranium company and an emerging gold producer. The company was created in 1988 through a merger of two Crown corporations, Eldorado Nuclear (federal) and Saskatchewan Mining Development Corporation (provincial). Shares were sold to the public in 1991 with the governments maintaining a minority interest. Government ownership interest has declined since through the periodic sale of their shares. Cameco has uranium and gold mining operations in northern Saskatchewan, a uranium processing plant in Ontario and, as a joint venture partner, a gold mine under construction in Kyrgyzstan. The company is currently exploring for minerals in Canada, the United States, Mexico, South America, Australia, and Central Asia.

Cameco's explanation as to why it implemented its Aboriginal relations program and what motivated the growth of that program over time was provided in the previous section but is worth repeating here:

> *Ten years ago — a legislated requirement*
> *Five years ago — began to see the strategic advantages*
> *Now — very much a strategic investment*
>
> (Cameco survey response, 1996)

This change over time has resulted in the company's current view that "partnerships with Aboriginal communities anchor support for its existing operations and facilitate the prospects of expansion and new mine development" (Sloan and Hill 1995, 35). Cameco has set out to earn this community support

> *by implementing policies which permit northerners to share in the benefits of development in the Athabaska Basin. Specifically, it is committed to staffing at least half the corporation's*

> *northern operations with local residents, to give preferential consideration to northern businesses and to promote dialogue between Cameco and northern leaders.* (Cameco 1995a, 25)

Cameco's program to implement these policies has the four familiar components — employment, education and training, business development, and communication, consultation and negotiation with communities and community leaders.

In 1989, in response to provincial government requirements, the company made a commitment to build a mine site workforce that employed at least 50% northerners (the vast majority of whom are Aboriginal). The mine site employment rate for northerners at that time was 32%. In order to achieve its objective, northerners were (and still are) given first priority to fill vacant positions at the mine sites. The company did not wait passively for northerners, and in particular Aboriginal people, to apply. Proactively, it developed

> *one of the largest employment data bases in the north and accepts referrals from northern outreach offices, band offices, tribal council offices and northern training institutions. This network of information allows us to determine the availability of qualified northern candidates for employment opportunities.*
> (Cameco 1993, 2)

Because northerners, particularly Aboriginal people, often lack the necessary qualifications "many technical positions are filled by northern trainees to give them the experience necessary to expand their qualifications" (Cameco 1993, 2).

By 1993, 43% of the minesite workforce were northerners. More importantly, to this discussion, 37% of the total mine site workforce was Aboriginal (Cameco 1993). By 1995, 50% of the mine site workforce was from the North and 40% was Aboriginal — a total of 450 Aboriginal people (Cameco 1996a, 1995b). With these numbers, Cameco became Canada's largest industrial employer of Aboriginal people, edging out Syncrude with approximately 340 Aboriginal employees. In addition to this direct hiring, Cameco requires all its contractors to (i) maximize their hiring of northerners and (ii) source their materials and subcontractors from the North, whenever possible. In 1993, Cameco estimated that of the average 300 contractor employees working on site at any particular time, 50% were northerners, most of them Aboriginal (Cameco 1993, 3).

Going beyond on-the-job training including the use of trainee positions as described, Cameco supports education and training in other significant ways. The company hires students for the summer and encourages them to stay in school. Cameco offers awards and post-secondary scholarships to 40 northern students each year. As well, along with other uranium mining companies and governments, Cameco is participating in a five-year, $10.5-million program. The purpose of the program is to identify specific occupations needed at future mining operations in the North and then to train northerners so that they will be qualified to fill these positions when the new mines open.

Cameco's efforts to support northern and Aboriginal businesses have been as successful as their Aboriginal employment activities. Through such measures as "tendering contracts only in the north and encouraging joint ventures between northern firms and southern suppliers" (Cameco 1993, 3), by 1995, "of the $92 million Cameco spent on goods and services in Saskatchewan, 52% was spent on purchases from northern Saskatchewan-based enterprises" (Cameco 1995a, 25). Several of these northern firms are joint ventures between either the La Ronge First Nation or the Prince Albert Grand Council and non-northern companies formed to exploit the opportunity offered by Cameco's "buy northern" policy.

Finally, Cameco works to strengthen its partnership with the Aboriginal and other northern people through communication. The company holds frequent community meetings, with translations into Cree and Dene, to discuss its future plans with the members of the communities impacted by its operations. In a further effort to enhance communication and consultation, Cameco has established a Northern Community Liaison Committee that "provides an opportunity for the 14 northern chiefs and mayors to meet with Cameco's executives three times a year to exchange information and ideas" (Cameco 1993, 3). Also, a prominent First Nation leader, Chief Harry Cook of the La Ronge First Nation is a director of the company and contributes a First Nations' perspective at the highest corporate level.

Cameco has been successful in achieving its northern and Aboriginal employment and business development objectives. Directly and through its contractors, it employs 700 northerners, over 600 of whom are Aboriginal. In addition, its injects more than $46-million into the northern economy through its purchases from "northern" businesses. These activities have had a tremendous impact in a region where unemployment is very high, high-paying jobs scarce and business opportunities limited. Clearly, the people in the North (including Aboriginal people) and Cameco are involved in a mutually beneficial partnership. Through jobs and business activity, Aboriginal people and other northern residents benefit from the long-term survival of the company.[10] In return, Cameco has earned the support of northern residents[11] allowing it to meet its primary goal; that is to "anchor support for its existing operations and facilitate the prospects of expansion and new mine development" (Sloan and Hill 1995, 35).

---

10 There is considerable debate about the impact of the employment of Aboriginal people in the northern mine on the socioeconomic conditions in northern communities. Not all the Aboriginal employees of the mines remain residents of their home communities. However, most, particularly those from First Nations, maintain strong connections to their communities through "citizenship" and extended family relationships. This means that at least some benefits flow to that "home community" even if the employed individual chooses to live elsewhere.

11 This is not to say that uranium mining and economic development associated with it is without detractors. As elsewhere, in northern Saskatchewan, there is considerable concern about the environmental impacts of uranium mining and the nuclear industry in general.

5.3.3.2. Interfor

Forestry is another industrial sector where increasing First Nations' control over land and resources has become a critical issue. The following paragraphs describe one company's response — International Forest Products Ltd. (Interfor). Although more advanced than some, its programs and alliances are typical of those emerging among forestry companies.[12]

Incorporated in 1963, Interfor has grown to become one of Canada's major forest companies with operations throughout British Columbia. The company has 59 logging operations and operates eight sawmills. The company employs approximately 4,400 people including 900 through the logging contractors under its direction. Annual sales of lumber, wood chips and logs in 1995 generated revenues of $930-million (Interfor 1995a).

Interfor has entered into a variety of arrangements with people of the First Nations in British Columbia. These arrangements were motivated by Interfor's desire to preserve its annual allowable cut, maintain its logging profits, increase the supply of logs to its mills and ensure uninterrupted operation of its mills. In order to accomplish these objectives "Interfor is willing to undertake a range of co-operative arrangements, including joint ventures, with any Aboriginal community or organization that holds cutting rights" (Sloan and Hill 1995, 195). Interfor fully expects, indeed wants, these partnership arrangements to provide the First Nations economic development (jobs and wealth), a sense of ownership and self-worth, control over Aboriginal land, and the preservation of cultural sites and artifacts (Interfor 1995c). This approach has not always succeeded at Interfor. In his questionnaire response, Fred Lowenbergen, Senior Vice President of Forestry and Land-Use, said that it began to emerge only between five and ten years ago in response to increasing Aboriginal control over forest resources, which is crucial to Interfor's long-term survival.

Interfor's logging and forestry operations have the company interacting with 30 First Nations, creating opportunities for co-operative arrangements ranging from simple logging contracts to complex business partnerships involving large capital investments and long-time horizons. According to Sloan and Hill and the company's own documents, its arrangements with First Nations already in place or under consideration include:

- At least nine brushing, planting and environmental contracts with Aboriginal companies.
- A co-operative venture with the Toqualt Band in the construction and operation of their sawmill and the marketing of their lumber.
- On occasion, supplying facilities and equipment to Aboriginal entrepreneurs.
- A joint working group with the Tla-o-qui-aht Band to review and pursue development proposals.

---

12 MacMillan Bloedel is a case in point. According to comments returned with its questionnaire response, MacMillan Bloedel and its partner Saskatchewan Forest Products are actively seeking Aboriginal partners to participate in a proposed oriented strandboard project in northeastern Saskatchewan.

- Preliminary discussions about a joint venture sawmill operation with the Anderson Lake Band.
- A contract with the Nisga'a Nation to do helilogging on their land secured by an agreement to contract part of the work to a 10–12 person Nisga'a crew.
- With the Sechelt Band:
  - a joint stewardship and economic alliance signed in 1994 involving logging roads, a lodge and other tourism facilities and the establishment of a joint planning process that reviews the company's 5-year plans,
  - technical advice to the band on the development of a value-added mill, and
  - assistance in training fisheries and forestry crews and then awarding them contracts.

The company's experience has convinced it that three factors are key to a successful partnership with Aboriginal people:

> - *There must be clear potential for mutual benefit.*
> - *The two parties must bring together a mix of capital, human resources, business skills and technology to ensure that the arrangement is profitable.*
> - *The relationship must be characterized by mutual respect and trust.* (Sloan and Hill 1995, 200)

With these factors present, the company expects to benefit from its co-operative ventures with Aboriginal people through improved access to timber, local workers and contractors. In turn, Interfor expects the benefits to Aboriginal people to include employment opportunities, skill development, the opportunity to develop businesses, and the development of management and business skills. The company's motive is clearly and unequivocally long-term corporate profitability secured through mutually beneficial partnerships with First Nations who control key forest resources.

5.3.4. Balanced Programs

5.3.4.1. B.C. Hydro

The fourth and final category of programs are those that emerge when Aboriginal people represent both a significant market and a source of critical resources. B.C. Hydro is a case in point. The company is a Crown corporation of the Province of British Columbia. It generates, transmits and distributes electricity. With revenues of $2.1-billion and a customer base of 1.3-million, it is the third largest utility company in Canada. The company has over 6,000 employees of whom fewer than 1% were Aboriginal in 1992.

In August 1992, the corporation launched its Aboriginal Relations Department with a mandate to "establish mutually beneficial business relationships with Aboriginal people that will be recognized as a model for others to follow" (Brooks 1994, 18). In June 1993, reflecting the importance of Aboriginal relations to the corporation, the position of Vice-President of Corporate and Aboriginal Affairs was created. According to Cheryl Brooks, the manager of the Aboriginal Relations Department, B. C. Hydro's strategy for forming mutually beneficial business arrangements with Aboriginal people was a pragmatic response to the fact that

> *First Nations people are gaining greater control and jurisdiction over land and resources, reestablishing their own governments, and acquiring the skills and education to become a part of B.C. Hydro's future workforce. They also make up an increasingly significant portion of B.C. Hydro's customer base.*
>
> (Brooks 1994, 18)

The company's program has the familiar elements of employment, training and education, business development and communication. In addition, B.C. Hydro's program has a grievance resolution component. This aspect flows from the fact that, in the past, First Nations received inadequate or no compensation for power line rights of way crossing their land and for the flooding of their traditional land by hydroelectric projects.

During the first one and a half year of its existence, the Aboriginal Relations Department concentrated its efforts on grievance resolution and communication. It was felt that these efforts were essential to the creation of a foundation on which future business partnerships could be built. The department also developed and delivered negotiations and cross-cultural training programs during this period and began to implement its strategy for generating an increasing number of business opportunities for Aboriginal suppliers. This latter strategy has three elements: (i) expand the opportunities for Aboriginal suppliers in capital projects, operating purchases and contract services; (ii) enhance the capability of Aboriginal businesses to meet B.C. Hydro's needs; and (iii) encourage "other Crown agencies and businesses in British Columbia to develop policies and actions that drive Aboriginal business development" (Brooks 1994, 20). In 1995, speaking business development, Brooks reported that "modest results have been achieved to date, and tangible goals have been set with the objective of achieving rapid progress in the next two years" (Brooks 1994, 20).

B.C. Hydro is also developing an Aboriginal employment strategy. Employment equity is one element, but the company is looking beyond equity issues to its future labour needs. It sees the Aboriginal population as an important source of employees, particularly in remote areas. To tap this resource, the company has recently introduced "an integrated recruitment, training, mentorship and placement program" (Brooks 1994, 21) for Aboriginal people.

5.3.5. Summary: "Best Case Programs"

The preceding are examples of good Aboriginal relations programs in each category. They are by no means unique. Cogema's program, although smaller than Cameco's, is equally impressive. Placer Dome is adopting similar strategies at its proposed new mine in Labrador. Syncrude's Aboriginal relations program and partnerships have long been touted as among the best in the country. Imperial Oil and other petroleum exploration and extraction companies are beginning to develop programs similar to those of Syncrude. MacMillan Bloedel and TimberWest, two other B.C. forest companies, have programs similar to Interfor's. In fact, the entire B.C. forest industry has come together to develop and publish *A Proposed Aboriginal Forestry Strategy for the BC Forest Industry* (B.C. Council of Forest Industries 1994) recommending similar practices. The other major banks as well as the accounting and business consulting firms all have or are developing programs similar to those of the Bank of Montreal's. The provincial utilities across the country have programs similar to those of SaskEnergy and B.C. Hydro.

5.4. Summary and Conclusions

It is clear from my research results that at least some corporations behave in a manner consistent with the contingency perspective and the expectations of Aboriginal people. Given the unfolding treaty negotiations and land claims and the resulting First Nations' control over key resources, it is safe to say that the number of corporations doing so will increase over time. It follows that First Nations taking an "assertively pragmatic approach" (Shatz 1987b) should be able to find corporate partners willing to enter into mutually beneficial alliances for sound business reasons. This augurs well for the success of the First Nations approach to economic development as described in chapter 2.

The contingency perspective suggests that in response to a broadening and deepening of what the public and governments believe to be socially responsible corporate behaviour, companies are more likely to enter into alliances and other participative processes with Aboriginal people than they were in the past. My research certainly confirms this fact. The corporations studied have clearly developed their corporate Aboriginal programs (which involve a strong component of partnership) in response to changing public expectations. In some cases, this has occurred as a direct response to Factors 2 and 3. In other cases, it has come about because companies believe that such behaviour will improve their access to key resources held by Aboriginal people (Factors 4 and 5). Over time and in the manner described by Brummer (1991) Belkaoui (1987) Goldman (1995) and others, companies by their words and deeds are indicating that they view the satisfaction of social responsibilities (by partnering with Aboriginal people) as essential to earning the returns necessary for long-term survival and not simply an obligation imposing current costs to be minimized in the interest of short-term profits.[13]

Two other aspects of the contingency perspective are worthy of consideration. The first relates to the notion that companies are adopting the strategies of flexible competition in response to changes in the global economy. Specifically, it is expected that companies will narrow their focus to concentrate on key competencies and core activities and, as a result, increasingly rely on "external" arrangements such as joint ventures and other partnerships, subcontracting, negotiated supplier contracts to meet needs once met "in-house." The results of my business survey indicate this to be the case. Ninety-four percent

13 See Figure 3-2, chapter 3.

of the respondents indicated that they are more likely to behave in this fashion now and in the future than they were 10 years ago.

The second aspect is the suggestion that this general tendency on the part of companies will result in the formation of alliances between particular companies and those who possess or control skills, resources, markets, public goodwill and/or the support of particular interest groups necessary for the long-term survival of these companies. My research results clearly bear this out. All the companies who have gone beyond simple employment equity programs to establish partnerships of one type or another with Aboriginal people say that they have done so for one or more of the following reasons: (i) increasing Aboriginal control of land and resources, (ii) increasing financial capacity through treaties and land claim settlements and (iii) a population growing in numbers and affluence.

It is also apparent from their responses that many of the corporations believe that leadership (Aboriginal and corporate) is a critical aspect of the process leading to the formation of successful partnerships. All the companies with well-developed programs stress the importance of senior management support and involvement and managerial accountability for results. They also stress the importance of communication, consultation and negotiation with Aboriginal leaders and have established mechanisms to assure that these happen. Most of the companies also acknowledge the need to consult directly with Aboriginal community members and groups (the civil sector) and not just leaders, to build support for their activities. This confirms the aspects of the contingency perspective relating to the importance of leadership and the civil sector.

5.5. Mutually Beneficial Alliances: Cases

The following cases provide examples of mutually beneficial corporate/Aboriginal alliances of various types from across the country.

Case 5–1: White Bear Oil and Gas (1997)[14]

Oil production has turned into a big business for the White Bear First Nation. Indeed, 1,700 barrels of oil per day are produced on the approximately 12,000-hectare (30,000 acre) reserve located 13 km north of Carlyle, Saskatchewan and they plan to drill 40 new wells within the next year. But the priorities of White Bear Oil and Gas (WBOG), the First Nation's oil company, are helping their community, protecting the environment and respecting Aboriginal traditions.

WBOG's success in the oil industry is largely due to a unique agreement they signed in December 1993 with Tri Link Resources Ltd., a Calgary-based oil company. The agreement allows Tri Link to drill for oil on the reserve and enables WBOG to take part in the oil production by sharing in the costs and profits and benefiting from the employment opportunities and economic spin-offs.

The agreement provides WBOG with a base royalty as well as options to participate in the oil production. By taking advantage of these options to participate WBOG has more than tripled their revenue. This revenue is either put

---

14 Source: DIAND Website, *http://www.inac.gc.ca/ecdev/entre/sk/wboilg.html* [edited].

back into oil production or used to help the community by, for example, assisting youth groups and Elders. WBOG also wanted to give something back to past generations that will never benefit from the oil that was a part of their land, so the company decided to put up headstone markers for those who have passed away.

"We want to put markers on these graves so that the people who are gone will never be forgotten, so that our history will never be lost," says Terry Littlechief, President of WBOG.

Chief Brian Standingready believes it is important that the First Nation focuses on helping their people, rather than making profits. "The oil won't be here forever, our people are our priority," says Chief Standingready. "We have to respect the land, our heritage sites, the environment. We always consider the future generations and ask what this is doing for them."

Mr. Littlechief agrees: "We believe that each action taken has many effects. What we do today will effect future generations. Following strict environmental guidelines and spending the revenue properly is very important to us, so that 20 years, 50 years, 100 years down the road our grandchildren won't question the decisions we made."

WBOG has managed to merge the oil business with their cultural beliefs. For many members of the First Nation, their land, and nature in general, is something sacred. For this reason, before any activity takes place on a future well site, an Elder goes to the area and prays to ask the land for forgiveness and to thank the land for its bounty. As well, sacred heritage sites are declared no-drill zones. Because preserving the natural beauty of White Bear Lake and the surrounding country is important to the First Nation on spiritual, environmental and economic levels, WBOG asks that abandoned well sites be restored to an environmental standard higher than oil industry standards.

Tri Link is sensitive toward White Bear's environmental and cultural concerns. Mr. Littlechief says that Tri Link has worked in partnership with White Bear to address these concerns and form a relationship built on trust.

In a letter to the White Bear First Nation Gary Burns, President and CEO of Tri Link, describes their relationship: "There are many aspects to the agreement; however, the foundation was one of trust — trust between an oil company and a First Nations people ... the White Bear Project is similar to a foreign operation ... we try to honour the traditional laws and cultural heritage as guests in another land."

Through continual communication and respect, Tri Link and White Bear have come to understand each other's aims. One of White Bear's goals in allowing the development of its oil and gas reserves is to create employment and training opportunities for First Nation members.

In his letter, Mr. Burns points to this goal: "Part of this agreement between Tri Link and the White Bear people outlines a moral commitment by Tri Link to help create longer-term employment, to encourage education and to be proactive on certain social issues."

Since White Bear began working with Tri Link, a number of First Nation members have been trained and employed in the oil industry. Tri Link hired two university graduates from White Bear to work in their Calgary office as a petroleum land administration assistant and as a geological technical assistant respectively. A summer student was hired to work out of their Kipling office to gain environmental and production experience.

Two White Bear members work out of WBOG's office and two members work as petroleum land administrators with the White Bear Pilot Project. These individuals all attended the Southern Alberta Institute of Technology for training sponsored by the White Bear First Nation and received certificates as petroleum land administrators.

Many White Bear First Nation members have gained training and work experience in the oil industry, thanks to WBOG. So far approximately 38 members have been trained and are employed to drill rigs for Tri Link. Another four have been trained and are working as contract battery operators. Recently four White Bear members were trained and certified as heavy equipment operators in a program jointly sponsored between Tri Link and the First Nation-run Kakakaway Learning Centre. In the past, the Kakakaway Learning Centre and Tri Link have teamed up to offer training to 30 individuals in the areas of chainsaw certification, chainsaw instructors certification and entry level training such as first aid, CPR and H2S Alive.

As well, the agreement provides White Bear companies and private contractors with the opportunity to bid for services required by Tri Link such as surface lease construction, pipeline construction, seismic line clearing, well site reclamation, trucking, well site maintenance and drilling and service contracting. As a result, seven new businesses have developed on the White Bear First Nation creating new employment opportunities and on-the-job work experience for many First Nation members. These activities have provided over 90 First Nation people with short- or long-term employment.

White Bear Oil and Gas is very pleased with the economic development that has resulted and hopes that this is only the beginning. Mr. Littlechief envisions a bright future for WBOG, a future that includes investing in the oil industry off reserve. But, he says that as WBOG grows, it will continue to base its business on the First Nation's values.

Indeed, WBOG's mission statement states that the company's goal is "to contribute to the present and future prosperity of White Bear First Nation by ensuring the quality of life for the people, environment and future generations through the guardianship and administration of our oil and gas resources, revenues and future developments."

"There are benefits to having oil revenue, but there is also a down side," says Mr. Littlechief. "We deal with weighing this balance everyday; whether the damage done to our land will be worth it in the end. For this reason we feel very strongly that the revenue has to be spent properly so that it can benefit us and our grandchildren down the road."

Case 5–2: Torngait Ujaganniavingit Corporation (TUC) (1997)[15]

In the Ten Mile Bay, a 15-minute boat ride from the small community of Nain, Newfoundland, lies a granite dimension stone quarry that has turned out to be

15 Source: DIAND Website, *http://www.inac.gc.ca/ecdev/entre/at/Tucqua.html* [edited].

very profitable and beneficial for both the owners and the employees of the quarry. That makes sense as, after all, they are the same people.

The initiative started back in November 1990, when the Labrador Inuit Development Corporation (LIDC) and the Department of Mines and Energy quarried a 10-tonne test block of Labradorite crystal anorthosite rock from Ten Mile Bay. Without the proper equipment available, this huge block had to be transported to Nain, Labrador, by using 45-gallon drums for floatation and making use of the tides. From Nain, the block made its way via various vessels to Italy, where it was processed and sold. All the effort to move the stone was worthwhile though, as the processed stone met with a market response even more positive than first anticipated.

When it was shown that the quarry would be a profitable investment, the LIDC, which is the corporate arm of the Labrador Inuit Association (LIA), formed a quarry company: TUC (Torngait Ujaganniavingit Corporation). The LIDC has more in mind than simply creating profit however. It has a mandate to improve the living conditions of the Inuit of Labrador by providing employment opportunities. The organization also promotes education and training of Inuit to meet the requirements of today's labour market.

With these goals in mind, TUC's Ten Mile Bay quarry employs 20 members of the LIA from the nearby community of Nain. "The employees who work at the quarry are working for themselves because they are LIA members," says Henry Lyall, Office Manager for TUC. "Right now, all the profits are being reinvested into the quarry, but eventually, the profits will go toward benefiting the community."

The employment provided at the quarry is quality employment as well. "This is good work because you can work during the day, and then go home at night instead of living in a camp," explains Pete Lyall, Quarry Master. This is a very important aspect of the job for the Inuit, as they are more than happy to put in hard 12-hour days of work if they can still maintain the close family contact that is essential to their culture.

The opening of the quarry was carried out under the supervision of two experienced quarrymen from a Quebec company. They stayed to oversee operations for a month and a half. During the winter of 1993, the 20 members of the quarry crew from Nain undertook further training to develop their skills. Two people went to Italy to work in granite quarries, and four people completed a surface drilling and blasting course in Springdale, Newfoundland.

The original financing of the equipment for the quarry came from the Atlantic Canada Opportunities Agency (ACOA), which contributed approximately 50% of the cost, and from Enterprise Newfoundland and Labrador, the Canadian Aboriginal Business Development Program, and the Department of Mines and Energy.

A marketing agreement for the processing and sale of the stone was signed with an Italian/German company, and soon half of this company will be transferred to TUC, so that it can take a more prominent role in the marketing aspect of the stone business. Now the quarry is in full production, and in 1996, estimated production was 830 cubic metres of stone with a value estimated at $1,270,000 Canadian.

TUC plans to expand to a new quarry sight in John Hay's Harbour, Labrador. So far, a $500,000 loan approved by ACOA to purchase equipment and a 20-year lease on the land has been approved by the Newfoundland government. The stone in John Hay's Harbour is similar to the Ten Mile Bay stone, but has a different colour and texture. This new material should therefore open up a new market which will not compete with the Ten Mile Bay stone. This new quarry site will create another 20 jobs.

Currently, the stone being shipped to Italy is processed and used for flooring, tables, fixtures, walls and other such applications. Before the stone is shipped, each block must be cut square. This creates some wasted stone. TUC is planning to build a processing plant in Hopedale, Labrador. This plant will take the smaller pieces of stone that would normally be considered waste and process them into smaller products such as headstones, tables and fixtures. This plant will create between 10 to 12 jobs.

Fred Hall, Director of the LIDC, hopes to see even more expansion into the stone industry over the next five years. This will lead to many more sustainable, quality, full-time jobs for the LIA members throughout Labrador.

Case 5–3: Xexe7ellp Ginseng: A Potent Recipe for Success (1996)[16]

Canada's First Nations have used ginseng in much the same way it has been used by the Chinese, as an herbal medicine, for thousands of years. Ginseng grows wild in eastern Canada and its close relative, the sarsa-parilla root, grows wild in western Canada. The use of the root can be traced back 3,000 years in Asian Pacific Rim countries, where it is the most widely used medicinal herb.

American ginseng, Panax quinquefolium L., has now taken root in the Skeetchestn First Nation's Reserve, about 400 km east of Vancouver. The world's largest ginseng growing company, Chai-Na-Ta Farms, Ltd., has joined with the Skeetchestn to form Xexe7ellp (potent) Ginseng. The First Nation provides 220 hectares of land, labour, and part of the financing. In turn, Chai-Na-Ta provides the balance of the financing, experience, and management for the venture and will buy all of the ginseng produced at a guaranteed rate to sell to markets in Asia and the United States.

Gerry Gill, president and CEO of Chai-Na-Ta, is enthusiastic about this venture with the Skeetchestn First Nation: "Ron (Chief Ron Ignace) and his council are looking for long-term potential for capital growth. I was really impressed. I saw a lot of creativity and ingenuity in how they were trying to reach self-sufficiency."

The gross revenue of ginseng is up to $66,000 per hectare, making ginseng a very profitable crop. But startup costs are high — it cost $30,000 to seed 20 hectares, planted last fall and ready for harvest in spring 1999. Profits will be split evenly between the two parties. The project is expected to take at least 10 years to complete and could generate as much as $50-million in revenue. Potentially, $5-million will be paid in salaries for at least 170 jobs. Much of that will end up in Skeetchestn members' pockets, as they have first right-of-refusal on jobs.

---

16 Source: DIAND Website, *http://www.inac.gc.ca/ecdev/entre/bc/Ginsen.html* [edited].

Ginseng is a tricky plant to farm. "It requires an arid growing climate, so the Skeetchestn land is ideal. It's hot and dry in the summer, and cold enough in the winter to put the plants into dormancy," explains Gill. Ginseng naturally grows under the canopy of hardwood forests, so 70% shade was reproduced by covering all of the plants with thick tarps dotted with holes. Seedlings were protected from the winter cold by a blanket of hay, a project which employed seven Skeetchestn people this fall. Soil preparation is also essential: 45 centimetres of nutrient rich soil was needed to plant in, so barley was cultivated and then mulched into the soil before the ginseng was planted. The Department of Indian Affairs and Northern Development (DIAND) provided $80,000 to clear stones from the soil at the site.

"We like to control the water on our farms," explains Gill so the First Nation built a 2.3-million-litre reservoir which is hooked up to nearly four kilometres of underground irrigation pipe. An existing 500-horsepower pump was reconditioned to bring the water from the Thompson River at Deadman's Creek inlet to the reservoir. The irrigation system saves money by using the power of gravity instead of costly electricity to hydrate the fields. "The water system is the key to unlock the potential of this area," says Chief Ignace. The reservoir will also provide water for a newly completed subdivision on reserve, and will service a proposed development to include a gas bar, store and restaurant. Construction on this commercial development should begin in 1997. The federal First Nations Infrastructure Initiative provided $250,000 for the reservoir.

The elixir of life, as ginseng is often called, is said to reduce stress, increase physical stamina and quiet the nerves. It is said to enhance blood flow, help control blood sugar and cholesterol levels, assist in regulating blood pressure, slow the degeneration of cells and increase longevity. For the Skeetchestn people, ginseng may also be the elixir of economic opportunity, strengthening the ties between the First Nation and the corporate world, and providing the financial base to ensure success in future endeavours.

Case 5–4: The Red Dog Inn: A Partnership Grows (1997)[17]

When John Chan befriended some Aboriginal customers at his restaurant in Thunder Bay in the 1970s, he had no idea that fate was smiling on him.

He just thought they were nice guys with a good sense of humour, and he enjoyed their company whenever they stopped in for a bite to eat. It never occurred to him to ask what they did for a living.

Then, a few years later, he took on a position as manager of the Red Dog Inn, a 67-room hotel in nearby Fort Frances. The hotel was having financial difficulties, and had changed hands several times.

That was when Chan found out that his friends, who had started eating at the hotel's two restaurants as soon as they heard that Chan was the manager, were leaders of several First Nations in the Fort Frances area.

Willie Wilson, Tribal Area Chief of the Grand Council Treaty 3 First Nations, and Tom Bruyere, Executive Director of the Chiefs Advisory Services,

---

17 Source: DIAND Website, *http://www.inac.gc.ca/ecdev/entre/on/reddog.html* [edited].

were two of them. They knew about the hotel's situation and approached Chan about joining the First Nations in making a bid for ownership of the hotel. Chan accepted. His new business partners were the First Nations of Rainy River, Nicickousemenecaning, Couchiching, Naicatchewenin and Seine River.

There were several advantages to the partnership. Chan's expertise in hotel and restaurant management were definite assets, helping smooth the way to a grant from Industry Canada's Aboriginal Business Canada program for the purchase of the hotel.

The First Nations had already learned a great deal by working together on other business ventures, and joining forces reduced the financial risks for everyone involved.

Since taking over the Red Dog, the new owners have put a fresh face on the hotel. The dining room, ballroom, conference rooms, nightclub, and all guest rooms have all been redecorated. Four chefs run the restaurants and catering service, and one of them, who happens to be Chan's wife, is a specialist in Chinese cuisine.

The hotel night club, dubbed "The Dawg," is a local hot spot, with large screen TVS, pool tables and a DJ three nights each week. Young people from across the U.S. border in International Falls, Minnesota flock there every weekend for a good time.

The hotel employs 12 to 15 First Nations people, depending on the season. Many of them are young people who work at the hotel while going to school and take away some business training and valuable work experience when they go.

Business is good, and Chan couldn't be happier about the way fate has smiled on himself and his old friends. "I'm very proud to say that the relationship is great ... they're nice people to be in business with," he said.

5

6

Entrepreneurship: New Venture Creation in an Aboriginal Context

Aboriginal people in Canada want to develop an economic system that will improve their peoples' socioeconomic circumstances, build economic self-reliance, support self-government, and preserve and strengthen traditional aspects of their society. Aboriginal control over their own development is an essential characteristic of this system. At the same time, Aboriginal people acknowledged that their economy must be integrated with the global economic system. The challenge facing Aboriginal people is to create viable businesses that will allow them to successfully integrate their economic activities into the global economy while retaining adequate control over development on their lands and attaining their development objectives.

The economic development experience of the Japanese following the Second World War offers some insight into the challenge facing Aboriginal people. In the chapter entitled "Identifying Opportunities: Knowing Where to Strike" from *The New Competition* (Kotler et al. 1985, 61–85), the authors describe Japan's situation following the Second World War as follows:

> *It's politics and economics were ruled by a foreign power. Its constitution, educational system, and other administrative structures and processes were fostered — some might say imposed — by the Occupation forces.*
>
> *Continuing well into the 1950's, the Japanese economy faced many constraints: Capital was in short supply, the technologies required to revitalize many industry segments were to be found only overseas, costs were too high in many industry segments, and balance of payments problems abound because the country imports more than it sells abroad.*
>
> *How was it to pull itself out of its economic doldrums? What industries might or should lead the way? What respective role should government agencies and the private sector play in making these choices? In search of these answers,* OPPORTU-

> NITY IDENTIFICATION AND MANAGEMENT *emerged as one of the most important factors.* (Kotler et al. 1985, 61)

There are remarkable similarities between the circumstances the Japanese faced then and those that Aboriginal people face now. It follows that opportunity identification and management (essential components of entrepreneurship as we will see later in this chapter) will be as critical to the Aboriginal economic development as they were to Japanese development.

Granting that Aboriginal people have undertaken effective capacity-building activities and acknowledging the willingness of non-Aboriginal companies to form mutually beneficial commercial alliances with Aboriginal companies, the ultimate success of the Aboriginal approach to economic development depends on opportunity identification and management, that is, entrepreneurship. For each business, opportunities will have to be identified and new ventures created, customers' needs assessed, products developed and marketed, employees hired, trained and directed, potential partners found, financing secured, and the like. These business management activities must be done properly over and over again to create and sustain the profitable businesses that are the key to the successful implementation of the First Nations' economic development strategy. Further, doing these activities successfully from a business perspective is not sufficient. They must be done in a way that is consistent with the traditional values and practices that the First Nations people deem important.

6.1. Entrepreneurship, Innovation, New Venture Creation and the Economy

According to Ken Blawatt (1998, xii):

> *Entrepreneurship is a series of skills, but more so an anthology of developed principles that have their origins in humankind's earliest evolution. Entrepreneurship itself is the genesis of business activity. More importantly it forms the basis of an economy and by some standards, is the economy of a nation.*
>
> (Blawatt 1998, xii)

He goes on to say that

- *Entrepreneurs drive the economy, creating new concepts, innovations, new ventures, employment and national wealth.*
- *Entrepreneurs bring a balance to a nation's economic system, offsetting concentrations of power, increasing competitiveness.*
- *Entrepreneurship serves the community first and society by providing an improved standard of living, social responsiveness, sustainable industry. It adds to the social and psychological well being of the community by providing an outlet for creative action.*
- *Entrepreneurship … offers third world countries the opportunity to become first world countries* (Blawatt 1998, 21)

6.2. Entrepreneurship

The single most important activity in the development of successful new ventures and the ongoing success of existing ones is the identification of viable opportunities. The discovery of such opportunities is the result of an outwardly focused search seeking to identify and meet the needs of a particular market.

This search process must be continuous. Yesterday's opportunities and the businesses developed to meet them are constantly supplanted because market needs change, competitors develop new products and/or better define market segments and their particular needs, and/or technology offers new products, methods and tools that better satisfy market needs. This change is relentless. It poses a continuous threat to existing businesses. Failure to take a proactive approach, that is, to continuously strive to better meet current and emerging needs, will inevitably result in the failure of what may once have been a successful business. At the same time, this ceaseless change is the source of tremendous opportunities for the creation of new, successful ventures and for the growth and continuing profitability of existing businesses. New, innovative and exciting business opportunities are always "out there"; the trick is to find them.

An outward looking, market-oriented search for opportunity is part of the process called *entrepreneurship*. This process involves the recognition of opportunity, the assembling of resources, and the assumption of risk in the pursuit of profit. It is characterized by:

1. The perception of opportunity where others see threats.
2. The recognition of change where others see a continuation of the same.
3. The identification of a dissatisfied or under-served market segment where others see satisfied customers.

6.3. Definitions of Entrepreneurship; Characteristics of an Entrepreneur

In recent years much has been written about entrepreneurship and entrepreneurs. Attempts to describe entrepreneurship and entrepreneurs generally fall into one of two categories: (i) traits-based — What are the characteristics of a person that makes him or her a successful entrepreneur? and (ii) process-based — How is entrepreneurship done successfully?

Raymond Kao (1989) in his book *Entrepreneurship and Enterprise Development* adopts a traits-based approach. Based on Secretan (1986), Kao says that an entrepreneur is

> *a person who combines risk, innovation, leadership artistry, skill and craftsmanship into a foundation upon which to build and motivate a team* (Kao 1989, 8)

Kao goes on to use the work of Hornday and Gibb (see Figure 6–1) to describe the attributes of an entrepreneur (Kao 1989, 9). Based on this list, Kao concludes that

FIGURE 6–1: The Attributes of an Entrepreneur

Hornday	**Gibb**
Self-confidence	Creativity
Perseverance, determination	Initiative
Energy, diligence	High achievement
Resourcefulness	Risk-taking (moderate)
Ability to take calculated risks	Leadership
Need to achieve	Autonomy and independence
Creativity	Analytical ability
Initiative	Hard work
Flexibility	Good communication skills
Positive responses to change	
Independence	
Foresight	
Dynamism, leadership	
Ability to get along with people	
Responsiveness to suggestions and criticism	
Profit orientation	
Perceptiveness	
Optimism	

> *entrepreneurs are people who act, people who get things done, often without paying much attention to "the rules." In the economic realm, they can spot a business opportunity — an unmet need — and act on it, putting together the resources required and building an organization.* (Kao 1989, 9)

While traits-based approaches are interesting and offer valuable insight, they offer little guidance to an individual, group or organization seeking to create viable new ventures. On the other hand, process-based approaches do.

Shifting to these process-based approaches, Peter Drucker (1993), in his classic work *Innovation and Entrepreneurship*, says that

> *Entrepreneurship rests on a theory of economy and society. That theory sees change as normal and indeed as healthy. And it sees the major task in society — and especially the economy — as doing something different rather than doing better what is already being done.* (Drucker 1986, 26)

Significantly, Drucker also says:

> *Entrepreneurship in society — and its is badly needed — requires above all the application of the basic concepts, the basic techné, of management to new problems and new opportunities.* (Drucker 1986, 17)

Timmons (1994) concurs, saying that

> *Entrepreneurship is creating and building something of value ... the process of creating and seizing an opportunity ... involves definition, creation and distribution of value and benefits to individuals, groups, organizations and society.*
>
> *Involves building a team of people with complementary skills and talents; of sensing an opportunity when others see chaos, contradiction and confusion; and finding, marshaling and controlling resources.* (Timmons 1994, 7)

It is clear from these two authors and others who discuss entrepreneurship as a process that it has two key aspects: (i) a search for innovative opportunities, and (ii) the application of the principles of management to convert such opportunities into a viable new ventures — the very activities that Kotler and his co-authors identified as key to the Japan's economic resurgence following the Second World War.

More importantly, the skills and techniques relating to the two aspects can be learned. For example, Drucker says the following about innovation and opportunity identification:

> *Innovation is a specific tool of entrepreneurs, the means by which they exploit change as an opportunity for a different business or a different service. It is capable of being presented as a discipline, capable of being learned, capable of being practiced.*
> (Drucker 1986, 19)

Further, Drucker, Timmons, Kao and others adopting the process-based approach to entrepreneurship, all emphasize the critical importance of the various management functions — organizational development, marketing in all its aspects, financing and financial management, operations management and human resources management — to the creation of a successful venture based on an innovative opportunity. These too, can be learned.

The notion that entrepreneurship is a process drawing on a defined and learnable set of skills and techniques as opposed to an outcome achieved by individuals with a specific set of traits, is important and encouraging to Aboriginal people as they seek to improve their socioeconomic circumstance. Entrepreneurship does not require that Aboriginal people develop an individualistic approach to business based on personality traits and attitudes that may conflict with their culture and values. Instead, the techniques and tools of entrepreneurship can be used just as effectively in a communal society — one that emphasizes group rather than individual ownership and sharing rather than individual rewards — as they can in an individualistic society.

The identification of opportunities and the structuring of business ventures to pursue these opportunities are the subjects of the remainder of this chapter. Details about the tools and techniques of management used to bring new ventures to life are beyond the scope of this book. Such information can be found in works on new venture creation.

6

6.4. Identifying Innovative Opportunities

Kotler (1985) describes five strategies for the identification and management of opportunities in the pursuit of economic growth. They are:

1. Provided Opportunities: Identify sub-markets that have been ignored or poorly served by existing firms and seek to establish a strong presence in that segment. Move to the larger markets from this established base.
2. Creating Opportunities — Product Development: Through research and technological development, create a new product that meets existing market needs in a new and superior manner. An example would be the compact disc as a substitute for the vinyl record.
3. Creating Opportunities — Market Development: Develop a creative version of an existing product satisfying a new market segment's needs. Johnson and Johnson's successful campaign to encourage adults' use of "Johnson's Baby Shampoo" fits this category.
4. Adapting to Changing Customers Preference: Understand what the customer wants and is willing to pay for. Constantly monitor to identify changes in society and the implication of these changes to needs. Look beyond current preferences for unserved or emerging preferences.
5. Learning from Competitors: Focus on a better understanding of the competition; how they conduct their business, what products they sell, what strategies they pursue, how they manufacture their product, and so on. What are their weaknesses and what opportunities do those weakness offer?

"Purposeful Innovation and the Seven Sources for Innovative Opportunity," and "Principles of Innovation" are two chapters from *Innovation and Entrepreneurship* (Drucker, 1985) that offer additional insight into the identification of opportunity. In the first chapter, Drucker discusses innovation. Several definitions for innovation are put forward. Two of them are as follows:

1. Innovation endows resources with a new capacity to create wealth — a supply-based definition.
2. Innovation changes (increases) the value and satisfaction obtained from resources by the consumer — a demand-based definition.

The second definition more completely captures the essence of innovation from the perspective of the creators of a business. A new venture and its products must, in the view of the market, deliver greater value or want satisfaction to the consumer than is delivered by existing offerings.

Drucker (1985) goes on to state that the search for innovative opportunity need not be intuitive. The process of innovation can be learned and pursued systematically. It must be viewed as a continuous activity involving the methodical evaluation of the environment, identifying and analysing changes and trends. Drucker suggests that the sources of innovative opportunity can be systematically categorized. He proposes seven categories, the first four focusing on sources inside the industry and the last three, outside. These seven sources are:

1. **An unexpected success, failure or other event** which indicates the occurrence of change; things are no longer as current wisdom would have them understood. An example can be found in the spectacular failure of the Edsel. This car was extensively researched and designed to meet the market needs as they were understood at the time. It was, however, a dismal flop. Ford viewed this unexpected failure as an indication of a significant shift in the nature of the automobile market. The company investigated and concluded that the old segmentation into economy, standard and luxury cars no longer adequately reflected the car market of the day. Instead, a lifestyle-based segmentation was more useful. They applied this new view of the market to the development of the Thunderbird, which became the most successful innovation in the automotive industry since Henry Ford's Model T.
2. **An incongruity**, a difference between what is and what "ought to be" reflecting a lack of understanding of the environment and/or the presence of change. The automobile industry can again provide an example of the exploitation of an incongruity between what is and what is expected. Prior to the energy crisis "everyone knew" that the North American consumer would not buy a small, low-powered car. The American manufacturers continued to believe this while concerns about pollution, energy conservation, and economy led to a new reality, one in which the American buyer was prepared to purchase a small car. The Japanese manufacturers saw this new reality and acted. The North American companies are still struggling to recover.
3. **An innovation based on a process need** which is known but to date unmet. The Glung-Us fish trap described in Case 2–5 is an example. With the decline in fish stocks, there is a need to fish selectively taking fish species from only those stock strong enough to support a harvest. Current commercial technology, particularly the seine net, does not permit such selective harvesting; the Glung-Us does.
4. **Changes in the industry or market structure** which catch established organizations unprepared and still concentrating on the "old." Westcoast Energy in its reaction to the Berger Inquiry is an example of this source. Westcoast realized that the forces that gave rise to the inquiry indicated a real change to the conditions under which their industry would operate in the future. The company saw these changes as an opportunity and became an early adopter of a strategy of alliance with Aboriginal people in the pursuit of oil and natural gas related opportunities.
5. **Demographic changes** are changes in population characteristics such as birth rate, family structure, work force structure, education levels, ethnic/cultural mix, etc. This source is particularly significant in the Aboriginal context. Take for example the case of B.C Hydro. The company realizes that the real employment issue for them in the future will not be equity, that is, to share fair proportion of their workforce with Aboriginal people. B.C. Hydro must figure out how to make employment in the company attractive to Aboriginal people. This is so because in the near future, in many of the areas where B.C. Hydro operates, Aboriginal people will makeup either the majority or a very large

minority of the potential workforce and competition for their services will be fierce.

6. **Changes in perception, values, needs.** An example close to the Indian community is the change in attitude, particularly in Europe, toward "animal rights" and the impact of this change on the trapping industry. European governments are passing laws restricting the fur industry in response to this change in the values of their citizens that are impacting detrimentally on this historically successful industry. Is there an opportunity hiding in this threat? Will Europeans be more receptive to other First Nation products because of the damage they have done to the fur industry? Does their increased sensitivity toward nature and the "wholeness of life" open possibilities for other Indian products, for example, in tourism?
7. **New scientific or nonscientific knowledge** creating the possibility of new products or services. Examples of technical innovations are numerous and include the computer chip, the microwave, the VCR, and so forth.

These seven sources are interrelated. In Drucker's view, they are best perceived as seven windows, each providing a slightly different outlook on the world and its changes.

In the chapter on "The Principles of Innovation," Drucker (1985) provides a lists of do's and don'ts necessary for the successful practice of purposeful innovation. The do's can be summarized as follows:

1. Purposeful, systematic innovation begins with the analysis of the opportunities. All the sources of innovative opportunity should be systematically analyzed and systematically studied.
2. Innovation is both conceptual and perceptual. The second imperative is therefore to go out to look, to ask, to listen. Go out and look at the customers, the users, to see what their expectations, their values, their needs are.
3. An innovation, to be effective, has to be simple and has to be focused. It should be focused on a specific need that it satisfies, on a specific end result that it produces.
4. Innovations had better be capable of being started small, requiring at first little money, few people, and only a small limited market. Otherwise, there will not be time to make the adjustments and changes that are almost always needed for an innovation to succeed.
5. All strategies aimed at exploiting an innovation, must achieve leadership within a given environment. Otherwise they will simply create an opportunity for the competition.

The cases presented in section 6.5 and throughout this book show by example that Aboriginal people can and have done these entrepreneurial "do's" very effectively.

In summary, the don'ts are:

1. Don't try to be too clever. Anything too clever, whether by design or execution, is almost bound to fail.

2. Don't diversify, don't splinter, don't try to do too many things at once. An innovation needs the concentrated energy of a unified effort behind it. It also requires that the people who put it into effect understand each other, and this, too, requires a unity, a common core.
3. Don't try to innovate for the future. Innovate for the present! Unless there is an immediate application in the present ... a brilliant idea but not an opportunity to operate a viable business.

Finally, Drucker ends by listing three necessary conditions. They are:

1. Innovation is work ... hard, focused, purposeful work making very great demands on diligence, on persistence, and on commitment. If these are lacking, no amount of talent, ingenuity, or knowledge will avail.
2. To succeed, innovators must build on their strengths. Which of these opportunities fit me, fit this company, puts to work what we (or I) are good at and have shown capacity for in performance?
3. Innovation has to be close to the market, focused on the market, indeed market driven.

The article "Tough-Minded Ways to Get Innovative" (Pearson 1988) from the *Harvard Business Review* offers a view of the innovative process within an existing organization. Its author, A.E. Pearson, was president of PepsiCo Ltd. He draws heavily on practical examples of innovation in that company's well-known subsidiaries that include Pizza Hut, Taco-Bell and Frito-Lay. Based on his experience, he concludes that there are five steps to making a company or organization more dynamic and innovative. They are:

1. Create a corporate environment that puts constant pressure on everyone to beat your specific competitors at innovation.
2. Structure your organization so that you can promote innovation instead of thwarting it.
3. Develop a realistic strategic focus to channel your innovative efforts.
4. Know where to look for good ideas and how to use your business system to leverage them once they are found.
5. Throw the book at good ideas once you've developed them.

Of particular interest is Pearson's answer to his rhetorical question — "How do you find good, concrete ideas?" He states that

> *the best backdrop for spurring innovation is knowledge — knowing your business cold. Good ideas most often flow from the process of taking a hard look at your customers, your competitors, and your business all at once.* (Pearson 1988, 103)

In doing this, he suggests concentrating on:

1. **What's already working in the market place that you can improve upon and expand?** PepsiCo regularly spotted promising new ideas in the market place, improved upon them, and then out-executed the competi-

tion. As an example, he refers to Frito-Lay's exploitation of Doritos, Tostitos and Sabitos. These products were originally introduced to a regional market by small producers. Frito-Lay recognized that products appealing to a local market might also appeal to a huge international mass market. They did, and now generate sales totalling approximately $1-billion.

2. **How you can segment your markets differently and gain a competitive advantage in the process?** Taco Bell examined the market and recognized the existence of a segment poorly served by their existing offerings. Working women felt the food was too heavy and spicy and did not patronize the outlets. Having identified this opportunity they created a "light" taco salad. This product met the segment need ideally and increased per-store sales by 20%, 70% to women. In its first year, this product added about $100-million to sales. More generally, Pearson concluded that successful segmentors offer their customers better value through lower prices, better performing products, and/or better features for certain uses (niches).
3. **How your business system compares with your competitors?** The business system includes all activities involved in getting the product to market. A distinctive system can provide advantage by allowing you to reach the market in ways difficult for your customers to duplicate. As an example, Pearson refers to Pizza Hut's development of a lunch pizza. Few customers purchased pizza for lunch. Investigation revealed that the reason was time-related. Traditional cooking techniques took 20 minutes. A segment existed that could be exploited if a product feature — quicker preparation — could be developed. A method used for cooking burgers was identified and adapted.

Pearson's (1988) three categories of innovative opportunity encompass the same basic elements as Drucker's seven sources and Kotler's five strategies for the identification and management of opportunity. Central to all is a fundamental concept — the search for opportunity must take place in the market. It is the needs and wants of current and potential consumers that create opportunities for the development of successful businesses.

The following five cases offer insight into Aboriginal entrepreneurship and new venture creation in all areas of the country.

6.5. Opportunity Identification in an Aboriginal Context: Sources and Examples

Case 6–1: Success Sweet For Saskatoon Berry Entrepreneurs (1996)[1]

Rodney and Colleen Parenteau have had a "taste of success" over the past few years.

---

1 Source: DIAND Website, *http://www.inac.gc.ca/ecdev/entre/sk/chocol.html* [edited].

In 1991, the Parenteaus started Saskatoon Berry Chocolates Inc. on their 64-hectare farm approximately 30 km northwest of Saskatoon. When Mr. and Mrs. Parenteau bought the farm in 1987, they weren't sure what to do with the 1.2-hectare Saskatoon berry orchard that was included with the farm.

"We thought we could make jams, but that requires a lot of berries, and there are already a lot of people who manufacture jams," says Mr. Parenteau, who is a Métis from the Duck Lake area. "With only three acres, we needed something innovative and unique that wouldn't require a lot of berries."

Inspiration struck while they were attending a cousin's wedding in Edmonton.

"They served gourmet chocolates at the reception and it was very classy," says Mr. Parenteau. "It was something very unique and we thought we could build a niche for ourselves."

In addition to personal equity, Mr. Parenteau received two grants from Aboriginal Business Canada (ABC) that totalled $50,000. The Parenteaus began by producing handmade Saskatoon berry-filled gourmet chocolates. The chocolates were a mouth-watering success.

Saskatoon Berry Chocolates Inc., which has been featured on a national public affairs program, has been expanding ever since. The Parenteaus make Saskatoon berry, blueberry, prairie berry (a blend of Saskatoon berry, blueberry, and chokecherry), strawberry and raspberry jams and syrups. The Parenteaus are also producing flavoured honeys which are used mainly for gourmet cooking. The flavours include Saskatoon berry, chokecherry, blueberry, raspberry, cinnamon and Belgian chocolate.

The company expanded in 1993 to include various types of caffeine-free herbal tea, including Saskatoon berry, prairie berry, blueberry and "merry berry," which is a blend of apple, orange and currants. The blends are unique because the Parenteaus add the natural herb, Seneca root, to the teas. The Seneca root is of special significance to Mr. Parenteau, because his ancestors used it for medicinal purposes.

The Parenteaus do business with approximately 10 gift shops in Saskatoon. In addition to the gift shops, a large portion of their clients comes from marketing their products through the Internet.

"Our clients come from all over the world, from as far away as Japan, New Zealand and Germany," says Mrs. Parenteau, who is actively involved with the Women Entrepreneurs of Saskatchewan. "There is a large group of Canadians living overseas, which is a big market for us, and they are eager to see anything distinctly Canadian, including Saskatoon berry chocolates."

The Parenteaus now maintain two separate orchards. They have 1.2 hectares in Langham and another 4 hectares in the Dalmeny area, which are managed by Mr. Parenteau's brother and sister-in-law, Vern and Laurie Parenteau.

The Parenteaus aren't finished yet, and they have plans to enter the winemaking arena. In 1991, Mr. Parenteau took a second-place prize in the "Country Classics" wine category of the Canadian Amateur Wine-Making Contest.

"Because the cost of berries is so high, it hasn't been easy to make a profit on the wine in the past," says Mr. Parenteau, who has his master's papers in masonry from the Moose Jaw Technical Institute. "But we've been patient and the price of the berries is going down so the wine market will be more competitive and then we'll dive in."

The home-based business keeps the Parenteaus busy all year round. From January to May, the company concentrates on attending conferences and trade shows in the United States and Canada's East Coast where they are able to make a large profit by selling their product directly to the customer. Yearly they attend between 20 and 30 conferences and trade shows. From May until August, the Parenteaus focus on tourism in the province, which included a contract with the Canadian Football League last year. August to December is spent gearing up for the Christmas season. The number of staff they employ varies from three full-time employees during the spring season to 10 to 12 full-time employees during peak season in the fall.

According to Mr. Parenteau, the road to success has been a long one.

"My family was very poor when I was growing up. I was working to help support my family by the time I was 11 (years old)," says Mr. Parenteau. "But this has taught me something valuable. I know how to work hard and I appreciate everything that I have and I don't take anything for granted."

Case 6–2: Reading, Writing, and Arithmetic Revamped (1996)[2]

The "3 Rs" used to be reading, writing and arithmetic, but all that has changed since Elaine Cowan and Ray Starr started Anokiiwin Training Institute in Winnipeg. "We are constantly revising, redesigning and recreating," says Ms. Cowan, president of Anokiiwin. "Our business plan is never stagnant and I think that is what's helping to make this a success."

Ms. Cowan and Mr. Starr, both from the Peguis First Nation north of Winnipeg, opened Anokiiwin in February 1995 using their own money and a grant from Aboriginal Business Canada (ABC).

"We wanted to take our vast experience working in the Aboriginal community and put it to good use," says Mr. Starr, who holds a Bachelor of Education degree and has worked in the public sector on adult education and training programs. "Knowing and recognizing the skills needed, we wanted to set up a private school and develop skills from the bottom up by tailoring our curriculum while providing employment for Aboriginal people."

The learning centre offers a wide range of accredited courses including life management skills, management training, tourism and hospitality, computerized accounting, small motor repair, mechanics, adult basic education, project management, medical services, and health-care aid.

Technology is also a big component of learning at Anokiiwin. The learning centre struck a deal with SHL Systemhouse, a division of MCI International based in Toronto, to market their computer curriculum. The curriculum has five methods of teaching: basic instruction led by textbook, multimedia style, computer interactive, self-teaching through discs for personal computers, and video.

---

2 Source: DIAND Website, *http://www.inac.gc.ca/ecdev/entre/mb/anokii.html* [edited].

"This is a custom course-maker so we can customize each student's textbook, computer application and specialty," says Ms. Cowan, who has developed numerous training programs for all levels of government, communities, private companies and the nonprofit sector. "This deal was a win-win situation because SHL didn't want to deal with small markets, but that's exactly what we wanted."

In 1969, according to the Department of Indian Affairs and Northern Development (DIAND), approximately 800 Aboriginal people had post-secondary education, but by 1991 that number has skyrocketed to 150,000 and Anokiiwin wanted in on the action.

"If we don't stay on the cutting edge, then our students can't be on the cutting edge," says Mr. Starr. "And if our students aren't up to speed then they will miss out on opportunities and then we haven't done our job."

Anokiiwin, which employs five instructors on a contract basis, entered a partnership with the University of Winnipeg in June 1996. "The university had a management studies program that we liked so we negotiated a partnership. We are now launching it jointly through the U of W Continuing Education," says Ms. Cowan. "[The university has] the product, but we will do the tailoring."

Customizing requires creativity, and that, Ms. Cowan says, is something Anokiiwin has in abundance. "Some institutions are so large that it's almost impossible to be creative," says Ms. Cowan. "But we are small, we have the network, access to Aboriginal communities, and Aboriginal educators."

The learning centre, which is housed in a 180-square-metre building in Winnipeg's downtown, also uses innovative measures in its teaching, such as the inclusion of Elders, mentors, Aboriginal values, and cultural sensitivity.

Ms. Cowan says she is working on a marketing strategy, but so far it hasn't been necessary to develop one. Word of mouth and connections currently bring in new students. Since Anokiiwin opened a year ago, the learning centre has graduated between 100 to 150 students. Today approximately 80% of those graduates are employed, she adds.

While Ms. Cowan says Anokiiwin has reached a measure of success, she says there is a long way to go. "We are providing a critical service to the Aboriginal community in Manitoba that is badly needed. We've made great strides, but we need to continue working toward a self-reliant workforce," she says.

Case 6–3: L&L Beverages, Suppliers of Water, Juice, Cola, and First Nations' Awareness (1997)[3]

The office is a flurry of activity. The phone seems to ring every few seconds, people come in and out of Larry Peters' office asking questions that only he as co-owner and president of L&L Beverages, can answer. He scarcely has time to sit for an interview. Yet, he is in his element — a big change from less than two years ago.

---

3 Source: DIAND Website, *http://www.inac.gc.ca/ecdev/entre/at/L&lbev.html* [edited].

Peters was laid off from his sales position of 13 years with Pepsi in January 1995 during a restructuring. But this didn't set him back for long. He saw a need for cola machines in First Nation communities and soon formed L&L Beverages with his brother Lynwood. They began to supply First Nations Cola to reserves via vending machine. However, it soon became apparent that with only one product line and a desire to serve all of the Maritimes, "Something needed to change, it was expand or die," explains Peters.

So when the opportunity to take over Connell Beverages' distribution arose in July 1996, it was too good to pass up, even with the limitations imposed on the purchase of the assets. "The offer was made the first of July, and they wanted a closing date of August first. It seemed impossible, but we did it," explains Peters. "We got one loan from the Ulnooweg Development Group and another from a bank, but the rest of the money to buy Connell Beverages came from heavy investments by my brother-in-law, Peter Clark, my brother Lynwood and I." It all seems worthwhile however, because business has been booming ever since.

With over 100 vending machines, more than 680 customers, and new customers every day, L&L is becoming better able to compete on a level playing field with the "big guys." "With our head office being off reserve, there aren't any special tax breaks. But this is the way we want it because we wanted to show we can compete just as well as anyone else," says Peters. "But it's not easy. Peter, as general manager, and I, as president, take only take enough to survive, and profits get reinvested. We really want to see this company grow and succeed."

So far L&L has sole distribution rights in the Maritimes for First Nations Cola, which is produced in Manitoba, Northern Chill from New Brunswick, and Mistic Juices from New York. They also distribute Culligan Water, "the only water doctors recommend for infant formulas because it doesn't need to be boiled like other waters," Peters points out. "It's distilled, not spring water, so at the end of the day it's just H_2O." Peters is looking to the expansion of First Nations Cola to 350-ml, 600-ml and 2-L bottles because the new markets available due to this expansion will help facilitate the expansion into the potato chip and snack market as well. "The name of the game is to have our supply trucks full when they leave to make deliveries."

There is more to this story than a successful business, however. With L&L's increased success, Larry Peters is also able to increase Aboriginal awareness. "After expanding our distribution network by acquiring Connell's territory, we're now able to get more of our product to more people, and this means that we can distribute more First Nations Cola as well. Over 60% of our sales of First Nations Cola is off reserve to grocery and convenience stores and restaurants." This means an increased awareness of the product, and therefore an increased awareness of First Nations.

Awareness is also increasing for First Nations peoples. As a First Nations person distributing a First Nations product, Peters wishes to give back to his community. "We're the only cola company that advertises in the Native newspapers. We also support events like native sports events and Pow-Wows. We sponsored the Tobique Music Festival by supplying pop and water there." He also wishes to set an example for other First Nations peoples. "Just as First Nations Cola is a nontraditional product, L&L is a nontraditional business for First Nations but I'm hoping that other Natives will follow my example and take advantage of the opportunities that exist out there."

Case 6–4: Selkirk First Nation Ventures into World Commodities Market (1996)[4]

The Selkirk First Nation recently dipped their toes into the world commodities market. Over the summer of 1996, the First Nation experimented in world markets by organizing the picking and sale of morel mushrooms growing wild on their territorial lands near Pelly Crossing, Yukon. The Selkirk First Nation organized the registration of pickers, distributed information packets and maps, set up camp sites for the pickers, set up and operated buying and drying stations, and kept up on current market price information.

Morel mushrooms are a delicacy in European cuisine. They flourish for a maximum of two seasons after a forest fire has occurred in an area. Last year, three large fires occurred in the Selkirk First Nation's territory. These tracts of land are now producing the much sought-after morel mushrooms. "It's a very competitive business," says Sandy Trerice, General Manager of the First Nation's Selkirk Development Corporation. "It was exhausting, but we learned a lot." The dried mushrooms are put in storage, until the fall peak-market period. They are worth more at this time because of an increased demand created by the wild meat season in Europe, beginning in October. "It is strategically good to hold on to some mushrooms," says Sandy. "This is the fun part!"

Being the new kids on the block, Sandy confessed that the Selkirk First Nation and the Development Corporation were a bit overwhelmed at first. "Because we were just starting out, sometimes we felt at the mercy of those already in the mushroom business. Some who are already in the industry are very protective of their position there — it's a very tight-knit group." Yet, Sandy believes that the First Nation and Development Corporation have an advantage: "Worldwide, the Yukon is renowned for its pristine environment. Because our mushrooms are grown in such an environment, we think they will be preferred by consumers."

Sandy credits the success of the mushroom season to good organization, daily involvement, and the dedicated participation of pickers, but adds that the season wasn't without complications. "What didn't work well was that we didn't know who to trust. It's like gold mining — it felt like people were trying to confuse you, and keep you confused. There weren't a lot of resources out there to consult. We had to rely on what other people told us, and a major downfall was the inconsistent information that we were getting."

However, Sandy views the experience in a positive light. "It was a lesson in a lot of things. Business. Human nature. I think the experience was more positive than negative. It was a good experience for me. I'm glad I was involved."

The Selkirk First Nation is the only Yukon First Nation to organize such an initiative. This venture into the world commodities market is the Development Corporation's third economic endeavour in its three-year history. It is an important and significant step in bringing prosperity and a sense of accomplish-

---

4 Source: DIAND Website, *http://www.inac.gc.ca/ecdev/entre/yt/Mshrm.html* [edited].

ment into the community. The morel mushroom industry is big world business. The Selkirk First Nation have not simply dipped their toes into the pool — they're making a big splash.

Case 6–5: A Thriving Business in La Romaine (1997)[5]

When customers open the door to Kamatshenan, a Montagnais term which signifies construction, they are greeted with a smile that suggests not only happiness, but also a strong sense of pride. The smile belongs to Bertrand Bellefleur, owner of the hardware store.

The store opened its doors to the public in December 1991 to offer a service that had not been provided in the community. Although Mr. Bellefleur has made some changes to meet the needs of his customers, his business continues to flourish.

"I first realized the need for this type of business while I was working for the Band Council as a technician. Before I opened the hardware store, all materials required for construction were purchased outside the community," said Mr. Bellefleur.

Like most other entrepreneurs, Mr. Bellefleur has been faced with a few obstacles along the way. He soon realized that, with determination and innovative ideas, these could be surpassed. "Because I was a new entrepreneur with few assets, it was difficult to find sources of funding," explained Mr. Bellefleur.

Determined to make a success of the business, Mr. Bellefleur decided to use the savings that he had to make improvements. He began by selling cigarettes in the store. This soon escalated to the sale of bread, pop and candy. Bertrand closely followed the market demand and its evolution. By identifying his customers' needs, he was able to respond.

Kamatshenan hardware store was soon transformed into a grocery store. "To help with the transition, I received a grant in the sum of $19,000 from the Aboriginal Economic Development Program," said Mr. Bellefleur. With the funding, he was able to purchase shelving units, additional refrigerators and freezers. Mr. Bellefleur also purchased a computer for accounting purposes and expanded the building to allow for the storage.

"La Romaine (the community where he and his family live) can only be accessed by plane or boat. As a result, we must order sufficient provisions to last four months. The expansion was necessary to store the food," explained Mr. Bellefleur.

Mr. Bellefleur's business is continuing to expand with a gas bar expected to be opened within the next month. He confides that the true secret to successfully managing a business is to be aware of the indirect expenses incurred by the business, such as administrative and transportation costs. It is equally important to endure the negative aspects of business management so as to profit from the many positive aspects.

"I think that my business sets a good example for the children in the community who one day wish to become entrepreneurs. I encourage them to ask questions in order to learn more about entrepreneurism," said Mr. Bellefleur.

---

5 Source: DIAND Website, *http://www.inac.gc.ca/ecdev/entre/pq/Bellef.html* [edited].

Kamatshenan continues to provide customers with hardware materials upon request; however, the main revenue is from the groceries. The store currently employs five Aboriginals on a full-time basis and operates according to the lifestyle of the community. For example, it is tradition among the natives to go fishing on Sunday afternoons, so the store is closed during Sunday afternoons.

6.6. Forms of Business Organization

Part of the process of new venture creation is the determination of the form of business organization that best suits the needs and objectives of those creating the business. The various possible forms of organization and there implications in an Aboriginal context are discussed in the following sections.

6.6.1. Sole Proprietorship

A sole proprietorship is a business owned by a single individual. It is the simplest form of organization. It is inexpensive to establish and reflects the desires of the owner who is the sole decision-maker. A proprietorship ceases to exist on the death or incapacity of the proprietor. The owner is also the sole recipient of any profits and bearer of any losses. He/she is personally liable for all the debts of the business. If the assets of the business are not adequate to cover all such debts then the personal assets of the individual must be used. The sole proprietorship does not pay federal or provincial income taxes. Instead the profit, calculated using acceptable accounting procedures (except where tax law requires a specific treatment), is added to and taxed as part of the personal income of the owner. If the proprietor is an Indian and the income is situated "on reserve," no federal or provincial income taxes will have to be paid.

6.6.2. Partnerships

A partnership is similar in many respects to a proprietorship. The significant differences relate to the fact that the business is owned by two or more people who have joined together with the objective of earning a profit from business, rather than a single individual. It must be registered with the appropriate provincial authority, listing the names and addresses of all partners. If a partner leaves or a new one joins, the old partnership terminates and a new one is created. As with a proprietorship, the owners receive the profit or bear the loss from the business.

Because of the complexity of issues relating to the division of profit or loss and the responsibilities of partners, a written agreement is advisable. The agreement should cover the following issues:

1. The name of the firm and its purpose.
2. The investment of each partner.
3. The particular duties and authorities of each partner.
4. The beginning and ending of the partnership; time frame, conditions for terminating, etc.

5. The settlement process on the death, incapacity, or retirement of a partner.
6. The procedure in the event of dispute between or among partners.
7. The disposition of profits and losses, interest on investment, and payment for services provided.
8. Any other matters which might be anticipated given the specific nature of the business and the partners involved.

If no specific partnership agreement exists, the following general rules apply:

1. The partners share equally in profit or loss.
2. One partner binds all, if acting in the normal course of running the business.
3. Every partner may take part in the management of the firm.
4. No new partner can be admitted without the consent of all current partners.
5. A majority of the partners is adequate to settle most disputes but any changes to the partnership of "a fundamental nature" require unanimous agreement.
6. Any partner can dissolve the partnership at any time by giving notice to other partners.
7. A partner carrying on a business of the same nature as that of the partnership must share the income from that activity with the other partners.

It is possible for a particular partner to limit his/her risk through the use of a specific form of organization, called a "Limited Partnership." The limited partners are at risk only to the extent of their investment. To qualify for and retain this limit to liability, the following conditions must be met:

1. There must be one or more general partners liable for the debts and other obligations of the partnership to the full extent of their assets (invested in the partnership and personal).
2. The limited partner may invest only cash.
3. The name of the limited partner cannot appear in the name of the firm or be otherwise promoted for business gain.
4. The limited partner must not participate in the management of the firm but can be an employee and is entitled to examine the financial records of the business.
5. The limited partner cannot withdraw any part of his/her investment, but can draw a share of the profits.
6. The partnership must be registered with the information provided to include the names and dollar investments of any limited partners.
7. Any change in membership, the nature of the business, or any other matter specified in the original registration requires a new registration or the limited partners will become liable as general partners.

All of the assets of the firm belong to the partnership, whether it is an ordinary or limited partnership. Depreciation (for tax purposes, Capital Cost Allowance) is deducted at the partnership (not personal) level in calculating business profit. A partner may be employed by the firm and paid a wage; however, this amount is not deductible for the purposes of calculating business profit, instead it is considered a "draw" against that partner's share of the business's profit.

Once profit is calculated for the business as a whole, each partner's share is determined and that amount is added to his/her personal income as "income from business" for the purpose of calculating income tax liability. If the business and related income is situated on reserve, no income tax will be have to be paid any Indian partners. A partner need not withdraw as cash all of his/her share of profit. Any amount not withdrawn increases a partner's investment in the business. If the business experiences a loss, each partner's share of the loss plus any cash withdrawn during the year reduces his/her investment in the firm.

6.6.3. Corporations

Corporations or limited companies are created to overcome three problems associated with partnerships and proprietorships. Those problems were, and still are:

1. The unlimited liability of the owner(s) for the liabilities and other obligations of the firm.
2. The limited life of the firm (terminated by death, incapacity, or withdrawal of the sole proprietor or of a partner).
3. The difficulties in raising large amounts of capital for major projects due to the two preceding issues and the inability to easily sell small parts of the business to investors.

Incorporation produces a business that is a legal entity separate from its owners. It is the corporation which conducts the business, incurs the liabilities and earns the profit. Ownership interest in the firm is acquired through the purchase of shares. The shareholders control the business through the election of the board of directors and a direct vote on certain important matters. The owners' liability is limited to the amount they paid for their shares in the business.

Corporations can be split into two categories: privately held and publicly traded. Both have to be registered with either the federal or a provincial government. This registration involves, among other things, the development of a constitution specifying such things as the purpose of the company, the authorized number of shares, the voting rights, the procedure for selecting directors, the composition of the board, the duties of directors, and so forth.

The shares of a private corporation are usually held by a small number of individuals closely associated with the firm. Generally, there are restrictions on an individual shareholder's freedom to sell shares to an outsider and on the firm's ability to issue additional shares to new shareholders. The purpose of incorporation as a private corporation is usually related to the limiting of liability and, possibly, to some tax advantages, as opposed to the facilitation of the raising of additional capital.

This latter issue, raising the capital, is the reason why many businesses elect to become publicly-traded corporations. The shares of such a corporation are bought and sold on a public market. This means that the firm can raise additional capital by selling shares to the "public." The new investors become owners and are entitled to a share of the profits through dividends. Control of the company can be retained by the original developers if they retain a majority of the voting shares.

A corporation is a separate legal entity and as such is subject to federal and provincial tax on its profit. The business calculates that profit using acceptable accounting procedures modified by special tax rules. The board of directors decides whether to distribute the after-tax profit to shareholders as a dividend or reinvest some or all of it in the business. A corporation, although a "legal individual," is not recognized as an Indian, no matter who owns the shares or where it operates. Any incorporated First Nation/Inuit-owned business, therefore, has to pay corporate income tax on its profits.

Wages are a legitimately deductible expense for a corporation, as they are for any other form of business. Further, unlike a proprietorship or a partnership, a corporation can deduct as expenses the wages and bonuses paid to its shareholders so long as such payments are for work done and/or services rendered and are reasonable. If the corporation is "situated on reserve" and the recipients of the such wages and bonuses are "Indians," no income tax will have to be paid on the amount distributed as wages or bonuses by either the corporation or the recipients.

Corporations "located on reserve" have been used to convert what would have been taxable income from off-reserve activity to nontaxable wage payments to First Nation members. For example, if a First Nation member was to operate a service station as a proprietorship on a highway adjacent to, but not on First Nation land, the profits would be taxable when added to the individual's income. On the other hand, if the same service station was organized as a corporation with its head office "located on reserve," the wages paid to Indians would not be subject to income tax. If the proprietor was instead the controlling shareholder and an employee, some, if not all, of the amount that was profit and taxable under a proprietorship would become nontaxable wage. The taxable profits of the proprietorship can, in this manner, be converted to nontaxable wages of a corporation. Any profit remaining from the payment of reasonable wages and other expenses will be subject to income tax.

A 1992 Supreme court decision regarding unemployment insurance payments has called into question the legality of this practice. Revenue Canada served notice that beginning in 1994, they will expect Indians who earn income for work performed off-reserve to pay income tax even if they work for a corporation resident on-reserve. This decision is being challenged by First Nation groups.

6.6.4. Joint Ventures

A joint venture is a contractual arrangement between two or more investors to share the control an activity. The joint venture has many of the features of a partnership. The investors share in the decision making, the profits, and the losses. On the other hand, the investors are usually companies, often incorporated, or other bodies and the joint venture itself is often incorporated. Usually a venture is formed for a particular business purpose or project. As with partnerships, a written legal agreement clarifying the terms of the venture including the rights and responsibilities of the investors is critical.

A joint venture can permit the investors to:

1. Spread the risk where individual projects are risky and entail a large capital investment.
2. Combine the various particular strengths of the investors into the package necessary for the project.
3. Invest in "foreign" jurisdictions where laws require a certain level of local participation.

Joint ventures are of particular interest to Aboriginal people developing businesses. For example, they can permit the combination of the respective advantages of the Aboriginal and non-Aboriginal investors. The Aboriginal investor brings to the venture the potential of preferential tax treatment, an underutilized labour force and often the legal control of a particular natural resource. The non-Aboriginal investors usually bring financial resources, technical expertise and market access to the venture.

The partners retain title to the assets they bring to the venture. Depreciation (Capital Cost Allowance) is not deducted in calculating venture income. Instead, it is deducted by each participant, for the assets it owns, from its share of the venture profit. This creates the potential for mutual gain for both First Nation and non-First Nation investors. If the venture is "situated on reserve," then the First Nation investors may not need the capital cost allowance as a deduction to reduce taxable income, whereas non-First Nation investors do. If the joint venture is structured so that non-First Nation investors provide and retain title to the depreciable assets, they will be able to utilize the full deduction. In this way the outside investors can shelter additional income from tax, making the investment more attractive than a similar investment with non-First Nation participants.

6.6.5. Co-operatives

The co-operative is a special form of business organization similar to a corporation but with the following distinct features:

1. The owners are members, each possessing one vote regardless of the amount invested.
2. The owners must be present to vote; there is no proxy voting.
3. The surplus (profit) is either retained and reinvested or distributed in the form of (i) interest on investment and/or (ii) a patronage dividend based on the volume of business done by the individual with the co-operative.

Co-operatives are generally formed by individuals who perceive potential economic benefits from the pooling of their purchasing power or their marketable resources. In the first type, it is expected that purchase cost will decline as the volume purchased is increased. Some of the cost reduction will go toward the operating costs of the business with the remainder going to individual members through reduced prices, interest on their investment and/or patronage dividends. In the second type of co-operative, individuals pool their resources believing that a common front will permit the delivery of the output to the market in the most profitable manner. One producer co-operative that is familiar to many Aboriginal people is the Freshwater Fish Marketing Coop. There are also numerous Aboriginal co-operatives across the country formed to market handicrafts and art works.

6.6.6. Development Corporations

As the name suggests, development corporations are a particular type of corporation and thus all the characteristics of the corporate form of business organization apply. They play a prominent role in new venture creation among Aboriginal people. According to a recent study of the First Nations in Saskatchewan,[6] 84% of the First Nations in the province have created development corporations to own and operate businesses on their behalf. In addition, 72% of the First Nations in Saskatchewan are members of one or another of the Tribal Councils that have established development corporations to conduct business on behalf of their member First Nations. Combining these two types of development corporations, 86% of the First Nations are involved in economic development activities carried out through a development corporation.

The purpose of development corporations is to remove day-to-day business decision-making from the political arena. Subject to broad objectives and policy guidelines determined by the political leaders, a development corporation and its businesses are expected to concentrate on profitability, growth, long-term survival and employment creation. For example, Decter and Kowall (1989) suggest that the most important lesson that can be learned from the success of the Kitsaki Development Corporation of the La Ronge First Nation is

> *The value of creating an arm's length corporation separate from the political governmental structure of the Band. By creating a separate organization focused on economic development, the Band can place a higher priority on such development. As well, the corporation can be run on sound business principles and freed to some extent from politics.*
>
> (Decter and Kowall 1989, 41)

The two cases that follow provide a better understanding of the role of Aboriginal development corporations, as do the descriptions of CREECO, Makivik and the Inuvialuit Development Corporation in chapter 4.

---

6 See chapter 7 for an in-depth discussion of the results of this research.

6.6.7. Development Corporations: Examples

Case 6–6: LIDC — Labrador Inuit Development Corporation (1996)[7]

The Labrador Inuit Development Corporation (LIDC) was incorporated under Canadian law in 1982 as the economic development arm of the Labrador Inuit Association (LIA).

The mandate of LIDC is to improve the living conditions of Inuit of Labrador by providing employment opportunities, with a focus on traditional Inuit skills. The organization also promotes education and training of Inuit to meet the requirements of today's labour market.

LIDC is 100% owned and controlled by the LIA to ensure the goals of the association are followed by the development corporation. LIDC currently employs 46 people directly, and 43 of these positions are filled by LIA members. The greatest concentration of employees are from Inuit communities on the north coast of Labrador.

LIDC is involved in various subsidiary companies and economic development projects. One example is the PiKalujak Fisheries, a shrimp fishery that is 50% owned by LIDC. Last year LIDC realized $400,000 in profits from this project and currently 10 jobs are sustained by the fishery.

Another example of one of LIDC's successful projects is the Torngait Ujaganniavingit Corporation stone quarries. For the past five years one quarry has been operating at Ten Mile Bay while a second quarry is being planned for John Hay's Harbour. In addition, the company plans to build a small processing plant to begin production in 1998. This year the quarry's estimated production is 850 cubic metres of stone with an estimated value of $1.2-million. The unique stone cut at the Ten Mile Bay quarry is black with crystals of gray and blue through it. Italy creates the greatest demand for the stone where it is used to build stone walls, buildings and floors.

The shrimp fishery and the stone quarry are both projects that reflect the traditional way of Inuit life. Hunting and fishing were key ingredients of survival and stone carving has been passed on through generations.

Financially, LIDC is now in an excellent position to begin investing in some new projects. Some other projects that LIDC is presently involved in include operation and maintenance of the north warning radar system; operation, maintenance and services supplier in support of mining exploration; Inuit art; caribou harvest; and turbot and char fisheries.

LIDC members are hopeful for the corporation's future, especially now, since the corporation is in the financial position to invest in new projects. Board members feel that these new projects will create the employment and revenues necessary for successful survival of the northern Inuit communities of Labrador.

---

7 Source: DIAND Website, *http://www.inac.gc.ca/ecdev/entre/at/Lidc.html* [editied].

Case 6–7: Four Winds Trading Company (1997)[8]

Historically, Aboriginal trade in Manitoba depended heavily on the region's rivers. Travelers, including traders and their goods used the rivers for transport. The junction of the Red and Assiniboine Rivers in Winnipeg, known as The Forks today, was an Aboriginal trading site for centuries.

The Forks is still a trading post of sorts. It has been designated a National Historic Site and is home to a variety of markets and eclectic shops. One of those shops, Four Winds Trading Company, continues the tradition of Aboriginal trade, twentieth-century style. Four Winds sell arts and crafts made by Aboriginal artisans from all over North America — everything from pottery to traditional costumes. Some items are commercially made, but most are handcrafted by individual craftspeople, many of them from Manitoba.

West Region Economic Development Corporation operates the store. Six First Nations in western Manitoba own the corporation. Richard Gaywish, the Development Corporation's general manager, says that Four Winds provide an important market for local artisans: "When we talk about what kind of employment we've created with the store, it's not only what we've created with the business, but what we've created for the craftspeople in our communities. They now have somewhere to go to sell their products at a reasonable price rather than being ripped off."

Four Winds have been in operation for over five years now, and Gaywish is confident it will do well in the future: "It's always a struggle, but in comparison to other craft stores, I think we're doing well. We create employment for Native people in the city of Winnipeg." Four Winds employ five people full-time, year-round, and three people part-time in the summer. All of the employees are Aboriginal. Not only does the store provide employment, it has also paid off its initial bank loan of $80,000 and is turning a profit.

In fact, two years after Four Winds opened at The Forks, it was doing so well that West Region Economic Development Corporation, decided to open an additional store. Like the original store, the new store is at the intersection of some important trade routes. However, these trade routes are only decades, not centuries, old. The location chosen for the second store is at the Winnipeg International Airport.

When West Region Economic Development Corporation first looked at the idea of opening an art and crafts store, they consulted with other Aboriginal people who have experience in both business, and arts and crafts. "At the time, there were a lot of Native arts and crafts stores out there, but not a lot in Manitoba," says Gaywish. "We traveled and we met with different people, and sort of got an idea of what their wholesale and retail prices were. Based on those findings, we set up our store here."

Since Four Winds have been in operation, it has been a learning experience for everyone involved in the business. According to Morris Shannacappo, a senior economic development officer with West Region Economic Development Corporation, one of the most important things they've learned, is how to appraise the art that people want to sell them. "It was a good experience, try-

---

8 Source: DIAND Website, *http://www.inac.gc.ca/ecdev/entre/mb/4winds.html* [edited].

ing to find out what is a reasonable price for art, and learning how to haggle with the artists. By now, we've seen a lot of art, and we know what's good art."

Now that they have an increased understanding of the industry, Gaywish says they hope to expand the business, and possibly even make Four Winds into a franchise. "One of the reasons we went into the airport was to get our feet wet, so we could go into a bigger centre like Toronto or Vancouver," he says.

Gaywish and Shannacappo believe the market for Aboriginal arts and crafts is growing. Shannacappo believes that Four Winds success is partly due to their devotion to one basic principle when it comes to the artwork they sell: "Authenticity. We've tried to stay as close as possible to authenticity." People want real, traditional Aboriginal art, and Four Winds delivers.

Gaywish says they also keep in mind the fact that their business will only succeed if they keep ahead of the fads. He cites dream catchers as an example. "We've been marketing dream catchers for years. We've sold thousands of them," he says. "But one of these days that's going to wear itself out, and we have to be ready for what comes next." If their success thus far is any indication, they will be ready.

7 First Nations' Economic Development in Saskatchewan

This chapter is organized in seven sections. In the first section, the overall economic and business development strategies of the First Nations in Saskatchewan are described and discussed. In the second, the First Nations and Tribal Councils are ranked based on their level of economic development activity and the differences between the high- and low-ranked Nations investigated. The ranking of these Nations are compared with respect to changes in income and employment levels between 1986 and 1991 in the third section. The fourth section presents a more detailed discussion of the nature of First Nations' business development. The focus is on forms of ownership, market and business size. The fifth section considers the issues of risk and performance by First Nations' businesses. The sixth addresses development capacity, particularly human, financial and physical resources. In the final section, the eight characteristics of First Nations' economic development and the proposed contingency perspective are evaluated in light of my research results.

7.1. Planning, Organization and Ownership

My research into the nature of economic development among First Nations in Saskatchewan and their resulting business economy began in January 1994. It continued through the summer of 1996. My initial objective was to create a database about the economic development activities of the 70 First Nations located in Saskatchewan. To gather information, I prepared and distributed a questionnaire to each First Nation in Saskatchewan. I combined the results of this survey with data obtained from TransGas and the FSIN to create a database. Tables 7–1 to 7–3 in this section as well as Tables 7–12 to 7–19 in section 7.4 are drawn from this database.

7.1.1. Development Plans

Both community and economic development plans are common among the First Nations in Saskatchewan. In their community development plans, the First

Nations establish broad objectives in areas that include (i) economic self-sufficiency and an end to dependency on social assistance, (ii) self-government, (iii) respect for Elders and traditional practices, and (iv) social development including health and addictions, justice and policing, housing and community infrastructure, and education.

Either as part of their community development plans or as a separate economic development plan, most First Nations discuss economic and business development. They make a clear connection between economic and business development and their broader community development objectives. Business development is expected to provide jobs and create wealth through profits and growth. Economic development is a broader concept. It includes capacity building activities such as education and training, institution-building, infrastructure development and the acquisition of physical and financial resources.

A sense of the relationship between business and economic development is captured by William Hatton, a past director of economic development for the La Ronge First Nation, when he says:

> *Economic development is the process of creating institutions that do business development — not business development itself.*
>
> *If business development is a wrench — economic development is the machine tool which creates it.*
>
> (Decter and Kowall 1989, 1)

Together, business and economic development are expected to create the economic self-reliance that, in turn, is to form the foundation for community development and self-government.

One purpose of my survey was to determine just how widespread economic development planning is among the 70 First Nations in Saskatchewan. According to my results (see Table 7–1), by 1995, 73% of the First Nations had prepared a community development plan. Ninety-three percent of these plans contained specific economic development goals and strategies for attaining these goals. In addition, 31 First Nations reported having an economic development

TABLE 7–1: Saskatchewan First Nations' (FN) Economic Development Planning, 1995

	Community Development Plan		**Community Development Plan with Econ. Dev. Goals**		**Economic Development Plan**	
	Yes	**No**	**Yes**	**No**	**Yes**	**No**
Total	52	11	48	15	31	32
Proportion	73%	15%	68%	21%	44%	45%
Total FN	70					

plan separate from their community development plan. In 1995, only 18 of the 70 First Nations reported lacking a formal plan that set economic development goals and strategies.

A follow-up investigation of these 18 First Nations revealed the following facts. Three did not respond to that portion of the questionnaire. Another three were newly established First Nations. At the time of my survey, their energies were directed to acquiring land to establish their communities, and not on economic development. All the remaining 12 First Nations reported owning and operating at least one business. Seven of the 12 had also created development corporations. Based on this evidence, 12 of the 18 First Nations were clearly involved in economic and business development activities even though they did not have formal development plans. Combining these 12 with those reporting economic development plans, 91% of the 70 First Nations in Saskatchewan have formal or informal economic development goals and business development strategies.

7.1.2. Economic Development Responsibilities and Structures

After having addressed planning, my questionnaire sought out information about the organizational structures that First Nations have adopted for economic development. Table 7–2 summarizes these results. Eighty-two percent of the First Nations indicated that responsibility for economic development has been assigned to a particular elected band councilor or a committee of councilors. Most of the remainder said that the economic development activities are the responsibility of the council as a whole. This is an indication of the collective nature of their approach to development and its close ties to First Nations' governments. Thirty First Nations reported that they have assigned operational responsibility for economic development to a particular employee, indicating the commitment of significant human and financial resources to the development process.

Fifty-nine of the First Nations have created development corporations to own and operate businesses on their behalf. In addition, 72% of the First Na-

TABLE 7–2: Saskatchewan First Nations' Development Organization, 1995

	Economic Development Portfolio		Economic Development Employee		First Nation Development Corporation		Tribal Council Development Corporation	
	Yes	No	Yes	No	Yes	No	yes	No
Total	58	5	30	33	42	21	50	20
Proportion	82%	7%	42%	46%	59%	30%	72%	28%
Total FN	70							

tions are members of one or another of the Tribal Councils that have established development corporations to conduct business on behalf of their member First Nations. Combining these two types of development corporations, 86% of the First Nations are involved in economic development activities carried out through a development corporation.

The stated purpose of these development corporations is to remove day-to-day business decision-making from the political arena. Subject to broad objectives and policy guidelines determined by the political leaders, a development corporation and its businesses are expected to concentrate on profitability, growth, long-term survival and employment creation. For example, Decter and Kowall suggest that the most important lesson that can be learned from the success of the Kitsaki Development Corporation of the La Ronge First Nation is

> *The value of creating an arm's length corporation separate from the political governmental structure of the Band. By creating a separate organization focused on economic development, the Band can place a higher priority on such development. As well, the corporation can be run on sound business principles and freed to some extent from politics.*
>
> (Decter and Kowall 1989, 41)

Given their prevalence, it is apparent that this view of the utility of development corporations is widely held among the First Nations in Saskatchewan.

7.1.3. Forms of Business Ownership

Going beyond this general consideration of organization for business and economic development, Table 7–3 considers the business ownership strategies adopted by First Nations. It provides information about the relative significance of four types of business ownership. The first type are those businesses owned by an individual or individuals from a particular First Nation, that is, private ownership. The other three types all involve collective (government) ownership.

TABLE 7–3: Business Ownership as Reported by Each First Nation, 1995

Individual Owner of Businesses		Individual FN Owner of Businesses		FN JV with Others (Not TC)		FN JV with Tribal Council		FN JV with Tribal Council or Others	
Yes	**No**	**Yes**	**No**	**Yes**	**No**	**Yes**	**No**	**Yes**	**No**
49	20	52	18	25	44	50	19	57	12
71%	29%	75%	26%	36%	64%	72%	28%	83%	17%

FN: First Nation; JV: Joint Venture

They are those owned by (i) an individual First Nation, (ii) a First Nation in joint venture with others but not through their Tribal Council and (iii) Tribal Council joint ventures. If the First Nations in Saskatchewan are implementing a planned a purposeful economic development strategy consistent with the approach described in chapter 2, the last three forms of ownership should play a prominent role in their business economy, and my results indicate that they do.

Seventy-one percent of the First Nations reported at least one business venture owned and operated by an individual (or individuals). Seventy-five percent of the First Nations reported being the sole owner of at least one business. Thirty-six percent indicated that they are involved in at least one joint venture with others (excluding their Tribal Council) while 72% of the First Nations are involved in joint ventures through their Tribal Councils. Combining these two types of joint ventures, 83% of the First Nations in Saskatchewan reported participating in at least one joint business venture.

7.1.4. Summary: Planning Organization and Ownership

The information from my survey presented in Tables 7–1, 7–2 and 7–3 provide strong evidence of the pervasive nature of economic development among the First Nations in Saskatchewan. All but a negligible few are actively involved in the creation of businesses for the purpose of improving the socioeconomic circumstances of their people. Further, collective ownership by individual First Nations and through joint ventures plays a prominent role in this business development strategy. A more thorough investigation of the First Nations' approach to economic development can be found later in this chapter and in chapter 8, the Meadowlake Tribal Council case study.

7.2. Comparative Business Development Performance

Before going on to investigate in more detail the nature of First Nations' businesses, it is important to obtain a sense of the distribution of economic development activity among the First Nations. Are all equally active or does the level of activity vary with location, size, education level and/or other factors? Further, is a higher level of economic development activity by a First Nation associated to a correspondingly greater improvement in its members' socioeconomic circumstances, particularly employment and income levels? This section addresses the first question and section 7.3, the second one.

7.2.1. First Nation and Tribal Council Rankings

To address the first question, the 70 First Nations have been ranked by level of economic development activity. For each First Nation, a score of one was assigned for each yes to the items in Tables 7–1 and 7–2. In addition, one point was added for each business owned under the four categories in Table 7–

TABLE 7–4: First Nation Rankings

Top Ten Overall

FN Name	Tribal Council Name	Score	Rank
Muskeg Lake FN	Saskatoon Tribal Council	30	1
Kinistin FN	Saskatoon Tribal Council	27	2
Yellow Quil FN	Saskatoon Tribal Council	27	2
Mistawasis FN	Saskatoon Tribal Council	26	3
Muskowekw AN FN	Touchwood File Hills Qu'Appelle	24	4
James Smith FN	Prince Albert Grand Council	24	4
Sweetgrass FN	Battlefords Tribal Council	24	4
Lac La Ronge FN	Prince Albert Grand Council	23	5
Peepeekisis FN	Touchwood File Hills Qu'Appelle	23	5
Fishing Lake FN	Touchwood File Hills Qu'Appelle	23	5

Lowest Ten Overall

Birch Narrows FN	Meadow Lake Tribal Council	9	19
Kahkewistaha W FN	Yorkton Tribal Council	9	19
Sakimay FN	Yorkton Tribal Council	9	19
Keesekoose FN	Yorkton Tribal Council	8	20
English River FN	Meadow Lake Tribal Council	7	21
Peter Ballantyne FN	Prince Albert Grand Council	7	21
Ahtahkakoop FN	Independent	7	21
Cowessess FN	Yorton Tribal Council	6	22
Red Pheasant FN	Confederation of Tribal Nations	6	22
Joseph Bighead FN	Independent	5	23

3. The First Nations were then ranked from highest to lowest based on total scores. The rankings for the 70 Nations extended from 1 to 25 because of numerous ties. The median rank was 13. The scores of the 10 top and lowest ranked First Nations are provided in Table 7–4.

The ranking process was extended to the 10 Tribal Councils and the independent First Nations (see Table 7–5). The total score for each council is the sum of the scores of its member First Nations. These totals were then divided by the number of First Nations in the council and the councils ranked them based on the result. Not unexpectedly, the highest-ranked First Nations belonged to highest-ranked councils and the lowest to the lowest-ranked (or

TABLE 7–5: Tribal Council Rankings

		TC Rank Overall Activity		TC Rank/# of FN	
Tribal Council Name	**# of FN**	**Score**	**Rank**	**Score**	**Rank**
Saskatoon Tribal Council	7	155	3	22	1
Battlefords Tribal Council	4	67	6	17	2
Touchwood File Hills Qu'Appelle	16	255	1	16	3
Prince Albert Grand Council	12	183	2	15	4
Meadow Lake Tribal Council	9	119	4	13	5
Confederation of Tribal Nations	6	72	5	12	6
South East Treaty 4 Tribal Council	2	24	9	12	6
Willow Cree Tribal Council	1	12	11	12	6
Agency Chiefs Tribal Council	3	29	8	10	7
Yorkton Tribal Council	6	55	7	9	8
Independent	4	17	10	4	9

were independent). In fact, all the top 10 First Nations are members of the top four Tribal Councils. Furthermore, 34 of the 37 First Nations at or above the median score are from the top five Tribal Councils, while only three of the other First Nations at or above the median level of activity are from the other five councils or the independent First Nations. The question is, Why are the First Nations that are members of these five Tribal Councils so much more active in economic development than the other First Nations in the province?

7.2.2. Analysis of Relative Business Development Activity

My search for an explanation for the difference in business development activity among First Nations and Tribal Councils focuses on three broad areas: (i) leadership, planning and organization, and implementation; (ii) geographic location; and (iii) socioeconomic circumstances, particularly population, education level and land-base. In the sections that follow, these three categories of causal factors are examined.

7.2.2.1. Leadership, Planning and Organization, and Implementation

Leadership, economic development planning and organization, and business development activities vary among the 70 First Nations. Some leaders and their Nations opted for a business-oriented development approach in the 1980s or earlier while others have turned to this strategy just recently. In particular, among First Nations, Muskeg Lake and La Ronge were early adopters of this approach, as were the Saskatoon, Meadow Lake, Prince Albert and

Touchwood File Hills Qu'Appelle Tribal Councils. The early adoption of a business-based development strategy is reflected in their current rankings (see Tables 7–4 and 7–5).

The four highest-ranked First Nations are members of the Saskatoon Tribal Council (STC) and the STC is the highest-ranked Tribal Council. The remaining three First Nations of the STC ranked sixth, twelfth and thirteenth, which meant that all seven members of the STC ranked in the top half of all Saskatchewan First Nations in economic development activity.

Under the leadership of Lester Lafond, Chief Harry Lafond and others, the top-ranked First Nation — Muskeg Lake — was an early and aggressive adopter of a business development approach to economic development (Saskatoon Sun 1996). Muskeg Lake's successes include the creation of an urban Reserve in 1988. This reserve has been developed into a commercial/light industrial park that has become a model for other First Nations. Chief Lafond (Lafond 1996), in his address to students of the Saskatchewan Indian Federated College, says the urban reserve is the centrepiece of Muskeg Lake's economic development strategy that involves both First Nation and private ownership. Muskeg Lake was able to make this groundbreaking move because it received a portion of its Treaty Land Entitlement (TLE) compensation (the urban reserve land) in the early 1980s. The other 27 First Nations that are signatories to the 1992 TLE Framework Agreement had to wait until the mid-1990s before receiving their compensation with payment spread over 12 years. Several entitlement Nations are now following the lead of Muskeg Lake (e.g. Peter Ballantyne in Prince Albert and Star Blanket in Fort Qu'Appelle).

The commercial/industrial park provides employment and income directly and supports the development of privately owned businesses. The Muskeg Lake First Nation earns income from the urban reserve in two principal ways: (i) land and commercial space is leased to tenants and (ii) tenants are charged the equivalent of a property tax. In turn, Muskeg Lake provides tenants with a variety of services — sewer and water, roads, policy and fire protection, etc. — under a servicing agreement it has with the City of Saskatoon. Profits from the venture are either reinvested in expansion or accrue to the First Nation.

According to Chief Lafond, some of these profits are being used by Muskeg Lake as an economic development fund to encourage and support individual entrepreneurship and private business development. The fund provides equity capital to Muskeg Lake citizens who wish to start businesses. With this equity in hand and a viable business plan,[1] these business proponents can then pursue the remaining capital they require from SIEF, the banks, credit unions and other sources. According to Chief Lafond, some of the profits from the industrial park will also be used to support members who chose to follow a more traditional lifestyle "on reserve." Overall, Muskeg Lake is following a balanced approach to development involving First Nation-owned and private businesses.

---

1 Recognizing the importance of business planning to the successful creation and expansion of private and publicly owned business, Muskeg Lake and the other First Nations of the STC offer business plan preparation seminars and ongoing support to their members.

A balanced approach is not limited to Muskeg Lake. The other three in the top 10 ranked STC First Nations placed among the top five Saskatchewan First Nations when ranked on businesses owned by individuals. These three and Muskeg Lake also ranked at or above the median level in businesses owned by the First Nation and in joint ventures. This balanced approach extends to the remaining STC Nations (all of them were above the median level of activity but not in the top ten). These results are a reflection of the strategy adopted by the STC that includes the promotion and support of business development by individuals and at the First Nation level as well as joint ventures at the Tribal Council level. As a result of this strategy, the STC ranked first among Tribal Councils in businesses owned by First Nations, second in joint ventures as well as second in businesses owned by individuals.

The Touchwood File Hills Qu'appelle Tribal Council (TFHQ) ranks first among tribal councils on raw score and third when that score is divided by the number of member Nations. Three First Nations from the TFHQ are among the top 10 with eight more at or above the median score of 13. Five TFHQ First Nations fall below the median score. The TFHQ Nations have adopted a strategy that emphasizes joint venture business development at the Tribal Council level. The average number of joint venture arrangements per First Nation for TFHQ members is 6.4, the highest for all Tribal Councils. Muskowekwan, the highest-ranked TFHQ Nation, ranks second among all First Nations in both non-Tribal Council and total joint ventures but only average or lower in the two non-joint venture ownership categories. All of the other TFHQ Nations that ranked above the median in overall activity fall below the median in all ownership types except Tribal Council joint ventures. It is only TFHQ's strong joint venture foundation that places them in the top 50%. Again, this is a clear example of a discernible strategy being responsible for the above average performance of individual Nations and the Tribal Council as a whole.

There are two First Nations from the Prince Albert Grand Council (PAGC) among the 10 top-ranked Nations. Of the remaining 10 PAGC First Nations, seven are just at the median level of overall activity, and three are below. The two highest-ranked PAGC Nations have adopted sharply contrasting strategies.

The La Ronge First Nation, a member of the PAGC, is the largest First Nation (in terms of population) in the province. Under the leadership of Chief Harry Cook and others, this First Nation has been a recognized leader in business development for many years (Decter and Kowell 1989). Through its Kitsaki Development Corporation, it either owns a substantial interest or in full a number of successful businesses including Northern Resource Trucking, Six Seasons Catering, Athabaska Catering, Kitsaki Meats, Northern Lights Wild Rice, Keethanow Bingo North, the La Ronge Motor Hotel, First Nations Insurance, and NAPA Auto Parts. The formation of joint ventures with non-First Nation companies in larger businesses serving regional, national and international markets is the La Ronge First Nation's preferred strategy. As a result, it leads all First Nations with seven non-Tribal Council joint ventures. The next highest in this category is Muskowekwan with only three. The La Ronge First Nation also ranks first in total joint ventures with 10, closely followed by Muskowekwan with nine.

James Smith First Nation is another PAGC top-ten ranked First Nation. My research indicates that it leads all First Nations in businesses owned by First Nation individuals. However, it ranks well below the median level in business owned by the First Nation and has no non-Tribal Council joint ventures. Clearly, a very different approach to that of the La Ronge First Nation.

Overall, the ranking for PAGC reflects the contrasting approaches of its two most active members. Largely because of the number of businesses owned by James Smith, PAGC ranks third in businesses owned by individuals behind STC and TFHQ. It ranks fourth in Tribal Council and total joint ventures, and fourth in First Nation-owned businesses behind TFHQ, STC, and MLTC. The PAGC ranks first by a wide margin in non-Tribal Council joint ventures with 19. The next closest in this category is TFHQ with six. Interestingly, even without the seven joint ventures of the La Ronge First Nation, PAGC's number of non-Tribal Council joint ventures would still be twice that of TFHQ. There is an explanation for this.

The La Ronge First Nation has actively recruited other northern First Nations into its joint ventures. For example, it has invited several groups to become partners in Northern Resource Trucking, an insurance brokerage, and in its mine catering companies. The La Ronge First Nation has several reasons for doing this including (i) acquisition of additional capital for the business from the new partner(s), (ii) reduction of the likelihood of other First Nations forming competing companies and (iii) a genuine desire to show leadership and assist other less experienced northern First Nations achieve their economic development objectives. By example, it has also encouraged other PAGC members to form joint ventures among themselves and with outside groups. As a result, non-Tribal Council rather than Tribal Council joint ventures dominate among the Nations of the PAGC.

This is not to say that the PAGC has not been active in development activities. It has.[2] Through its development corporation, it is involved in several large projects including the Prince Albert Inn, the Northern Lights Casino and PAGC Security Services, and is actively considering others. In fact, in several instances, Tribal Council joint ventures (e.g. trucking and catering) have operated in direct competition with similar joint ventures involving one or more of the PAGC members. It is apparent that the PAGC's fourth place ranking among Tribal Councils can be attributed as much to the activities of the La Ronge First Nation as to any discernible Tribal Council strategy common to all its members.

There is one First Nation (with a total membership of three) from the Battleford Tribal Council (BTC) among the top ten. The Sweetgrass First Nation is tied with James Smith of the PAGC for the top rank in businesses owned by individuals. Like James Smith, it ranks below the median in all other categories. The other two members of the Tribal Council are also above the median level in overall ranking. They also emphasize ownership by individuals and have lower results in the other categories. As a result, among Tribal Councils, the BTC ranks first in the ownership by individual category. It ranks no

---

2 See Case 2–3 for a description of the development activities conducted by PADC, the development corporation of the Prince Albert Grand Council.

higher than fourth in the other categories. Overall, the BTC ranks second in level of economic development activity among Tribal Councils based on the First Nation category but only sixth in total activity.

There are no members of the Meadow Lake Tribal Council (ranked fourth on total score and fifth on score per First Nation) among the top ten First Nations. Four member Nations are ranked above the median level and the remaining five below. In spite of the relatively low ranking of its individual members, the MLTC is considered by many to have the most successful business development program of all the Tribal Councils. In fact, it was named the "National Economic Developer of the Year" at the 1995 conference of the Council for the Advancement of Native Development Officers. It is the nature of the MLTC's joint venture businesses and the planned relationship between these businesses and those owned by individual First Nations and First Nation individuals that have raised the profile of the MLTC and created its reputation for success. The MLTC ranks second in Tribal Council joint ventures behind TFHQ and third in First Nation's owned businesses. The Council's development activities are considered in depth in chapter 7.

It is interesting to note that there are signs that the lower-ranked Tribal Councils and First Nations are beginning to adopt strategies similar to those ranked higher. For example, the Agency Chiefs Tribal Council (ACTC), currently ranked seventh among Tribal Councils, is aggressively pursuing a development strategy which should improve its position in the rankings in the future. As part of this strategy, the ACTC has just purchased production equipment to establish a disposable diaper factory. After extensive negotiations with communities in the region, it was decided to locate the plant in North Battleford rather than on any of the three member Nations' reserves. Access to transportation, an adequate source of electric power and the availability of a suitable vacant building were among the determining factors. Once operational, the plant will employ 27 people with planned expansion expected to increase this number to 60. The company will have a preferential hiring policy that favours the members of the ACTC First Nations. This project is the latest of several economic development initiatives undertaken by the ACTC in the past several years. According to the Saskatoon Star Phoenix:

> *Although it is the smallest tribal council in Canada, it has created 134 jobs over the last three years, mainly in forestry. It is a major contractor for Weyerhauser in Prince Albert.*
> (Star Phoenix 1996c, B5)

Similar signs are emerging in the Southeast Tribal Council (SETC) and among the independent First Nations (currently ranked sixth and ninth, respectively). From the SETC, the White Bear First Nation has some exciting ventures including a golf course, resort hotel and a joint venture in the petroleum sector.[3] Ochapowace owns and operates a successful ski resort, a retail mall containing several businesses and has recently purchased a large hotel in Regina (the Landmark Inn). In fact, these First Nations are ranked second and first

3 See Case 5–1 for a description of Whitebear Oil and Gas.

respectively for businesses owned by a First Nation. At the time of my survey, neither was involved in joint ventures through the SETC or otherwise. This is likely to change. Both will be involved in a casino to be operated as an FSIN/SETC joint venture and both are considering other joint venture projects. Ocean Man, one of the new independent First Nations in the south of the province, has also embarked on a significant joint venture. The First Nation has invested $1-million in a joint venture with the City of Weyburn and a corporate partner to build and operate an ethanol plant in Weyburn. From these examples, the development approach adopted by the top-ranked Nations seems to be diffusing to other First Nations.

In summary, the top-ranked Nations and Tribal Councils have two things in common that differentiate them from the lower ranked ones. The first is a discernible and effective development strategy. The second is having leaders committed to economic development. This second factor becomes evident in discussions with members and others about the reasons why certain First Nations and Tribal Councils have been more active and successful than others in their development activities. In each case, key individuals are widely credited as being "the champions of development"[4] who through their leadership have been instrumental in the success of their First Nation or Tribal Council.

It is important to determine if there are other factors that contributed to the difference in performance between the high- and low-ranked groups. Four factors were chosen for evaluation — location, population, land-base, and education level.

7.2.2.2. Location

On a province-wide basis there is a difference in performance between First Nations in the north (forested area) of the province and those in the south (agricultural area). Only one of the top performing First Nations (La Ronge) is in the north whereas four of the lowest ranked ones are. Not unexpectedly, remoteness and isolation do seem to play a role in level of business activity.

It has long been accepted that remoteness and isolation impose constraints on business and therefore economic development. Particularly significant are restricted access to: (i) markets, (ii) suppliers, (iii) a cost-effective and reliable transportation system, (iv) an appropriate labour force and (v) necessary government and non-government business support services. The La Ronge First Nation is the least disadvantaged of the northern Nations in these respects. The town of La Ronge is the administrative centre for northern Saskatchewan. By northern standards, it is well-served with banks, accounting firms, education institutions, and a full range of government services. It has good road access to

---

4 Among others, the following receive prominent mention: Chief Richard Gladue, Vice Chief Oniel Gladue and Executive Director Ray Ahenakew of the MLTC; Chiefs Miles Venne, Tom McKenzie and Harry Cook of the La Ronge First Nation and Dave MacIlmoyl and Al Solhiem of its Kitsaki Development Corporation; Lester Lafond and Chief Harry Lafond of the Muskeg Lake First Nation and Director of Economic Development Darrell Balkwill of the STC; and Chief Denton George of the Ochapowace First Nation.

southern markets and suppliers. The community has scheduled air service. The opposite in every respect is true for the four lower-ranked First Nations in the North.

A similar pattern of north-south performance is evident among the nine First Nations of the MLTC. The four members ranked above the median level in economic development activity are all in the southern part of the Tribal Council region. All are in or near the agricultural zone and are well-served by roads with good access to Meadow Lake and larger centres. All are within the prime supply area for both the saw and pulp mills in Meadow Lake. In contrast, the five MLTC Nations ranked below the median are further north. They are more poorly endowed in all aspects. In particular, they are at the northern edge of, or beyond, the current economic limit for forestry.

Location is not all bad for the First Nations of the North. With remoteness, a northern location brings increased opportunities to participate in resource-based development projects. The demand for forest and mineral resources, a change in corporate attitudes, land-claim results, and government requirements are all coming together to create a new environment favouring mutually beneficial alliances between First Nations and large resource companies.[5] The La Ronge First Nation was an early and successful participant in such alliances with multinational mining companies. Other members of the Prince Albert Grand Council are following suit. The foundation of the Meadow Lake Tribal Council's development activities is a network of forestry-based alliances with several partners. In addition, cultural and eco-tourism present opportunities for the more northerly and isolated First Nations, and several projects are under consideration.[6]

Beyond the effect of northern isolation just discussed, location, including relative proximity to an urban centre, seems to have had little impact on First Nations' economic development activities. To the north and west of Saskatoon, good and poor performers are equally represented and in close geographic proximity. Two of the top performers in the area are from the STC and one is from the BTC. One of the poor performers is from BTC, one is independent and the other is from the Confederation of Tribal Nations (CTN). To the south and east of Saskatoon, there is a string of six high performers (members of either the STC or TFHQ) and then a group of poor performers, members of the Yorkton and South East Tribal Councils or an independent. Based on this geographical distribution, Tribal Council affiliation and all that that says about respective approaches to development seems to be much more important than location to a First Nation's level of economic and business development activity, at least in the south of the province.

What about population, land base and education level? Do they offer an explanation for the difference in ranking between the high- and the low-performing First Nations? I analysed the data from the 1986 and 1991 censuses

---

5 See chapter 5 for a more detailed discussion.

6 As part of its coordinating and facilitating activities, the FSIN has established a tourism taskforce to investigate opportunities in this sector. As well, the MLTC has identified tourism as one of the sectors of opportunity in its 20-year economic development plan.

in search of an answer to this question. Usable figures were available for four low-ranked First Nations (Red Pheasant, Cowessess, Ahtahkakoop, and Sakimay) and five high-ranked groups (James Smith, Muskowekwan, Mistawasis, Kinistino, and Muskeg Lake).[7]

7.2.2.3. Population, Land Base and Education

Table 7–6 presents population data for the nine First Nations to be considered. Poor performers have, on average, a larger population than good performers — 415 to 301 in 1991. However, there are clear exceptions negating any association between size and performance. Sakimay, the smallest of the First Nations, is a poor performer while James Smith and Mistawasis, both good performers, are larger than several of the poor performers. In short, population does not appear to offer insight into the difference between the high and low performers.

The data on land-base size are surprising and somewhat counterintuitive (see Table 7–7). The lower-ranked Nations have a considerably larger land base on average than those ranked higher. The two highest ranked overall — Muskeg Lake and Kinistin — are by far the smallest in land area. Clearly a larger land base does not necessarily result in a higher level of economic activity. This calls into question the commonly held view among First Nations that they require an expanded land base as a foundation on which to build their economies. Land for land's sake does not appear to be the answer. On the other hand, strategically selected parcels, often as small as in the case Muskeg Lake's urban reserve, can have a huge impact on economic development.

TABLE 7–6: Low- versus High-Ranked First Nations by Population on Reserve

Low-Ranked FN	**Red Pheasant**	**Cowessess**	**Ahtahkakoop**	**Sakimay**		**Total**	**Average**
Population, 1981	460	342	927	105		1834	459
Population, 1986	394	377	953	151		1875	469
Population, 1991	308	379	824	147		1658	415
High-Ranked FN	**James Smith**	**Muskowekwan**	**Mistawasis**	**Kinistino**	**Muskeg Lake**	**Total**	**Average**
Population, 1981	349	265	413	235	260	1522	304
Population, 1986	370	250	465	169	223	1477	295
Population, 1991	395	296	448	186	180	1505	301

Source: The 1986 and 1991 Censuses of Canada.

7 For the remaining five top and six low-performing Nations, data for one or more of the categories for one or both years were not published.

TABLE 7–7: Low- versus High-Ranked First Nations by Land Base

Low-Ranked FN	**Red Pheasant**	**Cowessess**	**Ahtahkakoop**	**Sakimay**		**Total**	**Average**
Square Kilometers	97	116	181	90		485	121
High-Ranked FN	**James Smith**	**Muskowekwan**	**Mistawasis**	**Kinistino**	**Muskeg Lake**	**Total**	**Average**
Square Kilometers	60	62	126	33	50	331	66

Source: The 1986 and 1991 Censuses of Canada.

TABLE 7–8: Low- versus High-Ranked First Nations by Education Level

	1986 (%)		**1991 (%)**		**% Change**	
	Low	**High**	**Low**	**High**	**Low**	**High**
Less than grade 9	44	46	29	32	–37	–23
Grades 9–13 without secondary school certificate	28	38	29	27	–2	–22
Grades 9–13 with secondary school certificate	2	2	4	5	125	233
Trades certificate or diploma	2	1	2	3	–20	200
Other non-university education without diploma	7	5	4	8	–50	88
Other non-university education with diploma	10	2	11	11	9	450
University without degree	6	4	18	11	192	247
University with degree	2	1	2	3	0	150

Source: The 1986 and 1991 Censuses of Canada.

The role of education in the relative performance of the First Nations is the final question to be addressed using census data (see Table 7–8). As with location, population and land area, it appears that a relatively higher education level is not associated with a higher ranking in economic development activity. In 1986, 72% of the over 15-year-old population of the lower-ranked First Nations reported an education level of less than grade 12, while the figure for the higher-ranked First Nations was 84%. In 1991, the figure improved to 58% for those ranked lower and 59% for the higher ones. At the upper end of education levels, in 1986, 14% of those over 15 years old in the lower-ranked Nations had completed a post-secondary program of one type or other. Only 4% had done so among the higher-ranked ones. By 1991, this had changed remarkably. While the proportion with a completed post-secondary program remained virtually unchanged (an increase from 14% to 15%) among the lower-ranked First Nations, it had risen dramatically among the higher ranked — from 4% to 17%.

From this comparison of education levels, it is clear that the superior economic development performance of the higher-ranked Nations cannot be attributed even in part to a better-educated population. Instead, could it be that the superior improvement in education levels achieved by the people of the higher-ranked Nations between 1986 and 1991 can be attributed to some of the same things that account for their superior economic development during the same period; that is, leadership, planning and organization? It is interesting to note that it was during this period that many of the better organized and managed First Nations took control over their education systems.[8]

7.2.3. Summary

In conclusion, location, population, land base, and education do not explain the difference in economic development activity between the lower- and higher-ranked Nations. Instead, performance is contingent on leadership and the strategies adopted and actions taken at both the individual First Nation and Tribal Council level. This is consistent with the proposed contingency perspective which, in turn, is an extension of what Corbridge calls a powerful trend "towards theories of capitalist development which emphasize contingency ... a new emphasis on human agency and the provisional and highly skilled task of reproducing social relations" (Corbridge 1989, 633). These results are also consistent with the findings of Cornell and Kalt (1989) of the Harvard Project on American Indian Economic Development. Manley Begay, executive director of the project, referring to the work of these authors says that

> *some tribes were found to be constructing effective institutions and others were not as productive ... there is evidence that the tribes which have poor economic performance, lack institutions capable of effectively regulating both individual and collective behaviour.* (Begay 1991, 4–5)

7.3. Comparative Economic Development Results

Using 1986 and 1991 censuses data, I have made an attempt to see if the activities of the higher-ranked Nations have resulted in a change in their socioeconomic circumstances that was different from any change experienced by the lower-ranked ones. Household income, employment, unemployment and participation rates were considered. A word of caution is necessary. Even among the most active First Nations and Tribal Councils, organized and aggressive business

8 For example, see chapter 8 for a description of the MLTC's education-related activities.

development at any significant scale is a relatively new phenomenon. Since most of the commercial ventures by First Nations began in the mid-to-late 1980s, any impact they may have on individuals has only begun to be felt. Therefore, my comparison of the two sets of census data can only be expected to uncover possible emerging trends rather than major socioeconomic shifts. Any definitive assessment of the impact will have to await the publication of the 1996 Census data.

7.3.1. Household Income

Table 7–9 reports the average distribution of household income for the higher- and lower-ranked Nations for 1986 and 1991 and the percent change over the period. There is no remarkable difference in the distribution between the two groups in either year. However, the change over the period contains a hint of a difference. While the proportion reporting income below $20,000 declined by 40% and 41% for the low- and high-ranked groups respectively, there is a difference in the change in the proportion reporting incomes of $40,000 or higher. There was an 83% increase (from 6% to 11%) in the percentage of households in this income range among the high performers and only a 13% increase (from 8% to 9%) among the low ones. In actual numbers of households, the difference is even more pronounced. Among the lower-ranked Nations, the number of households reporting income above $40,000 remained the same at 30, while the number among those ranked higher doubled from 15 to 30, from 1986 to 1991. It will be interesting to see if this difference in performance at higher-income levels between the higher- and lower-ranked Nations will be confirmed by the 1996 data.

TABLE 7–9: Low- versus High-Ranked First Nations by Household Income

	1986 (%)		1991 (%)		% Change	
Household Income	**Low**	**High**	**Low**	**High**	**Low**	**High**
Under $10,000	30	34	23	26	–22	–24
$10,000 to $14,999	20	22	22	22	8	1
$15,000 to $19,999	20	18	15	15	–26	–18
$20,000 to $29,999	16	14	21	19	28	32
$30,000 to $39,999	7	6	11	7	57	23
$40,000 to $49,999	5	2	3	7	–45	270
$50,000 and over	3	4	6	4	100	0
Average income	$19,455	$18,200	$19,792	$18,840	2	4
Median income	$15,234	$14,455	$16,119	$15,629	6	8

Source: The 1986 and 1991 Censuses of Canada.

7.3.2. Labour Force and Participation, Employment and Unemployment Rates

In an attempt to assess employment-related performance, Table 7–10 presents potential and actual labour force, employment and unemployment figures for 1986 and 1991, as well as changes over the period. While it is too soon to confirm a real difference in performance between the high- and low-ranked Nations, interesting indications of such difference are present.

In 1986, the unemployment rate for the lower-ranked Nations was 28%, much lower than the 35% rate for the higher-ranked ones. By 1991, this situation had reversed. The unemployment rate had increased to 37% for the lower ranked groups and decreased to 29% for those ranked higher. Underlying this shift in percentage was a net decline of 45 (14%) in the number of people employed among the lower-ranked Nations and an increase of 55 (28%) among those employed in the higher-ranked group. This suggests a trend toward increasing employment opportunities among the higher-ranked First Nations.

The increase in participation rates was the same for both at 13%. However, there is an interesting difference in underlying this performance. Among the higher-ranked Nations, the increase in participation was matched by an increase in employment; that is there was no change in the number unemployed (100 people). Job creation was able to keep up with the growth in the labour market and perhaps even encouraged that growth. In contrast, among those ranked lower the number of unemployed increased by 27% (from 130 to 165 people) even though the labour force declined by 15 people over the same period. Again, there is a clear difference in performance in favour of the higher-ranked Nations. Will this difference in performance be confirmed by the 1996 Census data? Time will tell.

TABLE 7–10: Low- versus High-Ranked First Nations by Employment

	1986		1991		% Change	
	Low	High	Low	High	Low	High
Total 15 years and over	1130	845	970	890	–14	5
In the labour force	460	285	445	340	–3	19
Employed	330	200	285	255	–14	28
Unemployed	130	100	165	100	27	0
Participation rate	41%	34%	46%	38%	13	13
Unemployment rate	28%	35%	37%	29%	31	–16

Source: The 1986 and 1991 Censuses of Canada.

7.3.3. Summary: Comparative Performance, 1986 to 1991

While it is too soon to form a definite conclusion, the higher-ranked First Nations appear to be outperforming those ranked lower at least in terms of income and employment creation. The higher-ranked Nations are those with effective leadership, well-developed strategies and an organized approach to economic development. It seems that such an approach to development is paying dividends in terms of socioeconomic performance. It is also true that at least some First Nations that have been performing at a lower level are following the lead of these better performers. This is certainly the case for the Nations of the ACTC and the SETC, as well as several in the PAGC that are emulating the La Ronge First Nation.

7.4. Forms of Ownership, Markets and Business Size

This section presents a more detailed exploration of the results of my research into the business development activities of the First Nations in Saskatchewan begun in 1994 and concluded in 1996. This study investigated the issues of forms of ownership, market scale (local, regional and national/international) and business size.

My investigation of these issues builds on the material presented in sections 7.1 and 7.2. From these earlier sections it is apparent that there are clear differences in business development strategies among the First Nations. Some favour individual private ownership while others emphasize ownership by the First Nation. Still others concentrate on joint ventures, some through their Tribal Council and others outside their Tribal Council. Finally, some seem to pursue a balanced strategy with all ownership types evident. Similar differences are evident at the Tribal Council level. Are there reasons to assume that one strategy will be more likely than another to deliver the economic development benefits that all the First Nations seek? This is the question to be addressed in the remainder of this section.

7.4.1. Forms of Ownership

Table 7–11 provides information about the forms of non-farm business ownership arrangements from the perspective of the individual First Nation. Arrangements differ from and exceed the number of businesses. This is so because a single joint venture business is the result of several First Nations' decision to participate in a particular business arrangement. In fact, the 59 joint venture businesses reported by the First Nations in Saskatchewan were the result of 269 separate decisions by individual First Nations to enter into a business arrangement. When assessing First Nations business development activities, the number of arrangements is at least as important as the actual number of businesses resulting from them. Arrangements are important because they are the outcome of decisions taken by First Nations leaders and members to parti-

TABLE 7–11: Non-Farm Business Arrangements by Type of Ownership, 1995

Type of Ownership	Number of Arrangements	Proportion of Total (%)
FN Joint Venture with Others (not Tribal Council)	45	8
FN Joint Venture with Tribal Council	224	40
FN Total Joint Ventures	269	48
FN Owner of Businesses	116	21
Total Owned by First Nations	385	69
Individually Owned Businesses	173	31
Total Business Arrangements	558	100

TABLE 7–12: Non-Farm Businesses by Type of Ownership, 1995

Type of Ownership	Number of Businesses	Proportion of Total (%)
FN Joint Venture with Others (not Tribal Council)	36	10
FN Joint Venture with Tribal Council	23	7
FN Total Joint Ventures	59	17
FN Owner of Businesses	116	33
Total Owned by First Nations	175	50
Individually Owned Businesses	173	50
Total	348	100

cipate in particular business ventures. As such, they are the result of a particular First Nation implementing its business development strategy.

First Nations and their individual citizens are involved in 558 business arrangements. Of this total, 31% involve businesses owned and operated by First Nation individuals (private ownership). The remaining 69% of the arrangements involve First Nations' government ownership in one form or another. Joint ventures account for 70% of these government ownership arrangements and 48% of all business arrangements.

Table 7–12 reports the numbers of business (as opposed to arrangements) by type of ownership. Of the total 348 identified First Nation businesses, 59 or

17% are joint ventures while 33% are owned by individual First Nations. Taken together these numbers indicate that 50% of all businesses involve government (collective) ownership. The remaining 50% are owned by First Nation individuals. From the information about business ownership in Tables 7–12 and 7–13 as well as the material in the previous section, it is clear that the First Nations in Saskatchewan have adopted a planned, purposeful and collective approach to business development in which First Nation government ownership and joint ventures play a prominent role.

7.4.2. Market Scale and Ownership

Tables 7–13 and 7–14 delve more deeply into the nature of the First Nation businesses, in particular on the relationship between the form of business ownership and the geographic scale of the market (local, regional, national/international) that the business serves. The point in question is: Are some types of ownership arrangements more likely than others to allow the First Nations the access to national and international markets they seek as part of their approach described in chapter 2?

Businesses categorized as local are those that serve the citizens of a particular First Nation. Included are such things as school buses, medical transportation, water and septic services, firewood wood-hauling, and retail stores with annual sales under $100,000. Regional businesses include those intended to serve the First Nation and surrounding areas but not the larger national/international market. Included are retail stores with annual sales in excess of $100,000, golf courses, resorts, and road and home construction companies. The national/international category includes all businesses competing directly in the global economy. Most businesses in this category are either in the forestry, mining, petroleum, or agriculture sectors.

Results indicate that 18% of the First Nation business arrangements target national/international markets, 58% regional markets and 24% local markets (see Table 7–13). This is evidence of the external focus of First Nations as they identify opportunities and create businesses. Eighty-five percent of the national/international business are joint ventures. In addition, joint ventures account for 58% of all regional businesses. First Nation-owned businesses account for 6% and 18% of the national/international and regional categories respectively. Taken together, collective arrangements involving First Nations' government ownership (joint ventures and First Nation-owned) account for 91% of national/international and 76% of regional business arrangements. Businesses owned by First Nations individuals dominate the local category at 63%.

Table 7–14 shifts the focus from business arrangements by First Nations to the businesses that have emerged from these arrangements. Twelve percent of the First Nation businesses serve national/international markets; 49%, the regional market; and 39%, the local one. Joint venture companies account for 63% of the non-farm nation/international businesses and 20% of the regional ones, while 15% of national/international (non-farm) and 34% of the regional businesses are owned by individual First Nations. In combination, businesses owned in whole or in part by the government (joint ventures and individual First Nation-owned) account for 78% and 54% of the non-farm nation/interna-

TABLE 7–13: Non-Farm Business Arrangements by Type of Ownership and Market Scale, 1995

Market Scale	Joint Ventures		Owned by Individual First Nation	Owned by Individuals	Total	%
	Other	Tribal Council				
National/International	21	63	6	9	99	18
Regional	24	161	59	78	322	58
Local	0	0	51	86	137	24
Total	269		116	173	558	

TABLE 7–14: Non-Farm Businesses by Type of Ownership and Market Scale, 1995

Market Scale	Joint Ventures		Owned by Individual First Nation	Owned by Individuals	Total	%
	Other	Tribal Council				
National/International	18	7	6	9	40	12
Regional	18	16	59	78	171	49
Local	0	0	51	86	137	39
Total	59		116	173	348	

tional and regional businesses respectively. Businesses owned by First Nations individuals dominate the local market.

It is apparent that the First Nations in Saskatchewan have adopted an approach to development with an emphasis on First Nation-owned and joint venture businesses. Further, the majority of these collectively owned businesses compete in the regional, national and international markets, rather than in the local market. This is the ownership/market pattern that one would expect as an outcome of the approach to economic development described in chapter 2. Moving from the aggregate to specific First Nations and Tribal Councils, it follows that those groups that pursue a strategy of government ownership and/or joint ventures are more likely to be involved in business competing in the broader economy than those that do not.

A word of caution is necessary. In one sense, Tables 7–11 to 7–14 may under-report the number of businesses owned by First Nations individuals and therefore their relative importance in the First Nations economy. In my research, I relied on the knowledge of responders from the First Nation (chief, councilors and/or employees) about businesses owned by individuals from their group. The secondary sources (the FSIN and TransGas databases) were each compiled by consultants who relied on a variety of sources. With three researchers independently pursuing the same information most, but not likely all, of the businesses owned by First Nation individuals should have been identified. In another and offsetting sense, these results understate the significance of the role of First Nations' governments in the reported business arrangements and resulting businesses. Many of the businesses owned and operated by First Nations individuals were created with First Nations' government support to serve a community need. In fact, 71 of the privately owned businesses (36%) provide either school bus, medical transportation, water delivery or septic tank pump-out services to First Nations' citizens on behalf of, and largely paid for by, that First Nation government. With these two "sources of error" about individually owned businesses working in opposite directions, the net effect of these two should be minimal when considering the relative importance of collective and private ownership among First Nations.

The next aspect to be considered is business size. The question to be addressed is, Is one form of ownership more likely than another to be associated with larger businesses?

7.4.3. Business Size and Ownership

Information about annual sales was available for 168 of the businesses in the survey. Table 7–15 provides information about the distribution of each ownership type over the revenue categories. Table 7–16 reports the proportion of each ownership type in each revenue category.

Based on the data presented in Table 7–15, there is a relationship between form of ownership and business size as measured by annual revenue. The businesses owned by First Nation individuals are overwhelmingly small. Eighty-seven percent of these businesses reported estimated annual revenues of less than $100,000 in 1995. An additional 12% expected their revenues to be

TABLE 7–15: Revenue Distribution by Ownership, 1995

Estimated Annual Revenue (1994)	Owned by Individuals		Owned by Individual FN		Joint Ventures	
Less than $100,000	95	87%	11	33%	4	15%
$100,001 to $400,000	13	12%	10	30%	8	31%
$400,001 to $750,000	0	0%	4	12%	2	8%
$750,001 to $2,000,000	1	1%	5	15%	3	12%
Over $2,000,000	0	0%	3	9%	9	35%
Total	109		33		26	

TABLE 7–16: Ownership Distribution by Revenue, 1995

Estimated Annual Revenue (1994)	Owned by Individuals		Owned by Individual FN		Joint Ventures		Total
Less than $100,000	95	86%	11	10%	4	4%	110
$100,001 to $400,000	13	42%	10	32%	8	26%	31
$400,001 to $750,000	0	0%	4	67%	2	33%	6
$750,001 to $2,000,000	1	11%	5	56%	3	33%	9
Over $2,000,000	0	0%	3	25%	9	75%	12

between $100,000 and $400,000. Only one of the 109 businesses in this category reported estimated revenue of more than $400,000. First Nation-owned business exhibited a different pattern. They are larger than those owned by individuals, with 67% reporting revenues greater than $100,000 and 36% revenues above $400,000. Finally, joint ventures are the largest. Eighty-five percent expected revenues greater than $100,000; 55%, revenues greater than $400,000; and 47%, revenues greater than $750,000. In contrast, only 24% of First Nation-owned business and 1% of individually owned ones projected revenues over $750,000.

Table 7–16 explores the relationship between size and type of ownership further. One hundred and ten businesses reported revenues of less than $100,000. Of this total, 86% were owned by First Nation individuals, 10% by individual First Nations and 4% were joint ventures. For those with revenues between $100,000 and $400,000, the distribution was 42%, 32% and 26% for individually owned, First Nation-owned and joint venture businesses respectively. A marked shift in the ownership distribution pattern becomes evident in the next category. Sixty-seven percent of the businesses in the category $400,001 to $750,000 were owned by individual First Nations and 33% were joint ventures. None was owned by individuals. The pattern is similar for the next category with 56% being individual First Nation-owned and 33% joint ventures. One individual owned a business in this category. Finally, joint ventures accounted for 75% of the businesses with revenue over $2,000,000. The remaining 25% were owned by individual First Nations. None was owned by individuals.

From the results reported in Tables 7–15 and 7–16, it is apparent that the type of businesses favoured by the First Nations' approach to development — First Nation-owned and/or joint ventures — are the largest in terms of revenue. This augurs well for the ability of these businesses to deliver the employment and other socioeconomic benefits sought by the First Nations. It also suggests that the First Nations and Tribal Councils that are higher ranked in these categories of ownership should outperform (in terms of income, job creation, and other factors) those that are ranked lower.

7.4.4. Economic Impact and Ownership

Tables 7–17 and 7–18 summarize the relative importance of each ownership type to the First Nations' business economy. It is not the number of businesses in a category that determines that category's contribution to economic development. Rather it is the aggregate economic impact of all the businesses in the category that matters. In the material that follows, a two-step process is used to determine the economic contribution of the businesses in each ownership category.

First, the weighted average level of annual revenue is calculated for each ownership category (see Table 7–17). These averages are individually owned, $86,000; First Nation-owned, $552,000; and joint ventures, $983,000. Second, an estimated total annual revenue figure is determined for each category of ownership by multiplying the average revenue for each category by the number of businesses in that category (see Table 7–18).

Joint ventures, which constitute only 17% of First Nation businesses, account for 42% of the total estimated annual revenue. Businesses owned by individual First Nations, 33% of the total businesses, contribute 47% of the estimated revenue. Businesses owned by First Nations individuals contribute only 11% of the total estimated revenue in spite of the fact that they account for 50% of the businesses. Remembering the earlier caveat about the possible under-reporting of individually owned businesses, it is nonetheless clear that collectively owned businesses (by individual First Nations and in joint ventures) dominate the First Nations' business economy in Saskatchewan. These businesses are being created as a result of the planned and purposeful development efforts of the First Nations in Saskatchewan.

In summary, four points from this and the three preceding subsections need emphasis:

1. Fifty percent of all First Nation businesses in Saskatchewan involve government ownership or are joint ventures (collective ownership).

TABLE 7–17: Weighted Average Annual Revenue, 1995

Individually Owned Businesses

Annual Revenue Range (1994)	Median Revenue ($)	Owned by FN Individuals	Total Revenue ($)
Less than $100,000	50,000	95	4,750,000
$100,001 to 400,000	250,000	13	3,250,000
$400,001 to 750,000	575,000	0	0
$750,001 to 2,000,000	1,375,000	1	1,375,000
Over $2,000,000	2,000,000	0	0
Total		109	9,375,000
Weighted Average Revenue			86,000

TABLE 7–17 (continued)

Individual First Nation-Owned Businesses

Annual Revenue Range (1994)	Median Revenue ($)	Owned by Individual FN	Total Revenue ($)
Less than $100,000	50,000	11	550,000
$100,001 to 400,000	250,000	10	2,500,000
$400,001 to 750,000	575,000	4	2,300,000
$750,001 to 2,000,000	1,375,000	5	6,875,000
Over $2,000,000	2,000,000	3	6,000,000
Total		33	18,225,000
Weighted Average Revenue			552,000

Joint Ventures

Annual Revenue Range (1994)	Median Revenue ($)	Joint Ventures	Total Revenue ($)
Less than $100,000	50,000	4	200,000
$100,001 to 400,000	250,000	8	2,000,000
$400,001 to 750,000	575,000	2	1,150,000
$750,001 to 2,000,000	1,375,000	3	4,125,000
Over $2,000,000	2,000,000	9	18,000,000
Total		26	25,475,000
Weighted Average Revenue			980,000

TABLE 7–18: Contribution to the First Nation's Economy by Ownership Type, 1995

	Owned by Individuals	Owned by Individual FN	Joint Ventures	Total
Average Annual Revenue	$ 86,000	$ 552,000	$ 980,000	—
Number of Businesses	173	116	59	348
Total Annual Revenue	$14,878,000	$64,032,000	$57,820,000	$137,942,000
Proportion of Annual Revenue	11%	47%	42%	—

2. Seventy-six percent of all Saskatchewan First Nations' businesses compete in the region, national and international markets.
3. Ninety-six percent of the Saskatchewan First Nations' businesses earning revenues greater than $400,000 per year are government-owned or joint ventures (collective ownership).
4. Eighty-nine percent of the estimated total annual revenue of Saskatchewan First Nations' business economy in Saskatchewan is earned by government-owned businesses or joint ventures (collective ownership).

Clearly, in aggregate the First Nations and Tribal Councils in Saskatchewan have adopted a collective approach toward creating businesses to compete in the regional and national/international markets with a strong emphasis on joint ventures. In financial terms, these businesses overwhelmingly dominate the First Nations' business economy in Saskatchewan. This outcome is entirely consistent with the First Nations approach to development described in chapter 2.

7.4.5. Ownership, Market Scale, Business Size and Economic Development Success

First Nations and Tribal Councils in Saskatchewan differ as to the extent that they are following a collective (government-owned and joint venture) approach toward creating business to compete in the regional and national/international markets. Based on my research into ownership and business size, First Nations that pursue a balanced strategy with above-median activity in all categories ownership and those that pursue a strategy that emphasizes First Nation-owned and/or joint ventures usually outperform those that emphasize individual ownership.

Consider the First Nation rankings (see Table 7–4). The James Smith, Sweetgrass, Muskeg Lake, Mistawasis and La Ronge First Nations all rank in the top 10 in economic development activity. However, their ownership strategies differ. The first four each rank first or second in businesses owned by First Nations individuals. All four also rank at or above the median level for First Nation-owned businesses. Muskeg Lake ranks well above the median level for joint ventures while James Smith and Sweetgrass rank below and Mistawasis just at the median. In contrast to these four, the La Ronge First Nation ranks well below the median level in individually owned business. It ranks first in joint ventures and at the median level for First Nation-owned businesses. It follows from my research that the strategies of Muskeg Lake and La Ronge First Nations should be the most successful (in terms of revenue, jobs, and others) and James Smith's and Sweetgrass's the least. Mistawasis's results should fall in the middle.

The same differences in approach can be found at the aggregate level among the top five Tribal Councils. The STC's ranking reflects a balanced strategy that places it first in First Nation-owned businesses, second in joint ventures and second in individually owned businesses. The BTC (second overall) emphasizes individual ownership, ranking first in that category. It ranks well below the median level in joint ventures and at the median level in First Nation-owned business. TFHQ's strategy emphasizes joint ventures. It ranks first in that category and third and seventh in individually owned and First

Nation-owned businesses respectively. The PAGC shows a balance between joint ventures and individually owned, ranking fourth in both. It ranks sixth in First Nation-owned businesses. Finally, the MLTC ranks third in joint ventures and third in First Nation-owned businesses. It ranks seventh in individually owned businesses. As with individual First Nations, Tribal Councils emphasizing a strategy of joint ventures and First Nation-owned businesses competing in broader markets should outperform those emphasizing individually owned businesses. Based on this, the businesses of the STC, MLTC and TFHQ should outperform the PAGC and the BTC in terms of revenue, job creation and the like.

A comparison of 1986 to 1991 censuses data is inconclusive with respect to the relative performance of the top ranked First Nations and Tribal Councils. This is not surprising because the ownership strategies and income projections described reflect the strategies and actions of the late 1980s and the early 1990s. A meaningful comparison of the resulting relative performance will therefore have to wait for the 1996 census data and even then it might be too soon to capture the differences in outcome flowing from the alternative approaches. It will also be interesting to see if a strategy of First Nation government ownership and joint ventures becomes more prevalent over time as one would expect if the results achieved are in fact superior. Some evidence of the superior financial performance of joint ventures and larger businesses and the spread of both types of ownership is provided in the next section of this chapter and in chapter 8.

7.5. First Nations Business Performance to Date

Assuming that the Aboriginal approach to development is theoretically sound, its success in a particular place at a particular time depends on the creation and operation of profitable businesses. The purpose of this section is to evaluate the financial success and long-term survivability of Aboriginal businesses in order to assess the likelihood of the Aboriginal development process achieving its objectives. Such information is difficult to obtain for individual businesses. However, a useful and reasonably objective indication about the overall financial performance of First Nations businesses in Saskatchewan can be obtained from three sources.

The first two sources are the records of two First Nation-controlled financial institutions — the Saskatchewan Indian Equity Foundation (SIEF) and Peace Hills Trust (PHT). The SIEF is an Aboriginal Capital Corporation (ACC). It is the oldest and largest of the 30 such institutions operating in Canada. Since 1986, the organization has made over 2,000 loans to First Nation businesses in Saskatchewan that have created an estimated 7,000 jobs. PHT is a full-service trust company owned by the Samson First Nation from Alberta. The third source is a report on the Aboriginal Economic Development Program prepared for the federal Department of Industry, Science and Technology.

7.5.1. Saskatchewan Indian Equity Foundation and Peace Hills Trust

Both the SIEF and PHT lend to First Nation-owned businesses. The SIEF operates exclusively in Saskatchewan while PHT operates in all the western provinces. According to Tony Shirt, PHT's Saskatchewan manager, loan performance in Saskatchewan mirrors that of the trust company as a whole. Both SIEF and PHT report loan-loss figures in their audited annual reports. These loan-loss figures provide an indication about the performance of Indian-owned businesses in two ways. First, in any given year the loan-loss rate of these institutions can be compared with those of institutions lending to non-First Nation businesses providing insight into the relative performance of First Nation and non-First Nation businesses. Second, trends in the institutions' loss rates over time can be examined to determine if the financial performance of their First Nation business customers is improving or declining.

In recent annual reports, both institutions proudly declare that their loss rates compare favourably with the rates of non-Indian institutions. The SIEF says that it has "one of the lowest loan loss ratios in the ACC framework. This fact has made us competitive with Trust Companies, Banks and Credit Unions" (SIEF 1995, 6). With respect to the trend in loan loss over time, the same annual report (SIEF 1995, 17) shows that SIEF's loss rate has declined steadily over time from a high of 6.7% in 1990 to 1.15% in 1995. This is evidence of a steady improvement in the financial performance of its First Nations' business clients. Similarly, Peace Hills Trust in its 1992 Annual Report states that its loan portfolio "continues to operate very soundly with provisions for loss for the year amounting to $216,922 or .2%, well under the industry average" (PHT 1992, 2). According to subsequent annual reports, the loss rate on PHT's loan portfolio has remained at or below the industry average indicating continuing average or above average performance by its business customers. Based on the records of these two institutions, the financial performance of Indian-owned businesses in Saskatchewan compares favourably to that of non-Indian business.

7.5.2. Aboriginal Business Canada

In 1994, Aboriginal Business Canada (a division of the Federal Department of Industry and Science) commissioned a study to assess the financial performance and employment creation of firms that had obtained financing under the Aboriginal Business Development Program. The study evaluated the performance of over 350 Aboriginal-owned firms from across Canada that had been in existence for two years or more. Result of the study indicate that

> *Aboriginal businesses are surviving at very high rates — higher in fact than other Canadian businesses. These businesses are creating a significant amount of jobs as well.*
>
> (Aboriginal Business Canada 1995, 1)

The average number of employees per active firm was found to be seven, with half employed on- and half off-reserve. The report also indicated that

- *Construction and retail businesses did especially well.*
- *There was no measurable difference in the rate of survival between businesses located in the cities versus those in rural and remote locations.*
- *A profitable business in a remote location ... is more likely to be very profitable compared to a business located in the city.*

(Aboriginal Business Canada 1995, 1)

According to the study, the size of the business and the form of ownership played a critical role in financial success. Only 12% of the businesses with revenues greater than $200,000 experienced significant losses while 55% of those with revenues less than $200,000 experienced such losses. In addition, joint ventures between Aboriginal and non-Aboriginal partners were found to be more successful than non-joint venture businesses. These two findings are particularly significant given the results of my research reported in sections 7.3.3 and 7.3.4. Businesses with revenue over $200,000 and joint ventures account for 89% of the estimated annual revenue of the First Nation businesses in Saskatchewan. This shows that the First Nations in Saskatchewan are focusing their efforts on the size of business and forms of ownership that are most likely to succeed.

It is apparent from the information from SIEF, PHT and ABC that the strategy the Aboriginal people are adopting across Canada is working. The businesses created by the implementation of this strategy are competing successfully and profitably in local, and more importantly, regional, national and international markets. While individual business failures are inevitable, they are no more likely to occur among Aboriginal businesses than among those owned by others. Given this, there is no insurmountable reason why Aboriginal people in Canada cannot attain employment and income levels comparable to those found in the Canadian economy at large, if they so desire. On the other hand, there is no guarantee that they will. Capacity, the subject of the next section (as well as chapter 4), will play a key role in the realization of this potential.

7.6. Capacity Building

The Aboriginal people in Saskatchewan have not neglected capacity building in their struggle for economic development. Perhaps, the most significant, which is the pursuit of land and resources is ongoing and has been described in chapter 4. Two other areas of capacity building — education and financial institution building — are worthy of note and are discussed in the following subsections.

7.6.1. Education

The First Nations in Saskatchewan are recognized leaders in education capacity building. The FSIN has created two post-secondary institutions — the Saskatchewan Indian Institute of Technologies (SIIT) and the Saskatchewan Indian Federated College (SIFC). The Metis have created Gabriel Dumont Institute. All offer certificate, diploma and, in SIFC's case, undergraduate and graduate degree programs in economic development and business administration. In addition, all three institutions offer noncredit programs that provide training and direct support (e.g. assistance in the preparation of business plans) to Aboriginal development activities and business ventures. The number of students entering these institutions' business programs has been growing steadily. There are now at least 175 Aboriginal students in the administration and commerce diploma and degree programs of the SIFC and 125 in the business diploma programs offered by the SIIT. A similar number are enrolled at Gabriel Dumont's. As well, in the fall of 1996 the first group of students was admitted to a First Nations Masters of Business Administration Program jointly offered by the SIFC and the University of Saskatchewan. The SIFC is currently developing two new undergraduate programs. One is in Aboriginal banking in partnership with the Canadian Bankers Association. The other is in tourism in conjunction with the Canadian Aboriginal Tourism Association.

Similar education-related capacity building efforts are underway elsewhere in Canada. For example, the Council for the Advancement of Native Development Officers (CANDO) is forming a country-wide consortium of post-secondary educational institutions interested in offering a two-year "Native Economic Development Diploma." CANDO is also developing a professional certification process similar to that found in the accounting profession. Candidates with suitable education (i.e. the two year diploma or equivalent) and sufficient practical experience will have the opportunity to complete a "professional module" and then be certified as a professional "economic developer."

The continuing growth in the number of First Nation individuals with post-secondary economic development and business management education can only increase the capacity for business development success in the future.

7.6.2. Financial Institutions

In addition to the two post-secondary institutions, the First Nations in Saskatchewan have created other institutions in support of economic development. The most important of these is the Saskatchewan Indian Equity Foundation. As noted earlier, between 1986 and the end of its 1994–95 fiscal year, the SIEF has made more than 2,000 loans to Indian businesses and in doing so helped create 7,000 jobs. According to Clive Diller, the SIEF's general manager, loan demand continues to grow with applications for the first six months of 1996–97 totalling an estimated $34,000,000. To put this number in perspective, the SIEF's entire loan capital is $7,000,000 with all but $500,000 of that amount already loaned out as of March 1996. This critical shortfall in financing capacity must be addressed if the First Nations' business development strategy is to succeed. In Saskatchewan, this capacity issue is being addressed on two fronts — continued financial institution building and the realization of treaty and Aboriginal rights.

To build the capacity to meet the demand for business financing and to broaden the range of financial services available to Aboriginal customers, the FSIN (through SIEF) has entered into a joint venture with the Toronto Dominion Bank to create the First Nations Bank of Canada. Beginning in December 1996, this chartered bank will operate nationally, independent of the SIEF. It will have three classes of shares. Ownership of the voting common shares will be restricted to Aboriginal people and institutions (Status, Non-Status, Metis and Inuit). Nonvoting Preferred "A" Shares will be available to the general public. The Toronto Dominion Bank will own the voting Preferred "B" Shares. Initially, $2,000,000 in equity capital will be raised from the sale of Common Shares to FSIN/SIEF and $8,000,000 from the sale of Preferred B Shares to Toronto Dominion Bank. In addition, Toronto Dominion Bank will provide a $150,000,000 guarantee in order to secure deposit insurance protection for the new bank's customers. Over time as additional Aboriginal investors come forward, the Class "B" Preferred Shares will be retired and Common Shares issued reducing the bank's ownership position and increasing that of Aboriginal people. Under the terms of the joint venture agreement, after 10 years, control of the bank must be shifted entirely to Aboriginal investors through their ownership of the voting Common Shares. The Toronto Dominion Bank can remain a preferred shareholder and continue to provide management, cheque-clearing, computer networking and other services on a "fee-for-service" basis. Toronto Dominion Bank is making this considerable investment in a partnership with Aboriginal people for business reasons. They believe this to be the best way they can profitably participate in the rapidly expanding Aboriginal economy.

The First Nations Bank of Canada will accept deposits from all sources but will target Aboriginal customers. Of particular interest are (i) current First Nations institutions and governments and their existing and emerging activities and programs, (ii) First Nations businesses, (iii) the large and growing pool of capital from treaty land entitlement and other settlements, and (iv) non-First Nations companies doing significant business in "Indian Country."[9] The third item is particularly significant. The recently concluded Treaty Land Entitlement process in Saskatchewan will make $522-million available to 27 First Nations over the next 12 years. The land claims process is not unique to the TLE First Nations in Saskatchewan. Other First Nations in Saskatchewan are pursuing specific claims. Elsewhere in the country there are numerous land claims under negotiation, with those in British Columbia being particularly noteworthy.[10]

Deposits raised from such sources will provide the bank with the capital necessary to make loans to existing and new Aboriginal businesses across Canada. The bank's marketing projections for deposits and resulting loans are confidential but conservative expectations suggest a many-fold increase in the dollars available for loans to Aboriginal customers in Saskatchewan and elsewhere in Canada. The FSIN/Toronto Dominion Bank initiative has not escaped the notice of the other chartered banks. They are not prepared to yield the lucrative First Nation market to the First Nations Bank of Canada by default.[11]

---

9 According to Barry Maneri, the newly appointed president of the First Nations Bank of Canada, they have already been approached by several non-First Nation businesses interested in setting up accounts. The most notable to date has been Ontario Hydro which plans to set up an account valued in the tens of millions of dollars in support of the business it does with Aboriginal customers.

10 See chapter 4.

11 For example, see a description of the Bank of Montreal's programs in chapter 5.

7.7. Summary and Conclusion

My research summarized in this chapter supports the conclusion that the development activities of the First Nations in Saskatchewan are consistent with the eight characteristics of the emerging First Nations approach economic development as described in chapter 2.

The majority of the First Nations in Saskatchewan have community and/or economic development plans that established development goals and adopted strategies for the attainment of these goals. The pursuit of economic self-sufficiency in the support of self-government and the improvement of socio-economic conditions occupy prominent places in these goals. The extent of ownership by First Nations' government as opposed to individual ownership is evidence of a collective or national approach. Further, my research confirms that the First Nations in Saskatchewan are focusing on the ownership of profitable business competing in local, and particularly regional and national/international markets. Joint ventures play a prominent role. These businesses are being created as part of well-founded development plans at the First Nation, Tribal Council and FSIN levels. Beyond business creation, these plans include capacity-building strategies that have resulted in the building of educational financial institution and the pursuit of land claims and other Aboriginal rights.

My research also indicates that the development activities and outcomes of the First Nations in Saskatchewan are consistent with my contingency perspective as proposed in chapter 3. The First Nations acknowledge the necessity of participation in the global economy and are creating a mode of development for doing so that is consistent with their values, cultures, institutions and practices. First Nations are clearly taking advantage of the characteristics of the new flexible regime of accumulation as they form alliances and partnerships with other participants in the global economy. The prevalence of joint ventures indicates that they (the First Nations) are anticipating, and others are exhibiting, behaviour consistent with the Doctrine of Domicile. Because of the size of each individual Nation (its local or community scale) and traditional practices, the people at the "grassroots" level (the civil sector) remain actively involved in all facets of the development process and are able to, and do, intervene forcefully in the process if the activities or results are deemed unsatisfactory.[12] Finally, through Tribal Councils and the FSIN, First Nations have established supra-local mechanisms and institutions to encourage cooperation and reduce destructive competition, among themselves.[13]

---

12 See chapter 8 for a discussion of the role of the civil sector in the forestry activities of the Meadow Lake Tribal Council.

13 A very recent example is the Saskatchewan Indian Gaming Authority established by the FSIN to manage all Indian gaming operations in the province. A stated objective of the FSIN in establishing the Authority is to avoid a proliferation of Indian-owned casinos and damaging competition among them. Instead, the Authority is charged with seeing that all 70 First Nations (regardless of location) share in the benefits of four Indian-owned casinos.

Results to date suggest that the approach to development adopted by the First Nations in Saskatchewan is working. Their business development activities have been modestly successful. While the scale of the activities has been too small and their implementation too recent to have had a significant impact on the socioeconomic conditions of their members, a foundation has been created upon which future growth can occur.

Increased loan capital from the new First Nations Bank of Canada and from other financial institutions responding to this competitive challenge will improve the access to capital for First Nations' businesses. Increased human capital in the form of an educated workforce will help ensure the continued effective performance of collectively and privately owned businesses. Physical and financial resources acquired through of land claims settlements will also have a profound impact. As these capacity building efforts take effect, it seems reasonable to expect strong growth in the number and size of successful First Nations businesses and a related large increase in jobs and other economic benefits as well.

Finally, it is likely that the same pattern of ownership will continue for three reasons. First, the pattern is the natural outcome of the First Nations' approach to development described in chapter 2. Second, the investment of financial compensation from land claims settlements by First Nations in economic development activities will ensure a continuing significant role for First Nation-owned businesses. Third, joint ventures should remain a preferred strategy for First Nations for a number of reason including (i) the continuing need to acquire expertise and technology in particular industries, (ii) the need to access national and international markets, (iii) the opportunity to diversify and reduce risk by spreading limited (although increased) investment capital over a number of businesses and industrial sectors, and (iv) the increasing attractiveness of First Nations as partners to non-First Nation companies because of increasing First Nations' control over land and resources.

7

8

Economic Development Activities of the Meadow Lake Tribal Council

This chapter is a case study of the economic development activities of the Meadow Lake Tribal Council (MLTC) and its nine-member First Nations. My purpose is to offer a richer and more detailed picture of the development activities of these Nations that will provide additional insight into the Aboriginal approach to economic development and its likely outcomes.

The chapter begins with a description of the study area — its geographical location, communities as well as people and their demographic and socioeconomic characteristics. Using the 1986 Census data, attention is drawn to the significant differences between the socioeconomic circumstances of the people of the MLTC First Nations and the other people of the study area, and of the province as a whole. After this overview, attention shifts to the MLTC and its efforts to improve the socioeconomic circumstances of the people of its member First Nations.

The discussion of the MLTC's development efforts begins with a review of the Tribal Council's history and a description of its structure, mission, and development objectives and activities between 1986 and 1991. Socioeconomic data from the 1991 Census are compared with those from the 1986 Census to determine the impact of the MLTC's development efforts during that period.

Next, considerable attention is devoted to the MLTC's economic development activities in the forestry sector (particularly following 1991) and the preparation and content of its 20-year economic development plan entitled *From Vision to Reality* (MLTC, 1995b. These two subjects are interrelated. Forestry activities have been pursued as a key element of the Tribal Council's emerging and evolving development strategy. As the MLTC gained experience in forestry related and other economic development activities, it became apparent to them that they needed to undertake a more formal consultative planning process to determine development goals and to develop strategies for attaining those goals; hence, the preparation of the 20-year plan.

The forestry activities of the MLTC, centring as they do on a joint venture with a non-First Nation pulp and paper company, and the development of its

20-year plan provide an excellent example of the Aboriginal approach to economic development in action and further validation of proposed contingency perspective on development.

8.1. Study Area and Subjects

The study area is defined by the boundaries of the Meadow Lake Tribal Council (see Figure 8–1). The Nations of the MLTC are located in the Churchill River Basin.[1] The southern part of the MLTC territory is drained by the Beaver River and its tributaries (in particular the Waterhen and Meadow Rivers), into Lac Ile-a-La-Crosse. The northern section is drained by a number of rivers into La Loche, Turnor, Peter Pond and Churchill Lakes, which in turn drain into Lac Ile-a-La-Crosse and the Churchill River proper.

There are nine First Nations in MLTC, four Dene and five Cree (see Table 8–1). At the end of 1993, according to the MLTC, the total population of these First Nations was about 8,000, "with 3,907 living on their own reserve, 466 living on another reserve, and 3,275 living off reserve" (MLTC 1995b, iii). According to the 1986 Census, the reported on-reserve population of the nine was 4,972, up from 4,334 in the 1981 census.

Within the geographic boundaries of the MLTC there are also a number of non-First Nation communities and three rural municipalities (see Table 8–2). According to the 1986 Census, the non-First Nation population totalled 16,637 (9,923 in the south and 6,714 in the north). The demographic and socioeconomic conditions of the people living in the MLTC region are described in greater detail in the next section.

TABLE 8–1: MLTC First Nations

Cree First Nations	Dene First Nations
Canoe Lake	Birch Narrows
Flying Dust	Buffalo River
Island Lake	Clearwater River
Makwa Sahgaiehcan	English River
Waterhen Lake	

1 The far north of the MLTC District is drained by the Clearwater River, part of the Athabaska system. However, none of the reserves of the nine MLTC Nations are located that far north, nor are any currently economically viable timber blocks.

FIGURE 8–1: The Meadow Lake Tribal Council District

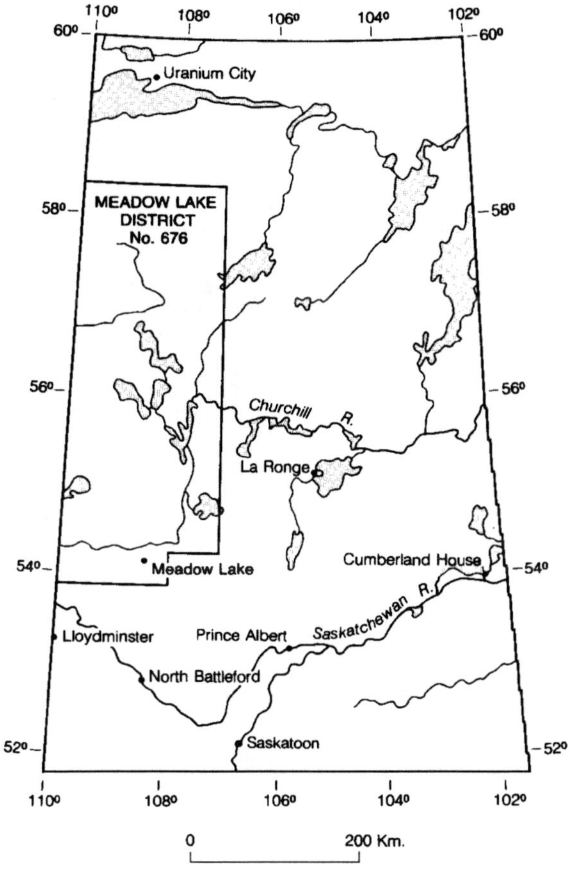

Source: Anderson and Bone 1995a, 126.

8.2. The Demographic and Socioeconomic Conditions

Information about the socioeconomic conditions of the people living within the study area has been drawn from the 1986 Census. The 1986 data are superior to that from 1991 because they deal with socioeconomic conditions as they were before the described development activities were undertaken.

TABLE 8–2: Non-First Nation Communities

South Urban (Towns, Villages and Hamlets)	Rural Municipalities
Meadow Lake	Meadow Lake #588
Gregg Lake	Loon Lake #561
Makwa	Beaver River # 622
Loon Lake	
Goodsoil	
Pierceland	
North (Villages and Hamlets)	
Green Lake	Patuanak
Cole Bay	Buffalo Narrows
Jans Bay	St. Georges Hill
Beauval	Michel Village
Pinehouse	La Loche
Ile a La Crosse	Turnor Lake

The communities within census divisions of the study area have been divided into four categories. The first category is "southern urban" and the second is "southern rural municipalities," where southern is defined by census division codes in the 17,000s. The third category is "northern villages and hamlets" (census district codes in the 18,000s). The fourth category is "First Nations" (Indian Bands), consisting of two sub-categories: (i) "southern First Nations" (CSD codes in the 17,800s) and (ii) "northern First Nations" (CSD codes in the 18,800s). Values for various socioeconomic variables for each census division within each category were combined and, when necessary, a weighted average calculated (e.g. household income) to arrive at the value for each variable for each of the community categories. The values for each variable for each category were then converted to proportions to permit comparisons among the categories of communities.

As a first step, chi-square test analysis was used to compare the socioeconomic data for the categories of communities with one another in various combinations. In all the combinations compared, the results indicate that there is a significant difference between the categories of communities for all the socioeconomic measures considered. The degree of difference varied. The least differences were between the northern villages and hamlets and northern reserves, among three Aboriginal categories, and between the two non-Aboriginal categories. The greatest difference appeared when all five categories were compared together, indicating a significant difference between the two more similar subcategories (Aboriginal and non-Aboriginal). In the subsequent description and

TABLE 8–3: Population in 1981 and 1986

	Population			
	1986	1981	Growth (%)	Aboriginal Origin (%)
Non-Aboriginal				
Rural Municipalities	4,676	4,694	–0.38	7
Town, Villages & Hamlets — South	5,247	5,029	4.30	22
Total Non-Aboriginal	9,923	9,723	2.06	15
Aboriginal				
Town, Villages & Hamlets — North	6,714	5,522	21.59	93
First Nations	4,972	4,334	14.72	99
Total Aboriginal	11,686	9,856	18.57	96
Study Area	21,609	19,579	10.37	59
Province	1,009,613	968,313	4.27	

Source: 1986 Census.

analysis, data for First Nations and northern villages and hamlets (the two Aboriginal categories) will be compared to each other and to the average of the data for the two non-Aboriginal categories and to data for the province as a whole.

Table 8–3 presents basic information about the population for the region in total and for the four categories. Two characteristics of the area's population are particularly worthy of note. First, and not surprisingly, the data indicate that the people of the rural municipalities and of the town, villages and hamlets in the southern part of the study area are predominately non-Aboriginal (93% and 78% respectively), while the people of the First Nations and the northern villages and hamlets are overwhelmingly Aboriginal (99% and 96% respectively). For the study area as a whole, almost 60% of the population is of Aboriginal ancestry.

The second item of note from Table 8–3 is the rate of population growth from 1981 to 1986. The rate for the region as a whole is 10.4%, well above the provincial average of 4.3%. Significantly, there is a great difference between rates of population growth of the Aboriginal and non-Aboriginal communities. From 1981 to 1986, the Aboriginal population increased by 18.6% (more than four times the provincial rate), while the non-Aboriginal population grew by only 2.1% (half the provincial rate).

The difference in the growth rates between Aboriginal and non-Aboriginal groups is reflected in the age distributions of their populations (see Figure 8–2). In 1986, 44% of the people of the region's First Nations and 38% of the

FIGURE 8–2: Age Distribution, 1986

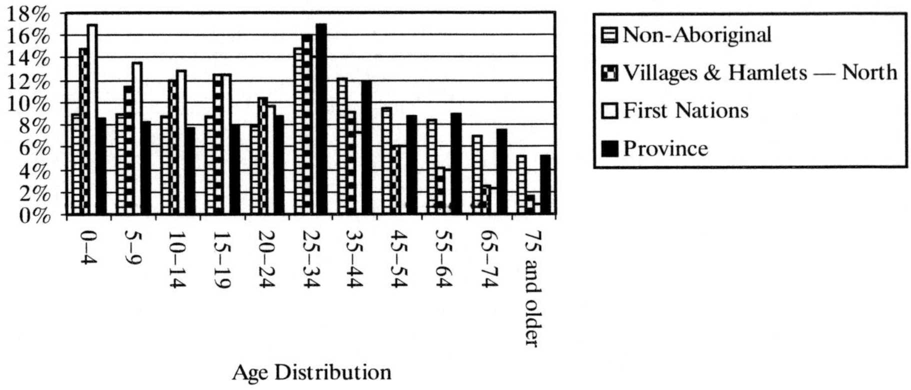

people of the northern villages and hamlets were under 15 years old. In contrast, only 27% of the people of the non-Aboriginal groups were under 15. The figure for the province as a whole was 25%. A similar difference exists at the older end of the age distribution. For both the province and the non-Aboriginal people of the study area, 20% of the population was older than 54. In contrast, only 7% for the population of Aboriginal ancestry was over that age. The youthfulness of the First Nation population and the high growth rate have obvious and significant implications. The most important of these is the looming growth in the potential labour force and resulting pressure on the already very high levels of unemployment.

Table 8–4 provides information about employment patterns within the study area. A clear difference is evident between the pattern for people who are of Aboriginal ancestry and those who are not. The population 15 years and older for each group is similar (6,955 for the former and 7,230 for the latter). However, only 38% of the people of the First Nations participated in the labour force, whereas 66% of non-Aboriginal people and 52% of the residents of northern villages and hamlets did. The difference in employment pattern between Aboriginal and non-Aboriginal people in the study area extends beyond participation rates to the unemployment rates. According to the 1986 Census, 33% of the people in the First Nation workforce were unemployed (32% in the northern villages and hamlets). This compares very unfavourably with the 9% unemployment rate for non-Aboriginal people.

Taken together the participation rate and unemployment rate for each group tell a graphic tale. In 1986, 68% of the potential non-Aboriginal labour force (age 15) of the study area was employed. The percentages for the two Aboriginal categories were drastically lower — 35% for northern villages and hamlets and only 26% for First Nations. This already highly unsatisfactory situation has the potential to deteriorate sharply, given the high rate of popula-

TABLE 8–4: Labour Force Participation and Unemployment Rates, 1986

	Rural Municipalities	Town, Villages & Hamlets — South	Non-Aboriginal	Town, Villages & Hamlets — North	First Nations	Aboriginal	Study Area	Province
Population 15 years and older	3,405	3,825	7,230	4,145	2,810	6,955	14,185	751,090
In the labour force	2,495	2,270	4,765	2,140	1,070	3,210	7,975	501,750
Employed	2,300	2,055	4,355	1,440	720	2,160	6,515	461,515
Unemployed	195	220	415	695	350	1,045	1,460	40,225
Participation rate	73%	59%	66%	52%	38%	46%	6%	67%
Unemployment rate	8%	10%	9%	32%	33%	33%	18%	8%
% of Population 15 years and older employed	68%	53%	60%	35%	26%	31%	46%	61%

Source: 1986 Census.

FIGURE 8–3: Source of Income, 1986

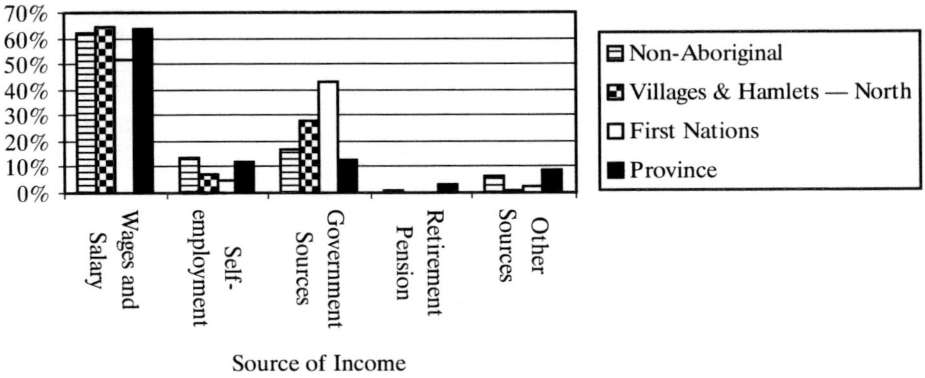

Source: 1986 Census.

tion growth and the related large and growing pool of Aboriginal young people who will be entering the labour force in next few years. The implications are obvious: There is a desperate need to create employment opportunities for Aboriginal people.

The sources of 1986 household income (see Figure 8–3) are consistent with the low participation and high unemployment rates described, and a resulting reliance by many Aboriginal people on various forms of government transfer payments (social assistance, unemployment insurance, training allowances and the like). Just over 50% of the people of the First Nations reported employment as their primary source of income. In contrast, the figures reported by non-Aboriginal people, the people of the northern villages and hamlets, and the province as a whole were 62%, 64% and 64%, respectively. As one would expect, this pattern reverses with respect to income from government sources as a primary source with First Nations reporting the highest level at 43%; non-Aboriginal people, 17%; northern villages and hamlets, 28%; and the province, 13%. There are also clear but smaller differences among the groups in the other income source categories. For example, self-employment income stands at 5% for First Nations in contrast to rates at more than twice that level for non-Aboriginal people and the province as a whole (13% and 12% respectively).

Household income (see Figure 8–4) and household size (see Figure 8–5) offer additional insight into the relative economic circumstances of the groups in the study area. In 1986, fully 52% of the people of the First Nations lived in households with an annual income less than $15,000. In contrast, only 36% of the residents of northern villages, 35% of non-Aboriginals in the study area, and 29% for the province as a whole, reported household incomes below $15,000. A similar pattern of inequality exists at the upper end of household in-

FIGURE 8–4: Household Income, 1986

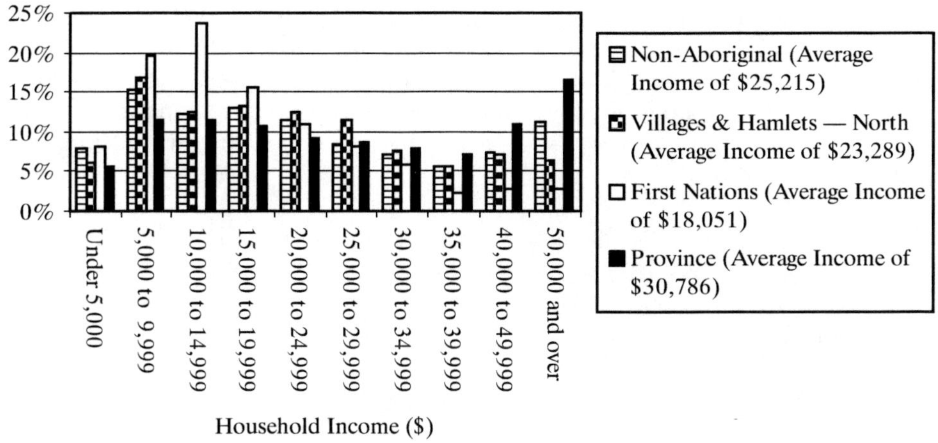

Source: 1986 Census.

FIGURE 8–5: Household Size, 1986

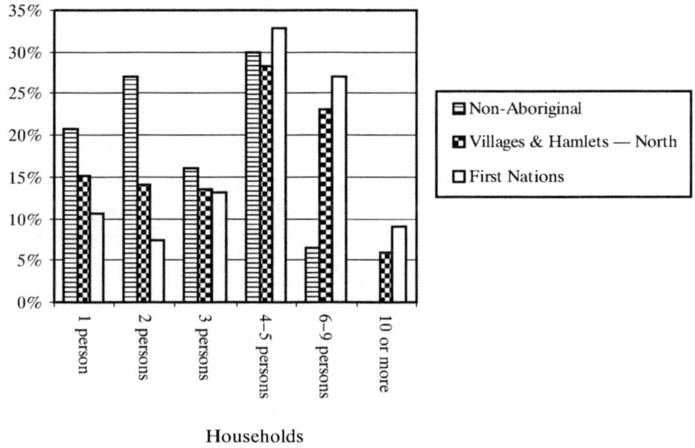

Source: 1986 Census.

come. Only 8% the people of the First Nations reported household income in excess of $35,000 as compared to 10% for those in the northern villages and hamlets, 25% for non-Aboriginal communities and 35% for the province.

As Figure 8–5 suggests, First Nations' households are much larger than those of the other groups. Thirty-six percent of all First Nations households in the study area consisted of six or more people. The figure for households of this size is also high for northern villages and hamlets at 28%. On the other hand, households of six or more people accounted for only 6% of the total among non-Aboriginal people in the study area. This means that the problem of significantly lower household income of First Nations is compounded by the fact that their income must support many more people. In fact, according to the MLTC in 1993:

> *The income per capita of the MLFN's is $2,618 while the average income per capita for the province is $12,147, The average combined earnings income and social assistance per capita for the MLFN is $6,418.* (MLTC 1995b, III–2)

Thus, the disparity between the economic circumstances of the people of the MLFNs is much greater than the simple comparison of household incomes (see Figure 8–4) suggests.

While the lack of employment opportunities in First Nation and northern communities is the major cause of the low participation and high unemployment rates of both Aboriginal groups, relative education levels were a contributing factor (see Figure 8–6). Fifty-three percent of First Nation members aged

FIGURE 8–6: Education Level, 1986

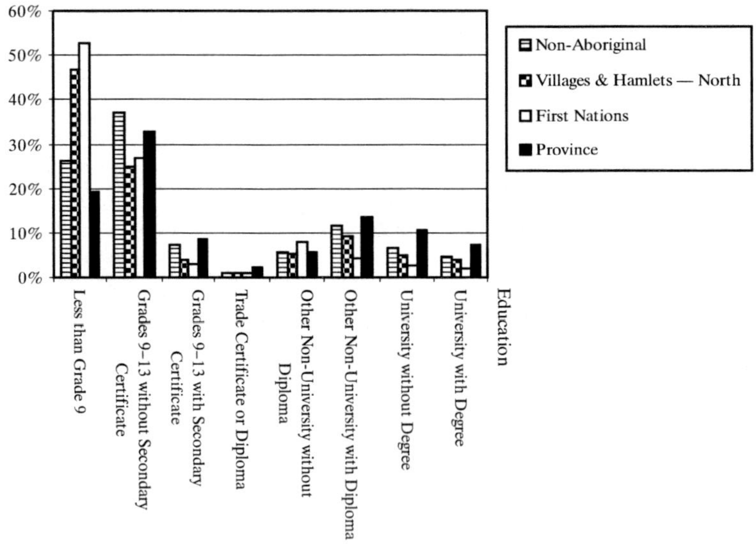

Source: 1986 Census.

15 and older had an education less than grade 9. The figure for the residents of the northern villages and hamlets was 47%. These levels compare unfavourably with the levels of the non-Aboriginal people of the study area and the people of the province as a whole, which were 26% and 19% respectively. Equally significant is the disparity between the proportion of people with an education level of grade 12 or higher — First Nations, 21%; northern villages and hamlets, 28%; non-Aboriginals in the study area, 37%; and the province, 48%.

As is evident from the preceding figures, the socioeconomic circumstances of the people of the First Nations of the MLTC were far from satisfactory in 1986. Further, it is obvious that given the age distribution and population growth rate, these circumstances were bound to worsen unless significant economic development occurred to create employment opportunities in large numbers. It is also evident that education levels would have to improve, if the people of the First Nations (existing participants and new entrants to the labour force) were to have the capacity to take advantage of any employment and business opportunities created. The efforts of the Meadow Lake Tribal Council, described in the following sections, were directed to these ends.

8.3. The Meadow Lake Tribal Council

According to its 1992–93 annual report, "the Meadow Lake Tribal Council is the political, service and corporate organization of the nine Meadow Lake First Nations" (MLTC 1993, 4). The Tribal Council was formed in 1986 as the result of the reorganization and expansion of Meadow Lake District Chiefs Joint Venture that had been formed in 1981. The responsibilities of the Tribal Council and the authority necessary to carry out those responsibilities are delegated to it by the people of its member First Nations:

> *The Tribal Council is governed by the nine First Nation Chiefs who are elected by the eligible membership of each First Nation. The Chiefs set policy and direction for the Tribal Council, bringing forward the issues and concerns from their First Nation members.* (MLTC 1995b, iii)

8.3.1. Economic Development Activities: 1986 to 1991

Since its inception in 1986, economic development for its member Nations has been one of the primary objectives of the Tribal Council. According to its 1990–91 Annual Report, the MLTC had been operating a business development program for the past six years. The objective of the program was to "stimulate economic growth for First Nations and to encourage an entrepreneurial spirit among our people" (MLTC 1991, 26). According to that same annual report, 106 business projects were undertaken during the six years of the program ending in 1991. Of this total, 65% were reported to be still operating at the time of the preparation of the 1990–91 report. Norsask Forest Products Ltd. and MLTC Logging and Reforestation Ltd. were among the projects begun during this period.

A comparison of 1991 census values with the already described 1986 values for selected socioeconomic measures provides an indication of the impact of the MLTC's development efforts during this five-year period (see Tables 8–5 and 8–6). This is not to say that the MLTC's business development activities were the sole cause for any improvement in employment and income. However, it is reasonable to assume that the approximately 66 businesses started by the MLTC between 1986 and 1991 created jobs and income that otherwise would not have been created.

There was a modest improvement in the employment, participation and unemployment rates of the people of the MLFNs between 1986 and 1991 (see Table 8–5). The potential labour force grew by 270 over five years, while the workforce grew by half that number (135). This is reflected in a 1.1 percentage point increase in the 1991 participation rate over that of 1986. Coincidentally, the number of people employed in 1991 also increased by 135 over 1986 levels. It seems likely that much of this increase was a result of the 66 new businesses created as a result of the MLTC business development program. As a result of this increase in employment, the unemployment rate fell by 4 percentage points and the proportion of the potential labour force employed increased by almost 2 percentage points over the period. It is noteworthy that in all aspects of employment reported in Figure 8–3, the improvement in performance of the First Nations over the period 1986 to 1991 exceeded that of the other Aboriginal group — those in northern villages and hamlets. However, in spite of this improvement, in 1991, the performance of the First Nations fell far short of that for the non-Aboriginal category.

There was also a change in household income distribution over the same period (see Table 8–6). The number of First Nations households reporting an income of less than $30,000 in 1991 declined by 9% from the number in 1986, while the number with income above that level increased by a similar amount. During the same period, there was a 6% decline in the number of northern village and hamlet households reporting income less than $30,000 and a decline of 20% in the number of non-Aboriginal households. As with the employment data, the performance of First Nations households is superior to that of households in the northern villages and hamlets category but falls short of that of non-Aboriginal households.

According to Table 8–7, between 1986 and 1991 there was also an increase in average household income for First Nations and northern villages and hamlets. The average household income of both Aboriginal groups increased by almost 20% over five years, a positive outcome. However this increase pales in comparison to the 46% increase experienced by the non-Aboriginal households in the study area.

In an effort to gain further insight in the change in income amount and composition, Table 8–8 compares average employment income and numbers between 1986 and 1991. The average full-time employment income in 1991 differs by slightly less than $3,000 between the First Nations and non-Aboriginal categories (up from a difference of $1,200 in 1986). This difference is substantially lower than the $10,000 difference in 1991 household income between the two categories. This can be attributed to at least two factors: (i) the lower participation rate and resulting greater reliance on non-employment (generally

TABLE 8–5: Unemployment and Population, 1986–1991

	1986			1991			Change		
	First Nations	North Villages and Hamlets	Non-Aboriginal	First Nations	North Villages and Hamlets	Non-Aboriginal	First Nations	North Villages and Hamlets	Non-Aboriginal
Population 15 years and older	2,810	4,145	7,230	3,080	4,230	7,250	270	85	50
In the labour force	1,070	2,140	4,765	1,205	2,015	5,185	135	–125	420
Employed	720	1,440	4,355	855	1,415	4,790	135	–25	435
Unemployed	350	695	415	350	575	400	0	–120	–15
Participation rate	38%	52%	66%	39.1%	48%	72%	1.1%	–3%	6%
Unemployment rate	33%	32%	9%	29.0%	29%	8%	–4%	–3%	–1%
% of Population 15 years and older employed	26%	35%	60%	27.8%	33%	66%	1.8%	–2%	6%

Source: 1986 and 1991 Censuses.

TABLE 8–6: Household Income, 1986–1991

	1986			1991			% Change		
	First Nations	North Villages and Hamlets	Non-Aboriginal	First Nations	North Villages and Hamlets	Non-Aboriginal	First Nations	North Villages and Hamlets	Non-Aboriginal
Less than $10,000	28	23	23	24	17	6	–4	–6	–17
$10,000 to $14,999	24	13	12	20	18	13	–4	5	1
$15,000 to $19,999	16	13	13	16	13	10	0	0	–3
$20,000 to $29,999	19	24	19	18	19	20	–1	–5	1
$40,000 to $49,999	3	7	8	6	8	13	3	1	5
$50,000 and over	3	6	11	6	13	21	3	7	10

Source: 1986 and 1991 Censuses.

TABLE 8–7: Change in Average Household Income, 1986–1991

	1986	1991	% Change
First Nation	$18,051	$21,276	18
Northern Villages and Hamlets	23,289	27,725	19
Non-Aboriginal	25,215	36,927	46

Source: 1986 and 1991 Censuses.

lower) income sources by First Nations' households and (ii) the larger number of two income households among non-Aboriginal people.

The differences between the changes in employment numbers between 1986 and 1991 for the two Aboriginal categories are striking in two ways. First, the average full-time employment income among First Nations increased by 16%, almost double the 9% rate of increase among the people of the northern villages and hamlets. Second, full-time employment among the people of the First Nations increased by 23% while full-time employment among those from the northern villages and hamlets fell by 20% over five years. This raises the question: Why was the employment and income performance of the First Nations over the period 1986–1991 superior to that of northern villages and hamlets?

Over the period 1986 to 1991, the two Aboriginal groups differed in their approach to economic development. The MLFNs through the MLTC had (and still have) a much more collective and planned approach to the process and that approach seems to have borne fruit. The leaders among the people of the northern hamlets and villages appear to agree with this conclusion. In the early 1990s, through an association of northern municipalities, they began to develop a common economic development strategy. In March 1990, the 14 members of the Northwest Saskatchewan Municipalities Association formed Keewatin Dahze Developers Inc. "as their formal body to address economic development initiatives" (K. D. Developers 1993, viii). One of the projects undertaken by K. D. Developers was the creation of Northwest Logging and Refor. The objective was (is) to create "a commercially viable woodland contracting operation" (K. D. Developers 1993, viii) providing the people of the member communities with an "opportunity to participate at an unprecedented level in the forest industry in Saskatchewan's northwest" (K. D. Developers 1993, x).

8.3.2. Capacity Building: Education

Recognizing that it takes well-educated, trained and effective people to develop the businesses central to their economic development plan and a trained and competent workforce to fill the jobs created by those businesses, the people of the MLTC have devoted (and continue to devote) considerable attention to education. Each First Nation controls its local school. In support of these

TABLE 8–8: Change in Average Employment Income and Numbers, 1986–1991

	1986			1991			% Change		
	First Nations	Northern Villages and Hamlets	Non-Aboriginal	First Nations	Northern Villages and Hamlets	Non-Aboriginal	First Nations	Northern Villages and Hamlets	Non-Aboriginal
Males — full year, full-time	160	560	1,410	160	380	1,570	0	–32	11
Average employment income	$20,185	$24,624	$21,111	$23,296	$27,441	$27,932	15	11	2
Males — part year or part-time	475	1,000	1,355	480	80	1,305	1	–32	–4
Average employment income	$ 6,320	$ 8,628	$11,043	$ 7,436	$ 9,275	$17,847	18	7	62
Females — full year, full-time	100	295	525	160	305	900	60	3	71
Average employment income	$17,160	$18,781	$18,337	$20,656	$21,920	$19,406	20	17	6
Females — part year or part-time	215	570	1,200	245	425	1,270	14	–25	6
Average employment income	$ 6,267	$ 7,296	$ 7,270	$ 6,317	$ 8,220	$ 9,511	1	13	31
All — full year	260	855	1,935	320	685	2,470	23	–20	28
Average employment income	$19,022	$22,608	$20,358	$21,976	$24,983	$24,826	16	11	22
All — part year or part-time	690	1,570	2,555	725	1,105	2,575	5	–30	1
Average employment income	$ 6,304	$ 8,144	$ 9,271	$ 7,316	$ 8,869	$13,735	16	9	48

Source: 1986 and 1991 Censuses.

local boards, the Tribal Council formed the MLTC Board of Education made up of representatives from each First Nation. This board provides a wide variety of professional and advisory services (e.g. speech pathologist, educational psychologist, education support unit) to local boards. Beyond advisory and support activities, the Tribal Council Board of Education manages the post-secondary funding program for all member Nations except English River, operates the Beauval Indian Education Center (a High School), and offers a three-year University Entrance/Business Administration Diploma Program and a one-year Integrated Resource Management Program. According to the MLTC 1993/94 Annual Report, there were approximately 1,300 students in the seven First Nation community schools, 147 in the Beauval Indian Education Center (40 in grade 12), and 95 MLTC students in post-secondary programs.

MLTC's efforts are reducing the disparity in education levels between the people of the MLTC First Nations and residents of the province as a whole. Figures from the MLTC annual reports provide an indication of this success. For example, according to the 1986 census, only 80 members of the MLTC First Nations reported a complete grade 12 as their education level. According to the annual reports, the Beauval Indian Education Centre graduated at least that many students in the four years from 1989 to 1992, a 100% increase. Similarly, by the spring of 1994, the MLTC forestry program had graduated 26 students with technical diplomas, more than doubling the number reported in 1986. Both these figures are conservative because many First Nations students attended other high schools and technical programs. Therefore, the actual number of graduates of both types is higher than those reported in the annual reports.

Figures from the 1991 census confirm this improvement in education level (see Table 8–9). In 1986, 80% of the people of the MLFN reported their education as less than a complete grade 12. By 1991, this number had fallen to 72%. The number of students reporting a complete grade 12 as their highest level increased from 80 (3%) to 135 (4%). Those reporting a non-university diploma increased from 4% to 10% (an increase of 200 people), and those with a trade certificate from 1% to 3% (an increase of 65). The number reporting partial university increased from 75 (3%) to 145 (5%). Continuing improvements in education levels can be expected as the number of students increase, more First Nation role models emerge, and employment opportunities requiring grade 12 or higher education increase as a result of development activities.

In summary, the results achieved between 1986 and 1991 were encouraging for the people of the MLFNs. Their education levels improved, the unemployment rate declined, the level of employment rose, the distribution of income shifted from lower to higher levels and the average household income increased. However, these outcomes fell far short of what was needed if the people of the MLFNs are to achieve levels of education, employment and income comparable to non-Aboriginal people.

8.3.3. After 1991: Looking into the Future

Building on the modest success achieved between 1986 and 1991 and in response to the larger unmet challenge of parity with non-Aboriginal people, the economic development mission, objectives and strategies of the MLTC have evolved and matured. By 1993, a clear vision for the future was in place and

TABLE 8–9: Education Levels, 1986–1991

	1986		1991		
	Nos.	%	Nos.	%	Change Nos.
Population 15 and over	2,810		3,105		295
Less than Grade 9	1,480	53	1,390	45	–90
Partial Grade 12	755	27	850	27	95
Complete Grade 12	80	3	135	4	55
Trade Certificate/Diploma	25	1	90	3	65
Non-University, No Diploma	220	8	120	4	–100
Non-University with Diploma	120	4	320	10	200
University, No Degree	75	3	145	5	70
University with Degree	55	2	55	2	0

Source: 1986 and 1991 Censuses

the role to be played by economic and business development in the realization of that vision identified. According to its 1993–94 annual report:

> *MLTC's vision is to support its member individuals, families and communities in achieving health and a state of well-being. This state of well-being means achieving health and a balance in the spiritual, physical, mental and emotional aspects of life. The MLFNs wish to achieve increased self-reliance in all aspects of life as part of this approach and philosophy.* (MLTC 1994, 4)

In pursuit of this self-reliance

> *the Chiefs of the MLTC have jointly mandated a twenty year plan of economic development strategy aimed at achieving parity with the province in terms of employment rate and income level. In short, we are striving to create and maintain 3,240 good-paying jobs in the next 20 years.* (MLTC 1994, 20)

The basic strategy adopted to achieve this objective was to "develop and establish "anchor" businesses around which smaller enterprises can flourish bringing long lasting economic activities and benefits" (MLTC 1994, 20). The MLTC had decided, as far back as 1988 with the purchase of 50% of the Meadow Lake Sawmill, that forestry offered a particularly good opportunity for the creation of such an anchor business. The Tribal Council has been actively involved in or considering businesses in other sectors as well including mining (possible equity participation in new mines in their area), petroleum (including a joint venture with SaskEnergy for natural gas storage), spent nuclear reactor fuel storage (preliminary study underway), tourism, and various commercial activities (including a newspaper and printing business).

Since 1991, the MLFNs have greatly expanded their forestry activities. They have also prepared a comprehensive 20-year development plan indicating how they expect to achieve their objective of "socioeconomic parity" with the non-Aboriginal people of the province. The forestry activities of the MLTC and the 20-year plan and the process used to develop it are interrelated. Their experience in forestry development and the forestry-related crisis that occurred in 1992–93 (described in the following section) pointed out the need and provided the impetus for the 20-year plan. The MLTC's forestry activities and the development of its 20-year plan are the subjects of the next two sections of this chapter.

8.4. MLTC Forestry Developments

The MLTC's involvement in the forestry industry began in 1988 when the chiefs of MLTC First Nations negotiated the purchase of 50% of the Meadow Lake Sawmill from the provincial government. At the time of this sale, the mill had been losing money for a number of years and was virtually shut down (Price Waterhouse 1994b). The remaining 50% interest in the sawmill was purchased by Techfor Services Ltd., a company wholly owned by the mill employees. The company was renamed Norsask Forest Products Ltd. (Norsask).

Norsask's most valuable asset was, and still is, the Forest Management License Agreement (FMLA) that it holds from the Province of Saskatchewan. This FMLA gives Norsask the harvesting rights (for both softwood and hardwood) and reforestation responsibilities for 3.3-million hectares of Crown Land in the Meadow Lake District (see Figure 8–7). While its mill only used softwood, the FMLA required that Norsask develop the capacity to use the hardwood (poplar) in the license area within four years or the rights to it would be lost (Star Phoenix 1993, A2). In addition, the FMLA required that residents of the license area be given priority for employment and that a co-management process be established involving "complete consultation between the sawmill [Norsask] and northern communities over issues including harvesting, hauling, reforestation, road construction, as well as trapping and fishing" (Price Waterhouse 1994a, 5).

Norsask's rights and responsibilities under the FMLA were central to the MLTC's forestry-based development strategy. They set the stage for the formation of a network of business alliances and joint ventures among the First Nations of the MLTC, between them (through Norsask) and a non-First Nation corporate partner — Millar Western Ltd., and among the non-First Nation residents of the communities in the FMLA area. The key alliance in the network was the joint venture between Norsask Forest Products Ltd. and Millar Western Ltd. The formation of this joint venture and the emergence of the other elements of the network are described in the material that follows.

FIGURE 8–7: Norsask's FMLA

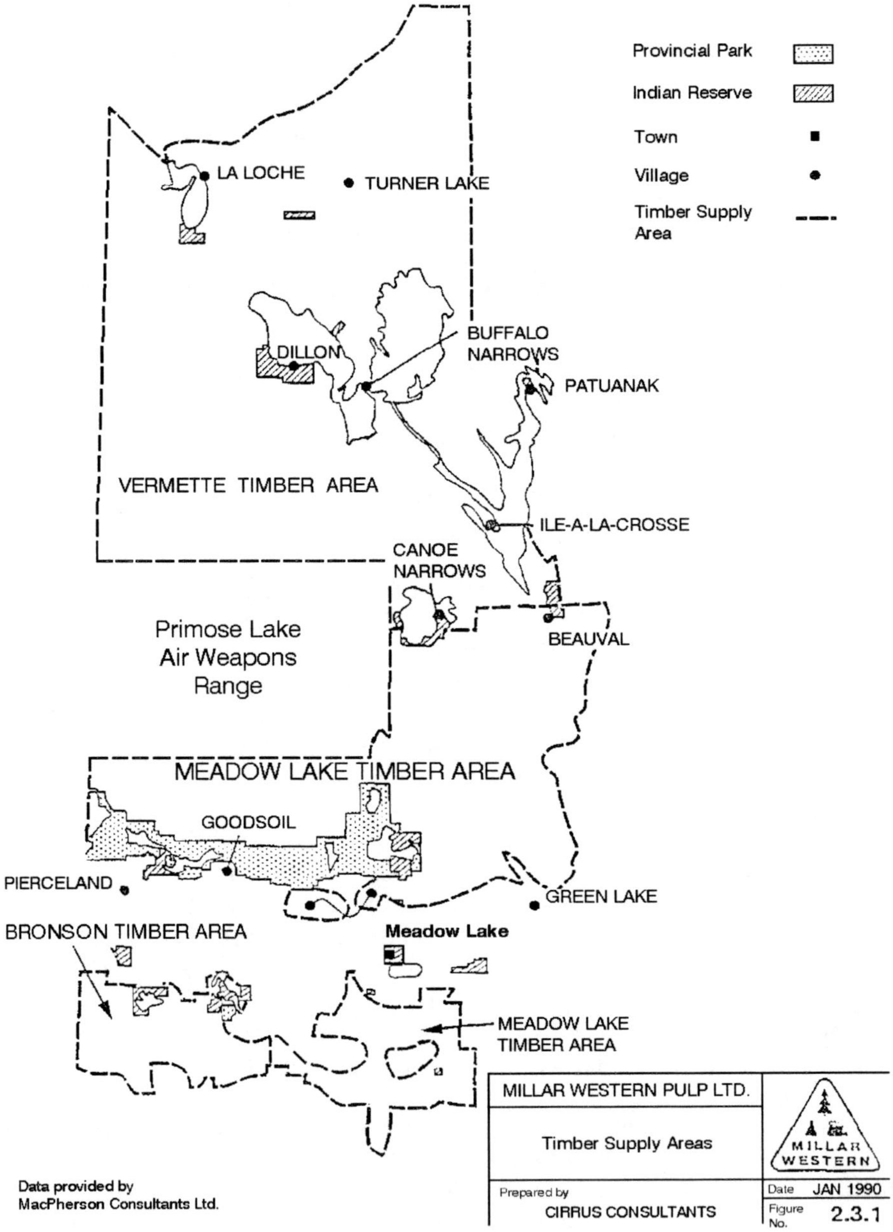

At the time that MLTC was searching for a way to exploit the business and employment opportunities presented by the FMLA, Millar-Western Ltd. a privately owned Alberta corporation, wanted to build a "zero pollution" pulp mill that used poplar instead of softwood as a raw material. The company saw this mill as the cornerstone of its strategic plan for the future. Throughout its market area (particularly in the United States) increasingly rigorous environmental regulations were rendering older paper plants using the chlorine-based bleaching process economically obsolete. For Millar Western, the cost of refitting an old plant to meet new standards compared to the cost of a new chlorine-free plant favoured the latter. However, forest resources suitable to supply a new plant were not available in Alberta. All had already been licensed to other pulp producers. Therefore the company's owners had to look elsewhere for an assured supply of poplar. They found such a supply just over the provincial border in Saskatchewan in the hands of the MLTC. The potential for a mutually beneficial alliance in these circumstance was obvious to the leaders of both parties.

Millar Western required access to an assured supply of poplar at a globally competitive price. They had the expertise and capital necessary to develop the pulp mill. Consistent with subcontracting/strategic alliances as elements of flexible production, the company was quite prepared to subcontract the harvesting and reforestation activities to outside organizations while it focused on its core activity, the production and sale of pulp. Millar Western was willing to accept conditions that served the needs and objectives of the MLTC, so long as it received competitively priced feed stock. On their part, the MLTC controlled the access to a suitable supply of poplar (Millar Western). They needed a use for this hardwood to satisfy the requirements of the FMLA and to realize its inherent employment and business development potential. However, they lacked the capital and expertise to develop this capacity. The leaders of the MLTC recognized that an arrangement with an outside company was the answer to their needs. The leaders of the two groups negotiated an agreement with terms and conditions intended to satisfy the objectives of both. Figure 8–8 illustrates the structure that emerged from these negotiations.

Millar Western, along with the Crown Investment Corporation of the Province of Saskatchewan, established a company called Millar Western Pulp Ltd. to build and operate the pulp mill at Meadow Lake. Millar Western owns a controlling interest (51%) in Millar Western Pulp. Millar Western Pulp acquired a 20% interest in Norsask Forest Products (10% from each of the two original owners Techfor and Norsask). This left the MLTC with a 40% interest in Norsask.

Norsask Forest Products and Millar Western Pulp then established a joint venture company called Mistik Management Ltd. (Mistik means "wood" in Cree), with each parent holding a 50% interest. Mistik was assigned the responsibility to manage all forest operations under the terms and conditions of the FMLA. Mistik was not expected to do the actual work but rather to contract to have it done through operating companies. It is through these operating companies that most benefits (employment, business creation and profits) were expected to reach the people of the MLFNs.

In June 1990, the MLTC created its own operating company, the MLTC Logging and Reforestation Ltd., to realize the benefits from forest operations

FIGURE 8–8: Forestry Industry Structure in the Meadow Lake District

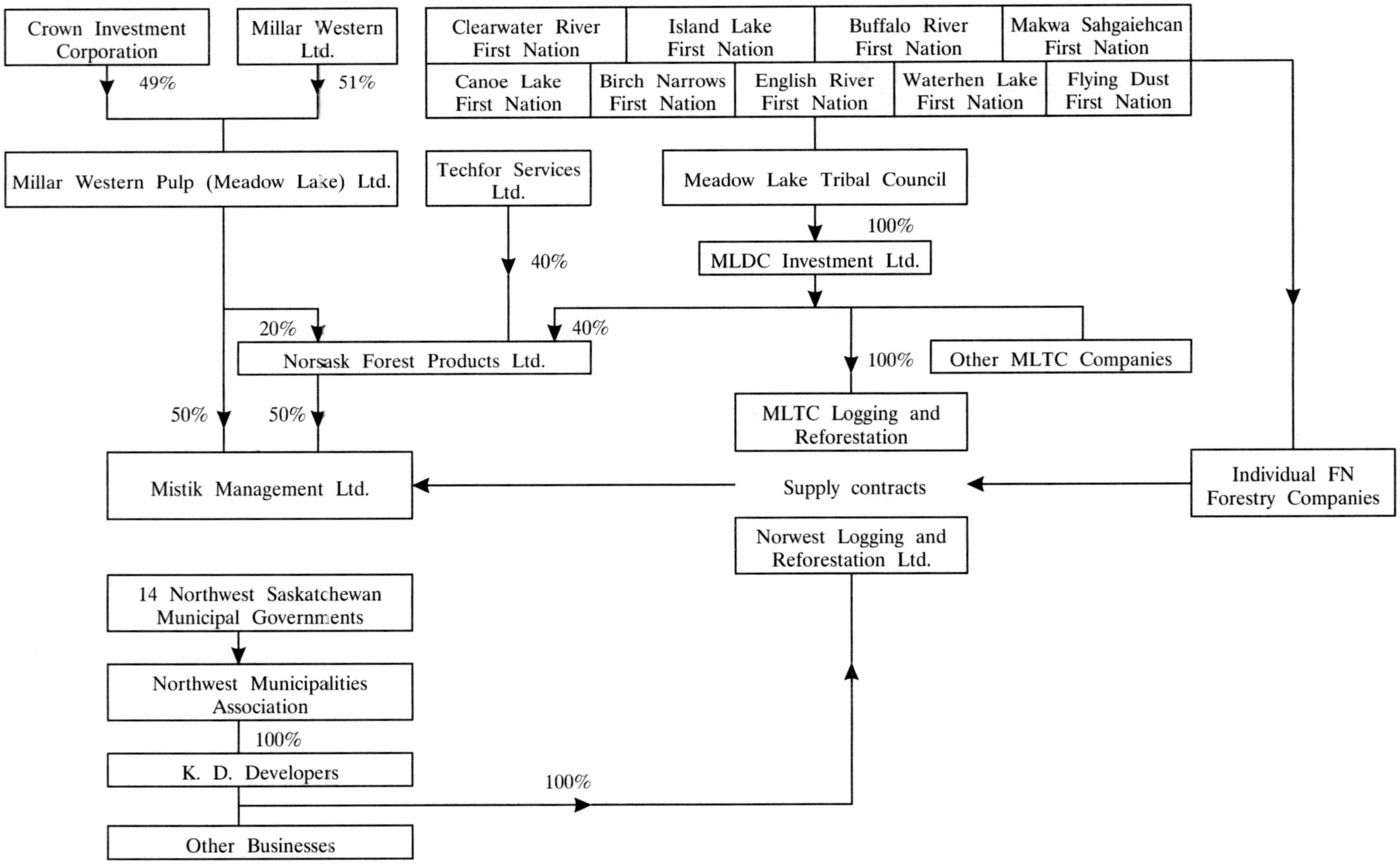

Source: Anderson and Bone 1995b, 133

for the citizens of its member First Nations. Under contract with Mistik, the company provides logs to both mills and undertakes other activities such as road building, log hauling and reforestation. Some individual First Nations, as well as some First Nations individuals, also created operating companies. As well, non-First Nations people (mostly Metis and non-status Indians) living in the 14 northern villages and hamlets of the area saw participation in forestry as a key to employment and economic development. Though an association of their municipal governments, they created an operating company called Norwest Logging and Reforestation Ltd.:

> *The company* [Norwest Logging and Reforestation Ltd.] *signed a contract with Mistik "for the provision of logging services starting in 1991/92 (year 1). The contract includes a schedule of annual wood volume allocations which increase from an initial volume of 50,000 m^3 to a maximum of 250,000 m^3 in year four and thereafter.* (K. D. Developers 1991, x)

Individuals from these communities also formed companies to participate in forestry activities.

To build the capacity of their people to participate in forestry industry as employees and business persons, the Tribal Council developed and offered two post-secondary education programs. One was a diploma program in Integrated Resource Management, developed and offered in partnership with the Saskatchewan Indian Institute of Technology. The other was a three-year university Diploma in Business Administration program in partnership with the Saskatchewan Indian Federated College.

By 1994, the Millar Western Pulp Ltd. mill was fully operational. The total harvest in the FMLA area that year was 1,000,000 cubic metres, up from the 300,000 cubic metres harvested in 1990. Of the 48 contractors involved in meeting this demand in 1994, MLTC Logging and Reforestation was by far the largest. The company harvested 300,000 cubic metres in 1994, up from the 50,000 cubic metres harvested in 1992.

This increase in activity as a result of the joint venture between MLTC (through Norsask) and Millar Western had a significant impact on First Nation employment building on the modest gains achieved between 1986 and 1991. MLTC Logging and Reforestation's output in 1994 provided employment for 140 people and placed the company among the top 10% of logging companies in Canada. By the same date Norsask Forest Products was ranked in the top 6% of Canadian saw mills employing 103 people (Price Waterhouse, 1994a). According to the same Price Waterhouse report, in addition to these 243 direct jobs, these First Nation companies created an additional 730 indirect jobs in the region (most of them since 1993). Employment is expected to remain stable at this level in the future.

Almost all of the 243 direct jobs created by Norsask Forest Products and MLTC Logging and Reforestation are held by members of the First Nations of the MLTC, as are at least 50% or 365 (a very conservative estimate) of the indirect jobs. The sawmill and supporting forest operations were virtually shutdown in 1986 so these are "new jobs" since the 1986 census. Given that only 730 members of the MLTC First Nations reported themselves employed in the

1986 census, the creation of these 600 or more good-paying, permanent jobs for people from the MLFN is a considerable accomplishment. At the same time, these results serve to bring home the scale of the challenge facing the people of the MLFNs as they struggle are to achieve their 20 year objective of employment parity with the province — 600 jobs created, 2,640 permanent, good-paying jobs to go.

In addition to the jobs created and other spin-off benefits to the region, "during the last three years, the companies [Norsask and MLTC Logging and Reforestation], in aggregate, have paid $10.7 million in corporate taxes and withheld income taxes on wages" (Price Waterhouse 1994b, 8). The MLTC is justifiably proud of these taxes paid, arguing that they represent an excellent return to the government of Canada on the $1.3-million in grants that the MLTC received to purchase and modernize Norsask. According to the leaders of the MLTC, these results provide evidence of the benefits to all people in Canada — First Nation and non-First Nation — of a policy of support for First Nations' business development by the federal and provincial governments. This is an example of the outcome that is anticipated by The Royal Commission on Aboriginal People. The thrust of the commission's conclusions is that additional money — up to $2-billion more per year for the next 20 years — invested now in capacity building and economic development by Aboriginal people will profit manyfold in the future through (i) reduced government expenditures to deal with the otherwise exploding unemployment and other social costs and (ii) increased tax revenues.

While many were satisfied with the increase in employment and business activity generated through forestry, a significant number of people of the MLFN were unhappy with certain operating decisions and actions taken by Mistik Management and MLTC Logging and Reforestation. Their immediate concerns centered on two issues. The first was the effect that clear-cut logging with mechanical harvesters was having on the land and their ability to continue traditional practices. Second and beyond the specific issue of clear cutting, the people directly affected by logging felt that they lacked an effective method of influencing the operating decisions taken by Mistik Management and MLTC Logging and Reforestation and that they were not receiving a fair share of the benefits from forestry activities in their area.

By May 13, 1992, dissatisfaction had become so intense that protesters, led by Elders from the Canoe Lake First Nation, established a blockade on Highway 903, 65 km north of Meadow Lake that halted the operations of MLTC Logging and Reforestation in the area (Windspeaker 1992a, 12). The protesters formed an organization called "The Protectors of Mother Earth." Allan Morin, head of the organization, in describing its members' demands, said that

> *The Elders object to clear cutting and the use of mechanical harvesters. They want control over their own resources, compensation for their people,* [and] *financial and technical compensation for local people who want to start their own forestry related businesses.* (Windspeaker 1993b, r2)

It is important to note that the protesters from Canoe Lake were not demanding an end to forestry activities in their area. Rather, they sought to change the terms of their participation in the activity in order to increase the benefits to, and decrease the negative impacts on, their community and its people. This is a clear case of the "civil sector" acting to protect its interests when arrangements arrived at by the other two sectors (the state in the form of their own government the MLTC and the market) were viewed as unacceptable.

Speaking about the blockade on behalf of the MLTC, Vice-Chief Oniell Gladdue "blamed the dispute on a lack of communication. He said many of the concerns will be resolved once the communities get more information" (Windspeaker 1992b, 12). He was speaking about the plans being put in place to incorporate community involvement in the decision-making process. A process had just begun (to be completed by the end of the winter of 1992/93) to establish co-management boards as required under the FMLA in each of the communities in the area covered by the license agreement. Barry Peel, president of Mistik Management, said that these co-management boards would give the people of the communities in the region "a say on issues such as where and how logging should take place, including the size and shape of cuts, location of roads, harvesting methods, reforestation and operating plans" (Star Phoenix 1992b, E1). Peel credited the Canoe Lake blockade with speeding up the introduction of the co-management process.

In late August 1992, while these co-management boards were being introduced, a meeting was held between the Protectors of Mother Earth, Norsask Forest Products, Mistik Management, and the MLTC. At this meeting all agreed that the proposed co-management boards and process would adequately address the issues underlying the blockade. The Protectors of Mother Earth asked that Norsask and Mistik stop logging in the disputed area until the negotiations establishing their co-management board and processes were concluded. The companies refused citing their responsibilities to the mills and to their employees. The meeting ended without resolving the conflict (Star Phoenix 1992a, A4).

The blockade continued through the winter of 1992–93. Much of this period was marked by legal actions. On December 9, 1992, the provincial government asked the courts to evict the protesters, claiming that they were illegally occupying Crown land. The protesters countered by filing a complaint with the Saskatchewan Human Rights Commission. According to Cecilia Iron, a spokesperson for the protesters, the complaint alleged that

> *The government* [Saskatchewan] *has repeatedly ignored our rights under the treaties, under the Natural Resources Transfer Agreement, and under the constitution. An agreement* [the FMLA] *between the government and a local forestry company* [Norsask Forest Products] *completely ignores Aboriginal rights and licenses to trap, hunt fish for food and harvest wild rice.*
> (Windspeaker 1992c, 2)

The Court of Queens Bench ruled on May 12, 1993, that the protesters must remove their blockade within 15 days unless an appeal was launched. The Elders refused to leave the blockade site, and negotiations with Norsask Forest Products resumed (Windspeaker 1993a, 3). On October 12, 1993, a tentative agreement was reached between the protesters and Norsask Forest Products.

According to Ray Cariou, chairman of Norsask, the people of the Canoe Lake First Nation, through a co-management board, would have the right to participate in decisions about such things as logging methods, the location of roads, and the accommodation of traplines and other traditional land uses (Windspeaker 1993c, r2).

It is significant that Millar Western remained one step removed from the dispute throughout. The company was neither the target of the protesters nor the negotiator of the settlement. It was able to concentrate on its core activities and leave local and regional issues in the hands of it partners, an outcome entirely consistent with flexible competition and the company's expectations when it entered into its alliance with the MLTC. Instead, the dispute and its resolution involved the people of the region and their own bodies — corporate (Norsask Forest Products), governmental (MLTC), and civil (the Protectors of the Mother Earth). The issues were identified and a solution found by the people directly affected — a local/regional mode of social regulation in action.

It remains to be seen if the local/regional mode of social regulation emerging in Canoe Lake, and throughout the FMLA area, will be successful in the long-run. To be judged so, it must simultaneously satisfy the requirements of the mills as they compete in the global economy, the development objectives of the MLTC, the needs and objectives (traditional and modern) of the people of the First Nation and non-First Nation communities of the region, and the requirements of the FMLA. While there are bound to be disagreements among the involved parties in the future as well as occasional economic difficulties, prospects for continuing success seem good based on the successful resolution of the Canoe Lake conflict and recent financial and job creation results.

The unfolding of events in forestry, particularly the Canoe Lake protest and its resolution, had significant impact beyond that sector. The experience resulted in the maturation and refinement of the MLTC's economic development mission, objectives, strategies and processes — particularly those relating to consultation, participation and traditional values. This impact is evident in the content of the MLTC's 20-year development plan *From Vision to Reality* and the process used to prepare it between April 1993 and October 1995.

8.5. MLTC Twenty-Year Plan

The MLTC 20-year development plan (both its content and the process by which it was developed) is an excellent example of the emerging Aboriginal approach to economic development. All eight characteristics described in chapter 2 are clearly and strongly present. The MLTC's answers to the three key questions raised in chapter 2 can be found in the plan.

The process that culminated in the completion of the MLTC's 20-year plan *From Vision to Reality* in October 1995 began in early 1993. It involved extensive consultation with the Elders and members of the MLFNs. Key aspects of this consultative process included a meeting with the representatives from the nine MLFN in April 1993; a meeting with the Elders in January 1994; a survey of the members of the MLFN during 1994; and, in April 1995, a three-day economic development symposium for members of the MLFN.

According to the 20-year plan:

> *The Meadow Lake First Nations' (MLFN) vision of the future is one of "healthy individuals, families and communities." This state of well being reflects balance and harmony in the spiritual, physical, emotional and mental aspects of life. Our vision includes self-sufficiency, self-reliance, and self-government. We will have control over our own lives and over decisions that impact our quality of life. We will have hope for the future and for the future of our children.* (MLTC 1995b, i)

This vision had its birth in April 1993, when members of the MLFN met for three days to discuss "all areas of community and family life and relationships with the environment and each other" (MLTC 1995b, I-6).

The next key step in the development of the 20-year plan occurred in January of 1994 when the Elders of the MLFN met to discuss traditional culture and values:

> *The Elders were specifically asked about the important values that contributed to healthy individuals, families, and communities in the past. The event was critical to developing the values regarding future economic development planning within the MLTC District.* (MLTC 1995b, I-7)

Self-sufficiency and self-reliance, sharing, community decision making, respect for the environment, and the preservation of traditional lifestyles and culture, emerged as key values.

The Elders particularly stressed that the key to attaining the vision of "healthy individuals, families and communities" was the replacement of the current destructive dependency on welfare with self-reliance. Typical of the Elders' views, one said:

> *In the future, hunting, trapping, fishing and gathering will not provide the self-sufficiency that is required. Young people will not live the same as the Elders live. The people cannot go back to the old days. We cannot turn back. We need to look ahead and know where to go next.* (MLTC 1995b, II-15)

In looking ahead, the Elders concluded that employment opportunities created through economic development were necessary to "allow people to regain self-reliance and self-sufficiency, and increase individual and community pride" (MLTC 1995b, II-3). The Elders stressed that the economic development process must incorporate traditional values, particularly those of sharing, community decision making, and respect for the environment, if the vision is to be realized.

As the next step in the process of preparing the plan, over 500 people from the nine First Nations were interviewed. Among other things, respondents were asked to rate the relative importance of maintaining a number of traditional values as part of the economic development process. Those surveyed overwhelming rated the maintenance of the following as very important: obtaining advice on economic development from Elders, getting the approval of MLFN peoples for economic development projects, protecting the environment, sharing the benefits of economic development, developing "on-reserve" or community employment, and achieving First Nation self-sufficiency and self-reliance.

Those surveyed were also asked the question "Can traditional lifestyles co-exist with modern enterprises or businesses?" Seventy-five percent of the respondents answered yes to this question. Typical comments from those who answered yes included:

- *The two types of lifestyle already do and its working.*
- *We have to work with Native and non-Native lifestyles.*
- *Strong family relationships are needed.*
- *Mixing the two types of lifestyles requires honesty, cooperation and communication.*
- *It's up to us to make it work.* (MLTC 1995b, 9)

The concerns expressed by those who felt the two could not and/or should not be mixed included:

- *Modern lifestyles overpower traditional lifestyles.*
- *Our culture is being lost.*
- *People can't live both ways.*
- *The two lifestyles conflict.* (MLTC 1995b, 9)

Respondents were also asked to identify the obstacles to achieving economic development goals, and the roles and responsibilities of individuals, families, First Nations, the Tribal Council, the federal and provincial government, and the private sector in overcoming these obstacles. Those surveyed identified the following as the primary barriers to development:

- *Accessible education/job training.*
- *Alcohol-free and drug free society.*
- *Equality and fairness in job distribution.*
- *Availability of permanent jobs.*
- *Community members working together supportively.*
- *Self-sufficiency and self-reliance versus welfare.*
- *Funding and financial programs for small business.*

(MLTC 1995b, 15)

The key roles and responsibilities identified for individuals in overcoming these barriers include having positive attitudes and motivation, striving for self-sufficiency, obtaining education and training, and starting small businesses. Those identified for the family include the ones for individuals as well such as providing healthy family lifestyles, providing support (moral, emotional, financial), and preserving language, culture and traditions.

The roles and responsibilities of each First Nation in overcoming these barriers were felt to include:

1. Providing effective and responsible leadership with a particular focus on ensuring community based long-term economic development intended to provide members a good standard of living.
2. Providing and encouraging education, training and wellness programs.
3. Encouraging self-reliance through business planning and marketing assistance, offering workshops and training programs, providing information on funding and providing loans for small business.
4. Direct involvement in economic development through business development initiatives as individual Nations and in partnerships with others.
5. Protecting the environment.

Expectations relating to the role and responsibilities of the Tribal Council include those listed for individual First Nations. In addition, the Tribal Council is expected to undertake larger development initiatives often in joint venture with outside partners and to provide support to the First Nations and their members as they pursue their own initiatives.

The federal and provincial governments' roles and responsibilities were felt to include funding for education, assistance to start large businesses, providing grants and loans to businesses, providing marketing and other advice and support, and developing long-term economic development strategies. Among the expectations of the private sector are providing financing (banks and credit unions), serving as mentors, providing business planning assistance, providing employment, and participating in joint ventures.

The initial meeting with representatives of the First Nations, the consultation with Elders, and the survey of community members resulted in the formation of a widely held vision and a general consensus as to the objective of economic development — "the achievement of employment and income parity with the Province of Saskatchewan" (MLTC 1995b, ix). Further, it was clearly established that this was to be done in a manner consistent with important traditional values, particularly those of self-reliance and self-sufficiency, protection of the environment, sharing of economic benefits, community decision-making and respect for the wisdom of the Elders.

In April 1995, a three-day economic development symposium was held to provide members of the MLFN with information about progress on the plan and to receive additional input. Approximately 150 members of the nine MLFNs participated in workshops that identified current economic development activities, opportunities for future economic development, and barriers to economic development for the MLTC in general and, more importantly, from the perspective of each member First Nation.

Participants at the seminar endorsed the strategy that calls for the MLTC to establish the larger anchor business and individual First Nations and their members to create small and medium businesses associated with these anchors. Participants reconfirmed the importance of the key traditional values including consultation with Elders, local decision-making, sharing of economic benefits and care of the environment. They also stressed the importance of continued human and financial capacity building to the creation of viable businesses and the development of a workforce capable of taking advantage of the employment opportunities such businesses will create.

Following the economic development symposium, the final 20-year development plan was drafted. Building on the strategy of anchor businesses, the plan identifies four key sectors as the main pillars of the economic development strategy. They are tourism, mining, forestry, and traditional activities including hunting, fishing, trapping, and agriculture/gathering. The plan goes on to evaluate each of these sectors in detail (at the Tribal Council and First Nation levels) focusing on opportunities and the barriers to realizing these opportunities. The plan establishes short, medium and long-term business and job creation objectives for the four key sectors as well as for those sectors identified as secondary (retail/service, construction/trades, oil and gas, environmental, management, professional/scientific, and public administration).

The plan *From Visions to Reality* forms the foundation for the operational plans of the Tribal Council and its member First Nations as they strive to realize their vision over the next 20 years. Will the people of the MLFN succeed? Only time will tell, but theory and results to date (at the MLTC and elsewhere in Saskatchewan) suggest they can. One heartening example began unfolding in 1997.

In January 1997, the English River First Nation announced its purchase of Tron Power, a construction and janitorial company servicing northern mines and businesses. The company is also involved in Cameco's gold mine in Kyrgyzstan. In addition to its northern and international operations, Tron has industrial maintenance contracts in Saskatoon. This added to the company's appeal since the investment will also provide employment opportunities for English River citizens who chose to live in that city rather than "on Reserve."

According to English River's press release, the First Nation and Tron Power had been involved in successful joint ventures since 1995. Before that they were partners in an employment equity plan intended to increase Aboriginal employment at the mines in northern Saskatchewan.[2] In summarizing these circumstances, Chief Archie Campbell said:

> *Many English River citizens already work for Tron Power, and our joint venture has given First Nations people the opportunity to become supervisors, journeymen welders, electricians, carpenters and pipe fitters. The purchase of the company will include First Nations employment in skilled areas, including management.* (English River First Nation 1997, 3)

According to Frank Lai, Economic Development Director for English River, financing the purchase was made possible by the First Nation's treaty land entitlement settlement.[3] Frank also commented (as does the press release) on the fact that the recently announced federal government's *Procurement Strategy for Aboriginal Businesses* figured prominently in the decision to purchase the company. According to the press release:

---

2 Another example of the blossoming of a corporate Aboriginal alliance from modest beginnings is discussed at some length in chapter 5.

3 Evidence of the success of First Nation capacity-building efforts and in particular the treaty land entitlement process is described in chapter 4.

> *Tron will be an instrument for targeting other construction and janitorial projects under the "Set Aside Program" of the Federal Procurement Strategy announced last year by Minister Irwin.*
> (English River First Nation 1997, 4)

In this one project, it is possible to see the convergence of all the forces described in chapters 4, 5 and 8, all under the guiding and coordinating influence of the First Nations' approach to economic development as exemplified by the MLFNs in their 20-year plan.

8.6. Concluding Comments

The forestry development activities of the Meadow Lake Tribal Council provide an excellent example of the role that can be played by alliances in First Nations' economic development. The forestry activities of the MLTC consist of a number of joint ventures and alliances. First, the MLTC itself is an alliance of nine First Nations. In fact, when formed in 1981 it was called the Meadow Lake District Chiefs Joint Venture. The foundation of the forestry activities and the holder of the critical asset (the FMLA), Norsask Forest Products, was formed as a joint venture between the MLTC and Techfor. The impetus for growth in the forestry industry came from two interdependent alliances. One was between Millar Western and Crown Investments to build the pulp mill. The other was the joint venture between Norsask and Millar-Western to create Mistik Management to manage the forest resource under the terms of the FMLA. Finally, the benefits to the people of the region (particularly employment) have been delivered through arrangements (although not joint ventures) between Mistik Management and various operating companies including MLTC Logging and Reforestation (a joint venture of the MLFN) and Norwest Logging and Reforestation (a joint venture of the 14 northern villages and hamlets). Results to date indicate that this system of alliances has been successful from the perspective of Millar Western and the MLTC and its people.

The MLTC forestry activities and the process and content of the 20-year plan are consistent with the eight characteristics of First Nations economic development identified in chapter 2. The approach is national and collective with many of the businesses being owned by the Tribal Council or by individual First Nations. The activities take place on traditional lands. The purpose is to attain economic self-sufficiency in support of self-government and to improve socioeconomic conditions. The process adopted involves participation in the global economy through the creation of profitable businesses, often in partnership with outside companies. Business ownership has provided the Indian people greater control over the activities on their land. Culture and traditional values are incorporated in the structure (ownership by the First Nation(s), not private Indian citizens) and methods of operation (increasing sensitivity to traditional land uses and growing use of consensus-based decision-making processes).

It also clear that the Tribal Council has learned from their experience. In an evolutionary way, the MLTC's approach to economic development shows a strengthening of the eight characteristics associated with the First Nations' approach to economic development. In particular, the process has become more consultative, more strongly centered on traditional practices, more nationally oriented (from the perspective of the First Nations), and more strongly focused on business development and successful competition in the global economy.

The MLTC's development activities have also been consistent with the contingency perspective developed in chapter 3. The MLFNs acknowledged the necessity of participation in the global economy in order to realize their vision and have attempted to create a distinct mode of development that will permit them to do so. Central to this mode is the strategy of creating "anchor" businesses through various forms of partnerships and alliances (supply contracts, subcontracting, joint ventures, etc.) with other First and non-First Nations businesses. This strategy is clearly consistent with the characteristics of flexible accumulation. It also anticipates behaviour by at least some non-MLTC partners consistent with the Doctrine of Domicile. Arrangements intended to implement the mode of development involved negotiations between key First Nation and non-First Nation leaders. The MLFNs acknowledged the need for and developed mechanisms to coordinate their activities and reduce destructive competition among them. Finally, their values, traditions and organizational structures demanded input from, and control by, people at the "grassroots" (the civil sector). When the arrangements established through negotiation between First Nation and non-First Nation leaders produced outcomes unacceptable to a significant portion of the people of the First Nations, their reactions caused the MLTC leaders to modify these arrangements.

On its part, Millar Western behaved as one would expected based on the contingency perspective and the results reported in chapter 5. The MLTC controlled resources critical to the company's future profitability. Recognizing this, Millar Western willingly entered into a network partnerships intended to satisfy both its and the MLFN's needs.

8.7. Other Aboriginal Forestry Operations

The following three cases describe other Aboriginal forestry operations.

Case 8–1: Nootka Merchandising: Making Wood Go Farther (1996)[4]

If you haven't been to Tahsis lately, you might not recognize it. A new shake mill, Nootka Merchandising, which produces top-quality wood products out of waste wood, is now gracing the handsome harbour of this small town on northern Vancouver Island. In June of this year, Nootka Merchandising opened shop, complete with a champagne christening of the mill buildings, and mill tours for the public.

The company is owned equally by all seven Mowachaht/Muchalaht First Nation chiefs and councilors. Right now, the quarterly revenue for the company is $12,000. In the future it will receive 10% of the market value of the finished product. By the time the mill is running at full capacity, the owners expect to

---

4 Source: DIAND Website, *http://www.inac.gc.ca/ecdev/entre/bc/Nootka.html* [edited].

earn nearly $80,000 annually for assisting administration and securing fibre contracts, says Larry Andrews, board director and hereditary chief of the Mowachaht/Muchalaht First Nation.

The company has just added two new saws to the plant, and is expanding to include "sawing lumbers" to its list of duties. Nootka Merchandising also makes shake or shingle blocks and paneling. The latter are 4′ × 8′ sheets of plywood covered with a layer of clear wood. The finished product, which is used for siding and wall finishing, is worth a lot more money than the original scrap wood it's built from.

The company now has a contract to receive 40,000 cubic metres of low grade cedar, which it will transform into various products. That much wood is enough to keep the plant going for about seven-and-a-half months. The company is looking for contracts for an additional 10,000 to 15,000 cubic metres of wood, which would enable the plant to stay open for a season of at least 10 months.

Nootka Merchandising has a few people to thank for its success. Andrew Petter, then Deputy Minister of Forests, made the rounds of reserves in British Columbia, announcing the provincial government's desire to see diversification in forestry, and suggesting working with low grades as an alternative.

Almost three years ago the Clarke Group installed the infrastructure for the mill, to the tune of nearly half a million dollars, after being wooed by the promise of a 20,000-cubic-metre contract for timber. The Band members, in return, invested their knowledge of the industry, found the location for the mill and secured the fibre contracts.

"The idea was to get Native employees," says Larry Andrews. Although Mowachaht/Muchalaht people have the first right-of-refusal for jobs at the shake mill, the staff is mostly non-Native. The new Mowachaht/Muchalaht reserve community, Tsaxana, near Gold River, is so comfortable no one wants to move to Tahsis. This problem is being broached by a new added-value mill in Gold River, to start construction as early as this fall; equipment has already been ordered for the operation. Once completed, the mill will consist of a chop line, kiln dryer, ripping saw and molder. Knots will be chopped out of low grade wood and the remaining wood finger-jointed back together to yield a "clean," usable quality product.

A&A Trading, Ltd. of Vancouver has invested the capital cost into this project. A joint venture has been established with Nootka Forestry under the name of Ahaminaquus Reman, Ltd. which will employ young First Nations people trained for the job. A contract has been signed between A&A Trading and the Mowachaht/Muchalaht First Nation to make its 20,000 cubic metres of timber quota available for trade to supply the raw material required for this operation.

John Mohammed of A&A Trading says the finished product will be sold in established markets in China, Korea and Japan. He says the Japanese are especially fond of the wood paneling for the interior of their traditional Japanese homes. Standard-quality lumber produced by this operation will be laminated back into durable solid posts and used for dimensional purposes in homes. When a home uses these "engineered-wood products," its value increases, since it will undoubtedly be standing longer than one built of ordinary solid posts, which tend to twist and bow.

8

Case 8–2: A (Finger-)Joint Venture (1996)[5]

Scrap wood has become a valuable asset. At least it is, to the Nak'azdli First Nation. On its reserve, just south of Fort Saint James, British Columbia, the new Tl'oh plant is making finger-joined studs and I-joists. Tl'oh Forest Products, Inc. is a joint venture between Apollo Forest Products, Ltd. of Fort St. James and Nak'ol Koh Timber, Ltd., fully owned by the Nak'azdli First Nation.

The plant was built on time and slightly under budget. "Everything went like clockwork. No hang-ups," says Robert Antoine, Tl'oh president. Apollo Forest Products feels pretty good about the deal, too. Scott Shettell, general manager of Apollo and director of Tl'oh, says, "We've been able to work out all our issues and concerns on both sides." He adds, "The plant is doing very well. We turned a profit after four months and have been ever since. Our profits are reasonable and production capacity is at 90%."

Nak'ol Koh Timber has a small business forest license to cut 469,000 cubic metres of timber over seven years. The raw wood is first sold to Apollo Forest Products at current market prices, where it is turned into many different wood products. In turn, Apollo sells an equal volume of trim ends (waste wood) to Tl'oh where value-added products are manufactured. Apollo cannot supply enough trim ends to keep the plant busy, so it purchases more from other lumber companies.

"We are most happy about putting people to work," says Nak'azdli Chief Harold Prince, who adds that the First Nation members have first right-of-refusal on Tl'oh jobs. Of the 60 staff who now work in the plant, 85% are Nak'azdli members, including the two supervisors. "We will try to maintain a 75% average," says Prince.

"It makes quite a hole in the unemployment figures. The employees of this mill make very good salaries," says Antoine. He adds that the plant now runs two eight-hour shifts and could easily run 24 hours a day when the plant is running at full capacity.

To manufacture finger-joined lumber, trim ends are dumped by conveyor into a bin where they're divided according to size, then ripped into different sizes. Each trim block has "fingers" cut into it, after which they are all lined up, glued, finger-joined together, and cut into boards of 8′ to 14′.

The I-joist unit is the newest division of the plant. These products are made from random length two-by-threes and OSB (oriented-strand board — wood chips and sawdust glued and pressed into boards). This division started in April 1996, five months after the finger-joining operation started, and is the only plant in northern British Columbia which produces I-joists. "Prior to us opening you had to buy I-joists from Calgary," says Prince.

Apollo and the First Nation each contributed $2.9-million to the venture. The Nak'azdli had $400,000 cash, and needed to finance the rest. Aboriginal Business Canada provided a repayable contribution of $900,000, and Apollo Forest Products loaned $1-million (separate from their joint-venture contribution). The balance was borrowed from the Royal Bank of Canada.

---

5 Source: DIAND Website, *http://www.inac.gc.ca/ecdev/entre/bc/Tlohe.html* [edited].

When the finished products leave the plant, Crystal Forest Industries takes over the marketing. Bill Stewart, director of Crystal Forest Industries and a board member of Tl'oh Forest Products, Inc., says that the first Japanese order of finger-joined studs was sent out in early October. Other markets for these include the Vancouver region, the Prairie provinces, and the American states of California, Tennessee, Ohio and the Carolinas. The I-joists are going into central British Columbia, the Okanagan and the Lower Mainland at this time, but, says Stewart, "I have two exporters in the Japanese market looking into marketing them there, and another person trying to get them into Oregon."

Engineered-wood products like these are popular because they are sturdier than those made of solid, natural wood, which tends to warp and bow. Robert Antoine says that their finger-joined products sell at a markup over natural products. Finger-joined two-by-threes are purchased mainly for the manufacture of recreational trailers, and the two-by-fours are popular for commercial and residential buildings, particularly because of their straightness, quality, and various long lengths.

Stewart explained that there has also been a very favourable response to the I-joists. Carpenters like working with them, apparently because the Tl'oh plant makes shorter lengths than some other plants. "It is of a size and weight they can handle. They may take two short pieces instead of a longer piece. They are easier to manoeuvre."

Case 8–3: Pic Heron Bay Development Corporation — Forestry Operation (1997)[6]

Follow a rough, rutted track through a stand of trees on the land of the Ojibways of the Pic River First Nation, and you will eventually find it.

"Don't worry — you'll know it when you see it," laughs Economic Development Officer Byron LeClair to a young rookie from the city who doesn't know what to look for.

And he's right. It's impossible to miss the sudden clearing that opens suddenly in front of the path, as the trees disappear and grass takes over. This is what they call a clear-cut.

At first glance, it just looks like a field of brown grass and bushes. A few blueberries can be seen close to the ground, struggling against the coming winter.

But a closer look reveals what's really going on. New trees, planted just after the area was cut, are beginning to push their way out of the grass and take over the land once more.

New growth is something LeClair knows a thing or two about. As Economic Development Officer for the Ojibways of the Pic River First Nation and President of the Pic Heron Bay Development Corporation, he spends his days trying to cultivate new growth in his community. This timber harvest area is helping him do that.

---

6 Source: DIAND Website, *http://www.inac.gc.ca/ecdev/entre/on/Piclog.html* [edited].

In 1982, the First Nation negotiated a third-party logging license for a small piece of their land. They lost money at first, but they kept at it, and it started to grow.

In fact, it grew so quickly that in 1984, Pic Heron Bay Development Corporation was born. The company is licensed for up to $8-million worth of lumber per year from lands along the Pic and Black Rivers.

In 1996, they expected to sell about $3-million worth to paper mills in nearby Terrace Bay and White River. The corporation is also in the final stages of negotiating a deal with a new mill in nearby Wawa, to sell poplar for use in plywood.

The forestry operation employs 20 to 25 employees each year, on a seasonal basis. Contractors from outside the First Nation are also brought in when there is a need for specialty equipment that can't be found on the reserve.

Over the years, a co-operative relationship has developed between the First Nation and the nearby town of Marathon, thereby strengthening both communities and creating new opportunities. "It makes doing business so much easier," LeClair said.

And for LeClair, doing business means more than making money. It means opportunities for his people and a way to keep the community strong.

Many members of the First Nation leave the reserve in order to obtain post-secondary education. As Economic Development Officer, LeClair wants to make sure that when they return, they will have the chance to use the knowledge and skills they have gained to help the community.

Business ventures like Pic Heron Bay Development Corporation can provide those opportunities.

"(People here) take pride in their community and the area around them. I think there's a real sense of belonging to something," LeClair said. "There's a great possibility here for doing great things."

9

Summary and Conclusions

When I began this book I had four objectives. They were to:

1. Identify the approach to economic development that is emerging among Aboriginal people in Canada.
2. Develop a theoretical perspective capable of providing insight into this approach.
3. Investigate their economic development activities to determine if these activities are consistent with the identified Aboriginal approach to development and the proposed theoretical perspective.
4. Identify actual development outcomes and compare these outcomes with expectations to determine if the adopted approach is effective.

I believe that these objectives have been accomplished.

9.1. Economic Development Goals, Strategies and Structures

In summary, the results of my research indicate that a new approach to economic development is emerging among Aboriginal people in Canada. No longer taking a passive approach, most are eagerly engaging in a wide variety of commercial activities. In doing so, Aboriginal people have adopted and are implementing a predominantly collective approach that is closely tied to each groups traditional lands, its identity as a Nation and its peoples' desire to be self-sufficient and self-governing.

This development approach is intended to serve three purposes: (i) the attainment of economic self-sufficiency as a necessary condition for the realization of self-government at the First Nation level, (ii) the improvement of socioeconomic circumstances, and (iii) the preservation and strengthening of traditional culture, values and languages. More and more, Aboriginal people believe that they can achieve these purposes through participation in the global capitalist economy and as a result they are aggressively creating businesses to compete profitably in that economy. They expect these businesses to generate the wealth necessary to support self-government and improve socioeconomic conditions. Further, as demonstrated in the MLTC case, they believe that their traditional values can be respected and supported by and used in their business activities, and they are acting on that belief.

It is clear from my research that Aboriginal people expect to exercise control over the development process to ensure that benefits accrue to their people in two ways: (i) ownership resulting in control over the business activities and the right to share in the profits from businesses and (ii) control over land and resources through land claims, treaty negotiations and Aboriginal government jurisdiction.

As is readily apparent from the results reported in chapters 5, 7 and 8, partnerships and other alliances are a very important component of the Aboriginal approach to economic development. They allow for an adequate level of Aboriginal control over business activities without requiring 100% ownership. They also allow for a more diversified and therefore less risky "portfolio" of businesses for the same capital investment. At the same time, partnerships create a synergy that combines the strengths of each of the partners and allays their weaknesses, resulting in a more successful business than any individual partner could have developed on its own. As the results reported in chapter 6 indicate, partnerships with non-Aboriginal businesses will become increasingly significant in the future as First Nations acquire additional human, financial and physical resources.

9.2. Economic Development Theory

Neither the modernization or dependency perspectives on development can be usefully applied to the emerging Aboriginal approach to development. The inadequacy of these perspectives is not limited to an Aboriginal context. As a result, many are struggling to create a perspective on economic development that is relevant in today's circumstances. I believe that my amalgam of regulation theory, the postimperial perspective and alternative/Indigenous approaches into a single "contingency perspective" is an acceptable extension of this struggle. Its development satisfies the second objective.

According to this contingency perspective, the outcomes Aboriginal people anticipate as a result of their development efforts are possible but not inevitable. Actual outcomes are contingent on the development process in all its complexities and will vary from place to place and over time. They can and will range from the bleak results anticipated by proponents of the dependency perspective, through those expected by Aboriginal people, to the equally unacceptably (to Aboriginal people) developed but homogenized outcomes anticipated by proponents of the modernization perspective. The critical question is whether the approach being adopted by Aboriginal people has the potential to deliver the results they desire. As concluded in chapter 3, at least theoretically, the answer to this question is yes. A strategy of competition in the global economy through a variety of joint ventures and alliances is well-founded.

9.3. Outcomes: On the Right Track

My third and fourth objectives were to answer this question: Are the actual outcomes experienced by Aboriginal people consistent with theoretical and/or their expectations?

With respect to theoretical expectations, at least those of the contingency perspective, the answer to this question will always, and in all circumstances, be yes. The essence of the perspective (and I believe the development process itself) is that there is a range of possible outcomes and, this being the case, whatever actually happens is consistent with theoretical expectations. Going further, the contingency perspective suggests that strategies like those adopted by Aboriginal people that are consistent with the requirements of flexible competition are more likely to be successful than those that are not. Finally, as described in chapters 5, 7, and 8, the behaviour of the corporate and Aboriginal leaders and the people as a whole (the civil sector), and the resulting socioeconomic outcomes, to the extent that they can be measured at this early stage of the process, are consistent with the perspective.

What is more important is whether the actual outcomes experienced by Aboriginal people are those they anticipated. Are they on the right track? I believe the answer "Yes, so far" is justified by my research results.

The MLTC case indicates outcomes that are consistent with the Tribal Council's expectations and the theories: Capacity is being built, jobs are being created, income and employment levels are improving and traditional practices are being respected by, and used in, the development process. The MLTC results, and the more general results for all Saskatchewan First Nations reported in chapter 7, indicate that First Nations can and are creating businesses that can compete successfully in the global economy. The type of businesses favoured by the Aboriginal approach — joint ventures/alliances and/or collectively owned competing in the global economy — dominate at the MLTC and provincial levels. Research indicates that they are the largest and most successful businesses from the perspective of long-term profitability and the creation of permanent employment. This business and employment success coupled with increasing capacity at the First Nations level through land claims and treaty settlements and a growing corporate willingness to form partnerships will ensure the continuing dominance of this strategy and its diffusion to the First Nations who have not yet adopted it. Indeed, evidence of such diffusion is widespread.

In closing, there is reason for optimism. As evidenced by the results achieved by the Inuvialuit Corporate Group, the Makivik Corporation, CREECO, the MLTC, the First Nations in Saskatchewan and the many Aboriginal ventures highlighted in the cases, the Aboriginal approach to development is working. Economic development does offer Aboriginal people hope for the future. However, a word of caution is necessary, The outcomes to date, as encouraging as they may be, fall far short of what is required to achieve even the modest goal set out by the Royal Commission on Aboriginal Peoples; that is, halving of the difference between the employment level of Aboriginal and non-Aboriginal people by the year 2015. Much remains to be done, and not just by Aboriginal people but all people living in Canada. As the report of the Royal Commission on Aboriginal Peoples so aptly points out, which the ARA and KPMG reports confirm, successful economic development by Aboriginal people will benefit all Canadians.

9

Appendices

Appendix 1

Economic Imperatives to Settle a Nisga'a Treaty†

In the spring of 1997, I submitted this letter to aid the Select Standing Committee on Aboriginal Affairs with its analysis of the social and economic impacts of the Nisga'a Agreement in Principle and future land claim settlements in British Columbia.

It had come to my attention that one key issue which the Committee has thus far had trouble addressing effectively is that of economic certainty.

Economic certainty is crucial to the success of any business endeavor. In the global marketplace, international companies who may wish to invest [in] B.C. are well aware of, and seriously concerned about, the economic uncertainty that surrounds the province as a result of unresolved land claims. The assumption is that once resolved, following any initial disruption, land claims will pave the way for future investment based on a solid foundation of common understanding.

The bottom line is that political instability is always a strike against any area that is hoping to attract investment or generate and support a lively and successful business community.

As the CEO of an investment management firm, I can point to examples such as emerging markets mutual funds, which invest primarily in developing countries. Of the 12 Hong Kong Bank mutual funds on offer, the Emerging Markets Fund is the smallest: our clients have invested $9.7 million in that fund as of the end of 1996, compared to $493 million in the domestic money market fund. Part of the difference is attributable to the safety of money market funds compared to equities, but the reality is that people do not invest their money if there is a good chance that, due to political instability, they may

---

† Milton K. Wong, Vice-president of the Hong Kong Bank of Canada, urges the B.C. government to settle the Nisga'a Land Question.
Source: http://www.ntc.bc.ca/settle.html

lose it. Keeping a close eye on political and social conditions is one of the most important jobs for fund managers responsible for such funds.

Treaties do bring change, and as a result even the most dynamic members of some societies may be understandably wary of them, fearing substantial shifts in political, social or economic conditions. It is also a commonly expressed worry among British Columbians that any gains achieved by the First Nations through treaties could result in some quantifiable loss to the rest of the population. These and similar natural fears increase the level of uncertainty and to some extent, hostility, surrounding land claims. International corporations do not want to invest in geographic regions that are prone to this kind of instability.

A Vancouver accounting firm, KPMG, has completed a Benefits & Costs analysis on the impact of treaty settlements on B.C. Consider their findings:

- When all of the financial impacts on B.C. are considered, the province can expect about three dollars worth of total financial benefit for every dollar of provincial cost. The net financial benefit to British Columbia would be between $3.9-billion and $5.3-billion over 40 years.
- The benefit arises mainly from cash awarded to First Nations. The inflow of money will spawn economic development in First Nations communities. Also, British Columbians as a whole will benefit; take-home paycheques will be up to $400 million higher, at the end of the day.
- Treaties will allow native people access to the economic and employment mainstream. As income disparity diminishes, savings in social expenditures, and less reliance on government support, will bring additional economic benefits.
- At the same time, the certainty that treaties will bring to the province's land and resources will encourage increased investment as people with renewed financial confidence spend money. First Nations will invest settlement money in the province, which will result in a modest economic boom for business people in communities nearby.
- British Columbia should see a significant employment increase as a result of the treaties. KPMG estimates settlements will produce between 7,000 and 17,000 new jobs. There will be increased investment and employment in the province because of the economic certainty that treaties will bring to its land and primary resources.

Others produced similar findings:

- According to the Nisga'a Tribal Council, currently about $13 million is pumped into the regional economy annually (the Smithers-Terrace-Prince Rupert corridor) by the Nisga'a and other tribal groups.
- At least one other early economic study estimated that B.C. has lost about $1-billion in foregone investment because of uncertainty over unresolved land claims.
- There is the human cost to be considered. Social conditions in Aboriginal communities have long been below that of other British Columbia communities, with higher infant mortality, suicide and birth rates, below average

life expectancy, welfare dependency and higher rates of unemployment. Settlements will go a long way toward resolving some of these difficulties.

Above all else, treaties are about establishing a solid, certain framework for future relations between native and non-native Canadians; and I believe that in the context of such a framework, we can establish a social, political and economic certainty that will encourage investment in British Columbia and therefore be of enormous help to business communities across the province.

Appendix 2

Comprehensive Claims Policy and Status of Claims[†]

ISSUE

What is the federal government's policy for the negotiation of comprehensive claims and the status of claims in Canada?

BACKGROUND

A federal policy for the settlement of Aboriginal land claims was established in 1973. The policy divides claims into two broad categories — specific and comprehensive.

Comprehensive land claims are based on the assertion of continuing Aboriginal title to lands and natural resources. The federal policy stipulates that land claims may be negotiated with Aboriginal groups in areas where claims to Aboriginal title have not been addressed by treaty or through other legal means.

The federal government has, however, accepted some claims for negotiation as comprehensive claims in areas affected by treaties. The claims of the Dene and Metis in Treaties 8 and 11 within the Northwest Territories were accepted for negotiation on the basis that the land provisions of the treaties had not been implemented. Claims from Treaty 8 and Douglas Treaty First Nations in British Columbia have also been accepted for negotiation within the British Columbia Treaty Commission process on the basis that it is necessary to negotiate consistent new relationships with Aboriginal groups in that province, particularly with respect to resource management.

The thrust of the 1973 Comprehensive Claims Policy, which was reaffirmed in 1981, was to exchange claims to undefined Aboriginal rights for a clearly

---

† November 21, 1997. Source: http://www.inac.gc.ca/subject/claims/comp/ccpol.html#issue

defined package of rights and benefits set out in a settlement agreement. A 1982 constitutional amendment provided that the rights of an Aboriginal group defined in its comprehensive claim agreement are constitutionally protected.

Significant amendments to the Comprehensive Claims Policy were announced in December 1986, following an extensive period of consultation with Aboriginal and other groups. The revised policy improved the negotiation process, allowed for greater flexibility in land tenure, and provided a clearer definition of the topics for negotiation. These changes have contributed to the achievement of settlements in recent years.

The 1986 Comprehensive Land Claims Policy allows for the retention of Aboriginal rights on land which Aboriginal people will hold following the conclusion of a claim settlement, to the extent that such rights are not inconsistent with the settlement agreement. The policy also ensures that any rights that are unrelated to land will not be affected by the settlement.

Under the Government of Canada's 1995 Inherent Right Policy, self-government arrangements may be negotiated simultaneously with comprehensive claims agreements. The Government of Canada is prepared, where the other parties agree, to constitutionally protect certain aspects of self-government agreements as treaty rights within the meaning of section 35 of the Constitution Act, 1982. Self-government arrangements may be protected under section 35 as part of comprehensive land claim agreements.

In the provinces, most of the lands and resources that are the subject of comprehensive claim negotiations are under provincial jurisdiction. Moreover, by establishing certainty of title to lands and resources, claims settlements benefit the provinces. It is the position of the federal government that provincial governments must participate in negotiations and contribute to the provision of benefits to Aboriginal groups.

On September 25, 1990, the federal government announced that the process for the negotiation of comprehensive claims would be expanded. The previous six-claim limit on the number of negotiations which could be undertaken at one time was eliminated.

Twelve claims have been settled, the most recent being those of the six Yukon First Nations.

A summary of the status of comprehensive land claims settled and those currently in negotiation is attached.

STATUS OF COMPREHENSIVE CLAIMS

Settled Claims

Twelve comprehensive claim agreements have come into effect since the announcement of the federal government's claims policy in 1973. These are:

The James Bay and Northern Quebec Agreement (1977);

The Northeastern Quebec Agreement (1978);

The Inuvialuit Final Agreement (1984);

The Gwich'in Agreement (1992);

The Nunavut Land Claims Agreement (1993);

The Sahtu Dene and Metis Agreement (1994);

Six Yukon First Nation Final Agreements based on the Council for Yukon Indians Umbrella Final Agreement (1993) and corresponding Self-Government Agreements for:

The Vuntut Gwich'in First Nation (1995);

The First Nation of Nacho Nyak Dun (1995);

The Teslin Tlingit Council (1995);

The Champagne and Aishihik First Nations (1995);

The Little Salmon/Carmacks First Nation (1997); and

The Selkirk First Nation (1997).

Description of Settled Claims

James Bay and Northern Quebec Claim

Area Claimed: 5,543 square kilometres of settlement land for the Cree, and 8,151 square kilometres of settlement land for the Inuit.

Population: 11,088 Cree and 7,268 Inuit

This was the first settled comprehensive claim. The final agreement was signed in 1975, and came into effect in 1977.

The settlement provided for $225 million (1975 dollars) for the Cree and the Inuit, which has been paid in full; full harvesting rights over 150,000 square kilometres; participation in an environmental and social protection regime; an income security program for hunters and trappers; and self-government under the Cree-Naskapi (of Quebec) Act.

Northeastern Quebec Claim

Area Claimed: Same as James Bay and Northern Quebec Agreement (JBNQA)

Population: 602 Naskapi

This agreement was signed in 1978 and amended the James Bay and Northern Quebec Agreement to integrate the Naskapi.

It provided the Naskapi people with $9 million, as well as settlement lands, rights and benefits equivalent to the JBNQA.

Inuvialuit Claim

Area Claimed: 11,000 square kilometres in fee simple and subsurface land; 91,000 square kilometres in settlement land; and 435,000 square kilometres in settlement area

Population: 2,500 Inuvialuit

The Inuvialuit claim was accepted for negotiation on May 13, 1976, and the final agreement, signed in June 1984, was effective July 1984. The settlement provided the Inuvialuit with approximately 91,000 square kilometres of land (of which 13,000 square kilometres includes mineral rights); and includes a financial component of $152 million (1984 dollars) and a one time payment of $10 million to an economic enhancement fund and $7.5 million to a social development fund. It also includes wildlife harvesting rights, socioeconomic initiatives, and participation in wildlife and environmental management.

Dene and Metis Claims

In 1976 and 1977, Canada accepted comprehensive claims from the Dene and Metis of the Mackenzie Valley in the Northwest Territories (NWT). Negotiation of a joint Dene/Metis claim began in 1981. An agreement was initialed by negotiators in April 1990. In July 1990, the Dene and Metis at their assemblies voted not to proceed with ratification of the agreement. The Gwich'in and Sahtu Dene and Metis did not agree with this action and withdrew from the Dene/Metis negotiating group; they requested regional settlements. In November 1990, the government discontinued negotiation of the Dene/Metis claim and authorized the negotiation of separate regional settlements, based on the April 1990 agreement, with any of the five Dene and Metis regions that might request it.

GWICH'IN CLAIM

Area claimed: 57,000 square kilometres in the Mackenzie Delta Region of the Northwest Territories; and a "primary use area" in the Yukon

Population: approximately 3,000

The Gwich'in of the Mackenzie Delta Region were the first Dene and Metis group to negotiate a regional comprehensive claim. Their final agreement was signed on April 22, 1992, and came into effect in December 1992.

The settlement provided the Gwich'in with approximately 24,000 square kilometres of land in the Northwest Territories, 4,299 square kilometres of which includes mineral rights, and 1,554 square kilometres of Tetlit Gwich'in Yukon Land in the Yukon; $75 million (1990 dollars) over 15 years; a share of resource royalties from the Mackenzie Valley; guaranteed wildlife harvesting rights; and participation in decision-making bodies dealing with renewable resources, land use planning, environmental impact and assessment review, and land and water use regulation.

SAHTU DENE AND METIS CLAIM

Area claimed: 280,278 square kilometres in the Great Bear Lake region of the Northwest Territories

Population: approximately 2,000

The Sahtu Dene and Metis were the second Dene and Metis group to seek a regional comprehensive land claim. Their final agreement was signed on September 6, 1993 and came into effect on June 23, 1994.

The settlement provided the Sahtu Dene and Metis with 41,437 square kilometres of land (of which 1,813 square kilometres includes mineral rights); $75 million (1990 dollars) over 15 years; a share of resource royalties from the Mackenzie Valley; guaranteed wildlife harvesting rights; and participation in decision-making bodies dealing with renewable resources, land use planning, environmental impact assessment and review, and land and water use regulation.

TUNGAVIK FEDERATION OF NUNAVUT (TFN) CLAIM

Area claimed: 1.9 million square kilometres in N.W.T., central and eastern Arctic

Date accepted: 1977

Population: 19,000 Inuit

This claim represents the largest comprehensive claim settlement in Canada. The settlement provides the Inuit with approximately 351,000 square kilometres of land (of which 37,000 square kilometres includes mineral rights); $1.17 billion ($580 million in 1989 dollars plus interest) in financial benefits over 14 years; a share of resource royalties; guaranteed wildlife harvesting rights; and participation in decision-making processes dealing with land and environmental management.

A political accord was signed by the federal and territorial governments and the TFN on October 30, 1992. The accord outlines the powers of and timing for the creation of a Nunavut Territorial Government. A referendum dealing with the boundary of the proposed new territory was approved by a majority of residents of the N.W.T. Both the Nunavut Land Claims Agreement Act (Bill C-133) and an Act to divide the N.W.T. and create the Territory of Nunavut (Bill C-132) were passed in June 1993.

On April 30, 1996, Iqaluit was officially declared the future capital of Nunavut. In a plebiscite held on December 11, 1995, residents voted 60.2% in favour of Iqaluit as their future capital. The government is committed to proceeding with what is essential to get the Government of Nunavut established and operational by April 1, 1999. $150 million will be provided by the federal government to cover costs associated with the creation of this new territory, including training, capital, operating and maintenance budgets and the establishment of the Office of the Interim Commissioner. Jack Anawak has been named Interim Commissioner.

COUNCIL FOR YUKON INDIANS (CYI) CLAIM

Area claimed: Whole of Yukon Territory

Date accepted: 1973

Population: approximately 8,000 Indians

On May 29, 1993, the federal government, the Yukon government, and the CYI signed an Umbrella Final Agreement (UFA) and final agreements with four Yukon First Nations (YFNs): the Vuntut Gwitchin First Nation; the First Nation of the Nacho Nyak Dun; the Champagne and Aishihik First Nations; and the Teslin Tlingit Council. The UFA establishes the basis for the negotiation of individual settlements with each of the 14 YFNs. It also provides for the negotiation of self-government agreements with Yukon First Nations. Self-government agreements were also signed with the four First Nations on May 29, 1993.

The settlement and self-government legislation was introduced into Parliament on May 31, 1994 and received Royal Assent on July 7, 1994. The surface rights legislation received Royal Assent on December 15, 1994. All three acts came into force concurrently on February 14, 1995.

On July 21, 1997, final and Self-government agreements were signed with Little Salmon/Carmacks (LSCFN) and Selkirk First Nations (SFN). The agreements for both LSCFN and SFN came into effect on October 1, 1997.

The final agreements provide the six YFNs (approximately 3,505 beneficiaries) with settlement land of 24,701 square kilometres (5.7% of the land mass of the Yukon), of which 16,576 square kilometres include ownership of mines and minerals. This is their share of the total settlement lands for all YFNs, which will amount to 41,595 square kilometres, of which 25,900 square kilometres includes mines and minerals. The six YFNs will receive financial benefits of $112,068,620 (1989 dollars) to be paid out in 15 annual installments, as their share of the total $242,673,000 (1989 dollars) for all YFNs. In addition, these YFNs will benefit from rights in the management of national parks and wildlife areas, specific rights for fish and wildlife harvesting, and special economic and employment opportunities.

Claims In Negotiation

Dogrib Claim Treaty 11

Area claimed: 210,000 square kilometres in the North Slave region of the Northwest Territories

Date accepted: June 1992

Population: 3,000

The Dogrib Treaty 11 land claim and self-government negotiations have been proceeding at an accelerated pace since a new federal negotiating mandate was approved in April 1997. Substantial agreement has been reached on the core land claim subjects. The parties commenced negotiations of self-government subjects in the fall of 1997. It is expected that an agreement-in-principle will be concluded in 1998.

Presently, two interim agreements are in place. The Interim Land Withdrawal Agreement removes from future disposition 13,000 square kilometres of land surrounding the four Dogrib communities. The Interim Protection Agreement provides the Dogrib Treaty 11 Council the ability to participate in the regulatory processes in the North Slave Region.

Treaty 8 Dene

Treaty 8 Dene (N'dilo, Dettah, Lutsel K'e, and Deninu Kue First Nations) are members of the Akaitcho Territory Tribal Corporation who were formerly part of the Dene-Métis Agreement of April 1990, which was not ratified.

From 1992 to 1996, the Akaitcho Dene First Nations (DFN) were pursuing a Treaty Land Entitlement settlement, in part to avoid the extinguishment clause in comprehensive claims settlements. These talks were unsuccessful, and in November 1996, representatives of Akaitcho DFN (including the Chiefs of N'dilo, Dettah, Lutsel K'e, and Deninu Kue First Nations), the Government of the Northwest Territories and the federal government participated in an interest-based exploratory workshop. A joint workplan to further explore interests was agreed upon, including the creation of a tripartite working group to explore the claims settlement interests; establish common interests and objectives; and sketch out the general parameters of a settlement package. Discussions have been proceeding well. An exchange of correspondence between the Akaitcho DFN and the Minister took place on the resumption of formal negotiations. The Akaitcho DFN and the Minister met August 13, 1997 and announced the resumption of formal negotiations. The GNWT is a party to these negotiations.

Yukon First Nations Claim

Land claim, self-government and implementation negotiations have been concluded with Tr'ondëk Hewch'in First Nation (Dawson) and the agreements will be initialed by negotiators in the near future. Land claim and self-government negotiations with Ta'an Kwach'an (TK) substantially concluded on May 21, 1996. Implementation plan negotiations are now substantially complete, however, the TK agreements can not be concluded until the band separation issue with Kwanlin Dun is resolved.

The remaining six YFNs are in various stages of active negotiations. Of these, we expect that two, Kluane and White River, will conclude negotiations by the end of 1997.

Atikamekw and Montagnais Claims

Area claimed: 700,000 square kilometres in Quebec and Labrador

Date accepted: 1979

Population: 18,284

The Atikamekw and Montagnais Claim (AMC) involves 12 communities. A framework agreement was signed with the Conseil des Atikamekw et des Montagnais (CAM), the Province of Quebec and the Government of Canada in September 1988 outlining the parameters of the negotiations. An interim measures agreement was signed in 1989 and expired in 1991. On December 15, 1994 Quebec tabled a global offer to the Atikamekw and the Montagnais covering the major aspects of an agreement-in-principle (AIP). The CAM was dissolved in late 1994 and replaced by three tribal groups: Assemblé Mamu Pakatatau Mamit representing the Mamit Innuat First Nation (Lower North Shore); the Conseil de la Nation Atikamekw (CNA) representing Atikamekw

Iriniw; and the Mamuitum Tribal Council (Centre Bloc) representing the Innu Montagnais.

The Assemblé Mamu Pakatatau Mamit submitted a proposal in November 1995 in response to the Quebec Offer of December 1994. Tripartite negotiations are presently being pursued on the basis of their AIP proposal with both governments and the objective is to reach an AIP by December 1998. The Conseil Tribal Mamuitun also submitted a proposal in February 1997 in response to the Quebec Offer of December 1994. Tripartite negotiations are presently being pursued on the basis of their AIP proposal with both governments and the objective is to reach an AIP by the summer of 1998. The Conseil de la Nation Atikamekw submitted their proposal in January 1996. On September 11, 1997, a Political Protocol was signed between the Quebec government, the federal government and the CNA. This protocol is instrumental as a negotiation accelerator for the Atikamekw party. Tripartite negotiations are presently being pursued on the basis of their AIP proposal with both governments and the objective is to reach an AIP by the summer of 1998.

Makivik Claim — Offshore (N.W.T.) and Labrador (Onshore and Offshore)

Area claimed: Offshore area adjacent to Quebec and Labrador, and inland northeast Labrador.

Date accepted: 1992 (N.W.T. portion) and 1993 (Labrador portion)

Population: 7,500

In 1974 Canada agreed to negotiate with the Inuit of Northern Quebec, represented by Makivik Corporation, with respect to certain offshore islands along the coast of Quebec in the Northwest Territories. Following the announcement of the 1986 Comprehensive Claims Policy, the claim was considerably revised and accepted again in January, 1992 (N.W.T. portion) and June 1993 (Labrador portion). It now includes the offshore islands and offshore areas along the coast of northern Quebec and Labrador, and an inland area in northern Labrador. A framework agreement was signed in August 1993 and agreement-in-principle negotiations are proceeding on a monthly basis for the N.W.T. portion. The Government of the Northwest Territories participates as part of the federal government negotiating team. Subjects under federal jurisdiction are also under negotiation for the Labrador portion.

Labrador Inuit Association (LIA) Claim

Area claimed: Coast line, interior, and offshore of northern Labrador

Date accepted: 1978

Population: 5,000 Inuit and Native settlers

A framework agreement setting out the scope, process, topics, and parameters for negotiation was signed in November 1990, by the LIA and the Governments of Canada, and Newfoundland and Labrador (Newfoundland).

In November 1991, a sub-agreement was initialed on eligibility and enrollment. In May 1992, Canada discontinued its participation in formal tripartite negotiations of land claims in Labrador as governments were unable to reach agreement on their respective roles and responsibilities, including the sharing of settlement costs.

On December 20, 1993, former Minister, Ronald A. Irwin, announced the resumption of AIP negotiations and Canada's return to the table without preconditions. This fulfilled a commitment in the Aboriginal Policy of the Liberal Plan for Canada. Negotiations continued at an even pace through the early stages of the discovery of nickel, cobalt and copper at Voisey's Bay in 1994.

In September 1996, fast-track negotiations commenced in St. John's with a target date for reaching an AIP by March 31, 1977. Although the target date was not met, the parties continued to negotiate a number of issues. In order to facilitate the conclusion of an AIP, senior officials and negotiators for the three parties met in Ottawa in October 1997. On October 28, 1997, a document was initialed which sets out agreements and understandings that will serve as directives for negotiators during further negotiation of the AIP. Negotiations are scheduled to resume the week of November 24th with the focus on self-government related issues.

Innu Nation Claim

Area claimed: Central Labrador and Quebec lower north shore

Date accepted: 1978

Population: 1,600 (500 Naskapi, 1,100 Montagnais)

Canada conditionally accepted the Innu land claim for negotiation in 1978, subject to provincial participation and a land use and occupancy study. The Government of Newfoundland and Labrador confirmed its willingness to negotiate in September 1990 and the Innu completed their occupancy study in October 1990.

The federal and provincial governments and the Innu Nation began negotiating toward a framework agreement in July 1991 and the parties made significant progress toward an agreement. However, on two separate occasions, negotiations were suspended: between May 1992 and March 1994; and again between September 1994 and May 1995. Tripartite negotiations among the Innu Nation and the federal and provincial governments resumed in May 1995 and on October 19, 1995, negotiators initialed a framework agreement. On March 29, 1996, the President of the Innu Nation, Peter Penashue, Premier Brian Tobin of Newfoundland and former Minister Irwin signed the framework agreement for the Innu Nation land claim at a signing ceremony held in St. John's. A self-government framework agreement was also signed on February 27, 1997.

Negotiations toward an agreement-in-principle (AIP) are proceeding well. The parties are presently looking at ways of fast-tracking these negotiations.

Nisga'a Claim

AIP signed March 22, 1996

Date accepted: 1976

Population: 6,000

Canada began negotiating with NTC in 1976, well before the establishment of the British Columbia Treaty Commission process. Negotiations continued on a bilateral basis until British Columbia formally joined the process in 1990. In 1991 the three parties signed a framework agreement which identified the topics for substantive negotiation toward the AIP. Between 1992 and 1995, the parties conducted approximately 200 consultation meetings and public events concerning the Nisga'a negotiations.

On March 22, 1996 Ronald Irwin, former Minister of Indian Affairs and Northern Development, John Cashore, B.C. Minister of Aboriginal Affairs and Chief Joe Gosnell, Nisga'a Tribal Council, signed the agreement-in-principle (AIP) which will form the basis for the first modern-day treaty in British Columbia. The AIP calls for a payment to the Nisga'a of $190 million in cash and the establishment of a Nisga'a Central Government with ownership of and self-government over 1,900 square kilometres of land in the Nass River Valley. The agreement also outlines the Nisga'a ownership of surface and subsurface resources on Nisga'a lands and spells out entitlements to Nass River salmon stocks and wildlife harvests. The parties are presently negotiating the final agreement.

CLAIMS IN BRITISH COLUMBIA (B.C.)

The tripartite British Columbia Claims Task Force Report, released on July 3, 1991, contained 19 recommendations on how to negotiate the settlement on the land question in B.C.. A key recommendation was to establish an arm's-length British Columbia Treaty Commission (BCTC) to facilitate and monitor treaty negotiations and to allocate negotiation funding to B.C. Aboriginal groups.

On September 21, 1992, the governments of Canada and British Columbia, and the First Nations' Summit formally supported the establishment of the Commission by signing the British Columbia Treaty Commission Agreement. The BCTC was established on an interim basis by provincial and federal orders-in-council on April 13 and 14, 1993 respectively, and by Resolution of the Summit on April 5, 1993. On October 19, 1995 the federal government introduced the BCTC legislation. Bill C107 received Royal Assent on December 15, 1995.

The BCTC consists of five Commissioners: two nominated by the Summit; one nominated by each of the federal and provincial governments; and a Chief Commissioner chosen by all three principals. The BCTC will facilitate, not negotiate, modern-day treaties. Its main functions are to assess the readiness of parties to begin negotiations, allocate negotiation funding to Aboriginal groups, assist parties to obtain dispute resolution services at the request of all parties, and monitor and report on the status of negotiations. The treaty negotiation process is open to all B.C. First Nations, the majority of which have never signed or adhered to treaties.

On June 21, 1993, Canada and B.C. signed a memorandum of understanding (MOU) on the sharing of costs as well as roles and responsibilities for treaty settlements. This provides a substantive basis for beginning new treaty negotiations in B.C. On June 29, 1993, the two governments created a cross-sectoral structure for joint third-party consultation: the Treaty Negotiation Advisory Committee (TNAC). The role of the TNAC is to provide policy and negotiating advice to governments on treaty-related matters that may directly affect third parties.

The BCTC opened its doors in December 1993. To date, 51 Statements of Intent to negotiate, representing over 70% of B.C. First Nations, have been accepted by the BCTC. Initial meetings have been held with all of the First Nations whose Statements of Intent have been accepted as complete. The submission of a Statement of Intent is the first stage of the six-stage B.C. treaty-making process.

The BCTC is currently determining the readiness of all parties to negotiate. To date, 42 negotiating tables have been declared ready. Framework agreements have been initialed by the negotiators in the Cariboo Tribal Council, Nazko, Sto:lo, Hul'quimi'num and Esketemc negotiations, and signed with Gitanyow, Champagne and Aishihik, Sechelt, Gitxsan, Wet'suwet'en, Ditidaht/Patcheenaht, Teslin Tlingit, Kaska Dena, Homalco, Nuu-chah-nulth Tribal Council, In-Shuck-Ch/N'Quatqua, Sliammon, Lheit-Lit'en, Ts'kw'aylaxw, Yekoochete'en, Haisla, Te'mexw, Yale, Klahoose, Tsimshian, Tsleil Waututh, Tsay-Keh Dene, Taku River, Nanaimo, Westbank, Carrier Sekani Tribal Council, Heiltsuk, Xaxli'p (Fountain Band), and Tsawwassen negotiations.

Appendix 3

UN Experts Seminar: Indigenous Land Claims†

Dear Friends,

We are pleased to enclose for your information the conclusions emanated from the U.N. Experts Seminar on Land Rights and Claims, which took part in Whitehorse, Yukon, March 24–28, 1996.

As these conclusions are the result[s] of consensual agreement among all the participants present at the end of the meeting, they are not open to revision, however, they represent fully the wishes of indigenous peoples around the table.

We hope you will be able to be in a position to give this document the widest possible circulation.

We thank you for your cooperation,

Rodrigo Contreras
Executive Director
WCIP Headquarters
100 Argyle Avenue
Ottawa, Ontario
Canada, K2P 1B6
Tel: (613) 230–9030
Fax: (613) 230–9340

CONCLUSIONS AND RECOMMENDATIONS

The United Nations Expert Seminar on Practical Experiences regarding Indigenous Land Rights and Claims meeting at Whitehorse, Canada, from 24 to 28 March 1996, bearing in mind and building upon important work already accom-

† Ottawa, 1 April 1996. Source: http://ces.iisc.ernet.in/hpg/envis/doc33.html

plished by the United Nations system, in particular in the area of standard-setting and within the context of other expert seminars such as the Expert meeting on indigenous self-government held in Nuuk, Greenland, and meetings taking into account the new partnerships between indigenous peoples and the international community based on mutual respect, reciprocity and harmonious, accessible and equitable process offers the following conclusions and recommendations for the consideration of governments, indigenous peoples and their organizations, and intergovernmental and non-governmental organizations.

1. Indigenous peoples have a distinctive spiritual and material relationship with their lands, and with the air, waters, coastal sea, ice, flora, fauna and other resources.

2. The importance of the issue of the link between self-determination and the right to land is recognized.

3. The promotion and protection of rights over lands and resources of indigenous peoples are vital for their development and cultural survival.

4. Indigenous peoples continue to be affected by the consequences of colonialism and are often deprived of a land and resource base.

5. Governments should recognize the lands rights and titles of indigenous peoples and implement effective and appropriate procedures and mechanisms, including constitutional, legal or treaty agreements.

6. Throughout the whole process, the procedures for the recognition of these rights, should provide for the effective representation and informed participation of indigenous peoples as equals. Without this, whatever legislation or treaty on this matter constitutes an imposition and not an enduring agreement.

7. States should make best efforts to guarantee access to land of indigenous peoples deprived of their land or who lack sufficient land and depend upon it for their survival, in order to guarantee their cultural and material development. Mechanisms such as land funds a claim settlement process where they exist are encouraged.

8. The recognition of rights of indigenous peoples to specific lands which they occupy cannot be separated from the recognition of other rights, within larger areas necessary for their material and cultural development.

9. Governments should review their laws and policies in order to address the concept of the inherent rights to self-government and self-management of indigenous peoples.

10. The existence of a fair constitutional and legal system, including a fair judicial system, able to guarantee due process of law is an important framework for the success and implementation of land settlement processes. In some countries experience has shown that the establishment of fair judicial processes for the implementation of treaties, agreements and other constructive arrangements with indigenous peoples has been

a useful means toward the respect of such agreements and the education of the indigenous and non-indigenous communities.

11. Experience has shown that the equitable and fair conclusion and implementation of treaties, agreements and other constructive arrangements relating to land between states and indigenous peoples can contribute to environmentally sound and sustainable development for the benefit of all.

12. The International Decade of the World's Indigenous People is an important vehicle for substantive participation of indigenous peoples in the resolution of land settlements and for increasing constructive partnerships with states and non-indigenous communities.

13. I.L.O. Convention 169 is regarded by indigenous peoples as articulating some minimum standards respecting indigenous land rights. "The United Nations draft Declaration on the Rights of Indigenous Peoples" as adopted by the Sub-Commission on Prevention of Discrimination and Protection of Minorities could be considered an opportunity for States to adopt an instrument reflecting a broad consensus among indigenous peoples about their land and resource rights.

14. Land rights and compensation issues arising from the taking or use of indigenous lands for military or security purposes, whether in war or in peacetime, can raise special problems, which need to be addressed by Governments and the international community.

15. Where land agreements are intended to protect the way of life or cultural integrity of indigenous peoples, social issues should be given equal emphasis to economic and resource issues.

16. Political will, in the form of a genuine commitment on the part of Governments, to partnership, in decision making is essential to the success of co-management regimes, and to the avoidance of adversarial relations between the parties to such regimes.

17. Land rights settlements should be freely negotiated, in good faith and not imposed unilaterally by legislation or negotiated under duress or threat.

18. Governments should renounce discriminatory legal doctrines and policies which deny human rights or limit indigenous land and resource rights. In particular, they should consider adopting corrective legislation and policies, within the International Decade, regarding the following:
    (a) The doctrine of terra nullius.
    (b) The doctrine that indigenous communities do not have the capacity to own land or to own land in their collective capacity.
    (c) The doctrine that indigenous land, title or ownership may be taken or impaired by the state or third parties without due process of law and adequate and appropriate compensation.
    (d) Doctrines or policies that indigenous lands must be held in trust regardless of the will of the indigenous peoples concerned.

(e) Doctrines and policies imposing an extinguishment of indigenous land rights, title or ownership.
(f) Policies which exclude some indigenous peoples from the land claims process established by the state.

19. Principles or guidelines for land selection or demarcation of indigenous lands should be jointly negotiated in a fair and equitable process and without the imposition of arbitrary criteria.

20. Governments, with indigenous peoples, should establish fair procedures for reviewing situations and for taking corrective action in situations in which indigenous land or resources have been taken or extinguished through processes which are claimed or are found to be fundamentally unfair or discriminatory.

21. Governments have a responsibility to ensure indigenous peoples have access to adequate resources to research and negotiate their claims so that settlements are equitable, just and enduring.

22. The structure, mandate, objectives, representation and accountability of members and mode of operation, including funding, of co-management structures should be determined through a process of negotiation with the indigenous parties to support the principle of equal participation.

23. It is important that practical effect be given to the spirit and intent of treaties and land agreements. This requires a willingness by the parties to act as partners, not adversaries as well as a clear understanding of the spirit and intent of treaties and land agreements by all parties.

24. Parties should negotiate on a basis of equality acknowledging indigenous leadership, structures, languages, social and legal systems in all aspects of the negotiations and implementation. For example, every effort must be made for agreements relating to land rights to be drafted in the language of the indigenous peoples concerned and for the indigenous language version to have equal status to the state language versions.

25. Interim protection measures, such as moratoriums on land transfers and on implementation of proposed development projects, should be taken, as necessary to protect indigenous lands or lands claimed by indigenous peoples from environmental degradation and alienation to third parties. Such measures would contribute to an atmosphere of good faith and constructive spirit in the negotiation process.

26. Effective measures for implementation, dispute resolution, amendment and enforcement of land settlements and agreements should be provided.

27. There is serious need for training, education and the required resources so that indigenous peoples may enter negotiations processes fully informed and technically equipped about the whole spectrum of implications of land rights negotiations. Training and education should also figure prominently in settlements implementation.

28. The equal participation of indigenous women should be reflected in all aspects of negotiation and implementation of land agreements.

29. There is a need to inform the non-indigenous public about the significance of indigenous land rights for the very survival of indigenous peoples and respect [for] their human rights. Land agreements are a way of building new constructive relationships between indigenous and non-indigenous communities.

30. Governments are urged to consider the establishment of impartial mechanisms to oversee and facilitate fair and equitable conclusions to land claims processes and the implementation of land agreements, including international mechanisms as necessary.

31. In its consideration of the establishment of a permanent forum of indigenous peoples, the United Nations General Assembly should consider whether the forum could play a constructive role regarding problems pertaining to land rights.

32. The United Nations should prepare a study involving the direct participation of indigenous experts on the issue of extinguishment of land rights and its implications with a view to recommending new approaches in this area with particular regard to the recognition and implementation of rights.

33. The United Nations and its specialized agencies should consider providing technical assistance to states and indigenous peoples to contribute to the resolution of land claims.

34. The World Bank should consider providing loans to indigenous peoples directly, in particular in relation to collectively owned land.

35. The United Nations system, before funding demarcation projects, should have adequate consultative mechanisms at all stages of the planning and implementation of projects.

36. The I.L.O Committee of Experts should clarify the interpretation of Article 14, paragraph 1 of I.L.O. Convention No. 169.

37. [Missing in original document]

38. It should be recognized that indigenous resource management ensures the sustainability for future generations and is rich in practical applications of [wildlife], fish and habitat conservation.

39. Parties in land rights negotiation should make particular efforts to ascertain and act upon the views of elders in these matters.

40. International cooperation in support of the administrative management of their lands and resources should be done in full cooperation with indigenous peoples.

41. Indigenous peoples should participate in decision making and policy regarding land, resources and development at international, regional, na-

tional and local levels, including UN processes such as the CSD and the Convention on Biological Diversity.

42. The implementation of sustainable development should take fully into account Indigenous Peoples' values, knowledge and technologies, in order to ensure resources for future generations.

43. The United Nations, its Specialized Agencies and other Intergovernmental organizations should assure that indigenous peoples cultural diversity, traditional values and ways of life are protected in terms of Agenda 21 and the institutions established for its follow-up.

44. Where the division of indigenous lands and attempts to divide these lands through individual titles as well as the existence of land privatization policies menace the material and cultural survival of indigenous peoples this is a matter of grave concern.

45. Governments should welcome, encourage and open up trade among indigenous peoples and other parties from different countries and facilitate such trade.

46. For the purpose of developing resources of indigenous peoples and communities, States and Inter-governmental organizations which provide international aid for such purposes, should make best efforts to provide development assistance through organizations of indigenous peoples

47. The United Nations, in the framework of the International Decade, should consider holding further consultations, workshops and seminars relating to indigenous land rights and interests focusing on issues such as the negotiation process, co-management regimes and other matters.

48. The Expert Seminar requests that the present report be submitted to the 14th session of the Working Group on Indigenous Populations and annexed to the Secretary-General's report on the International Decade to be presented to the 51st session of the General Assembly and that it be published and given the widest possible dissemination.

49–55. Additional recommendations for the UN system based on the text submitted by the Expert Roger Plant to be included.

Final unedited version prepared by Preston Hardison from a document released by the World Council of Indigenous Peoples. The electronic version has been checked for errors, but this is not an official copy and any errors remain the responsibility of the typist. For more information, please contact the WCIP.

Appendix 4

Social and Economic Impacts of Aboriginal Land Claims Settlements†

A Case Study Analysis

British Columbia is on the verge of resolving Aboriginal land claims, one of the most contentious issues in the province's history. The debate over First Nations' demands for land settlements divided the province and the nation in the past, but the establishment of a process for negotiating treaties has provided a new and clear framework for bringing this controversial matter to a satisfactory close. Most of those who have raised objections to certain aspects of the treaty process have nonetheless acknowledged that settling Aboriginal land claims is a provincial priority. Moreover, there is widespread agreement within the province that negotiating treaties with the First Nations is in the best interests of all British Columbians.

The decision taken in the early 1990s to proceed with the settlement of Aboriginal land claims has not brought unanimous acceptance, but there remains a strong consensus that negotiated treaties are essential to end the uncertainty that surrounds the issues of land, resource use and self-government. British Columbians wonder how complex legal agreements will affect their lives and circumstances and some worry that the historic agreements will fundamentally alter the social, economic and political make-up of the province. These concerns are a logical result of the decades-long public debate about the meaning and nature of Aboriginal land claims and reflect the high public expectations that have developed around the treaty-making process.

---

† December 1995. Summary Report prepared for the Ministry of Aboriginal Affairs, Province of British Columbia, Federal Treaty Negotiation Office, Government of Canada. Original report was prepared by ARA Consulting Group, Inc. Summary report was prepared by Ken S. Coates. Source: http://www.aaf.gov.bc.ca/aaf/pubs arasumm.htm.

One valuable means of anticipating the potential consequences of the treaty-making process for British Columbia is to consider the nature and impact of modern land claims settlements elsewhere in Canada and in other countries. On the legal and administrative side, comparative analysis is crucial to the progress of negotiations. Lawyers have, for years, followed national and international precedents, building a case for Canadian action on the basis of decisions and actions in countries from New Zealand to the United States of America. First Nations, linked through national and international networks, have likewise tracked international developments with great interest. Northern Canadian First Nations, for example, drew heavily on the Alaska Native Claims Settlement Act in deciding what they wanted, and did not want, in their treaties.

The comparative dimension only occasionally enters into the realm of public and political discussion. British Columbians, like New Zealanders, Yukoners, Australians, Alaskans and others before them, tend to see the land claims issue and its resolution as unique to their province and their circumstances. Treaty negotiations are not particular to Canada, let alone British Columbia. Many of the same problems, uncertainties, fears and expectations currently being experienced in British Columbia have been encountered elsewhere. British Columbians have a great deal to learn from these examples, because the provincial treaty process arises out of and is influenced by international developments and settlements. There is much to gain from considering other treaties and land settlement processes. The final agreements in British Columbia will respond to the specific historical and contemporary realities of the province and of the First Nations.

A NEW ZEALAND EXAMPLE

Consider, by way of illustration, a very recent example from the South Pacific. In October 1995, the Tainui (Maori) people of the Waikato District in New Zealand signed a treaty with the Government of New Zealand. The negotiation process was long and arduous and appeared, at several points, destined to run off the rails. Non-Maori (Pakeha) protests occasionally stilled the government's hand, and disagreements among the Tainui threatened to break off discussions. But proponents of a final settlement pushed ahead, leading to a final agreement in the winter of 1995. The settlement agreement received all-party endorsement and the legislation passed unanimously, and was hailed by Maori and Pakeha alike as a major step forward.

Within a matter of days, the Tainui announced their plans for the implementation of the economic portions of the final settlement, which included the transfer of some Crown lands to them, the use of settlement funds to purchase commercial properties, and the establishment of major educational endowments for Tainui development. The final signatures transformed a conceptual enterprise — the negotiation of a land settlement — into a practical matter. The Tainui quickly assumed a role as development partners in the Waikato, investigating the prospects of participating in an expansion of the Hamilton airport, participating in a major joint venture with the regional health board, and otherwise getting on with the business of implementing the long-awaited land claims deal.

The Tainui settlement, which took place thousands of miles away from British Columbia, nonetheless offers important lessons and perspectives. The grievances behind the final agreement are very old, going back to the Treaty of Waitangi (an agreement signed in 1840 by representatives of the British government and some 550 Maori chiefs which recognized the Maori as equal citizens of New Zealand and gave assurances about control over certain land and resources) and 19th century Maori-British wars. Negotiations had continued for many years and seemed, to some observers, to be blocked by impenetrable barriers of expectations, public resentment, and government fiscal constraints. The idea of the Maori as partners and major land owners (as part of the settlement, the Tainui gained control of the campus of the University of Waikato) upset an age-old pattern of Maori-Pakeha relations. Yet the agreement and its implementation was hailed by almost all observers as a major advance.

At some point in the future — perhaps next month, next year, in five years' time, or two decades from now — British Columbians will go through a similar process to that of the New Zealanders. The Nisga'a land claim, very close to resolution at several points in the past few years, may well provide a Tainui-like example more relevant to British Columbia. What is quite clear is that other Canadian and international examples provide a great deal of insight and information into the likely path of British Columbia's treaty process and final settlement0s.

UNDERSTANDING MODERN TREATIES

Treaties represent change and most societies, even the most innovative and forward-looking, are naturally wary of changes which can lead to substantial shifts in material, political or social conditions. The sentiment, often expressed in British Columbia, that the gains achieved by the First Nations through treaties represent a quantifiable loss to the rest of the population increases the level of uncertainty and, in some quarters, hostility surrounding land claims. British Columbians appear to support the resolution of land claims. They do, however, have questions about the content and impact of treaty settlements.

To better understand the possible impact of modern treaties in British Columbia, the governments of Canada and British Columbia commissioned a study of the Aboriginal settlements implemented in the past 25 years. The investigation, conducted by ARA Consulting Group, Inc., proceeded by way of a series of case studies, and involved both an analysis of the contents of the treaties and the reaction of indigenous and non-indigenous people to the settlements. The investigation did not seek to provide a quantitative evaluation of, for example, economic changes associated with the settlements. Instead, it offered a qualitative assessment of the post-treaty situation. This approach enabled the investigators to assess how the people and organizations directly affected by the settlements — Aboriginal and non-Aboriginal politicians, business and community leaders — felt about the implementation and impact of the treaties.

The modern treaty process (which is substantially different than the pre-1940s treaties signed with indigenous peoples) began in the 1960s, when national governments began to acknowledge the legitimacy of Aboriginal demands for land settlements. The first of the "modern" treaties was signed in Alaska in 1971 (The Alaska Native Claims Settlement Act). Two other major agreements, the James Bay Northern Claims Settlement Act (1976) and the Aboriginal Land Rights (Northern Territory) Act (1976) followed in Australia a few years later. The Western Arctic (Inuvialuit) Claims Settlement Act, also known as the Inuvialuit Final Agreement, was signed in 1984. The passage of time in the case of these four agreements is sufficient to evaluate the impact of the settlements.

Two other agreements are more recent: the Council for Yukon Indians Umbrella Final Agreement of 1993 and New Zealand's Waikato-Tainui Deed of Settlement of 1995. The full impact of these latter two treaties will not, of course, be known for quite some time. They nonetheless provide an excellent indication of recent settlements. Taken as a group, the modern treaties have demonstrated that governments and indigenous peoples can reach agreements. They also illustrate the vital role that community participation and understanding plays in the final resolution of Aboriginal land claims.

The pattern of settlements in Canada and overseas also points to a very basic reality. It is much easier to reach agreements with indigenous peoples in sparsely populated, remote regions than it is in more densely-settled agricultural and urban areas. (The Tainui settlement in New Zealand is an important exception to this general rule.) The reasons for this pattern are several-fold. National governments in Canada, the United States and Australia have greater constitutional control over territories (and greater control over the land in Alaska) than they do over states or provinces, giving them a freer hand to negotiate. Secondly, the presence of an indigenous majority or sizable First Nations minority gives greater urgency to the resolution of outstanding claims. As well, the comparative absence of third-party interests permits greater focus to the negotiations. Finally, the national electorate does not generally see their interests as adversely effected by treaties covering lands and peoples far removed from major population centres.

British Columbia, then, represents a major shift in emphasis — from negotiations with indigenous groups in relatively isolated, thinly-populated regions to treaty discussions with First Nations living with and amongst the 3.5 million people of a resource-rich province. Third-party interests, while important in other jurisdictions, are of vital significance in the British Columbia case. So, too, not surprisingly, is the high degree of uncertainty and public concern about the process and likely consequences — attributes shared with every other political jurisdiction that has concluded treaty negotiations.

A SUMMARY OF THE SETTLEMENTS

The past quarter century has seen a significant number of major treaty settlements. A selection of these agreements, summarized below, provide[s] a quick overview of the nature, extent and variety of modern treaties. There are other settlements that could be included (with the Gwitch'in, Nunavut, and Sahtu Dene and Metis in the Northwest Territories, for example), but the basic structure and contents of these agreements are very close to other settlements. The examples selected for detailed analysis helps to illustrate the context within which the British Columbia treaty process is taking place and what lies ahead for the province. The settlements brought to an end lengthy, often difficult negotiations. For the indigenous peoples involved, the treaties provided financial resources, land and other considerations that, they felt, provide a foundation for approaching the future. For the governments and, through them, the non-indigenous peoples in the affected areas, the settlements resolved outstanding disputes over land tenure and resource control, gave business much-desired certainty and economic stability, and offered a new framework of relations with indigenous peoples.

Alaska Native Claims Settlement Act (1971) — the United States

The discovery of a major oil deposit at Prudoe Bay on Alaska's North Slope in 1967 brought indigenous land rights to the fore. Four years later, in 1971, a highly controversial settlement was implemented. Under the Alaska Native Claims Settlement Act (ANCSA), the Natives received over $960 million, revenue sharing from resource developments, and 44 million acres of land. The agreement also called for the establishment of regional/village corporations, which were allocated the money and the resources and were, in turn, controlled by shares allocated to indigenous beneficiaries.

Most of the corporations floundered financially. In the 1980s, when it appeared possible that some of the corporations would lose control of traditional lands and resources to outside interests, the law was amended to ensure continued Native ownership. ANCSA, as the first of the modern treaties, automatically became the benchmark against which other agreements would be judged. Because of the financial difficulties and because of Alaskan Natives' frustration about the imposition of the commercial structure of the village corporation, most indigenous people subsequently pointed to the Alaskan example as a model of what to avoid.

James Bay Northern Quebec Agreement (1975) — Canada

Similar to the situation in Alaska, the prospect of a major energy development (prodded by the Canadian courts) spurred the settlement of Aboriginal land claims in Northern Quebec. The provincial government's plan for a massive hydro-electric development ran up against strong First Nations opposition. Following several years of negotiation, the Cree and Inuit of the region agreed to the James Bay Northern Quebec Agreement, thus opening the door for the James Bay hydro project.

The settlement provided the indigenous peoples with direct ownership of 14,000 square kilometres, and exclusive harvesting rights over an additional 150,000 square kilometres. As well, the Cree and Inuit received preferential access to resources over a 1 million square kilometres area. Cash payments totalled $225-million, with the Cree receiving $135-million and the Inuit the remaining $90-million. One of the key elements in the deal was the establishment of the Hunters and Trappers Income Security Program, a settlement-funded support program for Native harvesters. The agreement also ensured

Aboriginal participation in resource management and government service delivery. As the first of the Canadian modern treaties, the James Bay and Northern Quebec Agreement established the level of expectation for other negotiations, although it turned out that the emphasis on the preservation of harvesting rights and lifestyle took greater priority in the Cree/Inuit settlement than in subsequent negotiations.

The Aboriginal Land Rights (Northern Territory) Act (1976) — Australia

Aboriginal people of the Northern Territory, a vast, largely desert area of Australia, began pushing for a land settlement in the 1960s. When a national referendum gave the federal government responsibility for Aboriginal affairs in 1967, Australian officials made the resolution of land matters a priority. The Aboriginal Land Rights (NT) Act, passed in 1976, afforded Aboriginal groups an opportunity to claim, and potentially gain control of, traditional lands. The initial grant accounted for 258,000 square kilometres, and was expanded through subsequent successful claims to 520,000 square kilometres. The act also established Land Councils to administer the land and certain Aboriginal affairs and assured Aboriginal peoples of both a voice in future development decisions and a share of royalties from resource projects. Non-indigenous interests, particularly in the mining sector, resented the level of control given to Aboriginal peoples and the government subsequently revised the act to give greater certainty to resource developers.

The Western Arctic (Inuvialuit) Native Claims Settlement Act (1984) — Canada

Conditions reminiscent of the Alaska situation — namely the discovery of oil in the Beaufort Sea — spurred the Canadian government to conclude its negotiations with the 2500 Inuvialuit of the Western Arctic. The Final Agreement, which immediately established a baseline for subsequent Canadian treaty negotiations, offered a mix of cash, land government control, and resource rights. The final settlement provided absolute title to 91,000 square kilometres of land and surface rights to an additional 13,000 square kilometres, a cash settlement of $152-million spread over the 1984–1997 period, special grants for economic development ($10 million) and social development ($7.5 million) and guarantees of Inuvialuit harvesting rights. In addition, the settlement assured the Inuvialuit of an ongoing role in resource management, primarily through fixed membership on environmental and resource management boards.

The Council for Yukon Indians Umbrella Final Agreement (1993) — Canada

The most dramatic and, for British Columbians, the most relevant of the modern treaties was implemented in the Yukon Territory in 1995. Negotiations on the Council for Yukon Indians claims started in 1973, floundered several times, came within a hairs-breadth of settlement at least once, expanded to include the involvement of the territorial government at the negotiating table and then finally reached a conclusion. The Yukon treaty actually came in two stages: an Umbrella Final Agreement, signed in 1991, which set out the general terms and conditions of the settlement, and final agreements with each of the 14 First Nations in the Yukon Territory. When the first four final agreements had been signed, the Umbrella Agreement came into full effect. The Yukon treaty is comprehensive, providing $242.7 million in cash, direct ownership of 41,400 square kilometres, surface rights to an additional 15,500 square kilometres, a share in government royalties from resource developments on owned lands, the opportunity to conclude self-government agreements, and a significant role in the management of the territory's renewable and non-renewable resources. The Yukon agreement, which in turn drew on the experience and details of earlier settlements, provides a valuable example that addresses many of the concerns and issues surrounding treaty negotiations in British Columbia.

The Waikato-Tainui Deed of Settlement (1995) — New Zealand

The general background of the Waikato-Tainui Deed of Settlement was described earlier. The basic elements of the agreement are relatively straightforward: NZ $170 million to be used toward the purchase of privately held lands for Tainui use and the allocation of approximately NZ $100 million worth of Crown lands (34,000 acres without improvements, 1,800 acres with improvements). The ongoing funding for the Tainui is to come largely from the leases and rentals of properties transferred from the Crown. The Tainui, like other Maori groups (including those who have not yet settled their land claim), have an assured role in the evaluation of proposals for resource development and participate in the delivery of social services. Of great symbolic importance, the Deed of Settlement also includes a formal apology for the confiscation of Tainui land and an explicit acknowledgment of the important role that the Maori have played in the development of New Zealand.

THE IMPACT OF TREATIES AND LAND CLAIMS SETTLEMENTS

The settlement packages outlined above vary greatly, reflecting time, place, legal requirements, economic urgency, political will, and national realities. In each case, however, the treaties or legislative acts ended a long-standing dispute over land and resources and provided a new framework for social, economic and political relations. So, one might fairly ask, what happened? Through the negotiation phase, proponents and opponents offered various post-settlement scenarios, ranging from economic chaos and political disharmony to cross-cultural understanding, prosperity and political cooperation. The reality, not surprisingly, is rather more complex. On some agreements — the Yukon and Tainui deals being the prime examples — the jury is still out. On the others, and on treaty settlements overall, there is enough history and experience to provide an overview.

One caveat is necessary. Because each treaty arises out of specific historical, political, cultural and legal circumstances, it would be wrong to see any agreement, or set of agreements, as a direct model for British Columbia. Special arrangements adopted for the James Bay Cree, the Aborigines of the Northern Territory (Australia), or the Inuvialuit (Western Arctic) may have only marginal applicability in the province. The very diversity of British Columbia adds an additional complexity. The following is a summary of the overall impacts derived from the comparative case study analysis.

- In no case has the resolution of land claims brought political or economic chaos, although the Alaska Native Corporations did face financial difficulties. People adjusted to the new arrangements, political systems [were] adapted, and businesses quickly found new ways of responding to the post-settlement environment. Determined opponents of land settlements, and there have been some in each case, found aspects of the settlement and implementation to criticize, but did not uncover a fatal flaw in any of the agreements. Some aspects have not worked out as planned — the Alaskan Native Corporation model was not a general success — and others have met expectations — like the James Bay Hunters and Trappers Income Security Program. Not unlike most other negotiated settlements, the treaties did not (and could not) anticipate all eventualities. The Inuvialuit claim assumed the rapid development of the Beaufort Sea oil field. It has not yet occurred on the scale predicted. Treaties are not perfect, but they do a firm, clear and identifiable foundation for approaching the problems of the present and the future.
- The business communities in the areas affected by land claims opposed negotiations initially. There was particular concern that the indigenous groups would oppose future resource development and thereby stall development. Over time, business leaders came around, either convinced about the argument in favour of treaties or simply desiring certainty in the economy. In the post-settlement era, non-indigenous business leaders capitalized on new opportunities (often joint ventures with Aboriginal companies), and discovered a common interest in sustainable, mutually-beneficial economic development. As negotiations progressed, community and regional leaders realized that the infusion of federal money into the region through the settlement would be a major incentive to economic growth and diversification.
- All of the modern treaties have respected and accepted private land holdings and leases. Although indigenous groups have been forthright in their demand for land and resources, they have in each case accepted the rights of existing property owners. In the Tainui case, for example, where the vast majority of farm land in the Waikato has long since passed into private hands, the Maori and the New Zealand government agreed that there would be no transfer of privately-held land. The Tainui were given a reasonable cash settlement, a substantial portion of which they intend to use to purchase agricultural land at prevailing market rates.
- The level of non-indigenous support for, or acceptance of, treaty negotiations and settlements is closely related to the availability of information.

In the early years of the modern treaty process, negotiations proceeded in secret and with little public education or consultation with affected interests. This served to heighten uncertainty and raise fears about the likely outcomes. In those areas — the Yukon Territory being a very good example — where the public was kept well-informed of the progress of the discussions, public opposition and third-party concern declined substantially. In such cases, the final settlement is generally well-received and is, as in the case of the Tainui agreement, a largely symbolic acceptance of terms that are already widely known.

- The most contentious issue surrounding treaty settlements relates to the management of resources. Non-indigenous fears that final agreements will block access to minerals, timber, fish, wildlife and other resources has, in almost every instance, added fuel to the fires of discontent. The existing agreements, which deal primarily with isolated, thinly-populated areas, contain numerous provisions relating to the control, regulation and exploitation of natural resources and give indigenous people a significant say in the use of those resources. The situations in other areas demonstrates that it is vital that the approaches re: resource use and control be fully explained in order to alleviate non-indigenous concerns about the future of businesses and communities that rely on resource development.
- The most important reality of the post-settlement period is that life, generally, has proceeded much as before. Some areas and groups have capitalized on opportunities quickly and dramatically; others have opted for slower, longer-term growth, and invested accordingly. Following several settlements, many people expected a vast increase in local spending associated with the treaty and were surprised when the indigenous groups invested their money more broadly — some funds on local development and training, and other capital on more financially profitable investments outside the region. Industry officials who felt that Aboriginal leaders, empowered by new political structures that gave them additional authority over resource developments, would stand in the way of economic growth have been proven correct in some jurisdictions and incorrect in others. In each instance, however, national governments maintained sufficient power in the final agreements to over-ride indigenous protests if national interests were deemed to be at stake.
- Treaties have provided indigenous groups with the financial and administrative means to begin charting a new economic future for their people and their regions. The establishment of for-profit companies, joint ventures with non-indigenous corporations, community development schemes, and the like are an integral part of the settlement process and treaty implementation. Indigenous peoples have used the land claims process as a basis for participating more fully in the broader economy and, typically, have become more heavily involved with the non-indigenous population as a result of the treaty.
- Indigenous groups learned from the experience of early settlements that education and training must figure prominently in post-settlement operations. Treaties typically involve an array of administrative powers and responsibilities, greater community autonomy, and economic resources. In

order to capitalize on the opportunities thus presented, however, First Nations must have trained people ready to assume the task of implementing the treaty. In recent years, indigenous groups have placed a strong emphasis on education and training while the negotiations proceeded.

- Underlying the treaty process is a heart-felt desire among the indigenous people to keep their language and culture strong, to recover from the difficulties of the past, and to interest non-indigenous people in their heritage. The very process of negotiating such considerations — funding for language training, control of education, resources for cultural activities — has awakened non-indigenous people to the passion and conviction of indigenous communities about their traditions and language. The negotiation process, while focusing heavily on legal, administrative and financial matters, has the potential to begin creating cultural bridges and to alerting non-indigenous peoples to the richness and depth of Aboriginal culture. This, perhaps more than any technical or legislative initiative, may well be the most important legacy of land claims negotiations, precisely because it helps to build lasting, culturally-based links between peoples.
- Taken as a group, then, the modern treaties have not caused the level of disruption, disharmony and dislocation that critics forecast although, to be fair, neither have they offered instant solutions to difficult problems, as some proponents seemed to expect. Contemporary agreements are best understood as evolutionary in nature, rather than revolutionary, modifying existing patterns of indigenous-government relations rather than overthrowing the political, economic and social status quo. Modern settlements are, in the final analysis, both less of a threat and less of a solution than opponents and advocates have claimed. They have been, though, in places as diverse as the Canadian Arctic and the Australian outback, the catalyst for a new relationship between indigenous and non-indigenous peoples.

CONCLUSION

By resolving long-standing disagreements through negotiation rather than legally or politically imposed conditions, modern treaties liberate both indigenous peoples and non-indigenous peoples from contentious and difficult debates about the past. These often heated discussions — about colonialism, dislocation, sovereignty, ownership, and the legitimacy of Native land claims — generate a great deal of rhetoric and anger but rarely provide lasting solutions. Treaties are, ultimately, about complex legal, political and financial agreements, about compromise, and about determined efforts to bridge the gap between indigenous and non-indigenous expectations and desires. They are, perhaps most importantly, about establishing a social, political and economic framework for future relations between indigenous and non-indigenous peoples.

The best agreements — the ones likely to be of the greatest lasting benefit — are those that become compacts between peoples and more than agreements between leaders and political institutions, for they then represent the desire to set aside existing difficulties and to embrace a shared vision of the future. In each of the modern treaty processes, discussions passed through stages — protest and confrontation, non-indigenous skepticism and uncertainty, difficult negotiations, public debate about deals and possible deals, and euphoria mixed with weariness when the final agreement was signed. And then, following the settlement, people generally got on with business and with life. There were changes and adaptations, to be sure. But to a degree that surely must have surprised close followers of the different treaty processes, people adapted quickly to the new conditions.

British Columbians need not think that they are alone in facing the changes and uncertainty surrounding treaty settlements. There is a way of understanding and anticipating the impact of treaty negotiations that are currently underway. The modern treaty process is national and international in scope and impact, and the people of the province stand to learn a great deal by considering the experiences of others who have been down this path before. The experience with other treaty settlements provides an important window on a situation that British Columbians should now contemplate. The case studies offer a vital reassurance that those changes, although substantial, need not be unsettling and provide a portrait of a post-settlement reality that is far from chaotic or disruptive. There are also lessons here about how to proceed, particularly through the involvement and education of the public, in order to ensure widespread acceptance of the final accords and about the manner in which business, community and other interests came to support both the treaty process and the final settlement. As British Columbia moves through the treaty negotiation process, it helps to know that other people and other jurisdictions have been here before. Treaties are not a panacea, and nor are they a massive threat. They provide an opportunity for indigenous and non-indigenous peoples to chart a common future and to establish a framework for working together, not for pulling apart.

Appendix 5

The James Bay and Northern Quebec Agreement†

HISTORY

The James Bay and Northern Quebec Agreement (JBNQA) and the Northeastern Quebec Agreement (NEQA) are Canada's first modern land claim settlements. Signed in 1975 and 1978 respectively, they fulfill a commitment to deal with land issues dating back to the late 1800s.

Native people have occupied the settlement region since time immemorial, sustaining themselves on the region's abundant wildlife and other resources. Before its enormous hydro-electric potential was recognized in the 1960s, few outsiders were interested in the territory. In fact, until early this century, the only non-Native presence consisted of the Hudson Bay Company, missionaries and the federal department responsible for Indian affairs.

At one time, the lands now covered by the JBNQA and the NEQA were considered part of Rupert's Land, the domain of the Hudson's Bay Company. In 1868, the Rupert's Land Act was passed by the British government and the area was ceded to Canada. In 1870, by Imperial Order-in-Council, it was stipulated that the government must obtain the surrender of Indian title to the lands that formerly composed this domain.

Through boundary extensions in 1898 (to the 52nd parallel) and in 1912 (north to the Hudson Strait), these lands were transferred to the Province of Quebec. A key condition of the transfer of 1912 was that Quebec recognize the rights of Native inhabitants on these lands and that, in return, the Native people release such rights to Quebec. Any agreement would have to be approved by the Governor in Council.

For nearly 60 years, until the Government of Quebec announced, in 1971, its intention to develop the hydro-electric potential of the rivers draining into James Bay, this commitment to recognize Native rights was not honored.

---

† Source: http://www.inac.gc.ca/pubs/information/info14.html

Shortly thereafter, the province created the James Bay Development Corporation to develop all the territory's resources, including hydro, forestry, mining and tourism.

In the fall of 1972, the Quebec Association of Indians applied to the Quebec Superior Court for an injunction to stop all construction in the James Bay region. The injunction was granted on the grounds that the Government of Quebec had committed itself to settling Native land claims. Although this decision was overturned a few days later paving the way for work to continue on the James Bay hydro-electric project, the determination of Natives to protect their historic land-based interests led to negotiations toward a land claim agreement.

By 1974, the governments of Canada and Quebec, the Cree and Inuit of Northern Quebec and Hydro-Québec concluded an agreement-in-principle which led to the signing of the landmark James Bay and Northern Quebec Agreement on November 11, 1975. The Naskapi Indian Band followed the Cree['s] example, negotiating the Northeastern Quebec Agreement (NEQA), signed on January 31, 1978, amending the JBNQA.

Signatories to the JBNQA included the Government of Quebec, the James Bay Energy Corporation, the James Bay Development Corporation, the Quebec Hydro-Electric Commission (Hydro-Québec), the Grand Council of the Crees (of Quebec), the Northern Quebec Inuit Association, and the Government of Canada.

The JBNQA included a total of $225 million as compensation to the James Bay Cree and the Inuit of Northern Quebec, to be paid by Canada and Quebec. Compensation funding for the Cree was paid to the Cree Regional Authority and for the Inuit it was paid to Makivik Corporation. Under the terms of the NEQA, Canada and Quebec paid a total of $9 million in compensation to the Naskapi of Quebec.

In addition to settling Native land claims and providing financial compensation, the agreements defined Native rights and established regimes for future relations between Natives and non-Natives in the region and among local, regional, provincial and federal governments. As of June 30, 1993, 11,458 Cree, 7,066 Inuit and 610 Naskapi beneficiaries were affected by the agreements.

MAJOR COMPONENTS OF THE AGREEMENTS

The Land Regime

The JBNQA and NEQA, the territory was divided into [Categories] I, II, and III lands.

- Category I lands are for the exclusive use and benefit of Aboriginal people.
- Category II lands belong to the province, but Native governments share management for hunting, fishing and trapping, tourism development and forestry. Native people have exclusive hunting, fishing and trapping rights on these lands.

- Category III lands are a special type of Quebec public lands. Both Native and non-Native people may hunt and fish here subject to regulations adopted in accordance with the agreements. Aboriginal groups have exclusive rights to harvest certain aquatic species and fur-bearing mammals and to participate in the administration and development of the land. The Quebec government, the James Bay Energy Corporation, Hydro-Québec and the James Bay Development Corporation have specific rights to develop resources on Category III lands. The federal and provincial governments, depending on jurisdiction, must assess the impact of resource development projects.

Environment and Social Protection

These provisions relate to the undesirable environmental impact and social effects of development. They attempt to maximize positive effects while assessing their impact.

There are two advisory committees: one for the area situated south of the 55th parallel and the other for the area located north of the 55th parallel. These committees review environmental issues, policies and regulations and advise governments. Each committee includes federal, provincial and Native representatives.

Local Government Provisions

Inuit communities are incorporated as municipalities under Quebec law and specific powers are delegated to them by Quebec legislation. A regional government structure was established under a provincial act concerning the Kativik regional government. Makivik Corporation was set up so that Inuit concerns dealing with the implementation of the agreement are considered. Under Quebec legislation, the province also established the Cree Regional Authority to assist in the development of common services for Cree communities.

In 1984, the Government of Canada proclaimed the Cree-Naskapi (of Quebec) Act pursuant to Section 9 of the JBNQA and Section 7 of the NEQA. The Act recognizes local Indian government powers and sets up a system of land management. The Indian Act no longer applies to the beneficiaries except concerning Indian status. The new Act recognized a form of Indian self-government for the first time in Canada.

Education

Sections 16 and 17 of the JBNQA established Cree and Inuit school boards. Although they are under Quebec jurisdiction and are similar to other Quebec school boards, these school boards have a special mandate and powers which enable them to adopt culturally appropriate educational programs.

Section 11 of the NEQA deals with the question of education for the Naskapi. It provides for a school to serve the needs of the Band and general administration of the facilities by the Eastern Quebec Regional School Board. A Naskapi Education Committee performs the consultative functions assigned to school committees by the Quebec Education Act. It also possesses special powers.

The school boards' operational and capital budgets are funded jointly by Canada and Quebec, with Canada paying 25% of the Inuit budget and 75% of the Cree and Naskapi budget. Responsibility for the management of education rests primarily with Quebec.

Hunting, Fishing and Trapping

Certain rights are provided for the harvesting of wildlife. A coordinating committee, composed of representatives from the federal and provincial governments and the three Native groups, was established. It administers, reviews and regulates wildlife harvesting. It may also set harvesting limits and advise governments on wildlife management.

Economic Development

The objective is to further short-term economic development and to support ongoing projects, including the establishment of Native organizations which promote activities such as renewable resource development, and arts and crafts.

Health and Social Services

Resulting from the signing of the agreements, responsibility for health and social services for residents of Category I lands was effectively turned over to Native agencies established by the province. The Cree Regional Board of Health and Social Services of James Bay is responsible for the administration of the delivery of services to the Cree. The Kativik Health and Social Services Council performs similar functions for the Inuit. For the Naskapi, a Health and Social Services Consultative Committee was established to represent their interests concerning services offered by other agencies.

The Federal Role

The 1975 and 1978 agreements significantly modified federal involvement in Northern Quebec. The federal government now subsidizes many services it formerly provided. These services are now administered by Native local governments and the Province of Quebec.

The departments of Indian Affairs and Northern Development, Environment, and Human Resources and Labour are only a few of the federal departments which play important roles in the various regimes established by the agreements. Overall responsibility for coordinating federal activity was assigned to the Minister of Indian Affairs and Northern Development by the James Bay and Northern Quebec Native Claims Settlement Act of 1977.

IMPLEMENTATION NEGOTIATIONS

Early on in the process of implementation, the Native parties identified problem areas and pressed the governments to fulfill all their obligations under the agreements. In 1982, an implementation review of the JBNQA recommended a number of initiatives to deal with the most pressing issues identified by the Cree and Inuit. However, the JBNQA Implementation Review focused on the adequacy of program support from 1975 to 1981, but did not resolve the fundamental problems of interpretation of the agreement or long term implementation.

In 1983, Aboriginal matters were the subject of the first amendments to the Constitution Act, 1982. Among them was the provision that rights arising from existing and future land claims would be interpreted as treaty rights [Part II, Subsection 35 (3)]. As such, the JBNQA and the NEQA land claims acquired constitutional protection as "treaty rights."

In 1986, to address the persistent implementation problems, the federal Cabinet approved a process of mediated negotiations with the JBNQA and the NEQA beneficiaries. Four years of implementation negotiations led to agreements with the Inuit and the Naskapi in September 1990. As well as other items, the implementation agreements relieve the federal government from certain financial obligations pursuant to the JBNQA and the NEQA in exchange for one-time grant payments of $22.8 million to the Inuit and $1.7 million to the Naskapi. Once these agreements are implemented, all outstanding Inuit and Naskapi matters related to the implementation of the JBNQA and NEQA will have been dealt with. Moreover, a dispute resolution mechanism has been put in place to deal with any future issues.

Although negotiations with the Inuit and the Naskapi have been successful, they have not been completed with the Cree. The Cree insisted that what they consider to be outstanding operational matters must first be resolved before entering into discussions on JBNQA implementation. These included a long-standing dispute about the funding of local governments and regional structures, and of maintenance of the majority of the community facilities; a perceived shortfall in capital funding allocations, and the establishment of band status and the construction of a village for the Oujé-Bougoumou Cree.

The question of operation and maintenance was resolved in July 1988, and that of the Oujé-Bougoumou Cree band status and the construction of a village, in May 1992. Under the final agreement concluded in May 1992, the federal government agreed to pay $60 million over five years for the construction of 125 houses and municipal and school infrastructures, and for Oujé-Bougoumou band operations. DIAND also paid $12.3 million to the band to begin the socio-economic development of the community (that is $9.8 million in May 1992, and $2.5 million in April 1993).

Appendix 6

Nisga'a Final Agreement in Brief[†]

Preamble

The Final Agreement is intended to be the just and equitable settlement of the Nisga'a land question.

The Canadian courts have stated that reconciliation between Aboriginal and non-Aboriginal people is best achieved through negotiation and agreement, rather than through litigation and conflict. As such, the Parties intend the Final Agreement to establish a new relationship based on mutual sharing and recognition.

The Parties intend that the Final Agreement will provide certainty with respect to ownership and use of lands and resources, and the relationship of laws within the Nass area.

General Provisions

The Nisga'a will continue to be an Aboriginal people under the Constitution Act, 1982.

The Nisga'a will continue to enjoy the same rights and benefits as other Canadian citizens.

Lands owned by the Nisga'a will no longer be reserve lands under the Indian Act.

The Canadian Charter of Rights and Freedoms will apply to the Nisga'a Government and its institutions.

Federal and provincial laws (such as the Criminal Code of Canada) will continue to apply to Nisga'a citizens and others on Nisga'a Lands.

---

† 22 July 1998. Source: http://www.inac.gc.ca/subject/agree/nisgaa/nisgafb.html

The Treaty addresses the issue of certainty through a number of provisions. Key among these is a clause which provides that the Treaty is a full and final settlement of Nisga'a Aboriginal rights. Another provision clearly states that the Treaty exhaustively sets out the Nisga'a['s] section 35 rights of the Constitution Act, 1982. There is also an agreement that the Nisga'a Aboriginal rights and title are modified and continue as set out in the Treaty. Finally, the Nisga'a agree to release any Aboriginal rights, including Aboriginal title, that are not set out in the Treaty or which are different in attributes or geographical extent from the Nisga'a section 35 rights set out in the Treaty.

The Final Agreement can only be amended with the consent of all three Parties. Canada would give consent to any proposed amendments by order of the Governor in Council, and British Columbia would do so by resolution of the Legislature.

Lands

The Nisga'a will own approximately 1,992 square kilometres of land in the lower Nass Valley. The land will be held in fee simple by the Nisga'a — the same kind of land ownership enjoyed by other landowners.

Nisga'a Lands will include approximately 1,930 square kilometres of transferred Crown land and 62 square kilometres of Indian reserves that will cease to be reserves on the effective date of the Treaty.

Nisga'a Lands will not include existing fee simple lands, or lands subject to agricultural leases and wood lot licenses.

- **Mineral Resources**
  The Nisga'a will own all subsurface resources on the Nisga'a Lands.

- **Interests within Nisga'a Lands**
  Existing legal interests on Nisga'a Lands will continue or be re-issued on their current terms. The Nisga'a, as the owners of the Nisga'a Lands, will be able to set conditions on any new interests it grants in the future.

- **Fee Simple Lands Outside Nisga'a Lands**
  Land contained within 18 Indian reserves outside of the Nisga'a Lands, and a small amount of adjacent land, will become fee simple lands owned by the Nisga'a and subject to provincial laws. The Nisga'a will own the subsurface resources of these lands.

  The Nisga'a will also own an additional 15 parcels of fee simple land, totalling approximately 2.5 square kilometres. Subsurface resources on these lands will continue to be owned by the province and will be under provincial jurisdiction.

- **Commercial Recreation Tenure**
  The Nisga'a will receive a commercial recreation tenure for guiding which will operate under provincial laws.

- **Heritage Sites and Key Geographic Features**
  Important cultural sites will be protected through heritage site designation.

Some key geographic features will be renamed with Nisga'a names.

- **Parks and Ecological Reserve**
  British Columbia's authority and responsibilities over the Nisga'a Memorial Lava Bed Park and Gingietl Creek Ecological Reserve will continue.
  Nisga'a history and culture are, and will be promoted as, the primary cultural features of the Park.
  Nisga'a citizens have the right to use the lands and resources within the Park and Ecological Reserve for traditional purposes.

- **Water Volumes**
  Existing water licenses will remain in place.
  British Columbia will establish a Nisga'a water reservation of 300,000 cubic decametres of water per year to meet domestic, industrial and agricultural purposes.

Land Title

Nisga'a Lands will be owned by the Nisga'a. Any fee simple parcels within Nisga'a Lands that exist on the effective date will continue to be subject to the Land Title Act and the provincial land title system generally.

Individual parcels within Nisga'a Lands will initially be registered under a Nisga'a land title system and, following a transition period, may be registered under the provincial land title system.

Forest Resources

The Nisga'a will own all forest resources on Nisga'a Lands.

Existing licenses will be in effect for a five year transition period to allow licensees to adjust their operations and will then be replaced by new licenses. The licensees are required to meet certain obligations under the licenses through the transition period and beyond, including silviculture obligations.

Following the transition period, the Nisga'a will manage forestry on Nisga'a Lands.

The Nisga'a Government will be able to implement forest management standards, provided that these meet or exceed provincial standards such as the Forest Practices Code.

- **Timber Processing**
  Provincial laws pertaining to the manufacture of timber products harvested on Crown lands will apply equally to timber harvested on Nisga'a Lands.
  The Nisga'a will not establish a primary timber processing facility for 10 years after the effective date of the Treaty.

- **Forest Resources Outside Nisga'a Lands**
  The province agrees in principle to the Nisga'a purchase of forest tenure(s) with an aggregate allowable annual cut of up to 150,000 cubic metres. Any such acquisition would be subject to the Forest Act.

Access

There will be reasonable public access to Nisga'a Public Lands for non-commercial purposes such as hunting, fishing and recreation.

Residents of Nisga'a Lands who are not Nisga'a will have access to their private land.

The Nisga'a Government may make laws regulating public access for the purposes of public safety, protection of environmental, cultural or historic features, and protection of habitat.

The federal and provincial governments will have access to Nisga'a Lands for purposes such as the delivery or management of government services and emergency response. Likewise, representatives of the Nisga'a Government may, in accordance with the laws of general application, have temporary access to lands other than Nisga'a Lands for similar purposes.

Roads and Rights of Way

The province will continue to own the Nisga'a Highway (which is the main road through Nisga'a Lands) and will maintain the secondary provincial roads. The province may also acquire portions of Nisga'a Lands to create additional rights of way for road or public utility purposes.

The Nisga'a Government will regulate and maintain all Nisga'a roads.

Fisheries

Nisga'a citizens will have the right to harvest fish and aquatic plants subject to conservation requirements and legislation enacted to protect public health and safety.

- **Salmon**
  The Nisga'a will receive an annual allocation of salmon under the Treaty and harvest agreement, which will, on average, comprise approximately 26% of the Canadian Nass River total allowable catch. In addition, the Nisga'a will be able to sell their salmon, subject to monitoring, enforcement and laws of general application. A Harvest Agreement, separate from the Final Agreement, allows for the harvesting of sockeye and pink salmon.

  If, in any year, there are no directed Canadian commercial or recreational fisheries for a species of Nass salmon, a Nisga'a commercial fishery will not be permitted for that species.

- **Steelhead**
  The Nisga'a have the right to harvest steelhead for domestic purposes.

- **Enhancement**
  The Nisga'a Government may conduct enhancement activities for Nass salmon with the approval of the Minister of Fisheries and Oceans.

- **Non-Salmon Species and Aquatic Plants**
  The Nisga'a may harvest non-salmon species. The allocation will be for domestic purposes, meaning that the harvest cannot be sold. The Final Agreement provides for a shellfish allocation and the Nisga'a may negotiate an allocation for other species, such as halibut and crab.

- **Fisheries Management**
  The Minister of Fisheries and Oceans and the province will retain responsibility for conservation and management of the fisheries and fish habitat, according to their respective jurisdictions. In addition, the Nisga'a Government may make laws to manage the Nisga'a harvest, if those laws are consistent with the Nisga'a Annual Fishing Plan approved by the Minister.
  The Parties will establish and be represented on a Joint Fisheries Management Committee (JFMC) to facilitate the co-operative planning and conduct of Nisga'a fisheries and enhancement activities. The committee will make recommendations to the federal and provincial governments on these matters.

The Nisga'a will prepare a Nisga'a Annual Fishing Plan for all species of salmon and other fish. The Nisga'a Annual Fishing Plan will be reviewed by the JFMC and, if satisfactory, will be approved by the Minister of Fisheries and Oceans.

The agreement also provides for Nisga'a participation in any future regional or watershed-based fisheries management, should the need arise.

- **Lisims Fisheries Conservation Trust**
  The Trust will be established to promote conservation and protection of Nass area fish species, facilitate sustainable management of the fisheries for the benefit of all Canadians, and promote and support Nisga'a participation in the stewardship of the Nass fisheries.
  Canada will contribute $10 million to this initiative and the Nisga'a will contribute $3 million.

- **Nisga'a Participation in the General Commercial Fishery**
  The Nisga'a will receive $11.5 million from Canada and B.C. toward participation in the coastal commercial fishing industry to provide for the purchase of vessels and licenses.
  The Nisga'a will not establish large-scale fish-processing facilities within eight years of the effective date of the Treaty.

Wildlife and Migratory Birds

The Nisga'a will receive a wildlife hunting allocation for domestic purposes in the Nass Wildlife Area. There are specific allocations for moose, grizzly bear and mountain goat. In the future, mammals other than these may be designated and an allocation established.

Hunting will be subject to conservation requirements and legislation enacted for the purposes of public health and safety. The Nisga'a right to hunt cannot interfere with other authorized uses of Crown land and does not preclude the Crown from authorizing uses of or disposing of Crown land, subject to certain considerations.

The Nisga'a may also harvest migratory birds, subject to laws of general application and appropriate international conventions.

- **Wildlife Management**
  The Minister of Environment, Lands and Parks is responsible for all wildlife. A wildlife committee will be established to promote co-operative management of the resource in the Nass area and advise the Minister on management and Nisga'a hunting matters. The committee will have equal representation from the Nisga'a and the province, with one representative from Canada.

  The Nisga'a will develop an annual management plan for their hunt which will require provincial approval. The management plan will be reviewed by the wildlife committee and approved by the provincial Minister.

  Nisga'a citizens who hunt outside the management area will be subject to provincial laws.

- **Trade, Barter and Sale**
  The Nisga'a will be able to trade or barter wildlife, wildlife parts and migratory birds among themselves, or with other Aboriginal people. The Nisga'a harvest of wildlife is for domestic purposes.

- **Trapping**
  Trapping will be regulated in accordance with provincial laws.

- **Guiding**
  Guiding activities will continue to be subject to laws of general application.

  The Nisga'a may receive a guide outfitter's certificate in the Nisga'a Lands, if a current certificate ceases to apply.

  The Nisga'a will receive an angling license for certain watercourses outside of the Nisga'a Lands.

Environmental Assessment and Protection

The Nisga'a Government will have the power to make laws relating to environmental assessment and protection. The environmental standards defined in these laws must meet or exceed federal and provincial standards.

The Nisga'a may undertake environmental assessments of proposed projects on their lands. Assessments will include public participation; and, the results will be available to the public, except where information must remain confidential by law. Federal and provincial environmental assessment processes continue to apply on Nisga'a Lands.

Canada and British Columbia will participate in environmental assessments in cases where a project will have effects outside the Nisga'a Lands. To avoid duplication, the agreement provides for the harmonization of Nisga'a environmental assessments processes with those of Canada and British Columbia.

Nisga'a Government

The Nisga'a will be governed by the Nisga'a Lisims Government (central government) and four Nisga'a Village Governments.

- **Nisga'a Constitution**
  The Nisga'a will adopt a Constitution which will set out the terms of governance and recognize the rights and freedoms of Nisga'a citizens. The Constitution must be passed by at least 70% of Nisga'a eligible voters.

- **Relations with Individuals who are not Nisga'a Citizens**
  The Nisga'a Government will be required to consult with other residents of Nisga'a Lands about decisions that significantly and directly affect them. Likewise, residents who are not Nisga'a will be able to participate in elected bodies that directly and significantly affect them. The means of participation will include opportunities to make representations, to vote for or seek election on Nisga'a Public Institutions, and to have the same means of appeal as Nisga'a citizens. Some local laws, such as traffic and transportation will apply to other residents of Nisga'a Lands, but in the majority of cases Nisga'a laws will only pertain to Nisga'a citizens.

- **Transitional Provisions**
  The first elections for Nisga'a Government will be held no later than six months after the effective date of the Treaty. Prior to the elections, the Nisga'a Tribal Council will continue to manage Nisga'a affairs, in accordance with the transition provisions.

- **Legislative Jurisdiction and Authority**
  The Nisga'a Government will have the power to make laws required to carry out its responsibilities and exercise its authority under this agreement. In addition, the Nisga'a Government may make laws governing such things as Nisga'a citizenship; Nisga'a language and culture; Nisga'a property in Nisga'a Lands; public order, peace and safety; employment; traffic and transportation; the solemnization of marriages; child and family, social and health services; child custody, adoption, and education.

  Federal and provincial laws continue to apply to Nisga'a citizens and Nisga'a Lands, and the relationship between these laws and Nisga'a laws has been clearly set out in the Final Agreement.

Administration of Justice

The Nisga'a Government may provide policing, correctional, and court services on Nisga'a Lands in accordance with the terms of the Treaty.

- **Police Services**
  If the Nisga'a Government decides to provide its own policing within Nisga'a Lands, it may do so with the approval of the Lieutenant Governor

in Council. The Nisga'a Police Service will have the full range of police responsibilities and the authority to enforce Nisga'a, provincial and federal laws, including the Criminal Code of Canada, within the Nisga'a Lands. The police force will be required to meet provincial qualification, training and professional standards. It will also be independent and accountable.

- **Community Corrections Services**
  The Nisga'a may enter into agreements with Canada or British Columbia to provide community correctional services in accordance with generally accepted standards, and consistent with the needs and priorities of the Nisga'a Government.

- **Nisga'a Court**
  The Nisga'a may establish a Nisga'a Court for approval by the Lieutenant Governor in Council. The Nisga'a Court will adjudicate prosecutions and civil disputes arising under Nisga'a laws and review the administrative decisions of Nisga'a public institutions.

  The judges will be appointed by the Nisga'a Government, according to a method of selection approved by the Lieutenant Governor in Council, and will comply with generally recognized principles of judicial fairness, independence and impartiality.

  In proceedings where the accused could face imprisonment under Nisga'a law, he or she may elect to be tried in the Provincial Court of British Columbia.

  Final decisions by the Nisga'a Court may be appealed to the Supreme Court of British Columbia on the same basis as decisions made at the Provincial Court of British Columbia.

- **Indian Act Transition**
  Provisions will be made to facilitate the transition from jurisdiction under the Indian Act to provincial or Nisga'a jurisdiction for such things as wills, administration of estates, and governance arrangements.

Capital Transfer and Loan Repayment

The cash settlement benefit of $190 million will be paid through capital transfers over a period of 15 years according to a schedule agreed to by the Parties.

The loans made by the Nisga'a to support their participation in Treaty negotiations over the years will be fully repaid over 15 years according to a schedule agreed to by the Parties.

Fiscal Relations

The Nisga'a Government will be responsible for ensuring the provision of programs and services at levels reasonably comparable to those generally available in northwest British Columbia.

Every five years, the Treaty requires the Parties to negotiate a Fiscal Financing Agreement through which funding will be provided to the Nisga'a Government to enable the delivery of programs and services including health, education, social services, local services, capital asset maintenance and replacement, housing, and resource management.

The Fiscal Financing Agreement will take into account the Nisga'a Government's ability to raise its own revenues consistent with an own source revenue agreement. The first Own-Source Revenue Agreement will provide for a phased-in contribution of Nisga'a revenues over a period of 12 years. After the initial agreement, the Own-Source Revenue Agreement will be renegotiable every two years, if requested by any of the Parties.

The Treaty confirms that the funding of Nisga'a Government is a shared responsibility of the Parties and that it is the Parties' objective that, where feasible, the reliance of the Nisga'a Government and the Nisga'a Villages on transfers will be reduced over time.

Taxation

The Nisga'a Government will have the power to tax Nisga'a citizens on Nisga'a Lands.

The Nisga'a Government, Canada and British Columbia may negotiate tax delegation agreements for other taxes and the Parties may make agreements to coordinate their respective tax systems on Nisga'a Lands.

The Indian Act tax exemption for Nisga'a citizens will be eliminated after a transitional period of eight years for transaction (e.g. sales) taxes and 12 years for other (e.g. income) taxes.

Pursuant to a taxation agreement, the Nisga'a Government and Nisga'a Village Governments will be treated in the same way as municipalities for tax purposes.

Cultural Artifacts and Heritage

The Royal British Columbia Museum and the Canadian Museum of Civilization will return a portion of their collections of Nisga'a artifacts to the Nisga'a. The museums will also retain some collections of Nisga'a artifacts for public exhibitions.

The Nisga'a Government and the province will coordinate their activities to manage heritage sites within Nisga'a Lands to preserve their heritage value from activities which may otherwise adversely affect them.

Local and Regional Government Relations

Nisga'a Lands will continue to be part of the Electoral Area "A" in the Regional District of Kitimat-Stikine.

The Nisga'a and the Regional District may enter into servicing agreements or otherwise coordinate their activities with respect to common areas of responsibility.

Dispute Resolution

If disputes arise regarding the interpretation, application or implementation of the Treaty, the Parties will try to resolve them through cooperation and consultation. If the Parties are unable to resolve the dispute in this manner, they may resort to mediation or another form of dispute resolution that would facilitate the Parties' efforts to agree. If these efforts fail, the Parties will have recourse to arbitration, if they agree, or the British Columbia Supreme Court.

Eligibility and Enrollment

To be eligible to receive benefits from the Nisga'a Treaty, a person must meet enrollment criteria that are largely based on Nisga'a ancestry.

The task of determining eligibility will be carried out by an eight-member Enrollment Committee, which will create a register of names during an initial enrollment period. Thereafter, the Nisga'a Government will maintain the register. The decisions of the Enrollment Committee and the Nisga'a Government with respect to eligibility and enrollment are final and binding, within the bounds of an appeals process.

Ratification

The Final Agreement has no force or effect unless ratified by the Nisga'a, British Columbia, and Canada.

Those Nisga'a who are enrolled by the Enrollment Committee will vote on the agreement by secret ballot. A Ratification Committee, with Nisga'a, federal and provincial representatives, will oversee the conduct of the vote. To be approved, the agreement must be ratified by a majority, (i.e. 50% plus one vote) of all eligible voters.

British Columbia and Canada will ratify the agreement in the British Columbia Legislature and Parliament, respectively, by the enactment of legislation giving effect to the Treaty.

Implementation

The Treaty will be implemented according to an Implementation Plan that is separate from the Final Agreement. The Implementation Plan sets out the steps to be taken to properly make the Treaty work on the ground. The plan will be for a term of ten years starting from the effective date of the Treaty.

Appendix 7

The Benefits and Costs of Treaty Settlements in British Columbia†

It is clear to me that the benefits ... in self-reliance for aboriginal communities, in certainty and security for us all ... in a fairer, economically more-prosperous province ... far outweigh the costs.

Premier Mike Harcourt, December 1, 1995
in an address to the Premier's Working Session
on Treaties, Vancouver, British Columbia.

Spurred by court recommendations that existing Aboriginal rights are better defined through negotiation than through the court process, British Columbia has joined the Government of Canada and the First Nations Summit to resolve land claims.

While the federal government bears the primary responsibility for land claims, the Province joined the process to ensure the rights of all British Columbians are protected and to bring economic certainty to our lands and resources.

To date, 47 First Nations representing about 70% of the Aboriginal population have entered the British Columbia Treaty Commission process to settle century-old grievances.

The Province hired the Vancouver consulting firm KPMG to conduct an independent review of projected financial and economic impacts of treaty settlements. Their report is based on the study of other modern treaties, including those in northern Canada.

The provincial government is committed to comparable justice and taxation systems for all British Columbians and to maintain or enhance basic social program standards through the treaty process. It has announced a number of "bottom lines" to guide its negotiators, including:

---

† A Summary of the KPMG Report. Source: http://WWW.aaf.gov.bc.ca/aaf/pubs/kpmgsum.htm

- Treaties must be affordable to B.C. taxpayers.
- Private property is not on the table.
- Negotiations must be as open as possible to scrutiny by all citizens.
- The Canadian Constitution, the Charter of Rights and Freedoms and the Criminal Code will apply to all British Columbians.
- Current tax exemptions for Aboriginal people will be phased out.
- The total amount of land held by First Nations should be roughly proportional to their population (less than 5%).
- Access to all public roads as well as to land and resources for recreational use will be guaranteed for all British Columbians.
- Province-wide standards of resource management and environmental protection will apply.
- Disruptions to interests on Crown lands will be avoided. If disruption occurs, there will be fair and timely compensation.

The Benefits

"When all of the financial impacts in B.C. are considered, British Columbia can expect about three dollars worth of total financial benefit for every dollar of provincial financial cost," the report says. The net financial benefit to British Columbia ... including B.C.'s share of cash, pre-treaty and negotiation costs and a further deduction for its share of Federal costs paid by British Columbians as Federal taxpayers — is between $3.9 billion and $5.3 billion, when totalled over 40 years.

The benefit arises mainly from the cash benefits to First Nations. The inflow of money into the province will spawn economic development in First Nation communities. However, according to the study, British Columbians as a whole will benefit and take-home paycheques will be up to $400 million higher at the end of the day.

Not all the benefits of resolving land claims can be measured in dollars and cents. Social conditions in Aboriginal communities have long been below that of other British Columbians, with higher infant mortality, suicide and birth rates, below-average life expectancy, welfare dependency and high rates of unemployment.

Treaties will not end all of those problems. But they are expected to go a long way to increasing self-sufficiency in native communities and allowing native people access to the economic and employment mainstream. As the income disparity is diminished, savings in social expenditures — and less reliance on government support — will bring additional benefits.

At the same time, the certainty that treaties will bring to the province's land and resources will encourage increased investment as people with new financial confidence spend money. First Nations, too, will invest settlement money in the province, which will result in modest economic boom for business people in communities near First Nations.

British Columbia should also see a significant employment increase as a result of treaties, with a KPMG estimate of between 7,000 and 17,000 jobs.

Aboriginal Affairs Minister John Cashore said the study shows that all British Columbians will benefit when treaties are finally settled. "First Nation communities will finally be able to have a say in their own development and to forge new relationships with their neighbours. All British Columbians will gain in the increased investment and employment in our province and in the certainty treaties will bring to our lands and resources."

He said the KPMG report is consistent with a study of the potential social and economic impacts of treaties released earlier in January 1995. That report, prepared by ARA Consulting Group of Vancouver, looked at other modern treaties from northern Canada and around the world. The bottom-line message in that study was that treaties do work. It also showed that treaties do not cause the economic disruption that critics predict, but neither do they solve all the problems of Aboriginal people.

The Costs

In looking at the costs of resolving land claims, KPMG included anticipated cash costs involved in settlements, as well as other costs, including funding of the Treaty Commission, the costs of the government's broad-based consultations with stakeholders and third parties, communicating land claims information across the province, and purchasing third-party interests in tenures where necessary.

KPMG estimates total settlement cash costs to range between $5.7 and $6.2 billion. Canada will contribute the bulk of these costs, with B.C. providing the lesser share of those costs, estimated at between $0.8 and $1.4 billion. B.C.'s contribution includes credit for revenues on land which the province will contribute, reducing the province's share of the cash costs of treaties.

When all the costs are added up, including the costs of negotiating and implementing treaties, the consultants expect the dollar cost to British Columbia to range between $1.4 and $2.1 billion over the next 40 years. Even at the higher of these values, this averages out to $50 million a year over the period, or less than one-quarter of one percent (.25%) of the provincial budget, a figure which Premier Harcourt said he is sure all British Columbians will agree is affordable, considering the economic stimulus it will produce.

That averages out to about $35 a year for each household in the province.

"This government has consistently said it would not sign treaties which do not meet the test of fairness or of affordability. I'm sure British Columbians will agree that these estimates are well within our ability to pay while at the same time allowing us to continue to maintain our prudent approach to managing taxpayer dollars," Harcourt said.

Aboriginal Affairs Minister John Cashore said the study is important because it gives the public an idea of the dollar amounts involved in resolving land claims. But, he says, the study is not a government bargaining position. "Negotiators will receive mandates from Treasury Board on a treaty-by-treaty basis and will then negotiate land and cash amounts at the treaty table."

KPMG estimates that First Nations will receive between 24,000 and 29,000 square kilometres of rural land, which is roughly 3% of provincial Crown land.

Cashore pointed out that costs and benefits of resolving land claims must also be considered in the context of the cost of failing to conclude treaties ... including increased civil unrest in terms of blockades and other actions which tie up resources, the cost of fighting continual court actions brought by Aboriginal people seeking their rights and the cost of continued investment uncertainty.

The KPMG report concludes: "...the real challenge and opportunity for British Columbia is to maximize the social and economic development within First Nations' communities while, at the same time, adhering to the cost targets established for treaties."

Appendix 8

References

Aboriginal Business Canada. 1995. Spirit of Enterprise. Ottawa: Industry and Science Canada.

Aglietta, Michel. 1976. *A Theory of Capitalist Regulation.* London: NLB.

Agrawal, Arun. 1995. "Dismantling the Divide Between Indigenous and Scientific Knowledge." *Development and Change* 26(3): 413–39.

Altvater, Elmar. 1992. "Fordist and Post-Fordist International Division of Labor and Monetary Regimes." In *Pathways to Industrialization and Regional Development* edited by Michael Storper and Allen Scott, 21–45. London: Routledge.

Amin, Ash. 1994. "Post-Fordism: Models, Fantasies and Phantoms of Transition." In *Post-Fordism: A Reader*, edited by Ash Amin, 1–40. Oxford: Blackwell.

Amin, Ash, and Anders Malmberg. 1994. "Competing Structural and Institutional Influence of the Geography of Production in Europe." In *Post-Fordism: A Reader*, edited by Ash Amin, 227–48. Oxford: Blackwell.

Amin, Samir. 1985. *Delinking: Towards a Polycentric World.* London: Zed Books Ltd.

Anderson, Robert. B. 1998 (forthcoming). "First Nations Economic Development: Objectives, Activities, and Outcomes" *The Journal of Economic Development* 1(1).

———. 1997. "First Nations Economic Development: The Role of Corporate Aboriginal Partnerships." *World Development* 25(9): 1493–514.

———. 1996a. *Native Economic Development: A Contingency Perspective.* The CANDO Research Centre on Native Economic Issues Working Paper Series. Edmonton: CANDO.

———. 1996b. *Native Economic Development: First Nations Business Development in Saskatchewan.* The CANDO Research Centre on Native Economic Issues Working Paper Series. Edmonton: CANDO.

———. 1996c. *Native Economic Development: The Case of the Meadow Lake Tribal Council.* The CANDO Research Centre on Native Economic Issues Working Paper Series. Edmonton: CANDO.

———. 1995. "The Business Economy of the First Nations in Saskatchewan: A Contingency Perspective." *The Canadian Journal of Native Studies* 15(2): 309–46.

Anderson, Robert B., and Robert M. Bone. 1995a. "First Nations Economic Development: A Contingency Perspective." *The Canadian Geographer* 39(2): 120–30.

———. 1995b. "Aboriginal People and Forestry in the Churchill River Basin: The Case of the Meadow Lake Tribal Council." In *The Proceedings of the Churchill River Conference*, edited by Peter Jonker, 128–37. Saskatoon: University of Saskatchewan.

Armstrong, George R. 1982. "The Firm and Society." In *Forest Resource Management*, edited by William Duerr, 293–300. Corvallis Oregon: O.S.U. Book Stores, Inc.

Armstrong, Robin. 1989. "Factors in Indian Economic Development On-Reserve." In *Native Socioeconomic Development in Canada*, edited by Paul Kariya. Winnipeg: University of Winnipeg, Institute of Urban Studies.

———. 1996. *Aboriginal Affairs and Social Science Research: A Challenge for Geographers*, Paper presented at the Annual Meeting of the Canadian Association of Geographers, unpublished. Saskatoon.

Armstrong, Robin, and Tim Rogers. 1995. A First Nations Typology: Patterns of Well-Being. Draft for Discussion Only. Ottawa: DIAND.

Bank of Montreal. 1993. *Aboriginal Banking Review.* Toronto: Bank of Montreal.

Barber, Edward. 1989. "The Contribution of Environmental and Resource Economics to an Economics of Sustainable Development." *Development and Change* 20: 429–59.

B.C. Council of Forest Industries. 1994. *A Proposed Aboriginal Forest Strategy for the BC Forest Industry: An Interim Report/Discussion Document.* Vancouver: The Council of Forest Industries.

B.C. Ministry of Aboriginal Affairs. 1998a. "The Benefits and Costs of Treaty Settlements in British Columbia: A Summary of the KPMG Report." B.C. Ministry of Aboriginal Affairs Website: http://www.aaf.gov.bc.ca/aaf/pubs/kpmgsum.htm

Bebbington, Anthony. 1993. "Modernization from Below: An Alternative Indigenous Paradigm." *Economic Geography* 69(3): 274–92.

Becker, David, and Richard Sklar. 1987. "Why Postimperialism?" In *Postimperialism: International Capitalism and Development in the Late Twentieth Century*, edited by D. Becker and R. Sklar, 1–19. Boulder, Colorado: Lynne Rienner Publishers, Inc.

Becker, David. 1987. "Postimperialism: A First Quarterly Report." In *Postimperialism: International Capitalism and Development in the Late Twentieth Century*, edited by D. Becker and R. Sklar, 193–201. Boulder, Colorado: Lynne Rienner Publishers, Inc.

Begay, Manley A. 1991. "Designing Native American Management and Leadership Training." *Harvard Project on American Indian Economic Development, Project Report Series.* Cambridge: John F. Kennedy School of Government, Harvard University.

Belkaoui, Ahmed. 1987. *Socioeconomic Accounting.* Westport Connecticut: Quorum Books.

Berger, Thomas. 1977. "The Probable Economic Impact of the Mackenzie Valley Pipeline." In *The Arduous Journey: Canadian Indians and Decolonization*, edited by J. Rick Ponting. Toronto: McClelland and Stewart.

Bertramsen, Rene. 1991. "From Capitalist State to the Political Economy." In *State, Economy and Society*, edited by Rene Bertramsen, Jens Thomsen and Jacob Torfing, 94–138. London: Unwin Hyman.

Blawatt, Ken R. 1998. *Entrepreneurship: Process and Management*. Scarborough: Prentice-Hall Canada.

Bombay, Harry. 1994. "The Forest Resource." *Mawioni Journal* Winter.

Bone, Robert M. 1992. *The Geography of the Canadian North.* Toronto: Oxford University Press.

Brizinski, P. 1989. *Knots in String.* Saskatoon: Division of Extension and Community Services, University of Saskatchewan.

Brohman, John. 1996. *Popular Development: Rethinking the Theory and Practice of Development.* Oxford: Blackwell Publishers. Ltd.

Brooks, Cheryl. 1994. "A Corporate Policy on Aboriginal Relations." *Canadian Business Review* (summer): 18–21.

Brugger, Ernst. 1990. "Endogenous Development Between Myth and Reality: Pre-requisites for Endogenous Development Strategies." In *Innovation and Regional Development*, edited by Hans-Jurgen Ewers. Berlin: Walter de Gruyter.

Brummer, James. 1991. *Corporate Responsibility and Legitimacy.* New York: Greenwood Press.

CANDO. 1995a. "Community Economic Development Organizations." *Mawiomi Journal* 2(2): 10–14.

———. 1995b. "Indigenous International Trade." *Mawiomi Journal* 2(2): 15–18.

———. 1995c. *Partners for Progress.* Winnipeg: CANDO.

———. 1995d. *Education: A Foundation for Economic and Community Development.* Winnipeg: CANDO.

Cardoso, F. 1979. *The New Authoritarianism in Latin America.* Princeton, N.J.: Princeton University Press.

Cameco. 1995a. *1995 Annual Report,* Saskatoon: Cameco.

———. 1995b. *Explore Cameco.* Saskatoon: Cameco.

———. 1993. *Neighbours in the North.* Saskatoon: Cameco.

Casey, Allan. 1991. "Banding Together." *Saskatchewan Business* (June): 13–17.

CCAB. 1994. "Collective Wisdom." *Contact.* 10 (September). Toronto: Canadian Council For Aboriginal Business.

———. 1993. *Presentation to the Royal Commission on Aboriginal Peoples.* Toronto: Canadian Council For Aboriginal Business.

———. 1992a. *Against the Odds.* Toronto: Canadian Council For Aboriginal Business.

———. 1992b. *Doing Business with Aboriginal Canada.* Toronto: Canadian Council For Aboriginal Business.

———. 1989. *Standing Alone.* Toronto: Canadian Council For Aboriginal Business.

Colchester, Marcus. 1994. "Sustaining the Forests: The Community-based Approach in South and South-East Asia." *Development and Change* 25(1): 69–100.

Corbridge, Stuart. 1989. "Post-Marxism and Development Studies: Beyond the Impasse." *World Development* 18(5): 623–39.

———. 1986. *Capitalist World Development: A Critique of Radical Development Geography.* Totowa, New Jersey: Rowman and Littlefield.

Cornell, Stephen, and Joseph Kalt. 1989. "Pathways from Poverty: Development and Institution-Building on American Indian Reservations." *Harvard Project on American Indian Economic Development, Project Report Series.* Cambridge: John F. Kennedy School of Government, Harvard University.

CRA. 1998a. "Cree Regional Authority." Grand Council of the Crees Website: http://www.gcc.ca.

———. 1998b. "Cree Regional Economic Enterprises." Grand Council of the Crees Website: http://www.gcc.ca.

Cree-Naskapi Commission. 1997. *The 1996 Report of the Cree-Naskapi Commission.* Ottawa: Cree-Naskapi Commission.

Dacks, Gurston. 1981. *A Choice of Futures: Politics in the Canadian North.* Toronto: Methuen.

Davis, John. 1991. *Greening Business: Managing for Sustainable Development.* London: Basil Blackwell.

De George, Richard. 1990. *Business Ethics.* New York: MacMillan Publishing Company.

De Janvry, Alain, and Elisabeth Sadoulet. 1993. "Market, State and Civil Organizations in Latin America Beyond the Debt Crisis." *World Development* 21(4): 659–74.

De Janvry, Alain, Elisabeth Sadoulet and Erik Thorbecke. 1993. "Introduction." *World Development* 21(4): 565–75.

Decter, Michael, and Jeffrey Kowall. 1989. *A Case Study of the Kitsaki Development Corporation.* Ottawa: Economic Council of Canada.

DIAND. 1997. *Comprehensive Claims Policy and the Status of Claims.* Ottawa: Department of Indian Affairs and Northern Development.

———. 1996a. *Procurement Strategy For Aboriginal Business.* Ottawa: Department of Indian Affairs and Northern Development.

———. 1996b. *Comprehensive Claims (Modern Treaties) in Canada.* Ottawa: Department of Indian Affairs and Northern Development.

———. 1993a. *Canadian Aboriginal Economic Development Strategy.* Ottawa: Department of Indian Affairs and Northern Development.

———. 1993b. *The James Bay and Northern Quebec Agreement and the Northeastern Quebec Agreement.* Ottawa: Department of Indian Affairs and Northern Development.

Dicken, Peter. 1992. "International Production in a Volatile Regulatory Environment." *Geoforum* 23(3): 303–16.

———. 1993. "Global-Local Tensions: Firms and States in the Global Space-Economy." *Economic Geography* 70(2): 101–28.

Doeringer, Peter, and Paul Streeten. 1990. "How Economic Institutions Affect Economic Performance in Industrialized Countries: Lessons for Development." *World Development* 19(9): 1249–53.

Donner, Richard F., and Ansil Ramsay. 1993. "Postimperialism and Development in Thailand." *World Development* 21(5): 691–704.

Drache, Daniel. 1982. "Harold Innis and Canadian Capitalist Development." *Canadian Journal of Political and Social Theory* 6(1–2): 35–60.
———. 1991. "The Systematic Search for Flexibility: National Competitiveness and New Work Relations." In *The Era of Global Competition: State Policy and Market Power*, edited by Daniel Drache and Meric Gertler. Montreal and Kingston: McGill-Queens University Press.
Drache, Daniel, and Meric Gertler. 1991. "The World Economy and the Nation Sate: The New International Order." In *The Era of Global Competition: State Policy and Market Power* edited by Daniel Drache and Meric Gertler, 3–25. Montreal and Kingston: McGill-Queens University Press.
Drucker, Peter F. 1985. *Innovation and Entrepreneurship.* New York: Harper & Row, Publishers.
Dube, S.C. 1988. *Modernization and Development.* Tokyo: The United Nations University.
Elam, Mark. 1994. "Puzzling Out the Post-Fordist Debate." In *Post-Fordism: A Reader*, edited by Ash Amin, 43–70. Oxford: Blackwell.
Elias, Peter Douglas. 1991. *Development of Aboriginal People's Communities.* North York, Ont.: Captus Press Inc.
———. 1995. *Northern Aboriginal Communities: Economies and Development.* North York, Ont.: Captus Press.
Erasmus, George. 1989. "Twenty Years of Disappointed Hopes." In *Drum Beat: Anger and Renewal in Indian Country*, edited by B. Richardson, 1–15. Toronto: Summerhill Press.
Esser, Josef, and Joachim Hirsch. 1994. "The Crisis of Fordism and the Dimensions of a 'Post-Fordist' Regional and Urban Structure." In *Post-Fordism: A Reader*, edited by Ash Amin, 71–98. Oxford: Blackwell.
Frank, Andre G. 1966. "The Development of Underdevelopment." *Monthly Review* 18(4): 17–31.
Frideres, James. 1998. *Native People in Canada: Contemporary Conflicts.* Scarborough: Prentice-Hall Canada.
Frieden, Jeff. 1987. "International Capital and National Development: Comments on Postimperialism." In *Postimperialism: International Capitalism and Development in the Late Twentieth Century*, edited by D.G. Becker and R. Sklar, 193–201. Boulder, Colorado: Lynne Rienner Publishers, Inc.
Friedmann, John. 1992. *Empowerment: The Politics of Alternative Development.* Cambridge, MA: Blackwell.
FSIN. 1993. *Annual Report.* The Federation of Saskatchewan Indian Nations.
GCC. 1998a. "Growing Crisis Over Wealth-sharing from Resources of Cree Lands Concerns Annual General Assembly." Grand Council of the Crees Website: http://www.gcc.ca.
Getimis, P., and G. Kafkalas. 1992. "Local Development and Forms of Regulation." *Geoforum* 23(3): 347–363.
Goldman, Steven. 1995. *Agile Competition: The Emergence of a New Industrial Order.* Hamilton, Ont.: The Society of Management Accountants.
Gottdiener, M., and N. Komninos. 1989. *Capitalist Development and Crisis Theory.* New York: St. Martin's Press.

Gottdiener, M. 1989. "Crisis Theory and Socio-Spatial Restructuring." In *Capitalist Development and Crisis Theory*, edited by M. Gottdiener and N. Komninos, 365–90. New York: St. Martin's Press.

Goulet, Dennis. 1989. "Participation in Development: New Avenues." *World Development* 17(1): 165–178.

Hedican, Edward J. 1995. *Applied Anthropology in Canada: Understanding Aboriginal Issues.* Toronto: University of Toronto Press.

Hirst, Paul, and Jonathan Zeitlin. 1992. "Flexible Specialization Versus Post-Fordism." In *Pathways to Industrialization and Regional Development*, edited by Michael Storper and Allen Scott. London: Routledge.

ICG. 1997. *Inuvialuit Corporate Group: 1996 Annual Report.* Inuvik: Inuvialuit Corporate Group.

IDC. 1998. "Inuvialuit Development Corporation." Inuvialuit Development Corporation Website: http://www.idc.inuvialuit.com

Indigenous Times. 1996. "MLTC Ventures into Construction Industry." *Indigenous Times* (August): 19.

Innis, Harold. 1956. *The Fur Trade in Canada*, Second Edition. Toronto: The University of Toronto Press.

Interfor. 1995a. *Interfor Statutory Information.* Vancouver: International Forest Products.

———. 1995b. *Interfor Environmental Report.* Vancouver: International Forest Products.

———. 1995c. *IFP Policy Re: Working With First Nations.* Vancouver: International Forest Products.

Inuvialuit Corporate Group. 1997. *Inuvialuit Corporate Group: 1996 Annual Report.* Inuvik: Inuvialuit Regional Corporation.

IPC. 1998. "Inuvialuit Petroleum Corporation." Inuvialuit Corporate Group Website: http://www.inuvialuit.com/irc/ipcpg1.html

IRC. 1998. "Inuvialuit Regional Corporation." Inuvialuit Regional Corporation Website: http://www.irc.inuvialuit.com

Jamieson, Ron. 1994. "Mutual Opportunities Through Partnership." *Canadian Business Review* (summer): 14–17.

Jenkins, Rhys. 1988. "Comparing Foreign Subsidiaries and Local Firms in LDCs." *Journal of Developing Studies* (October): 205–27.

Jessop, Bob. 1989. "Conservative Regimes and the Transition to Post-Fordism." In *Capitalist Development and Crisis Theory*, edited by M. Gottdiener and N. Komninos, 261–29. New York: St. Martin's Press.

———. 1992. "Fordism and Post-Fordism." In *Pathways to Industrialization and Regional Development*, edited by Michael Storper and Allen Scott, 46–69. London: Routledge.

———. 1994. "Post-Fordism and the State." In *Post-Fordism: A Reader*, edited by Ash Amin, 251–79. Oxford: Blackwell.

Kao, Raymond. 1989. *Entrepreneurship and Enterprise Development*. Toronto: Holt, Rinehart and Winston.

Kay, Cristobal. 1991. "Reflections on the Latin American Contribution to Development Theory." *Development and Change* 22: 31–68.

K. D. Developers. 1993. *Executive Summary.* Meadow Lake: Keewatin Dahze Developers.

Knight, Rolf. 1996. *Indians at Work: An Informal History of Native Indian Labour in British Columbia, 1858–1930*. Vancouver: New Star Books.

Koche, George. 1998. "Back to the Future North of 60." *Alberta Report* (12 January): 11–12.

Komninos, Nicos. 1989. "From National to Local: The Janus Face of Crisis." In *Capitalist Development and Crisis Theory*, edited by M. Gottdiener and N. Komninos, 348–64. New York: St. Martin's Press.

Kotler, P., L. Fahey, and S. Jatusripitak. 1985. *The New Competition.* Englewood, Cliffs: Prentice-Hall, Inc.

Krause, Lawrence. 1991. "Introduction." In *Liberalization in the Process of Economic Development*, edited by Lawrence Krause and Kim Kihwan, 1–26. Berkeley: University of California Press.

Kuptana, Rosemarie. 1992. "The Aboriginal Community's Perspective." In *Trade, Environment and Competitiveness*, edited by John Kirton and Sarah Richardson. Ottawa: The National Round Table on the Environment and the Economy.

Lafond, Lester. 1985. "Self Government in Perspective." In *Native Self-Reliance Through Resource Development*, edited by W. Sinclair, 15–17. Vancouver: Hemlock Printers Ltd.

Laxer, Gordon. 1991. *Perspectives on Canadian Economic Development.* Toronto: Oxford University Press.

Leyshon, Andrew. 1992. "The Transformation of a Regulatory Order." *Geoforum* 23(3): 347–63.

Lipietz, Alain. 1994. "Post-Fordism and Democracy." In *Post-Fordism: A Reader*, edited by Ash Amin, 338–58. Oxford: Blackwell.

Lipschultz, Ronnie. 1991. "Bargaining Among Nations: Culture, History and Perception in Regime Formation." *Evaluation Review* 15(1): 46–74.

MacKintosh, W.A. 1991. "Economic Factors in Canadian History." In *Perspectives on Canadian Economic Development*, edited by Gordon Laxer, 68–79. Toronto: Oxford University Press.

Makivik. 1998a. "James Bay and Northern Quebec Agreement." Makivik Corporation Website: http://www.makivik.org

———. 1998b. "Makivik Corporation." Makivik Corporation Website: http://www.makivik.org

———. 1998c. "Investment of Inuit Compensation Funds." Makivik Corporation Website: http://www.makivik.org

———. 1998d. "Makivik Corporation's New Head Office in Kuujjuag Heralds New Era in Nunavik Development." Makivik Corporation Website: http://www.makivik.org

———. 1998e. "Makivik Corporation: Third Vice President's Report." Makivik Corporation Website: http://www.makivik.org

McBain, Leslie. 1995. *An Analysis of the Spatial Distribution of the Northern Labour Force Employed in Uranium Mining in Northern Saskatchewan.* Saskatoon: University of Saskatchewan.

Mercredi, Ovide. 1994. "A Conversation With National Chief Ovide Mercredi." *Mawioni Journal* (Winter): 4–9.

MLTC. 1995a. *Meadow Lake Tribal Council Annual Report, 1994–1995.* Meadow Lake: MLTC.

———. 1995b. *Meadow Lake First Nations 20 Year Plan: From Vision to Reality.* Meadow Lake: MLTC.
———. 1994. *Meadow Lake Tribal Council Annual Report, 1993–1994.* Meadow Lake: MLTC.
———. 1993. *Meadow Lake Tribal Council Annual Report, 1992–1993.* Meadow Lake: MLTC.
———. 1992. *Meadow Lake Tribal Council Annual Report, 1991–1992.* Meadow Lake: MLTC.
———. 1991. *Meadow Lake Tribal Council Annual Report, 1990–1991, 1989–1990.* Meadow Lake: MLTC.
Morss, Elliot. 1991. "The New Global Players: How They Compete and Collaborate." *World Development* 19(1): 55–64.
Myrdahl, Gunnar. 1968. *Asian Drama: An Inquiry into the Poverty of Nations.* New York: Twentieth Century Fund.
NAFT. 1996. *The Promise of the Future: Achieving Economic Self-Sufficiency Through Access to Capital.* Ottawa: National Aboriginal Financing Task Force.
Newell, Eric. 1994. "A New Spirit of Partnership." *Canadian Business Review* (summer): 8–11.
Norcliffe, Glen. 1994. "Regional Labour Market Adjustments in a Period of Structural Transformation: The Canadian Case." *The Canadian Geographer* 38(1): 2–17.
Notzke, Claudia. 1994. *Aboriginal Peoples and Natural Resources in Canada.* North York: Captus Press.
Nugent, Jeffrey B. 1993. "Between State, Markets and Households: A Neo-institutional Analysis of Local Organizations and Institutions." *World Development* (21): 623–32.
Page, Robert. 1986. *Northern Development: The Canadian Dilemma.* Toronto: McClelland and Stewart.
PATC. 1993. *Prince Albert Development Corporation: Company Profile.* Prince Albert: Prince Albert Tribal Council.
Pearson, Andrall E. 1998. "Tough-Minded Way to Get Innovative." *Harvard Business Review* May-June: 99–106.
Peet, Richard, and Michael Watts. 1993. "Development Theory and Environment in an Age of Market Triumphalism." *Economic Geography* 69(3): 227–53.
Peck, Jamie. 1992. "Labour and Agglomeration: Control and Flexibility in the Local Labour Markets." *Economic Geography* 68(4): 325–47.
Peck, Jamie, and Adam Tickell. 1994. "Searching for a New Institutional Fix: The After-Fordist Crisis and the Global-Local Disorder." In *Post-Fordism: A Reader*, edited by Ash Amin, 280–315. Oxford: Blackwell.
———. 1992. "Local Modes of Social Regulation." *Geoforum* 23(3): 347–63.
Peters, Celeste. 1996. "FSIN Deals a Winning Hand." *Aboriginal Times* 4(December): 6–9.
PHT. 1993. *Peace Hills Trust 1993 Annual Report.* Hobbema AB: Peace Hills Trust.
———. 1992. *Peace Hills Trust 1992 Annual Report.* Hobbema AB: Peace Hills Trust.

Pitelis, Christos. 1991. "Beyond the Nation-State: The Transnational Firm and the Nation State." *Capital and Class* 23(Spring): 131–52.

Ponting, J. Rick. 1986. "Economic Development Provisions of the New Claims Settlements." In *The Arduous Journey: Canadian Indians and Decolonization.* Toronto: McClelland and Stewart.

———. 1986. *The Arduous Journey: Canadian Indians and Decolonization.* Toronto: McClelland and Stewart.

Pretes, Michael. 1988. "Underdevelopment in the Two Norths: The Brazilian Amazon and the Canadian Arctic." *Arctic* 41(2): 109–16.

Price Waterhouse. 1994a. *MLTC Logging and Reforestation, Inc. and Norsask Forest Products, Inc.: Performance Evaluation Relative to Industry.* Saskatoon: Price Waterhouse.

———. 1994b. *MLTC Logging and Reforestation, Inc. and Norsask Forest Products, An Evaluation of Various Financial Results.* Saskatoon: Price Waterhouse.

Ranis, Gustav. 1991. "Towards a Model of Development." In *Liberalization in the Process of Economic Development*, edited by Lawrence Krause and Kim Kihwan, 59–101. Berkeley: University of California Press.

Randall, James E., and R. Geoff Ironside. 1996. "Communities on the Edge: An Economic Geography of Resource Dependent Communities in Canada." *The Canadian Geographer* 40(1): 17–35.

Randall, James E. 1994. Local "Responses to Global Attitudes: Economy and Environment in Resources Communities." Paper presented at the Annual meeting of the Association of American Geographers, San Francisco.

RCAP. 1996. *The Report of the Royal Commission on Aboriginal Peoples.* Ottawa: Government of Canada.

Robinson, Michael, and Elmer Ghostkeeper. 1988. "Implementing the Next Economy." *Arctic* 41(3): 173–82.

———. 1987. "Native and Local Economies: A Consideration of Economic Evolution and the Next Economy." *Arctic* 40(2): 138–44.

Rostow, W.W. 1953. *The Process of Economic Growth.* Oxford: Clarendon Press.

Ruccio, David, and Lawrence Simon. 1988. "Radical Theories of Development: Frank, the Modes of Production School and Amin." In *The Political Economy of Development and Underdevelopment*, edited by Charles Wilbur, 121–72. New York: McGraw-Hill Publishing Co.

Samatar, Abdi Ismail. 1993. "Structural Adjustment as a Development Strategy?" *Economic Geography* 69(1): 25–43.

Saskatoon Sun. 1996. "Muskeg Becomes Model for Canada." *Saskatoon Sun*, 23 June, 4.

SaskEnergy. 1995a. *A Formula For the Future: Aboriginal People and SaskEnergy.* Regina: SaskEnergy.

———. 1995b. *Doing Business With SaskEnergy.* Regina: SaskEnergy.

Sayer, Andrew. 1995. *Radical Political Economy: A Critique.* Oxford: Blackwell Publishers Ltd.

Sayer, Andrew, and Richard Walker. 1994. *The New Social Economy.* Oxford: Blackwell.

Scott, A.J. 1988. *New Industrial Spaces: Flexible Production Organization and Regional Development in North America and Western Europe.* London: Pion Ltd.

———. 1992. "The Collective Order of Flexible Production Agglomerations: Lessons for Local Economic Development Policy and Strategic Choice." *Economic Geography* 68(3): 219–33.

Scott, A.J., and M. Storper. 1992. "Industrialization and Regional Development." In *Pathways to Industrialization and Regional Development*, edited by Michael Storper and Allen Scott, 3–17. London: Routledge.

Shatz, Sayre. 1987a. "Socializing Adaptation: A Perspective on World Capitalism." In *Postimperialism: International Capitalism and Development in the Late Twentieth Century*, edited by D.G. Becker and R. Sklar, 161–77. Boulder, Colorado: Lynne Rienner Publishers, Inc.

———. 1987b. "Assertive Pragmatism and the Multinational Enterprise." In *Postimperialism: International Capitalism and Development in the Late Twentieth Century*, edited by D.G. Becker and R. Sklar, 93–105. Boulder, Colorado: Lynne Rienner Publishers, Inc.

SIAP. 1992. *Saskatchewan Indian Agriculture Program — 1992 Annual Report*, Regina: SIAP.

SIEF. 1995. *Saskatchewan Indian Equity Foundation 1994–95 Annual Report:* Saskatoon: Saskatchewan Indian Equity Foundation.

———. 1993. *Saskatchewan Indian Equity Foundation 1992–93 Annual Report:* Saskatoon: Saskatchewan Indian Equity Foundation.

Sinclair, William. 1985. "Native Self-Reliance Through Resource Development." In *Native Self-Reliance Through Resource Development*, edited by W. Sinclair. Vancouver: Hemlock Printers Ltd.

Sklar, Richard. 1987. "A Class Analysis of Multinational Corporate Expansion." In *Postimperialism: International Capitalism and Development in the Late Twentieth Century*, edited by D.G. Becker and R. Sklar, 19–39. Boulder, Colorado: Lynne Rienner Publishers, Inc.

Sloan, Pamela, and Roger Hill. 1995. *Corporate Aboriginal Relations.* Toronto: Hill-Sloan Associates Inc.

So, Alvin Y. 1990. *Social Change and Development: Modernization, Dependency, and World-System Theories.* Newbury Park: Sage Publication.

Stabler, Jack. 1990. "Dualism and Development in the Northwest Territories." In *Natural Resource Development and Social Impact in the North* edited by J.S. and J.E. DiSanto, 11–42. New York: Peter Lang.

Stander, H., and D. Becker. 1990. "Postimperialism Revisited: The Venezuelan Wheat Import Controversy of 1986." *World Development* 18(2): 197–213.

Star Phoenix. 1996a. "Agreement Allows Natives to Determine Job Training." *Star Phoenix*, 6 July, A4.

———. 1996b. "Millions Marked for Native Housing." *Star Phoenix*, 8 June, A1.

———. 1996c. "Diaper Plant to Open." *Star Phoenix*, 6 July, B5.

———. 1995. "30,000 New Jobs Targeted by FSIN." *Star Phoenix,* 7 January, A3.

———. 1993. "Protectors of Mother Earth Plan to Continue Blockade." *Star Phoenix*, 17 May: A2.

———. 1992a. "Talks on Forestry Issue, Blockade Make Little Progress." *Star Phoenix,* 29 August, A4.

———. 1992b. "Natives to Co-manage Future Forests." *Star Phoenix*, 25 September 25, E1.

Storper, Michael. 1992. "The Limits to Globalization: Technology Districts and International Trade." *Economic Geography* 68(1): 60–93.

———. 1994. "The Transition to Flexible Specialization in the U.S. Film Industry." In *Post-Fordism: A Reader*, edited by Ash Amin, 195–226. Oxford: Blackwell.

Storper, Michael, and Allen Scott. 1992. "Industrialization and Regional Development." In *Pathways to Industrialization and Regional Development*, edited by Michael Storper and Allen Scott, 3–17. London: Routledge.

Storper, Michael, and Richard Walker. 1989. *The Capitalist Imperative: Territory, Technology and Industrial Growth.* New York: Basil Blackwell.

Straussfogel, Debra. 1997. "World-Systems Theory: Toward a Heuristic and Pedagogic Conceptual Tool." *Economic Geography* 73(1): 118–30.

Syncrude. 1994. *Aboriginal Review: A Report on the Relationship Between Syncrude Canada Ltd. and the Aboriginal People of Northeastern Alberta.* Fort MacMurray: Syncrude.

Tavis, Lee. 1988. "The Role of Multinational Corporations in the Third World." In *Multinational Managers and Host Government Interactions*, edited by Lee Tavis. Notre Dame: University of Notre Dame Press.

Tavis, Lee, and William Glade. 1988. "Implications for Corporate Strategies." In *Multinational Managers and Host Government Interactions*, edited by Lee Tavis. Notre Dame: University of Notre Dame Press.

Taylor, Peter J. 1989. "The Error of Developmentalism in Human Geography." In *Horizons in Human Geography*, edited by Derek Gregory and Rex Walford, 303–19. Totowa, N.J.: Burns and Noble Books.

TFHQ. 1993. *1992/93 Annual Report.* Touchwood, File Hills and Qu'Appelle Tribal Council.

The Globe and Mail. 1996. *Creative Strategies for Aboriginal Business.* Toronto: The Globe and Mail.

Thomas, Ken. 1994. "The Emergence of Aboriginal Business in Canada." *Canadian Business Review* (summer): 12–13.

Thomsen, Jens. 1991. "A Strategic-relational Account of Economic State Interventions." In *State, Economy and Society*, edited by Rene Bertramsen, Jens Thomsen and Jacob Torfing, 146–93. London: Unwin Hyman.

Thrift, Nigel and Michael Taylor. 1989. "Battleships and Cruisers: The New Geography of Multinational Corporations." In *Horizons in Human Geography*, edited by Derek Gregory and Rex Walford, 279–97. Totowa, N.J.: Barnes and Noble Books.

Thunder Hill Development Corp. 1993. *Thunder Hill Development Corporation.* Key and Cote First Nations.

Timmins, Jeffry. 1994. *New Venture Creation.* Toronto: Irwin.

Torfing, Jacob. 1991. "A Hegemony Approach to Capitalist Regulation." In *State, Economy and Society*, edited by Rene Bertramsen, Jens Thomsen and Jacob Torfing, 35–91. London: Unwin Hyman.

Toye, John. 1993. *Dilemmas of Development*, Second edition. Oxford: Blackwell.

United Nations Centre on Transnational Corporations. 1989. *Transnational Corporations and International Economic Relations.* New York: United Nations.

Uphoff, Norman. 1993. "Grassroots Organizations and NGOs in Rural Development." *World Development* 21(4): 607–22.

Usher, Peter J. 1993. "Northern Development, Impact Assessment and Social Change." In *Anthropology, Public Policy and Native Peoples in Canada*, edited by James B. Waldram and Noel Dyck. Montreal and Kingston: McGill-Queens University Press.

Waldram, James B., and Noel Dyck. 1993. *Anthropology, Public Policy and Native Peoples in Canada.* Montreal and Kingston: McGill-Queens University Press.

Wallerstein, Immanuel. 1979. *The Capitalist World Economy.* New York: Cambridge University Press.

Watkins, Melville. 1963. "A Staple Theory of Economic Growth." In *Perspectives on Canadian Economic Development*, edited by Gordon Laxer, 80–100. Toronto: Oxford University Press.

Weissling, Lee E. 1989. "Arctic Canada and Zambia: A Comparison of Development Processes in the Fourth and Third Worlds." *Arctic* 42(3): 208–16.

Wiarda, Howard. 1988. "Toward a Nonethnocentric Theory of Development; Alternative Conceptions from the Third World." *Journal of Developing Areas* 17(July): 433–52.

Wilbur, Charles, and Kenneth Jameson. 1975. "Paradigms of Economic Development and Beyond." In *The Political Economy of Development and Underdevelopment*, edited by Charles Wilbur, 3–27. New York: McGraw-Hill Publishing Co..

Windspeaker. 1993a. "Blockade to Celebrate Birthday." *Windspeaker*, 26 April, 11(3): 3.

———. 1993b. "Saskatchewan Protesters Defy Court-ordered Eviction." *Windspeaker*, 7 June, 11(6): r2.

———. 1993c. "Meadow Lake Protesters Reach Agreement with Norsask." *Windspeaker*, 7 November, 11(10): r2.

———. 1992a. "Protesters Want Logging Control." *Windspeaker*, 8 June, 10(5).

———. 1992b. "Protesters Continue Blockade." *Windspeaker*, 20 July, 10(8): 12.

———. 1992c. "Logging Protesters Continue to do Battle." *Windspeaker*, 21 December, 10(19): 2.

Wuliger, Robert. 1991. "A World Economy: Paradigms Lost and Found. *Challenge* (January/February): 4–12.

Index